KU-527-187

RAMON LULL
A BIOGRAPHY

BY THE SAME AUTHOR

TRANSLATIONS FROM THE CATALAN OF RAMÓN LULL, WITH INTRODUCTORY ESSAYS. EACH, 3*s*. 6*d*.

THE BOOK OF THE LOVER AND THE BELOVED.

THE ART OF CONTEMPLATION.

THE TREE OF LOVE.

STUDIES OF THE SPANISH MYSTICS. VOL. I. 18*s*.

LONDON: S.P.C.K.

RAMON LULL

A BIOGRAPHY

BY

E. ALLISON PEERS, M.A.

SOMETIME SCHOLAR OF CHRIST'S COLLEGE, CAMBRIDGE
GILMOUR PROFESSOR OF SPANISH IN THE UNIVERSITY OF LIVERPOOL
CORRESPONDING MEMBER OF THE HISPANIC SOCIETY OF AMERICA

LONDON
SOCIETY FOR PROMOTING
CHRISTIAN KNOWLEDGE

NEW YORK AND TORONTO: THE MACMILLAN CO.

1929

PRINTED IN GREAT BRITAIN

TO

THE PEOPLE

OF THE ISLAND OF MALLORCA

—SO OFTEN AND SO WILLINGLY MY HOSTS—

IN WHOSE COURTESY, GENEROSITY AND SIMPLICITY

LIVES THE SPIRIT OF THE

BEAT RAMON

La patria es gran, es bella : té gorchs, y fondalades,
Y oliverars, y pobles, y temples, y castells ;
Y putjos que s'abeuren del cel en les boirades,
Com de la llet materna, alçantse assedegades,
Les boques dels vadells.

Té murs de roques fondes hont brama la riera ;
La espiga d'or s'engronsa fins als pinars reulls ;
Els taronjers verdegen, se vincla la palmera ;
La mar damunt la platja s'adorm, o escup brumera
Entre gegants esculls.

JOAN ALCOVER.

PREFACE

No serious, full-length biography of the Mallorcan martyr, Ramon Lull, has been published in any language since Pasqual's great work appeared in the eighteenth century. Such a book the eminent Lullist Mateu Obrador had planned to write, and might indeed have written, had not death cut short his career. In the manuscript notes of his preface, which, with a skeleton of the projected biography, he left among his papers,[1] he describes his predecessors as "in general more inclined to patriotic and devout panegyric than to the study and collation of authentic sources and documents." That is perhaps true enough, not only of biographers up to Obrador's own time, but also of one or two who have written since. The chief fault, however, of such works as Lull's countrymen have produced during the present century is rather their brevity. Mn. Galmés has written a most carefully compiled little handbook—yet it can be read in an hour. Mn. Riber has given us a biography which supplements it admirably, but again is a mere essay. The Catalan successor of the industrious Cistercian is still awaited, and the harvest which he has to reap is the rich one of a hundred and fifty years' progress.

My primary object in attempting a biography, not indeed of the length which I should wish, but at least of a greater length than anything in English, is to give those who read neither Catalan nor Latin with any fluency a comprehensive account of the life and principal works of

[1] These notes have been generously placed at my disposal by Mn. Salvador Galmés.

a man who, though born close on seven centuries ago, makes still a most potent appeal to-day, and that to persons differing widely in temperament, in race and in creed. To English and American readers he is known chiefly by a few of his translated works, and before all the rest by his little classic *The Book of the Lover and the Beloved.* This shows the heights to which Ramon Lull could soar ; the present book endeavours to describe the depth and breadth of his life and personality, and the immortality of his work and his message.

But I have also aimed, in this biography, at representing the life and work of Ramon Lull to a wider audience than one composed of my own countrymen. Starting with the Latin and Catalan biographies written in Lull's own lifetime, and known respectively as the *Vita Beati Raimundi Lullii* and the *Vida Coetània*,[1] I have tried to extract the most authentic and essential elements from the masses of material—often quite worthless—which lumber libraries and archives, to co-ordinate results of the most recent investigations, and, above all, to follow the new orientation which Lullists have adopted increasingly since the Catalan Renaissance, making thereby the Lull whom they have re-discovered as real and as living to the twentieth century as Master Ramon was to the students of Paris or the Illuminated Doctor to the generation following his death.

The task of rejection has not been easy, and that of collation, selection and comment has been harder still. By comparison with the magnitude of the work and the greatness of the personality which it describes, the book is a short one, and the limits imposed upon it by practical considerations have forced me merely to touch upon matters to which I would gladly have devoted chapters. Needless to say, the judgments passed upon Lull's work are purely personal : if I have been unduly cautious in reading his life into his writings, such conservatism was inevitable after the prevalence of that pseudo-criticism

[1] To these I refer jointly in the text as the "contemporary biography" where they agree.

which turns *Blanquerna* into its author's life-story, and describes every other anecdote which Lull relates as "seguràment autobiogràfica."

Even more compressed than the rest of the book are the last two chapters, each of which requires a volume to do its subject justice. But their inclusion was obviously necessary, not only to complete, as far as might be, the story of a life which is not yet ended, but to justify the standpoint which gives a page to the formidable and forbidding *Ars Magna* and a chapter each to *Blanquerna* and to *Felix*.

I have consistently, though not pedantically, used Catalan rather than Castilian orthography in writing both of modern Catalan persons and places, and of mediæval Catalonia, Valencia and Mallorca. Abbreviations, all of which are explained in a Bibliographical Note on pp. xvii–xviii, have been adopted with a view to economizing space, and quotations in the footnotes have been reduced to a minimum, by the substitution of references for them. My Bibliography is brief, and intended less for Catalan scholars than for English students. The biographical table is also for the convenience of the general reader rather than for the specialist.

It is in no spirit of formality, but with the deepest gratitude and affection, that I dedicate this book to the Mallorcan people, a dedication with which I know my Catalan friends in Barcelona and elsewhere on the mainland will associate themselves gladly. That I have never in Mallorca met with anything but kindness from professor, priest or peasant, and never once been rewarded with less than a welcome and a smile for all the trouble my researches have caused archivists and librarians, has been perhaps my principal encouragement to proceed. If first and foremost I thank my friend, Mn. Salvador Galmés, next the librarians of Palma, the good Franciscans of Cura, the companion of my pilgrimages, Dr. Miquel Sureda, and, in Barcelona, my constant helper, En Jordi Rubió i Balaguer, together with the entire staff of the Institut d'Estudis Catalans, both they and others will recognize that these acknowledgments are but representative and typical.

At home, I am more than usually indebted to the officials of the British Museum, and, in the initial stages of the work, to my wife. The manuscript of the book has been read in its entirety by my friends, Professor W. J. Entwistle, of Glasgow, Associate-Professor G. W. Coopland, Reader in Mediæval History at Liverpool University, Dr. Ferran Soldevila, Lecturer in Spanish at Liverpool University, and the Rev. E. Iliff Robson, all of whom have made useful suggestions. It should be added that the substance of five lectures on Ramon Lull—forming the first course of a series on Catalan literature delivered for the Fundació Bernat Metge—has been incorporated in the later chapters of this volume.

E. Allison Peers.

The University,
Liverpool,
October 1928.

TABLE OF CONTENTS

Chapter V

Chapter VI

Chapter VII

Chapter VIII

Chapter IX

Chapter X

Chapter XI

Chapter XII

Chapter XIII

Chapter XIV

Chapter XV

Chapter XVI

Chapter XVII

Chapter XVIII

Chapter XIX

CHRONOLOGICAL TABLE OF THE LIFE OF RAMON LULL ACCORDING TO THE PRESENT BOOK

[ONLY a few outstanding works by Ramon Lull are mentioned in this table. For the remainder, the reader should consult the INDEX at the end of the volume.]

	YEAR	AGE
Birth	1232	—
Enters King's service	*c.* 1246	*c.* 14
Accompanies Prince James to Mallorca	1256	24
Marriage to Blanca Picany	1257	25
Conversion (about July)	1263	31
Return to Mallorca from abroad (early in)	1265	33
Period of study, ending in suicide of Moorish slave	1265–74	33–42
Book of Contemplation	1272	40
Book of the Gentile and the three wise men	1272–3	40–1
Retirement to Mount Randa, visit to La Real, and return to Mount Randa	1274	42
Visit to Prince James. *Book of the Order of Chivalry, Doctrine for Boys*	1274–5	42–3
Foundation of the College of Miramar	1276	44
Journey to Rome	1277	45
Unknown period of Lull's life, probably spent mainly in travel	1277–82	45–50
Sees James II of Mallorca at Perpignan	1282	50
Sojourn at Montpellier. Attends Dominican Chapter-General (1283). Writes *Blanquerna*	1283–4	51–2
Visits Rome. Travels to Bologna for Dominican Chapter-General. Returns to Rome. Writes the *Hundred Names of God*	1285	53
Travels to Paris. Sees Philip the Fair. Writes *Felix*. Attends Dominican Chapter-General at Paris	1286	54
Visits Montpellier and attends Franciscan Chapter-General	1287	55
Visits Pope Nicholas IV at Rome	1288	56
Returns to Montpellier, attending, on the way, a Franciscan Chapter-General at Rieti	1289	57
Receives letters of introduction from Fra Ramon Gaufredi (October). Leaves soon afterwards for Rome. Presents a tract to the Pope on the conquering of the Holy Land	1290	58

Contemplation (**A.C.**) : London, S.P.C.K., 1925 ; Blanquerna (**Bl.**) : London, Jarrolds, 1926 ; Tree of Love (**T.L.**) : London, S.P.C.K., 1926 ; Book of the Beasts (**B.B.**) : London, Burns, Oates & Washbourne, 1927. References to the *Book of the Lover and the Beloved* are generally made, not to *B.L.B.*, but to the slightly different version of that work found, in English, in *Bl.*, and, in Catalan, in *Obres*, vol. ix.

RAMON LULL

CHAPTER I

1232–1263

Mallorca. Its early history. Reconquest from the Moors. Birth of Ramon Lull in Mallorca. Education. Years spent in the royal service. Marriage. Profligate life. Conversion.

"La patria es gran, es bella." Thus sings a modern Mallorcan poet; and there is truth, as well as pride, in his song. Extensive Mallorca may not be, as measured in square miles, but the extent of her riches is illimitable. And on no part of the region where the Catalan tongue is spoken have Catalan poets more often loved to dwell than on this fairest of island-gardens, which to many of them is home. No less justly than England, it may be apostrophized as

> This precious stone set in the silver sea,
> Which serves it in the office of a wall,
> Or as a moat defensive to a house
> Against the envy of less happier lands.

Mallorca wins every heart, with its serene blue sky and blue, calm sea; with the warm yet kindly climate which it owes to both; with its innumerable secluded haunts and sheltered valleys; its wild mountain-paths, its ravines and gorges, its snow-capped peaks. Acres of orange-trees in fragrant flower perfume its December; weeks pass, and there is spread before one a snow-white mass of almond bloom; while all the year round rich olive-groves of silver and steely-grey form a perpetual background to the flora of winter and of summer.

B

Beauty, sunshine and peace reign in Mallorca without rivals and have reigned there for centuries unchallenged. And many of life's weather-beaten travellers, who have discovered this Isle of Calm and anchored there a while, look gratefully back upon it ever after, and forward to it with a wistful longing as to the haven where they would be.

So fair an island has not unnaturally changed hands more than once in the course of its long history. Phœnicians and Carthaginians, Romans and Vandals ruled successively in it ere it was absorbed, with the mainland of Spain, by the Moorish invasion. As early as 797, it passed to the Moors, and the Moslem conquest brought it more than four long centuries of comparative security from invasion, though they were centuries marred by internal strife and unrest. Still, the tiny Mallorcan kingdom grew fat and flourished, and as a pirates' base exasperated all the states of the Mediterranean. One prince after another looked enviously across the sea and strove to possess it, nor can we suppose that the Christian hosts of a partially reconquered Spain failed to measure it from time to time with covetous eyes.

But none of them could take it. Not even the Cid Campeador was to add its conquest to his valiant achievements against the Moors, though he was near enough to it when he ruled within the walls of Valencia. His doughty contemporary, Count Ramon Berenguer III of Barcelona, did certainly succeed for a brief space, in 1115, aided by the Pisans, in gaining a foothold within the island and taking the capital—now known as Palma—by assault. A counter-move on Barcelona, however, was sufficient to divert the conqueror, and in his absence the Moors regained the city. With its sister islands, Mallorca became ever more dangerous to the Christians and more valuable as a shelter for audacious Moorish pirates. Yet another entire century went by before a fresh attempt was made to wrest the kingdom from Moslem hands, and this attempt was successful.

King James I of Aragon, who succeeded to his throne in 1213, at the age of five, was no sooner out of his boyhood than he began to consider the extension of his already wide dominions. These included Aragon and Catalonia, with Cerdagne, Roussillon, and the isolated territory of Montpellier. But the eastern states of Spain, in the early thirteenth century, were attuned to conquest. Aragon cast envious eyes upon the Moorish kingdom of Valencia, which it was soon to make its own. Catalonia, with its important seaboard, looked rather across the Mediterranean, where in later years it was to accomplish a series of conquests of which its sons have ever since been justly proud. Both Aragon and Catalonia were filled with that unconquerable spirit which in 1212 had won the great victory over the Moors at Las Navas de Tolosa —a victory in the perils of which James' father Peter had taken his full share, but which had brought nothing either to him or to his people—save honour. Small wonder, then, if, after a turbulent boyhood, spent in subduing refractory Aragonese nobles and rebellious cities, the young king, who was afterwards to be known as James the Conqueror, desired to occupy himself with expeditions against the Moors abroad. And, since he had naturally more sympathy with the Catalans than with his subjects in Aragon, he was ready enough to gaze with them across the Mediterranean, and, if they would unite in following him, to place himself at their head.

It was quite comprehensible that they should. James was a born soldier and a gifted leader of men. Seven feet in height, strong and muscular, well developed yet by no means devoid of grace, he was a hero whom men could hardly choose but admire, nor would their admiration be unmixed with wholesome fear. His flashing eyes and wealth of golden-red hair told unmistakably, and truly, of a rash, impulsive, bold and generous disposition, and the fact that his fearlessness in warfare was combined with a capacity for amours which can seldom have been exceeded in history made him none the less attractive in mediaeval eyes, especially to a Latin race. He was only a youth of twenty when, at a banquet given in Tarragona by a wealthy merchant, Peter Martell, his host began to describe the attractions of Mallorca so realistically that the barons present urged James to put into execution plans which he had already conceived for its re-conquest. In December of the same year (1228) the Catalan Corts were convened at Barcelona, and the King, all eagerness for the fray, promised generous portions in the island, when it should be conquered, to those who would help him take it. In the following summer the successful campaign began.

On September 12, 1229, the Christians, having landed at Santa Ponsa, gained a hard-fought battle near Porto Pí, and the siege of the City of Mallorca (as Palma was then called [1]) began. It was a longer one than might have been expected, for the city was not taken until December 31, and some years were to pass before its warlike defenders left the mountain fastnesses to which they had fled, and made their final peace with the Christian conquerors.

This is not the place to relate in full the story of the conquest, nor of the ineffective counter-attacks, and the more disastrous guerrilla warfare, plague, and pestilence which had to be faced by the conquerors. Our concern is rather with the way in which the King fulfilled his obligations, both to God and to man. Deeply religious, after his own manner and that of mediaeval warriors, he caused the chief mosque of the city, upon his entry, to be immediately cleansed, so that Mass might be said in it daily. This done, among his first thoughts was the building of a cathedral, for which he gave the ground in front of his own royal palace. To his example and encouragement were unquestionably due the rapid strides made by the Church and the religious orders in Mallorca during the early years of Christian rule. And this, from every point of view, was as it should have been, for, from the venerable Archbishop of Tarragona downwards, clergy and religious were, throughout the campaign, among King James' most ardent supporters.

When the island was definitely divided up, some nine months after the taking of Palma, it was found that few, if any, who had helped the King had been forgotten.

[1] The shorter name will be used for the city hereafter.

Everyone, says the *Chronicle of King James of Aragon*, received so large a part that no one could pick a quarrel with his neighbour.[1] The Knights Templars and the Order of St. John of Jerusalem were given equal shares of territory, and both Dominicans and Franciscans established convents in Palma immediately. Nor were individuals neglected. Some of James' foremost warriors, alas, had been slain in battle and siege—among them the valiant Guillem and Ramon de Montcada. But such losses, if grievous, were few, and the earliest Christian settlers in reconquered Mallorca were those who, for their constancy and valour, were best entitled to dwell in so favoured a land. " La patria es gran, es bella," they must often have cried. Had not James the Conqueror described it as " the most precious pearl in my crown " ?

Among these earliest settlers was one who, a few years after the Reconquest, became the father of Mallorca's greatest son. Ramon Lull the elder bore a name of great antiquity and honour in Catalonia.[2] He had sailed with King James' fleet in 1229, and, to judge from the extent of the lands assigned to him, was evidently a person of some importance, though perhaps little more than thirty years of age.[3] The *Libre del repartiment* gives his territory as including the *rafal* of Aliebiti, not far from Palma,[4] and Biniatró (then called Beni-Atron) between the modern Campanet and Pollensa. Other authorities credit him also with the freehold of places called Tell, Gebelli and

[1] Tr. Forster : lxxxviii. (i, p. 175).

[2] The old Catalan form is Lull, or perhaps Lul (*cf.* Keicher, p. 1, n. 1) ; the Latin forms Lullus and Lullius are both used by the Beatus in his Latin works. According to modern Catalan orthography, the name is Llull. The unfortunate spelling " Lully," affected by some writers in English, is unknown in Lull's own country. I adopt the Catalan form, without accent, of Ramon's Christian name except where quoting from authors who use the accented Castilian form.

[3] Av., p. 51, following Vernon and earlier writers, gives the date of his birth as 1196, but there seems to be no satisfactory evidence for the supposition.

[4] This no longer exists, nor is it known in what direction it lay. Mallorcan authorities, however, believe it to have been in the north-west suburbs of the capital. A farm called So'n Llull, in this quarter, may possibly perpetuate the existence of some such family possession.

that of 1232.[1] A number of days are credited by different traditions with the honour of being Ramon's birthday, but it is a highly suspicious fact that they are all prominent saints' days, and the consensus of belief which placed his birth on the Feast of the Conversion of St. Paul is now as generally discredited as that which assigned his conversion to the same day of the year—an attribution which we know to be erroneous.

The traditional site of Ramon's birthplace is shown in what is now the Plaça Major in Palma, where an inscription, dating from the year 1888, records the belief that "in this place stood the house in which was born the great sage and blessed martyr Ramon Lull, 1232–1315."[2] The tradition here embodied, however, dates only from the sixteenth century, and there is this against it, that the site would have been in the parish of St. Nicholas, whereas Ramon's parents were buried in St. Eulalia, of which church they would probably be parishioners.[3] Nevertheless, no alternative site has been suggested.[4]

[1] Gabriel Lull, in 1606 (see *B.S.A.L.*, vol. iii, pp. 262–4), gives the date as "despues de deu anys que fonch conquistat lo Regna de Mallorca" (*i.e.* 1239). But, as will later be seen, this witness is in other respects unreliable. Daça gives 1240; Wadding, 1236; Blanch and others vary between 1231 and 1232. Pasqual (i, pp. 7–14) gives reasons, to many entirely convincing, in favour of the year 1232, which he accordingly adopts. Of more modern writers, Quadrado takes 1235 as the date, and is followed by several influential critics, including Menéndez y Pelayo. Recent biographers, however, in the light of new knowledge about other parts of Ramon Lull's life, have swung back to earlier dates, and indeed it would be hard, if not impossible, to compile a chronological table based on any birth-year later than 1233. Mn. Galmés in his short biography (p. 11) adopts the year 1233. Mn. Riber, in both his books, records the date 1232, but considers it uncertain. P. Ephrem Longpré (col. 1074) adopts 1235, but Mn. Avinyó argues in favour of 1232 (Av., pp. 52–4, 507–8). To me the arguments in favour of that date are practically conclusive, the dates of the conversion and *Libre de Contemplació* and the reference at the end of the contemporary biography (*Life*, pp. 44–5, 85–6) making a later date more than improbable, and the unsettled state of Mallorca, before 1231, making even that year too early to be likely.

[2] En aquest lloch estava, segons tradició, la casa natalicia del gran savi y benaventurat martir Ramon Lull, 1232–1315.

[3] Terrassa (*cit. Cronicón Mayoricense*, Palma, 1881, p. 5) gets over the difficulty by supposing that the parish boundaries were different in his time (the eighteenth century) and in Lull's.

[4] Seguí, at the beginning of his biography, describes the birthplace as being "en la calle de San Miguel de la ciudad de Mallorca, en una callejuela que no tiene salida, más de la vista que da a la riera, o arroyo, que parte la villa

Some writers assert that N'Elisabet had been married for ten years before she became a mother,[1] and that the story of Aloma's childlessness in Ramon's great romance *Blanquerna* [2] is therefore founded upon fact. For this, however, there is no contemporary testimony of any kind. The most that can be said with confidence is that Ramon was almost certainly an only child, for, although in his numerous works he refers frequently to his father and mother, his wife and his children, he never once makes mention of either brothers or sisters. In that case we can further surmise that Ramon the elder and Elisabet may have been married shortly before the expedition of 1229, which would account for three of the childless years, and be quite sufficient, together with the story of Aloma, to give rise to the tradition. If N'Elisabet had other children before or after the birth of Ramon, they probably died in infancy.

Heir to his father's considerable estates, Ramon was clearly looked upon as a boy with a future. Both his religious and his secular education were carefully planned and rigorously carried out. "I crave Thy grace, Lord God," he says, "devoutly and with all my heart, that Thou wilt bless my father and my mother for bringing me up in the way of truth."[3] If tradition can be believed, Ramon the elder must have held some position near the

de abajo de la alta." Dameto (vol. ii, bk. ii, p. 39) has only the words: "Nació . . . en una callejuela que no tiene salida, a las espaldas de la Inquisición." These two descriptions, at first sight different, refer to the same site, as reference to a map of old Palma will show.

[1] Armengual (*cit.* Pasqual, i, p. 5) seems to be the fountain-head here; he has been followed with greater or less reserve by all biographers. The trait is of course common among legendary accretions in the lives of great men.

[2] See pp. 160–61, below.

[3] *L.C.*, chap. 25 (*Obres*, ii, p. 125). *Cf.* chap. 77 (*Obres*, iii, p. 98): "Thy servant blesses Thee for Thy grace in making him a faithful Catholic, by reason of his father and mother being faithful Christians." Further, the Biblical expression, which Lull continually uses, "I am Thy servant and the son of Thy handmaid," may not be wholly conventional.

For Lull's own ideas and conjectures on education, see *L.C.*, chap. 305, *passim*, *D.P.*, chaps. 73 ff., *Bl.*, chap. 2. It is not possible to say how far these passages are a description of his own education, or a reaction against it, or neither. There can be nothing gained by the gratuitous assumption (*e.g.* in Mn. Riber's *Vida abreujada del B.R.L.*, pp. 8–10) that they depict the author's own experiences.

King, or in other ways have had influence with him, so that he educated his son with a view to obtaining a position for him in the royal court. And he apparently succeeded betimes if it is true that the boy was no more than fourteen years old when James the Conqueror took him into his service as a page.[1]

For about eleven years, James had been married to Violante, daughter of Andrew II of Hungary, and, besides a boy named Alfonso, born of a previous marriage with Eleanor of Castile, he had, of Violante, among other children, two sons, Peter and James, both of whom were destined to reign after him. Ramon must have been a charming and well-bred boy,[2] and the opinion that his father was well descended is the more tenable, though not of course proven, if we accept the tradition that, at Queen Violante's request, he became the companion of the two young princes, aged respectively about ten and four.[3] Both were being educated as boys who would one day rule, for James I was to follow the common though unfortunate custom of dividing his kingdom at his death.[4] Ramon became perhaps something of an elder brother to them, and must have found ample scope for observation in their dissimilar, if not antipathetic temperaments. He was especially beloved by the docile and affectionate prince James, so that, whether for this reason, or because he was a native of Mallorca, of which the younger prince was to be king, he was eventually made his tutor. Between tutor and pupil there were scarcely more than ten years in age, and we can well understand how the intimacy formed in childhood would

[1] All biographers subscribe to this tradition, and though there seems to be little documentary evidence behind it, there is every probability of its truth. The earliest evidence dates from 1373 (Pasqual, *Vindiciae*, i, p. 21).

[2] His extremely lovable disposition in later life is sufficient proof of this.

[3] Peter was born in 1236. About the birth of James, with whom this narrative is more directly concerned, there is some doubt. Zurita and Pasqual both give 1240 ; Swift adopts the date May 30, 1242. The *Thalamus parvus* of Montpellier, however, followed by many writers, makes the day May 20, 1243 ("En l'an de M e CC e XLIII, la vigilia de Pantacosta, nasquet a Montpellier En Jacme lo bon rey"). This date, or Swift's, I take as approximately correct in the text above.

[4] See p. 128, below.

grow continually stronger, with the result that when the tutor was no longer needed he was retained in Prince James' service as "that most illustrious lord's seneschal and majordomo." [1] The friendship between the two never waned. Throughout his career Ramon received continual indications that his former pupil had not forgotten him; we may be sure that he upheld him loyally against the truculent and domineering Peter; and we know that one at least of the happiest experiences in his later life he owed entirely to James' generosity.

In the summer of 1256 [2] the young prince was proclaimed heir to the throne of Mallorca, and, according to some authorities,[3] Ramon accompanied him to Palma, where he received the homage of his future subjects and promised to continue the privileges granted them by his father. The only documentary testimony under this date shows that Lull was in Barcelona—an inconclusive fact—and that his father had then died,[4] which event, if it had taken place quite recently, would no doubt necessitate the son's visit to his birthplace. We may therefore take it as probable that, wherever his headquarters may have been and his wanderings have led him, as successively page, tutor and major-domo, he returned to Mallorca, not only in 1256 with his master, but at other times on his own account, to look after his property.

Some little knowledge of Ramon's life and habits

[1] *V.C.* i; Pasqual, i, pp. 32–4. This is the first thing that we learn about Ramon's life from the contemporary biography. (Cf. *Life*, p. 1.) *V.B.R.L.* has merely "senescallus mensae Regis Majoricarum" (p. 47). What Ramon's office actually was is very uncertain. Nothing is known of an office of seneschal in the court of Aragon at the time, though the major-domo's duties are well defined. (See Bofarull: *Colección de documentos inéditos del Archivo General de la Corona de Aragón*, Barcelona, 1850, Tom. v, pp. 11–18; "Leges Palatinae Jacobi II Regis Majoricae," Pt. i, pp. ix–xii [preface to *Acta Sanctorum*, Junii, vol. iii, Venitiis, 1743]: "De officio magistrorum hospitii sive majorum-domus.")

[2] "xii calendas septembris anno Domini MCCLVI" (*cf.* Miret i Sans, *Itinerari*, etc., p. 253).

[3] *E.g.* Clasqueri and Zurita (*cit.* Av., p. 64).

[4] See J. Miret y Sans, in *Boletín de la Academia de Buenas Letras*, Barcelona, vol. xv, p. 103. In the document, which is in the Barcelona Cathedral Archives, "Raimundus Lulli filius quondam Raimundi Lulli" makes a gift to his first cousin Arnau (Arnaldus), and a Guillem Lull, probably a young relative, is the first of the witnesses. The document bears Ramon's autograph.

during these years of royal service may be gained from autobiographical passages in his later writings, and occasionally from additional sources. In all chivalric accomplishments—witness his *Book of the Order of Chivalry*[1]—he would seem to have delighted. But his principal interest was more probably in the art of the troubadour,[2] which at that time, and above all in Catalonia, Provence and Languedoc, was in its very heyday. The beautiful Catalan language tripped gracefully in *alba*, *ballada* and *sirventés*, and Ramon's later verses, some of them written in the popular troubadour metres,[3] show that the songs of his wanton youth must have been as gay and elegant as any. He who in after life was to be, like St. Francis, a *joculator Domini*, was devoted to "cansons e dances e sons e voltes e lays."[4] That was, after all, perfectly natural. He never threw off entirely the troubadour's mantle, and, among the many attractive characters in his romances, one of the best is a *joglar*.

The instruction in the liberal arts with which Ramon's parents would have thought it necessary to provide him, even in preparation for a career at court, could not have been extensive, and would probably be of less importance than instruction in the accomplishments of a gentleman: reading, writing, ciphering and a little Latin grammar would no doubt make up its total. It is often asserted by his biographers, the early and the late alike, that he had a particular distaste for learning—a doubtfully relevant sentence from one of his works being, however, the only serious evidence that is offered.[5] From what we discover later of his passionately studious temperament, there

[1] See pp. 120–4, below.

[2] Cf. *V.C.*, i: "Com fos en la plenitut de la sua joventut e s fos donat en la art de trobar e compondre cançons e dictats de les follies d aquest mon" (*Life*, p. 1). Cf. *V.B.R.L.*, i (*Life*, p. 47).

[3] *E.g.* the two poems in *Blanquerna* (*Bl.*, pp. 300, 529–30) and some of the stanzas from the *Medicina de Peccat*, such as that beginning:

Quant par l'estela en l'albor . . .

translated in part on p. 300, below.

[4] *L.C.*, chap. 143 (*Obres*, iv, p. 261).

[5] *L.C.*, chap. 109 (*Obres*, iv, p. 41). The sentence is quoted on p. 21, below: it does not appear to me to refer necessarily to learning at all, still less to book-learning.

would appear to be little truth in such statements as Seguí's, that he refused to study and was put to court at his own earnest desire.[1] No doubt, however, it is true enough that if he once entered the King's service as page there would be neither need nor opportunity for study, and, even as the tutor of a prince, he would atone for a defective knowledge of books by proficiency in manly exercises, and by a knowledge and understanding of men.

This last the life of the court, and more particularly the travels which it involved, would give him. The kingdom of Aragon had been greatly extended since the years of Ramon's childhood. It now stretched well to the south of Valencia, westward beyond Saragossa, and northwards as far as Perpignan, while its isolated territories of Montpellier, Carlat and Gévaudan were by no means without importance. Further, James was generally either absent from his own domains or occupied in visiting them, energetically, almost feverishly. In his travels his page would share, and a love for travelling not unnatural in a boy may well have sown the seeds of Ramon's later activity. One of his descriptions of himself is of "a man that has made many journeys over hill and plain, to populous and to uninhabited lands, by river and sea alike, and has seen . . . many kings and barons of high degree."[2] These words refer almost certainly to his journeys in the King's service, for when they were written, in 1272, his travels on his own account had, so far as is known, been confined to a single period spent in religious pilgrimages.

Some memories of James' court he gives us also ; if they are less certainly unmixed with fiction, he could hardly fail to incorporate in his earliest writings upon the conduct of princes some of his personal experiences in the royal house of Aragon. To these we shall draw attention, more naturally than here, in a later chapter. All such reminiscences of court life and foreign travel can be amplified even by a reader with a sluggish imagination

[1] Seguí, *Vida y hechos del admirable doctor y mártir Ramon Lull*, Mallorca, 1606, fol. 2.

[2] *L.C.*, chap. 101 (*Obres*, iii, p. 230).

who considers King James' manifold activities between 1246, the traditional year of Ramon's arrival at court, and 1260 or thereabouts, by which time he was presumably occupied with the business of the young prince entirely.[1] If indeed he became the Conqueror's page at fourteen he would quickly have gained an intensive experience of travel, for the King spent the year 1246 in at least twelve places, revisiting some of them in addition.[2] Nor was he less active in the years which followed : his conquests temporarily concluded, a period during which he was occupied with internal affairs had begun, and he travelled none the less extensively for being mainly in his own dominions. Ramon may well have been with the Conqueror at Valencia, when he was occupied with the eviction from it of the rebellious Moors [3] ; at Osca (Huesca), in 1251, when King James was at Queen Violante's death-bed [4] ; at Soria, in 1256 (unless the Prince's major-domo was cut off from the court of Aragon), when James was reconciled with his son-in-law Alfonso, who for some time had been too ready to test his strength on the Conqueror's frontiers [5] ; at Corbeil, for the betrothal of the Princess Elizabeth to St. Louis' son, afterwards Philip III of France (May 11, 1258) [6] ; and at Barcelona, two months later (July 16), when James I ratified the contract and the political treaty which it involved.[7]

[1] See Miret i Sans, *Itinerari*, etc., pp. 176–310. For the activities of James I during this period, *cf.* also *Chronicle of King James of Aragon*, *passim* ; Swift, pp. 83 ff. ; Aigrefeuille, vol. i, *passim* ; Devic et Vaissette, vol. vi, *passim*.

[2] The Conqueror's itinerary (*op. cit.*, pp. 176–86) for that year being : Valencia, Montpellier, Perpignan, Gerona, Barcelona, Villafranca del Panadès, Xátiva, Valencia, Tortosa, Lleida (Lérida), Pina, Saragossa, Alagón, Saragossa.

James did not go to Valladolid in November 1246 for the betrothal of his young daughter Violante to the heir (afterwards known as Alfonso the Wise) of Castile (*op. cit.*, p. 185. *Cf.* Swift, p. 85).

[3] He must often have been there on other occasions, for James I spent long periods there from 1246 to 1250 and was often there for months at a time in the years following. Miret i Sans, *Itinerari*, pp. 552 ff.

[4] *Op. cit.*, p. 217.

[5] *Op. cit.*, p. 252. Swift (pp. 92–3) dates this event a year later (March 1257).

[6] *Op. cit.*, p. 272 (the date corrects that of earlier authorities).

[7] *Op. cit.*, p. 277.

These travels, in Catalonia, Aragon, Castile and France, did much to broaden Ramon's experience, and his easy and genial disposition must not only have endeared him to his chosen friends but also made him everywhere a welcome companion. There followed the inevitable demoralization of an easy-going temperament by a pleasant life ; and as Ramon grew up into manhood, he showed too evident signs of becoming a dissolute courtier.[1] He gave himself up, in his own words, " to sins and the companionship of vices." [2]

> When I was grown and tasted vanity,
> Then strayed I into sin, worked evilly,
> Forgat my glorious God, with lust made free.[3]

With his gay and thoughtless companions he grew to blaspheme the name of God and to mock the holy things which as a child he had been taught to honour.[4] He abandoned the ways of honesty and upright dealing : " I deceived and acted falsely to many of my own friends," he says, " speaking to them often both falsely and evilly and doing them many wrongs." [5] Most markedly of all, he committed sins of lust, bringing both himself and others into open shame.

In 1257, or rather earlier—probably while still in Mallorca with Prince James—Ramon married a lady of gentle birth, called Blanca Picany.[6] The marriage is

[1] Bouvelles (*Vita Raymundi Lulli*, Paris, 1511), together with those who follow him closely, dilates on this phase of Ramon's life : " Seculariter ergo in palatio regis educatus," he says, " pro more aulicorum mundialiumque virorum totus inter amores vivebat in que ipsis amoribus, non modo flagrantem inventam, sed et maiorem vitae partem inaniter consumpsit : in dictandis dioneis cantilenis praecipue intentus." But it will be noticed that *V.C.* and *V.B.R.L.*, which open so abruptly, show no desire to particularize in this way, and hurry on to Ramon's conversion.

[2] *L.C.*, chap. 106 (*Obres*, iv, p. 25).

[3] Can fui gran e sentí del món sa vanitat
comencé a far mal e entré en pecat,
oblidant Déus gloriós, siguent carnalitat.
Desconort, ii.

[4] *L.C.*, chap. 210 (*Obres*, v, pp. 357–8).

[5] *L.C.*, chap. 23 (*Obres*, ii, p. 115).

[6] The erroneous assertion that Lull's wife was called Catalina Labots should be mentioned, so widespread is it (see, *e.g.*, Gabriel Lull, *B.S.A.L.*,

said to have been arranged by the king, in order to check his vicious career, but, from what we know of James' own love affairs, such solicitude seems highly improbable. Perhaps it was the prince who sought in a characteristically gentle manner to reform him. In any case, the attempt can hardly have been a success. Shortly after his marriage, Lull returned to the gay city of Montpellier, where he no doubt witnessed the burghers' profession of allegiance to Prince James as their future king [1] (December 18, 1258). Revisiting Mallorca in the following year, he seems to have lived for a time with his wife and to have had of her, successively, a son and heir, Dominic,[2] and a daughter, Magdalena.[3] But both at Montpellier and in Mallorca he was continually unfaithful to her, and, although some of the incidents related of his early married

vol. iii, pp. 262–4; Seguí, chap. i, who adds that she was a former mistress of Ramon's; and Cornejo, who merely gives the name).

Most modern writers have corrected this. The correct details are given, *e.g.*, in *Cronicón Mayoricense*, Palma, 1881, p. 14: "Este mismo año de 1257, con instrumento que pára en la escribanía de cartas reales de 8 de las kalendas de Octubre, Blanca Picany, hija de Ferrer Picany, difunto, firmó poder general a favor de Ramon Lull, su marido, hijo de Ramon Lull difunto. Prueba este instrumento y otros que produciremos en el año de 1275 [for this see p. 131, below], que dicha Blanca fué la muger de nuestro Beato Ramon Lull, y no Catalina Labots como han escrito algunos."

The document of 1257, cited by Pasqual (*Vindiciae*, i, p. 22) and others, states that Blanca Picany makes her husband (both being described as above), "absent and present alike," her procurator, and goes on to mention "all the possessions that the said R. Lull holds in the city of Barcelona and its suburbs, and in Catalonia," thus showing how considerable were the estates which Ramon could now call his own.

[1] *Cf.* pp. 115–7, below.

[2] Because he dedicated several books to his son (e.g. *Doctrina pueril*, *Libre de primera i segona entenció*, *Arbre de filosofia desijada*) it is assumed that he had no other. Nor does he mention any other in his will, dated 1313 (see p. 364, below). The inference may be erroneous, but the names of the two children are certainly correct, and Gabriel Lull (*B.S.A.L.*, vol. iii, pp. 262–4) was quite mistaken when he wrote: "Li nasqueren dos fills: Ramon Lull, en 1263, y Guillem Lull, en 1266. Morí lo Ramon sens infans; y del Guillem Lull nasqueren Ramon y Domingo Lulls germans, en los anys 1295 y 1298. . . . Succey a dit Domingo Ramon Lull son germa, bon ciutada, del cual nasque en Ramonet Lull en lo any 1327, etc." Cornejo says that Lull lost his wife when the children were still young, but gives no kind of proof; and we know that she was living as late as 1275 (see p. 131, below). There are also mentions of wife and children in *Obres*, i, pp. 78, 83, iii, p. 175 (1275 and 1272 respectively), and in iv, p. 227, viii, p. 14 (1272), etc.

[3] Magdalena afterwards married a certain Pere [Peter] de Sentmenat, of Barcelona. See p. 364, below.

life may not be historical, it is impossible to question their implication.

Indeed, Ramon himself, as a man of forty, looks back upon these days and brings them only too clearly before us:

> The beauty of women, O Lord, has been a plague and tribulation to my eyes, for because of the beauty of women have I been forgetful of Thy great goodness and the beauty of Thy works.[1]

And nearly forty years after this was written, in his *Phantasticus*,[2] he returns once more to his disordered youth, and, from that distance of half a century, seeing himself vividly in his own remembrance, describes himself incisively and briefly :

> In matrimonio copulatus : prolem habui, competenter dives, lascivus et mundanus.

Two stories of Ramon's youthful ardour, both referring to a period subsequent to his marriage, have become famous. Neither is found in the contemporary biography, nor is either in any way established, but each is related by authorities sufficiently credible to make possible its truth. We reproduce them in their simplest form, stripped of the adornments, added by later biographers, which only disfigure their outline.

It appears, first, that Ramon was enamoured of a lady of rare beauty,[3] who, being herself happily married, had no desire for the attentions with which he persecuted her.[4] These reached their climax one day when, riding on horseback through the city, he espied her entering a church [5] for the purpose of devotion. Suddenly his passion overwhelmed him, and, putting spurs to his

[1] *L.C.*, chap. 104 (*Obres*, iv, p. 11). *Cf.*, among other passages, chap. 143, *passim*, where he goes into great detail on the inordinate love of women.

[2] See p. 356, below.

[3] Tradition makes her a Genoese, and gives her name as Ambrosia de Castello. Pasqual (i, p. 47) follows another tradition, which names her Leonor.

[4] "La estaba regalando como antes [de casarse]," says Seguí, "dando muchas músicas, insistiendo en saraos, componiendo cada día nuevos cantares en su servicio."

[5] The Cathedral, for High Mass, according to Seguí, who is always prodigal of local colour. St. Eulalia is the church generally associated with this episode, but the attribution is not taken seriously.

horse, he galloped right into the church, the sanctity of which he would no doubt have violated still further had not the worshippers, in a tumultuous scene, ejected him.[1]

This unhappy incident,[2] so runs the tradition, decided the lady that by some means or other Ramon's suit must be ended. How she brought this about is the subject of the second story.

After asking permission of her husband to employ a drastic remedy, she summoned her admirer to attend her in some secluded place—perhaps her own chamber—when, instead of yielding, as no doubt he expected, to his demands, she uncovered her bosom, and displayed a breast that was being slowly consumed by a loathsome cancer.[3] "See, Ramon," she cried, "the foulness of this body that has won thy affection ! How much better hadst thou done to have set thy love on Jesus Christ, of Whom thou mayest have a prize that is eternal ! "[4]

Of the two stories this latter seems the less improbable, one interesting argument in its favour being provided by a work of Lull's late middle life, *Felix, or the Book of Marvels*, in which a very similar incident is told in great detail.[5] Briefly—for this narrative is un-

[1] Bouvelles' account runs thus : "equo conscenso in foro spaciaretur : videretque eam quam fatuo amore diligebat, in vicinum templum divine precis causa profectam : mox (tametsi eques) illam in templum persecutus est, ex quo confestim (velut amens et incompos sui factus) cui ingenti omnium risu explodi meruit."

[2] Pasqual (*op. cit.*, i, pp. 47–8) gives no credence to the story, not only because it is not in the contemporary biography, but because Lull (he says) always recounted in his works the worst offences of his youth, and was in any case too much of a gentleman by birth and breeding to commit such an act as this. Though Bouvelles records the episode, it is not found in Pax, and I do not myself think it genuine.

[3] I use the mediaeval substantive. "Insanabilis erat haec cancri pestis in pectore mulieris," says Bouvelles, "sed longe insanabilior cupidinei amoris cancer mentem laniabat Ræmundi."

[4] This story also is not in Pax. Bouvelles (who seems to be the first to relate it) goes into some detail, as also does Cornejo, more gruesomely. The latter adds the words : "Give not to a woman the love that thou owest to God." Pasqual (i, p. 58) considers the story to be false.

[5] Very few writers have noticed this similarity. (A list is given by Longpré, col. 1075.) Menéndez y Pelayo (*Orígenes de la novela*, i, p. lxxxiv) quoted the episode, but considered the tradition of the cancer-story to be founded upon it. Mn. Riber (*Vida i actes*, etc., p. 109) also takes this view. To me it seems more likely that Ramon, in *Felix*, is narrating, in a carefully

pleasantly outspoken—a bishop is deeply enamoured of a lady who refuses to do his will though he has wooed her on many occasions with great vehemence. At last she invites him to her chamber, where, to his initial discomfiture, he finds no less than three witnesses—the lady's two waiting-maids and her nephew! In this company she disrobes before him, and reveals a sight perhaps even more revolting, if less spectacular, than the cancer. The lady then reproves him sternly for his sin "in desiring to bring her into the wrath of God and of her husband and of her friends, and into the blame of the people." Whereupon the repentant prelate has "great shame and contrition."[1]

Whether the incident of the cancer be historical or no, it was certainly not the immediate cause of Ramon Lull's reformation, which perhaps is an argument against the genuineness of the story. Nothing less than direct Divine intervention was to reclaim him. "It was Thy Passion, O Lord," he says himself, "that aroused and awakened Thy servant, when he was . . . dead in mortal sins."[2] The Passion of Christ was in fact "the beginning and the cause"[3] of his conversion, an event which came about "in the fulness of his youth,"[4] or, as nearly as can be determined, when he was about thirty years of age.[5] He was sitting, one summer

disguised form, an incident drawn from his own early life—a practice not uncommon with him: he does it in *Felix* (see pp. 217, 222, below)—than that out of the many hundreds of stories which he relates in his works this particular one should, for no discoverable reason, have become incorporated in the Lullian tradition. Further, it is usual for such stories to gain in force, and not to lose, with the re-telling; and anyone who has read in *Felix* the story related above will agree that it is more daring and (except perhaps to refined modern ears) more effective than the cancer-story.

[1] *Felix*, bk. viii, chap. 27 (*Obras*, iii b, pp. 120–1).

[2] *L.C.*, chap. 55 (*Obres*, ii, p. 287). [3] *Ibid.* (pp. 287–88).

[4] *V.C.*, i (*Life*, p. 1).

[5] This fact is stated on several occasions by Lull himself, and, if we give due weight to his actual words, we shall place his conversion in the thirty-first year of his age (*c.* 1263):

"Jo son estat foll del comensament de mos dies dentrò a xxx anys passats, que comensà en mi remembrament de la vostra saviea e desig de la vostra laor e membransa de la vostra passio." (*L.C.*, chap. 70: *Obres*, iii, p. 65.)

"Car xxx ans ha que jo no son en est mon estat fructuós, ans son estat noable a mos veyns e a mos amics." (*L.C.* chap. 107: *Obres*, iv, p. 27.)

evening,[1] in his chamber, humming an air, to which he was engaged in fitting some amorous verses in the vulgar tongue, addressed to whatever lady may have been temporarily mistress of his heart. Suddenly, "when his whole understanding was engaged and occupied in the composition of this vain song,"[2] he chanced to look up, still absorbed by his thoughts, and there, on his right side, was the figure of "our Lord God Jesus Christ hanging upon the Cross."[3] So great was the shock of the vision that his pen fell from his hand. No doubts as to its objectivity occurred to him; no theory that he could form would account for it. His brain reeled; his powers of reasoning were numbed and dead. To return to his writing was impossible. He left the papers as they were, scattered about him, and betook himself straightway to his couch.[4]

No doubt he decided, on reflection, that he had been overwrought by his passion, and, when he rose the next morning, sat down again immediately to his song, thinking no further of the vision. But, a week later,[5] at about the same hour, when he was sitting in the same place writing another part of his song,[6] he suddenly became conscious once again of the sacred Presence. This time he was still more alarmed.[7] Without staying for a moment's thought, he flung himself upon his bed, and buried his face in the bed-clothes so that he might not see the terrible and persistent vision.

[1] Comment has already been made on the tendency of Lull's less trustworthy biographers to make his birth, conversion and death fall on saints' days (p. 8, above). The day commonly assigned to the conversion is the Feast of the Conversion of St. Paul, Jan. 25. But from what follows it is clear that it must have taken place in June or July, a fact which Pasqual (i, pp. 54, 81) refuses to see, preferring to credit the tradition. Upon this tradition, some notes will be found in Av., pp. 74 ff.

[2] *V.C.*, i (*Life*, p. 2).

[3] *V.C.*, i (*Life*, p. 2). It adds the words "molt dolorat e apassionat," which are not in *V.B.R.L.* (*Life*, p. 48).

[4] *V.C.* is very vivid: "Lo qual vist, hac gran temor en sí metex, e lexant totes aquelles coses que tenía enfre les mans, anà s metre en lo llit e va s colgar." *V.B.R.L.* is identical (*Life*, pp. 2, 48).

[5] This detail is from *V.B.R.L.*: "Quasi post octo dies postea in loco, quo prius, etc." (*Life*, p. 48.) *V.C.* (*Life*, p. 2) has merely "altra vegada."

[6] *V.C.*: "aquella hora e en aquell loc metex." *V.B.R.L.*: "in loco, quo prius, et quasi hora eadem." (*Life*, pp. 2, 48.)

[7] *V.C.*: "molt pus espaventat que no de la primera [visió]." So *V.B.R.L.* (*loc. cit.*)

As Ramon confesses, and as his later history will show, it was a stubborn and determined will that was even now in the pangs of a new birth. "Neither blows," he says, "nor punishments, nor pleasures, nor caresses, nor wiles of any man avail either to mould my will or to check it."[1] The loose-living seneschal was in no way prepared for a heavenly vision as the neophyte Francis had been when his Master spoke to him from the crucifix of St. Damian. Three times more did he take up his pen and assay to complete his song. And three times there appeared that Figure upon the Cross in agony, mute but insistent in its appeal.[2] These appearances are among the best authenticated events of Lull's whole life,[3] for not only does the contemporary biography relate them in great detail, but Ramon himself records them in one of his poems :

> But Jesus Christ, of His great clemency,
> Five times upon the Cross appear'd to me,
> That I might think upon Him lovingly,
> And cause His Name proclaim'd abroad to be
> Through all the world.[4]

[1] *L.C.*, chap. 109 (*Obres*, iv, p. 41).

[2] The conversion is placed by *V.C.* after the fifth appearance, which is obviously correct (for *cf.* n. 3 below) : "Jatsía per axò, aquella folla voluntat ell no lexà, ans bé, aprés pocs jorns tornant ell en acabar aquella cançó e no curant d aquelles visions maravelloses, fins que terçament, quarta e quinta li aparec" (*V.C.* i : *Life*, p. 3). *V.B.R.L.* (i : *Life*, p. 48) differs slightly : "In quarta ergo vel etiam in quinta vice, sicut plus creditur, etc."

[3] The various sixteenth- and seventeenth-century biographers differ considerably as to where the five appearances took place, there being no reliable testimony : some of their views are discussed by Custurer, pp. 487–8. Bouvelles makes Christ appear first to Ramon in his house, and say : "Ramon, follow Me." Seguí and his many followers place three of the appearances in Mount Randa at a later date (see pp. 106 ff., below), and assign to each a separate and distinct purpose. This is evidently incorrect.

Bouvelles, Pax and others suggest further that the first vision came to Ramon when he was in a state of great depression, again contradicting the contemporary biography. Seguí says that he went straight to Randa after the cancer episode.

[4] Plac a Jesucrist per sa gran pietat
que es presentà a mi cinc vets crucifigat
per ço que el remembràs e en fos enamorat
tan fort que eu tractàs com ell fos preïcat
per tot lo món. . . . (*Desconort*, ii).

Cf. *Cant de Ramon*, i :
Jesús me venc crucificat,
volc que Déus fos per mi amat.

The repeated experience terrified him increasingly, roused him to think, and awakened his conscience into action. "The pricking of his conscience told him that our Lord God Jesus Christ desired none other thing than that he should wholly abandon the world and devote himself to His service."[1] For a whole night he debated the matter.[2] So insistent was the vision that it could be calling him to nothing less than a complete change of life : and its unvarying form could only mean that he was to set Christ crucified in the forefront of an existence which previously had been occupied by vanities.

One thought alone stood between him and the life which was soon to be his. Was he worthy ? Could his sins be forgiven ? Would one whose opportunities had been so great, yet whose past had been so utterly abandoned, be received into the company of Christ's servants ? It was this question, at first insuperable, which left him in such remorse as only great sinners and great penitents have known. Gradually there was borne upon him "the great tenderness, patience and mercy which our Lord has toward sinners."[3] And with the day there came an overwhelming calm, the joy that cometh in the morning.

Ramon had taken comfort. He had now "true confidence in our Lord that, notwithstanding the life which until that day he had led, it was His will that he should devote himself wholly to His service."[4] He began, as he tells us himself, by going to confession, and, shriven of his sins, took the first steps upon the road of his great future.

> Pardon I sought at break of day.
> Contrite and sad, I went straightway
> My sins before God's priest to lay.

[1] *V.C.*, *V.B.R.L.*, i (*Life*, pp. 3, 48–9).

[2] *V.B.R.L.*, i (*Life*, pp. 48–9) tells us this twice : "Secum tota illa nocte cogitando tractans, quidnam visiones istae toties iteratae significare deberent . . . Laboriosam illam noctem duxit insomnem." *V.C.* (*Life*, p. 3) has only : "Estec molt acongoxat tota aquella nit, pregant nostre Senyor que l illuminàs."

[3] *V.C.*, i (*Life*, p. 3). *V.B.R.L.* (*Life*, p. 49) is even more emphatic, reading ". . . quam habuit et habet circa quoslibet peccatores."

[4] *V.C.*, i (*Life*, p. 3).

Came God's great gifts with hope's glad ray—
Devotion, love and power to pray—
And these will ever with me stay.[1]

It was a hard road, we may be sure, that Ramon was now to follow, and for one who had been journeying for so long in the contrary direction there could not fail to be in store a time of severe spiritual stress. "Never at any time soever," he confesses some ten years later, "have I experienced such strivings as when I turned from sin to acts of penitence." [2] The passage of years might blur the impression of those struggles, but they could never obliterate them. Ten years pass, and we find Lull still recalling the agony of confessing Christ before men, and setting his face like a flint lest he should act as one unmindful of his good profession :

Great need have I, Lord, that Thou shouldst fill me within and without with truth, so that all the falsehoods and lies that are in me may leave me and never more return, and that I may confess all my faults, crying them aloud before men.[3]

Till I go crying Thy truth aloud through the city, and till I cry aloud likewise the falseness which is in us, I shall not believe that I am in the way of truth.[4]

Twenty years pass, and again we find lines, which probably Ramon wrote with the pangs of conversion in his remembrance, in his *Book of the Lover and the Beloved* :

"O bird that singest of love, ask thou of my Beloved, Who has taken me to be His servant, wherefore He tortures me with love." The bird replied : "If love made thee not to bear trials, wherewith couldst thou show thy love for Him ?" [5]

[1] *Cant de Ramon*, ii. The original is slightly terser in its expression :

Matí ané querre perdó
a Déu, e pris confessió
ab dolor e contrició.
De caritat, oració,
esperança, devoció,
Déus me fe conservació.

[2] *L.C.*, chap. 86 (*Obres*, iii, p. 147).
[3] *L.C.*, chap. 23 (*Obres*, ii, p. 116).
[4] *L.C.*, chap. 24 (*Obres*, ii, p. 121).
[5] *Bl.*, p. 416 (No. 35).

The Beloved sang, and said: "Little knows the Lover of love, if he be ashamed to praise his Beloved, or if he fear to do Him honour in those places wherein He is dishonoured most grievously; and little knows he of love who is impatient of tribulations; and he who loses trust in his Beloved makes no agreement between love and hope."[1]

In one brief colloquy he summarizes both his fears and the thoughts that quelled them:

The Beloved said to his Lover: "Thou shalt praise and defend Me in those places where men most fear to praise Me." The Lover answered: "Provide me then with love." The Beloved answered: "For love of thee I became incarnate, and endured the pains of death."[2]

And in a parable of four short lines he describes, not indeed the first overwhelming visions of the suffering Christ which turned him from his evil ways, but an ever-recurrent vision of the strengthening Christ which kept him in the new ways whither He had led him:

The Beloved revealed Himself to His Lover, clothed in new and scarlet robes. He stretched out His Arms to embrace him; He inclined His Head to kiss him; and He remained on high that he might ever seek Him.[3]

From the day of his conversion, the crucifix had for Ramon Lull a new and intimate meaning. "Beloved Lord!" he writes at a later date, in an intensely personal passage:

Even as a woman who looks upon herself in a mirror can see therein the beauty or the ugliness of her face and her features, even so, O Lord, when thy servant looks upon the Cross, can he see and perceive all within himself that is beautiful and all that is repulsive.[4]

And about the same time, at greater length, he describes in moving language the nature of one of his frequent meditations:

[1] *Bl.*, p. 423 (No. 80).
[2] *Bl.*, p. 431 (No. 135).
[3] *Bl.*, p. 425 (No. 91).
[4] *L.C.*, chap. 104 (*Obres*, iv, p. 13).

When I kneel before the sacred Figure upon the Cross and seek assurance of salvation in that part of the Cross whereon rested Thy wounded Head, I find there tokens of damnation, because I have not raised my mind from things that are low and mean that it might soar to the heights of Thy greatness (*les vostres altees*). When I seek it in the place where Thy Feet were nailed, I find likewise damnation, remembering that my feet have not run the way of Thy commandments. When I seek it in front of the Cross, where Thy Body hung, I find damnation, because in the forefront of my youth I placed, not love of Thee, but love of worldly vanities. When I seek it behind the Cross, where naught can be seen but the cruel nails that pierced Thee, there likewise I find damnation, remembering that I have cast Thy love behind my back and thought only upon things that are vile and unworthy. When I look to Thy right Hand, the Hand of justice, I see damnation, for I think upon the sins for the which I merit it. And when I look to Thy left Hand, the Hand of mercy, I see damnation, for I merit neither mercy, nor glory, nor Thy Presence.

But when . . . I am wholly confounded, and know not where to look or whither to turn myself, then do Thine Eyes behold me, and in those Eyes which wept for our sins, and that Heart which was wounded and cleft for us, do I seek and implore my salvation. And in those tears, and in that Thy love and mercy—there do I find my health and my salvation, and there only.[1]

[1] *L.C.*, chap. 189 (*Obres*, v, pp. 193–4).

CHAPTER II

1263–1274

Hopes and projects. Pilgrimage. Influence of St. Ramon de Penyafort. Return to Mallorca. Studies in Arabic, theology and philosophy. Episode of the Moorish slave.

THROUGHOUT his new life, Ramon Lull presents the strangest blend of extreme idealism and sound common sense, so that one can never quite determine whether to call him a practical man or a visionary. But his worst enemies would not deny that, from first to last, he was active and energetic, spending none of his time debating instead of doing, but pursuing the ideals which appeared to him as relentlessly as he is said to have pursued his lady. No sooner had he determined to rule his life by Christ than he set out to follow Him to the world's very end. Let the contemporary biography for a while tell its own story.

"When by reason of this deliberation and purpose," it runs, "he was enkindled and inflamed in love of the Crucified, he considered what act and what service he might do that would be pleasing and acceptable to the suffering Christ[1]; and while he thought upon this he remembered those words of the Gospel that greater love and charity can no man have toward another than that he lay down his life for him. Wherefore the said reverend master, now wholly enkindled in the ardour of love for the Cross, deliberated as to what greater or more pleasing act he could do than to convert infidels and unbelievers to the truth of the holy Catholic faith, and thereby place his person in peril of death.[2]

[1] *a l apassionat.*

[2] *V.C.*, i (*Life*, pp. 3–4); *V.B.R.L.* (*Life*, p. 49) is a little less explicit.

The idea that he would one day suffer martyrdom for Christ appears to have been with him from the beginning of his converted life and never for long to have left him. Evidently he was pursuing this idea in the meditation referred to by the contemporary biography. He would lay down his life, as a missionary and a preacher, for the Gospel. But then once more there came doubts, and doubts well-founded. How could he, Ramon Lull, do this ? He might, through God's grace, be given the love, but he had not the " ability and fitness," [1]—in other words, the necessary learning. Whether or no he had cared little, as a boy, for books, he had certainly had little use for them, and as a consequence had scarcely learned more than the rudiments of Latin grammar.[2] Alternately there came over him fits of despondency and of confidence. First, he is plunged into despair, and remorse again visits him, as he considers his wasted youth. Then he determines that he will by some means or other write books —" some good and others better "—which shall confute the errors of the unbelievers.[3] How this is to be done he cannot yet conceive, for he realizes that it will be necessary, at the very least, to learn Arabic and Latin, as well as the sciences, but, in his moments of strength, Divine inspiration confirms him in his purpose.[4]

Gradually, further ideas occur to his fertile mind. If he is not a scholar, he is at least a successful courtier. He may perchance be God's chosen vessel to bear Christian ideals before kings as well as Gentiles, and he will use in His service the favour which he can command

[1] *V.C.*, i (*Life*, p. 4).

[2] " un poc de gramàtica " (*V.C.*) ; " . . . nec etiam de grammatica aliquid nisi forte minimum didicisset " (*V.B.R.L.* : *Life*, pp. 4, 49).

[3] " Començà a haver tanta dolor, que quasi isqué de sí metex ; e pensant aquestes coses ab pensa dolorosa, confià e pensà que encara per avant ell faría libres, uns bons e altres millors, successivament contra les errors dels infeels." (*V.C.*, i. *V.B.R.L.* speaks only of " unum librum praestantem et meliorem de mundo contra errores infidelium," *Life*, pp. 4–5, 50.)

[4] "Açò, però, hagué ell per inspiració divinal, car com ell era en si metex no podía pensar com ni en quina manera ell ordinaría los dits libres, com no hagués sciencia, e pensant més avant que jatsía ell açò faés, pus no sabia la lengo morisca o aràbica, que res no li aprofitaría " (*V.C.* i; cf. *V.B.R.L.*, i : *Life*, pp. 5, 50).

On the question of Lull's learning, see also Index, *sub* Arabic, Latin.

in high places. He will still have influence, no doubt, with James the Conqueror, whose desires for the genuine conversion of Jews are well known, and who, quite apart from religious considerations, may be expected to favour any scheme which will further the subjugation of the Moslems. Prince James, whose tutor and companion Ramon has been, is just entering upon manhood, is meditating marriage [1] and will in due course be as influential as he is now impressionable. Further, the Conqueror's elder son, Peter, who has quite recently allied himself with a Sicilian princess, will succeed to dominions more important than those of his brother, while the daughters also have married into powerful dynasties and will not refuse the desire of his heart to one whom they have known from childhood. Violante's husband, Alfonso the Wise, has for the last eleven years been King of Castile ; Constance has married Alfonso's brother Manuel ; while Elizabeth will in course of time be Queen Consort of France. Added to all these possible sources of influence are the friendships that the royal seneschal will undoubtedly have made in past years, on his travels, at home and abroad, with the King. In at least one direction, then, his way lies clear before him. "The power to convert unbelievers is in the will of God. . . . And, since He wills thus, therefore has He given power to the Pope and the Cardinals and other prelates and clerks—to wit, riches and men and wise persons that have knowledge." [2] He will remember this. He will go abroad to the courts of Christian princes ; he will importune prelates in their very palaces ; he will obtain the ear of the Holy Father himself. He will beg them one and all to send out more and more missionaries who will preach the holy Catholic faith to the heathen. And, that their preaching may have greater efficacy, he will urge the foundation of colleges and monasteries in which they may learn sciences and the

[1] James the Conqueror was even then (1262–6) negotiating for Prince James' marriage with Beatrice of Savoy. But, in spite of the lengthiness of the negotiations, the alliance was never accomplished.

[2] *D.P.*, chap. 83 (*Obres*, i, p. 154).

languages of the heathen.[1] Such foundations have already been heard of,[2] and the practical side of Lull's nature tells him that they are an essential preliminary to evangelistic work in heathen countries if unbelievers are to be converted by preaching and disputation and not merely overcome by a crusade of force.

So much, as we know more or less certainly, Lull had thought out in some detail within a few days of his conversion. It may also have been at this time that there came to him a second idea which was destined to occupy an important place in his projects. This was the idea of using the sum of human knowledge in the composition of an "art" (that is, a method) whereby unbelievers should be confuted in argument and the truth of the Christian religion triumphantly established over all. If, at the time of which we are writing, this project was not yet fully evolved, and Ramon's only literary ambition was to "make books" (or "a book")[3] for the conversion of the heathen, it is certain that it developed very shortly afterwards, for in a few years' time it was not only to blend with his other religious ideals but to take the foremost place among them all.

Together with these desires, there came to Ramon Lull an overpowering longing to go himself to preach the Gospel in Africa, to suffer himself for the Master Who had suffered, both once long ago and many times afresh, for his sins ; and, if he were found worthy, to lay down his life and win the crown of martyrdom.[4] Again and again, at recurrent intervals, this desire swept over him, overwhelming him by sheer force. He could never forget that the Beloved—the Saviour Who had appeared to him—had clothed Himself in the raiment of His Lover, that he might be His companion in glory for ever. What

[1] ". . . diverses monastirs aon homens savis e literats estudiassen e aprenguessen la lingua aràbica e de tots los altres infeels per ço que posquessen entre ells preicar e manifestar la veritat de la sancta fè catòlica" (*V.C.*, i: *Life*, p. 5). Cf. *V.B.R.L.*, i: (*Life*, p. 50): "monasteria, in quibus electae personae religiosae et aliae ad hoc idoneae ponerentur ad addiscendum praedictorum Saracenorum et aliorum infidelium idiomata."

[2] See pp. 35–6, below.

[3] See p. 27, n. 3, above.

[4] *V.C.*, *V.B.R.L.*, i (*Life*, pp. 5, 57). *Cf.* p. 24, above, and *L.C.*, chap. 220 (*Obres*, v, p. 437).

more natural, to one for whom eternal truth was a present fact, than that the Lover should desire in his turn to wear crimson garments, and so be the more like to his Beloved ?[1]

Love urges and impels me, Lord, to go to my death for praising Thy honours. But wherefore, Lord, since I am unworthy to die a death that is so exceeding lovely and have neither the strength nor the power to die for love of Thee, does love reproach and torture me because I die not for Thy love ? And wherefore does the abundance of my will make me to desire that whereof I am not worthy ?[2]

There was no thought in his mind, it would seem, so early as this, of the inauguration of a new crusade of arms.[3] Ten years or more had passed since the last Holy War of this kind had come to an inglorious conclusion, and though the worst disasters had not yet happened—St. Louis was alive and Antioch, Tripoli and Acre were still Christian—it was becoming only too clear that, whatever the way of the Spirit might accomplish, the way of the Sword spelt failure. The Holy Land and the Holy Sepulchre were still unconquered ; the progress of Islam was accelerated rather than lessened ; while, with all their bloodshed and strife, their mingling of cruelty and idealism, the Crusades had done nothing, as it was at one time hoped that they might, to heal the schism of East and West. The most practical men of the time, as well as the most Christlike, began to see that the only way to possess the Holy Land was not by might, nor by power, but by the Spirit of the Lord of hosts. Ramon, as he meditated on his future, saw this also.

Many knights do I see who go to the Holy Land thinking to conquer it by force of arms. But, when I look at the end thereof, all of them are spent without attaining that which they desire. Wherefore, it appears to me, O Lord, that the conquest of that sacred land will not be achieved . . . save by love and prayer and

[1] *L.A.A.*, 262 (*Bl.*, p. 451).
[2] *L.C.*, chap. 220 (*Obres*, v, p. 437).
[3] I write this despite *Desconort*, iii, where Ramon says that he did desire to set on foot a crusade (*passatge*) " ab ferre e fust e ab ver argument," for that poem was written over thirty years after this date. See also p. 73, n. 1, below.

the shedding of tears as well as blood. . . . Let the knights become religious, let them be adorned with the sign of the Cross and filled with the grace of the Holy Spirit, and let them go among the infidels to preach truth concerning Thy Passion.[1]

With all these thoughts filling his mind—more particularly his three firmly fixed projects of books, colleges and martyrdom [2]—Ramon betook himself to a church not far from his house, " where, prostrate upon the ground, he besought with tears the suffering Christ," [3] Who had led him to make this act of dedication,[4] that He would bring his desires to a " good end and conclusion." [5]

As soon as he returned home,[6] he set about making the preparations which the sudden change in his life demanded. They were neither few nor short, and occupied him for no less than three months.[7] The anonymous Latin biography diverges here from the corresponding life written in Catalan by suggesting that, had he wished, he might have arranged his affairs more speedily, and calling him slothful, lukewarm and too much in love with the world.[8] This may well be the case, though the Catalan biography, which hints at no such thing, shows not the slightest disposition elsewhere to hide Ramon's faults.

[1] *L.C.*, chap. 112 (*Obres*, iv, pp. 58–9). Ramon had not changed his opinion ten years later.

[2] *V.B.R.L.*, i : " Hic igitur tribus supradictis articulis in animo suo firmiter jam conceptis . . ." Cf. *V.C.*, i (*Life*, pp. 5, 51).

[3] *V.C.*, i (*Life*, p. 6).

[4] *V.B.R.L.* (*Life*, p. 51). *V.C.* merely describes " these three things " as " resolved within his mind."

[5] *V.C.*, i (*Life*, p. 6).

[6] There is a tradition (Mut, *cit.* Pasqual, i, p. 82 ; *cf.* Custurer, p. 482) that, as he was returning from the church, the Virgin and Child appeared to him near the Almudaina Gate. For a long time, an image, now demolished, commemorated the spot. The fifteenth paragraph of *L.A.A.* (*Bl.*, p. 414) is often quoted as a testimony to that experience, but it is of so ordinary a nature as to make such an inference quite unnecessary.

[7] " . . . acabada la sua oració, tornant s en en sa casa, com los negocis mundanals lo tenguessen encara empatxat, estec per tres mesos que ab diligencia no posqué en les dites coses treballar " (*V.C.*, i : *Life*, p. 6).

[8] " Post haec ad sua reversus, cum nimis esset adhuc imbutus vita et lascivia saeculari, in praedictis tribus conceptis negotiis prosequendis per tres subsequentes menses, scilicet usque ad sequens festum Sancti Francisci, satis fuit tepidus et remissus " (*V.B.R.L.*, i. *Life*, p. 51).

Towards the end of this period came the Feast of St. Francis,[1] which had been instituted little more than thirty years before and was a festival of great popular interest. As one would expect, Ramon attended Mass on that day, perhaps in St. Francis' church, and it chanced that a bishop, who was preaching the sermon there, laid great stress on the completeness of St. Francis' surrender. He had given up, not only his inheritance, but everything he possessed : even of his clothes he had stripped himself, that he might serve his lady Poverty with undivided love. The words went home to the conscience of the now impressionable young man. If he had been trying, during these months of preparation, to make terms with the world—if he had even been hoping to serve two masters—the words of the bishop were sufficient to complete that conversion which the visions had begun. Francis had served Lady Poverty : Ramon would serve Lady Valour.[2] No longer does he think about this tie and that with his former life.[3] Such of his possessions as are needed by his wife and children for their support he puts aside for that purpose. The remainder he sells —not without a struggle, for he has loved his wealth [4]— and, distributing the proceeds among the poor,[5] abandons his native island for so long as it shall please God.[6]

[1] This falls on October 4. The appearances of Christ to the Beat Ramon would therefore have taken place about the beginning of July.

[2] Valour, in Lull's writings, has generally the sense of "true worth." See (*e.g.*) *Bl.*, chap. 48, pp. 175 ff. and 455 (No. 291).

[3] According to the Karlsruhe MS. (J. Rubió, "El Breviculum, etc," p. 84) he received the habit of a hermit from the Bishop who had preached the sermon : there is a realistic picture of this in the second illustration of the Karlsruhe series.

[4] See *L.C.*, chap. 84 (*Obres*, iii, p. 137) where Lull describes himself as having still a covetous nature, and being unused to giving alms. But it is fair to read, together with this, *Desconort*, xviii, written at a much later date.

[5] See *L.C.*, chap. 79 (*Obres*, iii, p. 110). Cf. *Desconort*, xiv and xviii, where he makes what happened perfectly clear. At the same time, it would appear from *L.C.*, chap. 315 (*Obres*, viii, p. 11) that he was not, even in 1272, "wholly rid of the possession of temporal wealth" : no doubt he aided his wife effectively to administer what he had given her.

[6] This narrative follows *V.C.*, i (*Life*, pp. 6–7) exactly. As to Ramon's departure, *V.C.* has : "E de fet, lexada certa part de bens per la sustentació de la muller e infants, anà s en . . . etc." *V.B.R.L.* (*Life*, p. 52) adds : "(abiit) cum intentione numquam revertendi ad propria."

Ramon's first act, upon leaving Mallorca, was to undertake a lengthy pilgrimage.[1] "Why dost thou weary thy body, cast away thy wealth and leave the joys of this world?" his former friends would ask him. "Why dost thou go as an outcast among the people?"[2] To escape from this eternal question, to be free for a time of open gibes and curious glances,[3] may perhaps have been, at least unconsciously, as strong a motive as the more usual one of kindling devotion at frequented shrines. Neither the itinerary nor the duration of his pilgrimage can be more than guessed at. From the contemporary Catalan biography[4] we learn that he went to "divers holy places," among which was the "Church of St. James"—no doubt Santiago de Compostela.[5] The only other place which this biography mentions is "Our Lady of Rocatallada," which most critics take to be the shrine of Montserrat. The Latin life, however, states that he went to Rocamadour,[6] a favourite mediaeval place of pilgrimage in the south of France, the chapel of which, set in a magnificent position upon a cliff, is said to commemorate a foundation made by the penitent Zacchæus of Scripture. It is likely enough that he went to either, or to both, though, for a Mallorcan, Montserrat would be the most natural place of devotion.[7] Where the "divers holy places" were is uncertain. It is conjectured that they included the sepulchre of St. Peter and St. Paul at Rome, and the holy places in Jerusalem, principally because, some eight or nine years after this date, when for seven years at least it is unlikely that he had left Mallorca, Lull writes as if from personal observation of the habits of pilgrims in these places:

[1] The Karlsruhe MS. (see J. Rubió: "El Breviculum, etc.," p. 83) places the pilgrimage before the Bishop's sermon, but this is most improbable.

[2] *L.A.A.*, 12 (*Bl.*, p. 413).

[3] *L.A.A.*, 177 (*Bl.*, p. 438).

[4] *V.C.*, i (*Life*, pp. 6–7).

[5] Cf. *Bl.*, chap. 88 (pp. 377–8), which may have been written from personal reminiscences of this pilgrimage.

[6] "Abiit . . . ad Sanctam Mariam de Ruppis amatore" (*Life*, p. 52).

[7] Custurer (p. 493) is so sure that Lull went to Montserrat that he contradicts the very Latin text which he prints. Pasqual (i, p. 90) also thinks that it was Montserrat. Modern opinion tends rather to follow *V.B.R.L.*, and Sollier, who supports it.

We see men go on pilgrimages, O Lord, for love of Thee and to honour Thee, in search of the holy places and the churches wherein Thou showest miracles. They go to visit Thy holy Sepulchre, and the church of Rome, and the holy apostle St. James, and other places wherein remembrance is made of the holy apostles, and of other saints, both men and women.[1]

The description which follows is long, intimate and detailed, and is unlikely to be founded only on hearsay, the more so because the book of which it forms part is, as we shall see at a later stage, full of reminiscences of Ramon's earlier life. But there is a brief passage in a book that is later still, more eloquent than many pages of description, which reveals to us vividly the inner history of that first long journey, and perhaps of others which succeeded it.

The Lover was in a far country, and he forgat his Beloved, but was sad at the absence of his lord, his wife, his children and his friends. But soon the memory of his Beloved returned to him, that he might be comforted, and that his exile might cause him neither yearning nor sorrow.[2]

We cannot tell with certainty when Ramon returned to Spain from his pilgrimage: probably it was in the winter of 1264–5. When he did so it was with the brave idea—carried out in a later day by St. Ignatius of Loyola—of putting himself to school, that he might the sooner and the more effectively realize his projects. This was natural enough, considered logically. He had purified his soul, made heartfelt reparation for his sins, and, by his temporary self-exile, divorced himself completely from surroundings which might have dragged him back to them. Now was to come the intellectual preparation,—the acquisition of "grammar and other sciences"—and it was characteristic of Ramon Lull's ambitious spirit that he determined to go to the best centre of learning available, "the great University of Paris." [3]

But his acquaintances and intimates ("friends and

[1] *L.C.*, chap. 113 (*Obres*, iv, p. 63). [2] *L.A.A.* 334 (*Bl.*, p. 463).
[3] *V.C.*, ii (*Life*, p. 8). So *V.B.R.L.* (*Life*, p. 52).

familiars ")[1] were alike opposed to this course, and among them was one venerable adviser, so greatly revered, and so completely in sympathy with Lull's own ideals, that it would have been almost impossible for him to run counter to his judgment. St. Ramon de Penyafort, an aged Dominican whose life was to cover an entire century (1175–1275),[2] is an interesting figure to study by the side of Ramon Lull, and, like him, is one of the great mediaeval characters of Catalonia. " Confessor of kings and popes," as he was called in his day, St. Ramon had been grand penitentiary and general of his order, and chaplain to Gregory IX. He had filled, among other positions, the responsible one of keeping the conscience of a powerful and amorous Conqueror : James I's predilection for Dominicans was always very marked, and none did he value more than the saint who kept him, in spite of his frequent rashness, on the right side of ecclesiastical authority. Together they had waged war upon heretics and begged the Pope to establish the Inquisition in Catalonia.[3] Since then, and especially since the Council of Tarragona in 1242, the elder Ramon had been a scourge to the unorthodox and a veritable sword of the Lord against Jews and Saracens. Yet his methods of conversion, like the methods favoured by James the Conqueror,[4] were peaceful : at least one king of Tunis was his personal friend and, in 1256, he had been able to report to his general that over two thousand Saracens had presented themselves to him for baptism.[5] Further, he had seen, no less clearly than his namesake saw later, the paramount importance of the study of Oriental languages : it was largely because of his suggestions that definite proposals for such study had been made by the Dominican provincial chapter of Spain which met at

[1] *V.C.* ii (*Life*, p. 8). *V.B.R.L.* (*Life*, p. 52) has " parentes et sui amici."

[2] " Et maxime Frater Raymundus de Ordine Predicatorum, qui quondam Domini Gregorii IX compilaverat Decretales " (*V.B.R.L.*, i). *V.C.* is slightly less explicit (*Life*, pp. 8, 52).

[3] Effected by the bull *Declinante jam mundi vespere* in 1232.

[4] See p. 297, below.

[5] Touron, *Histoire des hommes illustres de l'ordre de Saint Dominique*, *cit.* Torras i Bages, p. 179.

Toledo in 1250, and again at a chapter-general in Valencia nine years later.[1] It is even said, though with doubtful correctness, that he had himself founded two schools of Oriental languages, at Murcia and at Tunis.[2] Further, it is certain that St. Thomas Aquinas' *Summa contra gentiles* was written, when St. Ramon was general of his order, at his suggestion—one authority even holds that it was composed at his command.[3]

These particulars of the life of the Dominican saint, who, at the time of our narrative, would have been ninety years of age, will give some idea of the influence which his opinion would have upon Lull, who might well have derived most of his own ideals from the saint's achievements. Possibly the latter may have looked upon this young disciple as his successor: in any case, Lull's college of Miramar, to be founded some eleven years later, was at least as truly in the succession of his work as was the college of Arabic founded by Fra Joan de Puigventós in Valencia in 1281 and the school of Hebrew and Arabic established in 1291 at Xátiva. We do not know what arguments St. Ramon and Lull's other advisers used to dissuade him from going to Paris, but, if we may deduce anything from his actions on returning to his native city, it would seem that they had represented to him the incompleteness of his spiritual preparation,—possibly also the perils of contact with the growing force of Averroism.[4] Now that he has been strengthened by his experiences at the sacred shrines, he must learn first of all to live as a Christian among those who have known him as a worldling—he must bear witness in his own home to the reality of his conversion. For the rest, his ignorance being so great, he can study at present in Palma as easily and profitably as elsewhere, especially the

[1] Mortier, i, p. 519.

[2] Diago, *cit.* Torras i Bages, pp. 179–80. Some authors assert that he had also founded a school at Barcelona. See also *Acta Sanctorum*, January, i, 411; R. Otto, pp. 511–3.

[3] Diago, bk. ii, chap. 16, and Touron (*cit.* Torras i Bages, p. 181), where an interesting comparison is made between St. Thomas and St. Ramon.

[4] See pp. 345–9, below.

language of those whom he hopes to convert, since there are many Moors still in Mallorca.

This counsel prevailed, and, on his arrival in Palma,[1] he at once cast aside "all superfluous clothing, such as he had been accustomed to wear, and dressed himself in a habit that was very honest and of the coarsest cloth that he could find."[2] "I am clothed with vile raiment," he would reflect, "but love clothes my heart with thoughts of delight, and my body with tears, griefs and sufferings."[3] Several passages in his early works suggest that his humiliation gained for him the opprobrium of his fellow-citizens,[4] and indeed we can well imagine that the re-appearance in Palma of the former royal seneschal clad in sackcloth would not create a very favourable impression. He would be regarded as something worse than Ramon the Fool in *Blanquerna*. "Say, O Fool," hast thou riches?" his former friends would cry at him. And his answer, learned at the foot of the Cross, would be: "I have my Beloved."[5] He had not yet given proof of the great ability which was his, nor perhaps had his self-sacrifice and years of pilgrimage as yet convinced those around him of his high degree of earnestness and sincerity. He was neither a cleric nor a professed religious. Though apparently he still lived in his house, surrounded by his family and his servants,[6] he had abandoned the primary duties of his married state and had renounced his honourable calling for the fantastic

[1] Mn. Galmés, in his biography (p. 30), dates this *c.* 1266, but the dating of later events forces me to put it back to 1265, and probably very early in that year.

[2] *V.C.* ii (*Life*, p. 8).

[3] *L.A.A.*, 149 (*Bl.*, p. 433). Cf. *V.B.R.L.*, i (*Life*, p. 52): "Assumpsit sibi vilem habitum de grossiore panno, quem ipse poterat invenire." *L.A.A.*, 144 seems to be a reminiscence of the same period.

[4] The most striking is in *L.C.*, chap. 10 (*Obres*, ii, p. 47), quoted in the text below. Other references are in *L.C.*, chap. 126 (*Obres*, iv, p. 155) and in the prologue to the *Libre del Gentil* (*Obras*, i, p. 3).

[5] *L.A.A.*, 177 (*Bl.*, p. 438).

[6] So we gather from *L.C.*, chap. 138 (*Obres*, iv, p. 227). In chap. 143 (iv, p. 261) he writes of himself as being "bound and subjected to the order of matrimony," and wishes that he might forsake it for the company of religious. In chap. 316 (viii, p. 14) he regrets being "occupied by the necessities of his wife, his children, and his friends," and longs for solitude and freedom.

pursuit of an ideal. He was now leading nothing else than a life of idleness ! So at least those who of old had been his associates would have it : so, for that matter, would run the gossip in a similar situation to-day. Some thought Ramon merely simple : others held his " abundant fervour " to be " all but madness "[1] and were not slow to act accordingly. Persecution in the thirteenth century was cruder and less refined than now, and it is easy to imagine the scenes which moved Ramon to write thus during his sojourn in his native city :

> Ah, Lord God ! Thy servant thanks and blesses Thee for that it has pleased Thee to give him greater fear of Thy judgment alone than of all the people who mock at him in the streets,—yet once he had greater fear of their judgment than of Thine.[2]

As he rode alone on horseback through the streets, the sight of the poor would move him to sorrowful self-reproaches, and the very respect paid him by his own wondering servants would be bitter to him.[3] More welcome than such honour were the scorn and the disdain of his enemies, and if, now and then, these moved him to wrath, he quickly recollected himself :

> When my ears hear men dishonouring me, reproaching me, reviling me and cursing me, then my heart feels itself moved to wrath, ill-will and displeasure and it begins to desire and to work evil. But I reflect that . . . if I grow sad when I am reviled and reproached, who am a thing vile and mean, how much more should I be glad when I hear Thee praised and honoured and obeyed and blessed and loved ! But my soul is so full of sin that too often I shut my ears when men speak of Thy goodness and honour and virtue, and open them to hear vainglory and worldly honour ; and when I hear the contrary thereof my soul is displeased because it hears not that which it desires and loves.[4]

At such times of depression, he would retire into the solitude of his own heart, where he found consolations which no man on earth could give him :

[1] *L.C.*, chap. 220 (*Obres*, v, p. 435) : " Me tenen quax per orat."
[2] *L.C.*, chap. 10 (*Obres*, ii, p. 47).
[3] *L.C.*, chap. 138 (*Obres*, iv, p. 227).
[4] *L.C.*, chap. 125 (*Obres*, iv, p. 146).

So enkindled is thy servant, O Lord, with desire to be contemplating Thy honours and praises that he withdraws himself, retires and flees from men, both by night and by day, that he may contemplate Thee more steadfastly and more fervently.[1]

One thinks of that audacious paradox which Ramon wrote in a later day :

The Lover was all alone, in the shade of a fair tree. Men passed by that place, and asked him why he was alone. And the Lover answered : " I am alone, now that I have seen you and heard you ; until now, I was in the company of my Beloved." [2]

Such appearances, then, as Ramon made in public were probably as few as they were unhappy. Nor was he given a better welcome when he expounded to curious enquirers his ambitious projects for the conversion of the heathen. The disillusionment which in the future was again and again to damp, though never to quench, his idealism was already making itself felt during these early years of trial in Mallorca.[3] No enthusiasm he found, no zeal : more thought was given to the externals of religion than to its essentials.

For the churches I see divers images and paintings made, which will beautify them ; but I see few men who will learn divers languages, or who will go and preach to the infidels, or bring them into the true way of life and lead them from the error wherein they now are.[4]

This lament was but the forerunner of many.

Of the nature of Ramon's studies in Palma, apart from the fact that they included Latin and Arabic,[5] little is known. No doubt the resources of the Dominican

[1] *L.C.*, chap. 222 (*Obres*, v, p. 449). [2] *L.A.A.*, 47 (*Bl.*, p. 418).

[3] *L.C.*, chap. 138 (*Obres*, iv, p. 227).

[4] *L.C.*, chap. 106 (*Obres*, iv, p. 25).

[5] *V.C.*, ii, *V.B.R.L.*, i (*Life*, pp. 8–9, 52–3). It is supposed by some critics that he already knew Arabic, but I am entirely of the same opinion as P. Ephrem Longpré, whose concise summing-up of the arguments (col. 1076) it is needless to repeat. He seems to me less happy when (col. 1076) he supposes Lull to have studied a *Liber petitionum et quaestionum* and identifies it with the *Liber quaestionum veteris et novi Testamenti*, attributed at that time to St. Augustine. This book I believe to be by Lull himself (see p. 82, below).

convent, founded at the time of the Reconquest, were open to him, and with the Cistercian house of Nostra Dona de la Real, which lay some two miles outside the city, he seems to have been all his life long on terms of intimacy.[1] It is to be supposed from his writings that, besides Latin and Arabic, he studied principally philosophy and theology, reading widely and deeply in the Scriptures and perhaps also in the Fathers of the Church. It is asserted that he "had a perfect knowledge of Aristotle and Plato, read the works of Richard of St. Victor, Avicenna and others, and especially a treatise much in vogue among the schoolmen, the *De Scientiis*, of Alfarabi."[2] Of all this, however, we have no proof,[3] and when we consider the great progress which his actual achievements soon after this time suppose him to have made in literary Arabic—perhaps in Latin also—it is difficult to believe that he can have studied Aristotle and Plato very deeply, still less the works of mediaeval mystics. Further, if he was aiming at a broad general education, he probably laid the foundations of the knowledge of natural science on which he built more substantially later.[4]

His principal study, however, was undoubtedly Arabic—one of the languages, probably, to which he pathetically refers as seeming to him "like the voices and languages of beasts."[5] The study, to one unskilled in foreign tongues and undisciplined to habits of work,

[1] See pp. 109, 133, 365, below.

[2] Av., p. 104. Pasqual (i, pp. 103–4) gives references here to *L.C.*, chaps. 151, 331, where certain philosophers are mentioned, but the references do not seem to be of such a kind as to prove anything.

[3] Longpré (cols. 1076–7) makes the best of a bad collection of evidence, thus: "Il a aussi pris contact avec saint Anselme et Richard de Saint-Victor dont il se réclame dans un de ses premiers ouvrages, le *Liber mirandarum demonstrationum* (l. i, c. xiv, *Salz*, ii, p. 7) et avec Aristote dont il cite et résume les principaux écrits (*D.P.*, c. lxxv, pp. 197–99). Des analogies frappantes permettent encore de croire qu'il a étudié le *De divisione philosophiae* de Gundisalvi. La dialectique du *Liber de Gentili et tribus sapientibus* (Salz, vol. ii), ses exposés célèbres de la théologie musulmane (Golubovich, *op. cit.*, p. 376) supposent aussi une longue et pénétrante initiation aux grands courants de la pensée islamique." The last sentence is true enough, but the books cited are too late in date to make the remaining suppositions more than fairly likely.

[4] *Cf.* pp. 109, 365, below.

[5] *L.C.*, chap. 125 (*Obres*, iv, p. 148).

would indeed be a formidable undertaking. In order to succeed in it the more completely, he purchased a Moorish slave who lived in his household for nine years, and became the cause of a characteristic and dramatic incident which the contemporary biography relates in detail. One day, when Lull was away from his house, the Moor began to blaspheme the holy name of Jesus Christ. The offence was reported to his master, whose zeal showed itself at once in anger. He struck the Moor fiercely, " on the mouth, the head, the face, and on other parts of his body."

Now as the said Moor was of a very haughty spirit, and further, as he had been almost in the position of master to his lord in teaching him the Moorish tongue, he had great wrath at these blows, and bethought himself how and in what manner he could kill and slay him. And having in his possession, one day, a knife that was very sharp, and seeing his lord sitting alone in a chair, he leaped upon him with a great cry, saying : " Now shalt thou perish."

The said reverend master parried the blow as best he was able, notwithstanding which he was wounded therewith above the stomach, yet not mortally.[1] So he strove with the Moor, and overcame him, and took from him the knife. When the others that were in the house heard the noise, they came and desired to slay the Moor, but the said reverend master permitted it not, but caused him to be put in prison until he had deliberated what to do with him.[2]

The deliberation, as may be imagined, was not easy. On the one hand, Ramon had to consider the benefit which he had received from the Moor's instruction, and the debt of gratitude which he therefore owed him. It seemed impossible to put to death the man who had so helped him to honour God. On the other hand, if he yielded to this feeling, might not the slave make another attempt, and perhaps a successful one, to be avenged on him ?[3] In the end he went away into retreat, to the

[1] *Cf.* Pasqual, i, pp. 123–4.

[2] *V.C.*, ii (*Life*, pp. 9–10). The above is a literal translation : the remainder of the incident follows *V.C.* and *V.B.R.L.* closely.

[3] *V.C.*, ii ; *V.B.R.L.*, i (*Life*, pp. 10, 53–4).

monastery of La Real,[1] so that he might think out the problem more carefully and ask for guidance from heaven. But no such guidance came to him—rather, he was more perplexed than ever.

Disconsolately, at the end of three days, he returned home. On the way he had to pass the prison where his slave was lying in daily expectation of his sentence. For some motive—perhaps hoping that an interview with the Moor might decide him one way or the other—he entered the prison. To his unspeakable relief, he found that the heavy responsibility had been taken from him : the Moor, having evidently little faith in the quality of his master's mercy, had committed suicide by hanging himself with the cord which bound him.

[1] *V.B.R.L.* has merely "ascendit ad Abbatiam quandam, quae prope erat"; *V.C.*, however, is quite definite: "anà s en a nostra Dona de la Reyal" *Life*, pp. 10, 54) and *V.B.R.L.* refers later (p. 55) to "Abbatiam regalem supradictam."

CHAPTER III

The *Book of Contemplation*. Evidence as to date. Plan, method and scope of the book. Summary of its content. Lull's views on the conversion of unbelievers, especially of Moslems. Estimates of the *Book of Contemplation*. Maturity of its outlook and style. Its intrinsic value.

THE crime and suicide of the Moorish slave took place in all probability early in the year 1274,[1] and, whether by chance or no, seem to have coincided with the completion of Ramon's studies in his native city.[2] We can only guess at the rare happenings of interest which came to break the monotonous round of instruction and private study during those nine years in which a fervent spirit held in apprenticeship an active brain. How, in the winter of 1265–6, the student must have longed to throw away his newly acquired grammar-books and follow the royal princes on their adventurous southern campaign—to Alicante, Elche and the final siege of Murcia![3] Rarely, it would seem, did Prince James visit the island which was one day to be his, but twice at least (in 1267 and 1268) he was there, and we may be sure that Ramon was frequently in the royal household then, and unfolded his ideals and projects to the astonished prince, who by this time would have learned, as young men do, to

[1] This date is later than that given by various writers, notably Pasqual, who rejects the plain statement of the contemporary biography (*Life*, pp. 9, 53) that the Moor was with Ramon for nine years and is followed by some modern biographers (*e.g.* Mn. Galmés, p. 31). I have studied Pasqual's reasons for his chronology (*Vindiciae*, i, pp. 58–9) with great care, but can see next to nothing that can be said for them. Since Ramon's return from abroad cannot be placed earlier than early in 1265, therefore, the Moor's suicide will have taken place in 1274. Nor do I find any further chronological difficulty involved in the adoption of the later date.

[2] The natural inference would be that Ramon felt strong enough in Arabic not to need a new teacher.

[3] *Chronicle of King James of Aragon*, ccccix ff.

look upon his former tutor as a man of his own age. It is easy to imagine James' wonder at the completeness of the change which religion had wrought in his once gay and courtly companion. That he was not unsympathetic is a fair inference from later events. He could not then know that a similar renunciation, and one of much more brilliant worldly prospects than Ramon's, would in the future touch him most nearly; that in his late middle age, his own son James—"the best and the eldest, who should have reigned"—was to give up a possible crown and the fruits of a successful marriage in order to strip himself gladly of his possessions and serve the Lady Poverty in the Franciscan order. Be it said to his honour, the Mallorcan king supported and encouraged his son in this resolve: had he learned how to do so, we may wonder, years before, from the example of the royal seneschal?[1]

Such events as the visits to Mallorca of Prince James, or of St. Ramon de Penyafort,[2] and the more momentous appearance of the Conqueror in 1269,[3] to raise recruits and collect 50,000 *solds* and three ships for the Crusade which was to witness the lamented death of St. Louis,[4] can hardly have been to Ramon, deeply occupied with his work as he was, more than passing distractions, to be welcomed indeed for the moment, but esteemed of value only if they prospered his projects. In addition to his studies, he found, during his nine years in Palma, two new and engrossing activities. One of these was the holding of disputations with Jews and Saracens,[5] who continued to inhabit the city in great numbers.

[1] See Dameto, bk. iii, p. 525; Muntaner, chap. 182 (from which comes the quotation in this paragraph); Aigrefeuille, vol. i, p. 168; Lecoy de la Marche, i, p. 366; Finke, *Acta Arag.*, i, p. 145.

[2] Diago, bk. ii, chap. 17.

[3] For James' enthusiastic account of Mallorca's help, see *Chronicle of King James of Aragon*, cccclxxxiii (*ed. cit.*, ii, p. 601). *Cf.* Dameto, *cit.* Pasqual, i, p. 111.

[4] Dameto, bk. ii, p. 439. James did not, as it fell out, himself take part in this Crusade. He duly set sail, in September 1269, but encountered a tremendous storm and was fortunate to land at Aiguesmortes (Devic et Vaissette, bk. vi, p. 914).

[5] *Cf.* Pasqual, i, pp. 105–7.

It appears that these debates were held under the patronage of Prince James,[1] who as yet had had no proof of Ramon's powers, but saw no difficulty in granting his approval to such missionary efforts as he felt moved to make in Palma.[2]

Lull's second, and much more important, activity was the composition of his earliest works, of which he completed at least two while the Moorish slave was still living in his household. One of these, the great *Book of Contemplation*,[3] was actually first written, wholly or partly, in Arabic,[4] so that the help of the slave would be of the greatest value. Since it was afterwards translated into Catalan, and this task was completed in or about the year 1272,[5] it evidently represents the firstfruits of Lull's

[1] *Cf.* Pasqual, i, pp. 108–9.

[2] For possible reminiscences of these disputations, see *L.C.*, chap. 187 (*Obres*, v, pp. 169 ff).

[3] The Catalan text is to be found in *Obres*, vols. ii–viii; the Latin text in Salz., vols. ix, x.

[4] Probably most of it was composed in Arabic, for from the last words of the book it appears that the translation occupied Lull some eleven or twelve months only: "Finished and ended is this translation of the Book of Contemplation from Arabic into Romance, the which translation was completed on the first day of the year [*i.e.* March 25] and the composition in Arabic was completed and brought to an end on Good Friday." (*Obres*, viii, p. 645.) But that Lull did modify the form of the work in translating it is clear from the end of chap. 352 [*Obres*, viii, p. 456] where he says: "Thy servant, O Lord, in translating this work from Arabic into Romance . . ., alters and changes such arguments as are less lofty than those which he sets down in their stead." See on this point Obrador's comments in *Obres*, ii, p. xx.

[5] In *L.C.*, chap. 129 (*Obres*, iv, p. 172) Lull writes that he is "about forty years of age" (*cf.* chap. 106,—*Obres*, iv, p. 25—and *Obres*, ii, p. 369, n.). This he would have been in 1272. At the end of *V.B.R.L.* (*c.* 1311: *cf.* n. 1, p. 351, below) we learn that he has been engaged in writing for forty years, which again is approximately exact if *L.C.* was finished in 1272. *V.C.* is a little less explicit, but a comparison of *Life*, pp. 44, 85–6, will probably convince most readers that both versions mean to convey the same thing. Mn. Galmés (*op. cit.*, p. 39) puts the composition of the book after the supernatural illumination of Randa, and, in order to do this and to keep the date 1272 (as well as for other motives—see p. 43, n. 1, above) reduces the number of years spent by Lull at his studies from nine to seven. This, as has been said, directly contradicts *V.C.* and *V.B.R.L.* For my own part, I can see no difficulty in the assumption that *L.C.* was written before Lull ever went to Randa at all, and this is confirmed by the significant fact that, though the book is full of biographical detail, avowed as such or only thinly veiled, there is no reference in it either to Randa or to any such illumination as Lull is known to have received there, even in such places as the end of chaps. 100 and 101 (*Obres*, iii, pp. 225, 229), where he is referring specifically to the Divine help

genius as an author. Indeed, his output was so great, and the reminiscences of his early life in the book are so frequent, that we may wonder if it does not perhaps incorporate parts of some spiritual journal or day-book which he kept from the time of his conversion. This, however, is but conjecture. The bare facts are that neither of the exact date of the work, nor of the place and circumstances in which it was written, have we any record [1]; but the year 1272 fits best into our general biographical plan, and there are several signs that the book was begun, if not also ended, at an early stage in Lull's career.

First, there are many references in it to his court life which suggest that this had not yet receded into the background of his memory. Only one who had moved in court circles, or who at least was familiar with courtiers, would so frequently illustrate his reflections from the conduct of "kings and princes and noble barons of this world." [2] Their disdain for gifts of small worth is described,[3] their use of high-sounding titles,[4] the crying aloud of their ordinances through their cities,[5] their extravagant love of their possessions,[6] their inaccessibility,[7] the delight which men take in speaking with them,[8] the greed of an evil prince for conquest and dominion without regard to justice,[9] the intentions of an unworthy vassal in serving his lord and master, and the considerate treatment of a worthy vassal at the hands of a righteous prince,[10] who will even die for his subjects.[11] We see the king at his pleasures, with his falcons,[12] horses and dogs,[13] with

needed in the writing of his book. In the *Ars Magna*, on the other hand, there is a reference to *L.C.* (cf. *Obres*, ii, p. 373).

[1] For an account of the principal manuscripts and early Latin versions of the book, see *Obres*, ii, pp. 340–67 ; v, pp. v–ix ; vi, pp. i–ii.

[2] *L.C.*, chap. 91 (*Obres*, iii, p. 171 *et passim*). From here to the end of the chapter all references are to *L.C.* except where otherwise stated.

[3] *Ibid.*

[4] Chap. 92 (*Obres*, iii, p. 180).

[5] Chap. 350 (*Obres*, viii, p. 419).

[6] Chap. 104 (*Obres*, iv, p. 13).

[7] Chap. 111 (*Obres*, iv, p. 52).

[8] Chap. 97 (*Obres*, iii, p. 208).

[9] Chap. 292 (*Obres*, vii, p. 237 ; *cf.* pp. 239–40).

[10] Chap. 146 (*Obres*, iv, p. 276) ; *cf.* chap. 251 (*Obres*, vi, p. 233).

[11] Chap. 319 (*Obres*, viii, p. 55, *et passim*).

[12] Chap. 109 (*Obres*, iv, p. 42).

[13] Chap. 284 (*Obres*, vii, p. 146).

troubadours, singers and musicians on the viol and lute,[1] with *joglars* and "tellers of new things" to whom he gives money and garments "that they may spread abroad his fame over all the world."[2] The courtiers' garments are described, the "spacious and painted halls" of their mansions, the knights with their richly caparisoned steeds, the ladies, painting their faces or embroidering their dresses and taking care that no spot or stain shall defile them.[3] Rich banquets are set before us and "delicate wines" in goblets of gold.[4] When these are despatched and men rise from table, there come *joglars* and flatterers (*lagoters*) with instruments of music, singing songs and speaking of vanities. These things are by no means to be despised and condemned, so the author says, unless indeed men think of nothing else, but "spend and squander upon them their time, their health, their youth and their riches."[5]

Whole chapters discuss themes, to Ramon very obviously personal ones, such as the love between a prince and his people[6]: the faithful and admiring vassal, it may further be noted, is a continually recurring figure. Most striking of all are the three chapters devoted respectively to princes, knights and *joglars*[7] and their several vocations. In these we see less of the good side of the mediaeval court than of the evil. Princes who should guard their people from injustice appoint corruptible men as bailies, *veguers*, procurators and judges. Many princes are extravagant and wasteful, making war upon the slightest pretext rather than ensuring the safety of their subjects and improving conditions at home. The size of their retinues prevents them from getting into touch with their people; they hunt for their own amusement, while wolves, in the shape of conscienceless officials, devour their flock. So their lives pass in idleness, and they

[1] Chap. 215 (*Obres*, v, p. 391).
[2] Chap. 256 (*Obres*, vi, p. 275); *cf.* chaps. 292, 299, 300 (*Obres*, vii, pp. 239–40, 312, 326).
[3] Chap. 284 (*Obres*, vii, pp. 150–1); *cf.* chap. 292 (*Obres*, vii, p. 235).
[4] Chap. 299 (*Obres*, vii, p. 310); chap. 297 (*Obres*, vii, p. 293).
[5] Chap. 299 (*Obres*, vii, p. 312).
[6] Chap. 304 (*Obres*, vii, pp. 359–70).
[7] Chaps. 111, 112, 118.

think complacently that God will honour them in the next world as He has honoured them in this, in which belief they are disastrously mistaken.[1] Certainly it would appear that Ramon's travels have not shown him the better side of royalty :

> Many a time have I enquired of men who go about the world if they have seen a prince that is full of perfections, and never have I found any that could tell me of such a one.[2]

The knights he presents to us are not much better than the princes, for they dishonour themselves and each other by frequent quarrels and the use of "proud and evil words."[3] Created knights that they may root out evil men from the world, they appear rather to spend their time in slaying "the just men and those that love peace rather than war."[4] More degraded still has become the office of *joglar* ; for, while its earliest songs were in praise and honour of God, *joglars* sing now only of lusts and vanities, and their ballads and lays and music and dancing are held in the highest esteem.

Whether such criticisms were justified or no, it is clear that they must for the most part have been the outcome of personal reminiscence. Occasionally even, the vividness or the detail of a reference suggests a thinly disguised allusion to some recent event :

> I saw a stray dog enter the court of the king—old, lean, mangy, and very repulsive to look upon. And then I saw that the king and his knights cried out at it and all the dogs of the court attacked it and drove it from the palace.[5]
>
> All the knights [of a court] know full well that the king loves a knight who approaches him gracefully, and they have knowledge thereof in the king's countenance and in the welcome which he gives to that knight every time that he appears before him.[6]
>
> When an honoured king does honour to a vassal, and clothes him with royal vestments, and gives him a seat in his council, and makes him to share his secrets and admits him to his intimacy and love, then gives he him ever cause and occasion of joy and contentment and pleasure.[7]

[1] Chap. 111, *passim*.
[2] Chap. 111 (*Obres*, iv, p. 53).
[3] Chap. 112 (*Obres*, iv, p. 58).
[4] *Ibid* (p. 57).
[5] Chap. 108 (*Obres*, iv, p. 35).
[6] Chap. 169 (*Obres*, v, p. 11).
[7] Chap. 349 (*Obres*, viii, p. 415).

The marked strain of penitence which runs right through the *Book of Contemplation* is also suggestive of an early date, the more so because it is rather less marked in the later books than in the earlier. "Vile and poor am I," ends the prologue, "both by my nature and by my evil works, wherefore I am not worthy that my name be written in this book nor that the work be attributed to me." [1] "How hast Thou suffered me to remain upon the earth," cries Lull in the fourth chapter, "who have been disobedient to Thee that art so great?" [2] "Thou hast made me to remember," he says elsewhere, "the estate wherein I lived . . . companying with wild beasts and dead in my sins; for my solace and pleasure were with men who were beasts indeed." [3] The greater part of one entire chapter is occupied with similar lamentations. "The more apt I found myself to sin, the more I allowed my nature to obey the dictates of my body." [4] "A fool was I, to waste and squander everything that I have." [5]

These definite and unmistakable allusions to Ramon's youth must be supplemented by scores of others, less personal if considered one by one, but as cumulative evidence of early date quite convincing. There is no other of Lull's works in which he refers to himself so often as "vile and mean," [6] "full of sin and wholly sin," [7] in which he marvels "that so small a body can contain so much evil," [8] confesses that while his friends and relatives trusted him, he worked them nothing but harm,[9] and laments that in time past he has served the flesh and the devil.[10] His was not an unusually introspective nature and during the greater part of his long life he was able to forget the things that were behind in reaching forth to others that were before. If further proof were needed that the *Book of Contemplation* was begun soon after the return to Mallorca, it might be found in such

[1] Prologue (*Obres*, ii, p. 6); *cf.* chap. 366 (*Obres*, viii, p. 641).
[2] Chap. 4 (*Obres*, ii, p. 20).
[3] Chap. 10 (*Obres*, ii, p. 49).
[4] Chap. 71 (*Obres*, iii, p. 72).
[5] *Ibid.* (p. 69).
[6] Chap. 5 (*Obres*, ii, p. 25).
[7] Chap. 76 (*Obres*, iii, p. 97).
[8] Chap. 5 (*Obres*, ii, p. 25).
[9] Chap. 75 (*Obres*, iii, p. 91).
[10] Chaps. 66, 67 (*Obres*, iii, pp. 44–5, 49–50).

passages as these which follow, all from the early chapters of the work, and telling of a mind still under the influence of a violent reaction from sin :

Many a time have I loved this worldly life, so that I thought it to be life indeed. But now . . . I know that it is no life at all, and never shall I call it so again, but rather a lingering death.[1]

One of those am I who many a time through their faults have lost Thee. Wherefore I say now to my soul that it must never lose Thee more, lest . . . once Thou art lost Thou be never again found.[2]

But what of Thy servant, O Lord, whose life has been so unruly that he has placed his first intention in things vile and mean, and only his second intention in Thee ? [3]

Since my beginnings and my youth have been spent in the ways of foolishness and have been given up to the works of sin, I beg Thy favour, O Lord, to grant me wisdom, that in my old age and at my end I may walk ever in wisdom's way.[4]

In the best time of my age, O Lord, I gave myself up wholly to sin . . . but now I would fain give up to Thee both myself and all things that are mine.[5]

Since the nature and property of this world is to torture all those that would find happiness in it, Thy subject and Thy slave, O Lord, renounces the world wholly and will have none of its glory or its happiness.[6]

A few definitely autobiographical references, some of which are quoted elsewhere, confirm these suggestions of early date. The author describes how he has " endeavoured with all his might to learn the Arabic tongue, and to understand the words thereof," and begs God to grant him His grace and blessing, " to the end that soon, by the use of Arabic words, I may be able to . . . show forth the truth concerning Thy Sacred Passion and Holy Trinity." [7] Clearly, when the first draft of this passage was written, Lull's studies had not progressed far, and that he eventually allowed it to stand when translating the book into Catalan probably means that he felt his Arabic still to be far from perfect. Another significant

[1] Chap. 26 (*Obres*, ii, p. 16).
[2] Chap. 29 (*Obres*, ii, p. 144).
[3] Chap. 45 (*Obres*, ii, p. 238).
[4] Chap. 70 (*Obres*, iii, p. 64).
[5] Chap. 79 (*Obres*, iii, p. 110).
[6] Chap. 99 (*Obres*, iii, p. 219).
[7] Chap. 125 (*Obres*, iv, p. 148).

fact is that, fond as Lull always was, in his later works, of mentioning a number of others which he had already written, hardly a single citation or mention of his own works is made in the *Book of Contemplation*,[1] which, on the other hand, is itself quoted freely in the *Book of Doctrine for Boys* (*c.* 1275), *Blanquerna* (*c.* 1283), the *Art of finding truth* (*c.* 1287), and elsewhere.

Turning now to consider the *Book of Contemplation* as a whole, we are struck at once by its length, which alone, whatever its merits may be, entitles it to a detailed consideration. In the modern Catalan edition, the text, without index, expository note or commentary, occupies seven volumes containing in all not far short of three thousand pages and well nigh a million words. The careful arrangement of the book, as well as the extent and the importance of its content, suggests that the composition was spread over a long period of time. It could surely not have been written in one year, as is asserted by the tradition which no doubt derives from the fact of its having three hundred and sixty-six chapters : indeed, it is much more likely to have occupied its author—between planning, execution and translation—for the greater part of his nine years in Palma. Lull himself is very conscious of its length, and the weightiness of its matter, for he describes himself picturesquely as an ant carrying on its back a burden larger than itself, which, for all its readiness to undertake it, it can hardly bear.[2]

The divisions of the *Book of Contemplation* are marked by a typically mediaeval artificiality, not unlike that which disfigures the *Siete Partidas* of Alfonso the Wise. First, there is a chapter for reading on each day of the year, the last chapter (which, according to this system, will be read only in leap years) being divided into four parts, indicative of the nature of the three hundred and sixty-sixth day.[3] The main division of the work is into five books, in remembrance of the five wounds of Jesus Christ

[1] For such citations as are to be found, see p. 82, below.
[2] Chap. 220 (*Obres*, v, p. 436).
[3] Chap. 366 (*Obres*, viii, pp. 626, 637).

on the Cross. A second division is into forty sections or distinctions, signifying the forty days which He spent in the wilderness. The three hundred and sixty-six chapters are divided each into ten paragraphs, in significance of the ten commandments given by God to Moses ; each paragraph has three parts, in honour of the Holy Trinity ; and the resulting thirty-fold division of every chapter serves to represent the thirty pieces of silver for which Christ was betrayed by Judas. Still farther is the symbolism pressed in the number of distinctions which each book contains : Book I, with nine, represents the nine heavens ; Book II, with thirteen, Christ and the twelve Apostles ; Book III, with ten, the five physical and the five spiritual senses ; Book IV, with six, the six directions [1] ; and Book V, which has only two, the two intentions.[2]

Artificial as these divisions seem to-day, it must be remembered that their symbolism illustrates the "two motives alone" with which the book was written, to praise God and have God's blessing, motives which are emphasized by the fact that in every division of every paragraph God is addressed by name, so that technically the work is one long address to the Deity.[3] Its aim appears to have been to describe as much of God's nature and attributes as it is within the power of human mind to comprehend ; to show Him, further, in His dealings with men ; and, in a secondary and as it were a reflex sense, to describe man's relations and duties to God. In the fulfilment of this aim, as noble as it was ambitious, is implied the proof, by "necessary reasons" (*raons necessaries*) and incontrovertible argument, of the fourteen articles of the faith.

> He who will perceive (*apercebre*) the fourteen articles by necessary demonstrations, let him read in this *Book of Contemplation* ; for in various places therein he will find and perceive that all these articles are indeed truth.[4]

[1] See p. 25, above, for a passage in which these figure, also *L.A.A.*, 258–60 (*Bl.*, pp. 450–1).
[2] Pròlech. See, for a definition of these, p. 156, below.
[3] *Cf.* Pròlech, § 16 (*Obres*, ii, p. 5).
[4] Chap. 160 (*Obres*, v, p. 21).

And likewise a more general appeal, both to the heart and to the intellect, is intended :

As this *Book of Contemplation* is composed and made up of arguments both diverse and new, the which are set down and arranged so as to give fervour and devotion to men, as well as demonstration of the truth, to the end that they may learn to praise and love and serve Thee : therefore let him who desires his fervour and love and knowledge to grow and increase be a contemplator of this book to the glory and honour of his Lord God.[1]

He who has this book in his remembrance and understanding and love can be wise in things alike of the sense and of the intellect, and can confound and destroy all error in his soul and all evil thoughts and all temptations and all evil habits ; and the same can he do in the souls of his neighbours.[2]

A fair idea of the importance which Lull attributed to the *Book of Contemplation* may be gained from a study of its final chapter. Several pages are needed to describe its value (*bonea*). It will give joy and counsel and wisdom and consolation and hope. It will prove by "necessary reasons" the Unity and Trinity of God, and which "law" (*i.e.* religion) is the true one : for this reason Lull desires that it may be "given into the hands of faithful men"[3] and "disseminated throughout the world."[4] To those who conscientiously follow its teaching it will impart every virtue ; it will develop all their faculties, both of body and mind ; it will convert all who have strayed, bring sinners to repentance, and be "a rest from labour and a comfort and consolation to men and women who are orphans and poor." It teaches the distinction between greater good and lesser, between possible and impossible, between truth and falsehood. Nor do these assertions, each of which is developed at some length, exhaust the book's utility. "We have neither place nor time sufficient to recount all the ways wherein this book is good and great."[5]

[1] Chap. 222 (*Obres*, v, p. 454). ; *cf.* also chaps. 102, 144, 282, 362 (*Obres*, iii, p. 237 ; iv, p. 268 ; vii, p. 130).

[2] Chap. 291 (*Obres*, vii, p. 228).

[3] Chap. 360 (*Obres*, viii, p. 549).

[4] Chap. 366, iv (*Obres*, viii, p. 641) ; *cf.*, for a similar sentiment, chap. 101 (*Obres*, iii, p. 229).

[5] Chap. 366 (*Obres*, viii, pp. 626–31).

The *Book of Contemplation* is not only an exposition, but an "art" (by which word Lull always means "method"): indeed, it is several times described as "this Art of contemplation."[1] It is meant for use—daily use, as we have seen—"by men learned and men simple, secular and religious, rich and poor."[2] And full directions are given for that use by one who was a thorough believer, from the earliest days of his career until the latest, in the benefits which come from rule and order. To profit by it fully, he says, the reader should first gain from the chapter-headings a general idea of its contents; he may then study the whole book, devoting one day to each chapter for a year, and repeating the process for a second year if he so desire; after this he may study such paragraphs and arguments as appeal to him, seeking them out for the purpose. "Even as a man takes pleasure in finding one fair flower after another, even so may he have pleasure in the contemplation of one fair argument after another."[3]

To give in a few words an idea of the content of this vast encyclopædia is not easy. The first book is of the Divine attributes, each distinction describing one attribute: infinity, eternity, unity, trinity, power, knowledge, goodness and truth. The opening chapter—"Of Joy"—is an arresting prologue to the theme of the treatise and gives an illuminating insight into the means by which the author rises to the height of his great argument. Three things should give us cause to rejoice: the existence of God, the existence of ourselves, and the existence of our neighbour. If a man has delight at the discovery of a precious stone, how much the more should he be glad to discover the Being of an infinite God! If we rejoice to see trees in leaf, flower and fruit, and have delight in river, wood and meadow, the beauties of which are without ourselves, how much the more should we take pleasure in our own being, and in the beauty and goodness which

[1] *E.g.* chaps. 83, 100, 101, 102, 146, 220 (*Obres*, iii, 130, 225, 229, 237; iv, 277; v, 436); *cf.* chap. 282 (*Obres*, vii, p. 130): "This *Book of Contemplation* is an art whereby man may learn to love Thee."

[2] Chap. 102 (*Obres*, iii, p. 237).

[3] Chap. 366 (*Obres*, viii, p. 626).

are within us ![1] In giving thanks for life's exceptional and accidental blessings, we should not fail to remember those that are essential to—nay, inherent in—life itself.

These considerations lead naturally enough to the eight distinctions with the exposition of which the whole of the first book is occupied. The second book follows with equal suitability, considering the works of God in His creation of the world, His Providence and His Redemption of fallen man, and His attributes as illustrated by these works. The nature of creation is discussed in general terms before we pass to the creation of the world,—of the first matter of all, of the firmament, of the elements, of metals, of plants, of animals and of the angels. Next we come to the Divine ordinances in man. There is, first, the ordering of his body, with its five physical "powers": the *potencia vegetable*, by which he absorbs nourishment; the *potencia sensitiva*, which is served by the five senses; the imaginative power, corresponding to it in another sphere exactly; the power of reason, served by the "spiritual senses" to be described hereafter; and its complement, a *potencia mutiva*, which translates its mandates into action.

We pass to man's two intentions, the first of which is "to love, honour and serve God, and to know His goodness and nobility," and the second, "to possess those good things which come to him through the merits of the first intention." The principal importance of this division lies of course in the order in which the two intentions are placed. "As Thou hast created this world in regard of the next, and not the next in regard of this, even so hast Thou willed that the second intention in man should be in regard of the first, and not the first in regard of the second."[2] Another chapter describes the position of man "between two motions (*moviments*) . . ., that which moves him to do good and that . . . which moves him to do evil,"[3] while still another sets him "between will and power."[4] This leads up to a discussion of man's

[1] Chaps. 1, 2 (*Obres*, ii, pp. 7, 11).
[2] Chap. 45 (*Obres*, ii, p. 227); *cf.* p. 156, below.
[3] Chap. 46 (*Obres*, ii, pp. 232–3).
[4] Chap. 47 (*Obres*, ii, p. 238).

free will, and his power of choosing between truth and falsehood, good and evil, glory and punishment, a subject to which the author returns later. For the present he leaves it, stressing this point, that from God come all good things and nothing comes from Him that is evil.

Following his general scheme of progression, he next reaches the Incarnation and Passion of Christ,—subjects which, though of such transcendent importance, are treated here very briefly, and give place to the related themes of judgment, Paradise and the life to come. But a return is made almost immediately to the Redemption,—to its theology, that is to say, to the doctrine of original sin, the need for salvation and the sufficiency of the merits of Christ alone. Once again comes a very natural turn of thought. Lull is meditating upon the Person of Our Lord, in Whom is consummated our salvation :

> As the good knight in battle, through his ardour and his chivalry, receives many a blow and many a wound, even so, O Lord, was it needful that Thy Body should receive much torture and tribulation and trial, and be sorely wounded, since it had to bear so great a weight of sin as was Adam's and to set us free therefrom.[1]

This consideration leads him to think of the Divine attributes which that work of redemption illustrates—of the Divine will, first, which brought it to pass, and afterwards of the dominion of God, and of His wisdom, justice, bounty, humility and mercy. Here and there, in the development of these themes, Lull repeats arguments used in his earlier chapters. In the main, however, considering the proportions of the book, we have little repetition to complain of.

The longest chapters in the latter part of Book II are on the Divine justice and humility, and both are distinguished by great variety of treatment, and by their application to the life of Lull's own day of the considerations set forward. In the two chapters which complete this book, the author returns to the future life of the righteous man and to the sources and the nature of his

[1] Chap. 62 (*Obres*, iii, p. 62).

eternal happiness ; and finally he sums up the two books of his treatise by a discourse upon the complete perfection (*acabament*) of God. Once more we may draw attention to the ease with which this supreme topic is introduced : the chief source of the eternal bliss of the righteous is the Divine Essence, and that Essence is the master-theme of their praises because it is perfection.

The third book, which is of greater length than the first two combined—and, according to Lull himself, of greater value than either [1]—turns to the theme of man. It is, indeed, for the most part, a study of man, in his physical and spiritual natures, in his greatness and his littleness and in his various estates and callings. The plan which this third book follows is based upon the ten senses, and, at its beginning, for the space of many pages, it is interrupted while a long procession of characters, of every rank and occupation, files past the reader, who is invited to " take note of that which is done " by clerks, kings and princes, knights and pilgrims, judges, advocates and witnesses, physicians, merchants, and many persons besides. The chapters concerned with these characters, though in the nature of a lengthy digression, will, except perhaps to the philosopher and the theologian, be among the most interesting in the entire work.[2]

We are shown a great company of clerics, seculars and religious alike, bishops, priests and deacons, hermits, monks and friars. The prelates are for the most part rich, but " give to the poor for the love of God in times of necessity." The inferior clergy spend much of their lives in study, and, having no family cares like laymen, are able to abstain from worldly trafficking and thoughts of money. Religious—" friars minor, friars preachers and others "—give themselves to prayer, abstinence and mortification ; they are often despised by the world, even

[1] In chap. 366 (*Obres*, viii, pp. 626, 632), the second volume (bk. iii) is described as being of greater value, and also harder to understand, than the first (bks. i, ii), and the third (bks. iv, v) than the second.

[2] Cf. *Blanquerna*, chap. 83, where the Cardinal of Benedicimus Te commands " a great company of men " to " go through the streets " blessing the Name of God, because (among other reasons) He has created these very " offices."

treated cruelly and unjustly, but, their affections being fixed on the world to come, they can bear such treatment with fortitude. This composite picture of the clergy is an idealistic one indeed, hardly qualified by more than the suggestion that not all clerks are "good clerks." Lull was still in the early years of his experiences of ecclesiastics. He was to write of them very differently as time went on.

There follow in the procession kings and princes, who have already been described ; knights, "armed with wood and steel," fortifying castles, consulting omens, ever seeking an occasion to show their prowess ; crusaders setting out for the Holy Land against the advice of those that have lost faith in the force of arms [1] ; pilgrims, on horseback or on foot, each with staff and scrip, bound for distant shrines and for churches where miracles are worked,[2] some clad poorly and begging their way as they go, others "with sauces and barrels full of wine, with coin of gold and silver for their expenses." No chapter in the book is more vivid than this,[3] which describes how the pilgrims are deceived by "false men whom they meet in hostelries and churches," how they gaze at the pictures, images and sculpture of the churches, find a welcome in monastery or hospice, and, on the "rough and perilous way" to and from their destinations, meet with "many a trial and misfortune by reason both of cold and of heat."[4]

The strain of satire becomes more marked as we pass to the professions of medicine and of law.[5] Judges and advocates alike are too often corrupt or corruptible : "for a small reward they will cause a man to lose many possessions and much money." [6] "When I pass along streets and through public places," declares Lull, "I look for some upright judge or honest advocate. And I see none . . . for almost all are corrupt in their professions." [7] They are flattered by princes and wealthy men, ride on well-fed mules and palfreys, partake of delicate meats, clothe themselves in sumptuous garments and sleep in

[1] Chap. 112. [2] *Cf.* p. 34, above. [3] Chap. 113.
[4] *Ibid.* [5] Chap. 114.
[6] Chap. 114 (*Obres*, iv, p. 72). [7] *Ibid.* (*Obres*, iv, pp. 73–4).

soft, luxurious beds.[1] The physician is tainted with a similar love of luxury, and is by no means always as cunning in his art as he should be ; but for all the ignorance, greed and quarrelsomeness of the worst of his kind, Lull has a deep respect for the profession. In all its members he sees types of the Great Physician, and of the "healers of men's souls" who work at His bidding.[2]

There follow still in the long procession merchants with cloth, hides, beasts, jewels and what not ; money-changers in the city ; sailors on the ocean ; jesters and artists at court ; and shepherds and labourers in the fields.[3] We can only stay here to remark that Lull shows both interest in and knowledge of a sailor's life, and goes into it in more detail than into any other calling save that of the *joglar*. Next in the pageant come the *maestrals*, or workers with their hands—those skilled in wood and stone, silver and gold ; then scriveners with parchment and ink, writing "letters of buying and selling" ; shoemakers preparing, cutting and sewing their leather ; tailors making *gramalles*,[4] together with coats and breeches, cloaks, capes and mantles ; furriers, weavers, butchers, barbers, millers, glaziers, potters, bakers, gardeners, taverners, couriers, criers, waggoners, municipal officers, money-changers, gamesters, archers, calkers, porters, and a few more "offices" given only a passing mention : a notable assembly, both for its size and for the clearness with which, in a few bold strokes, each character is outlined.

The digression was worth making, not only for the information of an enquiring posterity, but also for those who, in studying the *Book of Contemplation* when it was written, would be led by it to ask themselves what is required of men in certain professions and what these professions symbolize. When the thread of the argument is taken up again, we find ourselves considering the sense of sight, and then, with a rapidity designed perhaps

[1] Chap. 114 (*Obres*, iv, p. 75). [2] Chap. 115. [3] Chaps. 116–21.

[4] The *gramalla* was a long garment not unlike a cassock, reaching to the feet, and worn in Catalonia in the Middle Ages by city councillors.

to atone for so many pages of portraits, the senses of hearing, smell and taste. At the fifth sense a halt is again made, and for many chapters we survey man's physical and moral sensibilities.[1] Heat and cold, hunger and thirst, health and disease and like contraries come first, after which are considered shame, fear, vainglory, sensuality, and six of the seven deadly sins.

By far the longest part of the third book, however, is concerned with man's five faculties, or "spiritual senses," of cogitation, perception, conscience, subtlety and fervour.[2] Under the first head comes a rather miscellaneous collection of subjects which are commonly included in man's cogitations : chief among these are the Divine Essence, the human nature of Jesus Christ, the works of angels and devils, the discordance between faith and reason, the problems of human frailty, the four last things, the nature of the three "virtues" or "faculties" (of memory, understanding and will) and the conflict between sense and intellect. The last topic leads Lull into a discussion of the functions of perception, and its application to natural and supernatural laws, before becoming theological once again, and applying the principles of perception to the attributes of God, to the Trinity, the Incarnation and the Deity of Jesus Christ. After a brief comparison (to which we shall return) of the Christian, Jewish and Mohammedan faiths, he passes to the domain of ethics and discusses man's capacity for distinguishing between good and evil, truth and falsehood, wisdom and foolishness, perfection and imperfection. Yet even here he returns more than once to theology, discussing the origin of the universe, the resurrection of the dead, and the nature of prayer. The sections of the book which deal with conscience, subtlety (or subjection of sense to spirit) and fervour (*coratgía, frevor*) are very much shorter and more obvious in their argument than those which precede them.

The fourth book is relatively short, and for most readers less easy to understand than the foregoing books, not only because it treats of philosophical and doctrinal

[1] *Obres*, iv (chap. 130). [2] *Obres*, iv (chaps. 149 ff.).

subjects, but because it makes use of the device of the tree, which the author of the *Book of Contemplation* was to employ frequently, and of which a more comprehensive example will be given in a later chapter. The greatest space in this fourth book is devoted to "proving the articles of the faith," to an exposition of the ten commandments and to a homily on predestination.

Finally, we come to the summit of Lull's achievement in this gigantic work, the two distinctions on love and prayer, which between them make up more than one third of the whole. The forty-six chapters on love are a treatise on the subject in themselves, developed in the careful, logical fashion from which Ramon never for long departs, even though it leads him into hopeless artificialities. The progression of argument in the early chapters of the section illustrates this : the love of God to Himself, the love that is between the Divine and human natures of Christ, the love of Christ's human nature to itself, and the love that is between Christ and the angels. Only when he has speculated upon these lofty themes docs the author descend to man, and here again, after considering the love for man of God the Father and God the Son, he pauses to consider the love of the angels for themselves and for man, before taking up the more profitable theme of the love which man must have to God.

Thereafter the plan of the distinction is straightforward and is interrupted very little : the love of man for God, for Jesus Christ, for the lovers of Jesus Christ, for Our Lady, for the virtues, for poverty and riches, for life and death. Some particular manifestations of love are next considered,—the love of prince and people, of parent and child, of oneself, of friends and of enemies—before the distinction ends, rather abruptly, with six chapters leading the reader to speculate upon love in its perfection and imperfection, in the hereafter and in its own consummation.

So beautifully, and with such manifest inspiration, was Ramon to write of love in later days, that the reader who already knows his subsequent works will turn with great expectancy to this fourth section of the *Book of*

Contemplation. It is to be feared that he will suffer disappointment. There are few purple passages in it, few vivid images—certainly no more here than elsewhere in the book—few chapters which give any sign of eloquence. Lull could write in 1272 that "as the mule is brought to birth by the horse and the she-ass, so is the love of this world brought to birth by the body and the soul."[1] He could find figures that were prosaic as well as apt, more readily than those composed of the stuff of the truest poetry. Here and there he uses the phraseology of *amic* and *amat*, by which he is probably destined to be remembered for more generations and in more countries than we can readily estimate. But he had not yet evolved that magic symbolism which makes the *Book of the Lover and the Beloved* so wonderful a collection of meditations. Indeed, the word *amat* in the *Book of Contemplation* is comparatively seldom used to indicate the Beloved, Christ. The finest passages of this fourth section of the work are probably those (to be described hereafter) on the theme of love for one's neighbour, as exemplified in the evangelization of the heathen.

The final section, of fifty-two chapters, on prayer, introduces so often the phrase "to adore and contemplate" that we may ask at this point the pertinent question : What meaning attaches, in this book, to the word "contemplation" ? The comparison of any considerable number of passages in which it occurs will show that the meaning is a very wide one, and, while in most of these passages it will be synonymous with "meditation,"[2] or even with "consideration," "thought" or "study,"[3] there are a few in which it must perforce be applied to a more definitely mystical process, while in still more it bears its ancient technical meaning of the entire range of the life of mental prayer.[4] So great is the field which the

[1] Chap. 189 (*Obres*, vii, p. 195).

[2] *E.g.* chaps. 211 (*Obres*, v, p. 366), 317 (viii, p. 30), 318 (viii, p. 45).

[3] *E.g.* chaps. 160 (*Obres*, iv, p. 365), 254 (vi, p. 256), 366 (of which the third section gives directions "how to contemplate this book"). In chap. 296 (vii, p. 276) the most suitable hours for "adoration and contemplation" are suggested.

[4] *Cf.* chap. 352 (*Obres*, viii, p. 446) and its "simple, contemplative prayer"; chap. 360 (viii, pp. 553–4) and its "ordering of prayer and contemplation."

book covers that its title can be interpreted only in the very widest sense. In such frequent phrases as "prayer and contemplation," "to adore and contemplate," the meaning is wide and indeterminate, including probably both the higher and the lower processes of mental prayer, and, as the context often shows, being susceptible of more than one interpretation.

The section on prayer begins by dividing prayer into three parts or "figures":

> The first of these is prayer of the senses (*oració sensual*), wherein man calls upon Thee, O Lord, and speaks to Thee, adoring Thy virtues and honours, and begging of Thee grace, pardon and blessing. The second is prayer of the intellect (*oració entellectual*) wherein man has remembrance, understanding and love of Thee in his prayer, and contemplates Thee, having his remembrance, understanding and will directed towards Thy honours and Thy virtues. The third is that wherein man does good works, and uses justice and mercy and truth and the remaining virtues. . . . For whensoever he does this, then does he adore Thee and pray to Thee and call upon Thee (even if at such a time he have not remembrance and understanding of Thee) in remembering, understanding and willing some other thing after a righteous and virtuous manner.[1]

Each of these "figures" (all of which, of course, are within the Catholic tradition) is applied in the chapters following, which present as matters for "adoration and contemplation" the Unity of God, the Blessed Trinity, God's Essence, infinity, eternity, power, wisdom, love and other attributes. A single chapter presents in a similar way Christ's human nature, after which are considered God's gifts to man. He aids him to do good and to fight against evil, gives him discernment between good and evil, grants him his soul's desires, promises him Paradise, aids him to bewail his shortcomings, forgives him his sins, inspires him to convert others, gives him the grace of continence and is ever his consolation. For all these gifts man must pray to God when he adores and contemplates Him. So far the distinction on prayer is easy enough to follow, apart from the free use of algebraical symbols to avoid repetition of words and

[1] Chap. 315 (*Obres*, viii, pp. 3–4, 6).

phrases, a process both unfamiliar and disconcerting to the ordinary reader.[1] The succeeding chapters return to artificiality, of a typically mediaeval kind, when they recommend the practice of "intellectual adoration and contemplation by means of etymology, allegory and anagogy"[2]; it seems that this excursion into the fantastic is a result of Lull's reading in Arabic,[3] his aim being to improve upon Oriental methods of devotion in the interests of Christianity. Unfortunately, he is very seldom happy in his attempts at adapting these methods.

In the concluding chapters of the book he is seen to better advantage. The chapter which shows "how good a thing is ordered contemplation and prayer"[4] returns to first principles, if at a somewhat late stage in the treatise, and the remaining chapters, the number or length of which might—with advantage—have been increased at the expense of certain others, describe some of the fruits of prayer: they show, for example, how it gives man knowledge whether or no his soul is pure and clean, and whether the works which he performs are of truth or of falsehood. The three hundred and sixty-fifth chapter describes the more direct blessings which the contemplative soul receives, and the final (or complementary) chapter deals with the use of the book as a whole.

Among the secondary themes of the *Book of Contemplation*, one stands out high above the rest: the conversion of unbelievers. So frequently does Lull return to the subject that from this book alone it would be clear that it was the ruling passion of his life. In view of his

[1] This begins in chap. 328, and recurs at intervals until the end of the book. At its most complicated points (*e.g.* chap. 335) as many as twenty-two symbols are used, and passages occur like this: "If in Thy three properties there were no difference. . . . the demonstration would give the D to the H of the A with the F and the G as it does with the E, and yet the K would not give significance to the H of any defect in the F or the G; but since diversity is shown in the demonstration that the D makes of the E and the F and the G with the I and the K, therefore the H has certain scientific knowledge of Thy holy and glorious Trinity." A fresh key to the notation is supplied with every chapter.

[2] Chap. 352: title.

[3] See chap. 352 (*Obres*, viii, p. 446).

[4] Chap. 360.

later works and history, great interest attaches to his ideas on this theme, as expressed in his first book of importance. It may reasonably be assumed that in places they represent not only his considered beliefs, but also the results of his experiences with the Moors and Jews of Mallorca, a presumed degree of actuality which gives them added interest.

The aspect of his theme to which Lull devotes most space is a description of the stumbling-blocks which unbelievers—chiefly Jews and Saracens—find in the Christian religion. Their great difficulties appear to lie in the acceptance of the doctrines of the Trinity, of Christ's Deity, of the Incarnation and of the Virgin Birth. All these are so closely related that Lull by no means always attempts to separate them. " If the infidels dare not believe in the Trinity, it is for fear lest they should believe in three Gods."[1] They do not realize that " Catholics dare not doubt the Trinity lest they should cease to believe in the Unity "[2]; that " however much virtue and nobility they themselves grant and attribute to the Divine Essence through faith, Catholics attribute as much thereto and more also "[3]; that Christians no more commit idolatry when they kneel before the Cross than Moslems when they prostrate themselves and raise their hands and eyes to the heavens[4]; that, because we hold that God the Father was before God the Son, " we do not therefore believe in three Gods."[5]

As great a stumbling-block as the idea of a Triune God is that of a God made Man. The miraculous in any form is hard enough for infidels to accept,[6] but " that Christ, before His Incarnation, was already in being "[7] they reject as impossible : " in impossibility they believe, but not in the perfection of Thy power."[8] For the same reason they deny that the Virgin could remain a virgin and yet conceive a son, " forgetting or disbelieving in the power of God."[9] But why do they stop there ? If

[1] Chap. 77 (*Obres*, iii, p. 102) ; *cf.* chap. 246 (vi, p. 187).
[2] *Ibid.* [3] *Ibid.* [4] Chap. 255 (*Obres*, vi, p. 272).
[5] Chap. 346 (*Obres*, viii, pp. 373–4). [6] Chap. 18 (*Obres*, ii, p. 90).
[7] *Ibid.* [8] *Ibid.* [9] *Ibid.* (p. 89).

indeed they believe that the Almighty has no power above Nature, " why do they not deny that the world was created out of nothing, or that there will be a Day of Judgment, for all this likewise is against Nature ? "[1] It is not as if they found in the God-Man any defect or sin[2] : they attribute corruption to human nature unthinkingly, and quite wrongly assume that God (according to the Christian belief) " was by His union with human nature corrupted and defiled."[3] In no way is this true. God's Humanity is not like " the humanity of Peter or William or any other creature soever." It is " ever-blessed as being united with the Deity in a way that no other humanity can be."

For other rational beings are created to enjoy happiness in Thy Deity, O Lord, and in Thy Humanity ; and Thy human nature was created only to have happiness in being united with Thy Deity and to give happiness to the saints in glory. Above all creatures hast Thou blessed Thy glorious Humanity, O humble Lord, with exceeding great honour, and the false Jews blaspheme and dishonour it and believe it to have the vileness which they attribute to it, while the Saracens believe it not to have been united with the Deity nor to have redeemed the world.[4]

They dishonour Christ's human nature, indeed, " with intention to honour the Divine Essence," but in truth they dishonour this also in dishonouring " that creature whereby the Divine Nature is most truly signified in its perfections and honours and nobility."[5]

In this particular, as in the other, the Catholic faith is wholly misunderstood by these unbelievers. " They think that we believe the Deity to have turned into humanity, and humanity into Deity. . . . But this would be as impossible to us as to them, and in truth we believe not this that they attribute to us."[6] " When they hear that we speak of Christ as suffering hunger and thirst, heat and cold, passion and death, they think that we believe the Deity to have hungered and thirsted and died.

[1] Chap. 65 (*Obres*, iii, p. 36).
[2] Chap. 195 (*Obres*, v, p. 245).
[3] *Ibid.* (pp. 245–6).
[4] Chap. 283 (*Obres*, vii, p. 139).
[5] *Ibid.* (p. 140).
[6] Chap. 65 (*Obres*, iii, p. 36).

How can their foolishness . . . be so great as to believe that we hold such errors? . . . They know naught of the wise and ordered manner wherein Christ's Advent came to pass . . . nor of the nature of the faithful Christian's belief in the Incarnation." [1]

Some of the Saracens, it would appear, with whom Lull has reasoned are prepared to go farther with him than one would expect.[2] They "deny Christ's sacred Passion," it is true, but "with intent to honour His humanity." [3] They "love (that) humanity, believing and understanding that it was conceived of the Holy Spirit, and that it was in this world without any sin. But . . . they attribute not to it that virtue and sanctity whereby it has the best and the greatest honour—namely, in being united with Thy Deity and in being the occasion of the redemption of the world." [4] They allow furthermore, we read with surprise, that Our Lady "was a virgin both before and after the Birth of Christ, that she conceived through the Word of God, that her Son was a prophet, and that she herself was very good, and sinless"; they deny only that her Son "was God and Man, and that He redeemed the world." [5] It is not strange to find that Lull thinks the Saracens "nearer the Christians than any other unbelieving people." [6]

The Jews, on the other hand, are quite immovable. "They love not Our Lady, but blaspheme and despise and scorn her, saying and affirming and believing that her glorious Son was not conceived by the Holy Spirit, but was the son of a man; and is not united with the Deity, but was false, and a liar and a deceiver, and a greater sinner and wrong-doer than any other man soever." [7]

[1] Chap. 54 (*Obres*, ii, p. 281).

[2] There is nothing in the text to show that Saracens in general are not referred to, but presumably the reference is to individuals.

[3] Chap. 317 (*Obres*, viii, p. 22), *cf.* Korân, Sura iii, 73.

[4] Chap. 278 (*Obres*, vii, p. 86).

[5] Chap. 287 (*Obres*, vii, p. 176). Lull goes on to say that their admissions are to their denials in importance "as a drop of water is to the sea." But he has also (p. 175) contrasted their attitude very favourably with that of the Jews (see text above).

[6] Chap. 346 (*Obres*, viii, p. 379).

[7] Chap. 287 (*Obres*, vii, p. 175).

Apparently such unbelievers (whether they reject much of the faith or little) do not realize how far they are removed from God. They no more believe in Him than if they worshipped the sun,[1] and He is wholly absent from them when they pray, even as is the sun from a man that is blind.[2] Their delusions that they are pleasing to God by their good works, and that they are "excused from God's justice" because they hold their ancestors' faith, are alike groundless and vain. They are condemned by the righteousness of God to "infinite punishment" and "everlasting pains," and the rectitude of their intentions lessens only the severity of this punishment, not its duration.[3]

A harsh creed is this, but at least it gives to those who hold it sincerely a passion for the saving of souls, making the best of them very tender with those who unknowingly are hastening towards eternal punishment, and disinclined to remember their past offences against themselves. Seldom, if ever, is Ramon impatient with those whose acceptance of Christian doctrines he so earnestly desires. Of their persecutions of Christians he writes tolerantly and calmly.[4] On their devotion and consistency, their love of justice, mercy and many other virtues he dwells with unaffected and unconcealed admiration.[5] Most of all he praises their steadfast and unshakable belief in the Unity of God, whom faithful and unfaithful alike are called to love.[6] In this respect, as in certain others, "Christians, Jews and Saracens agree in their beliefs."[7] "If infidels allow and confess that God is one, without fellow or peer, even so likewise do the faithful."[8] And too often the tenacity of Jews and Saracens to their creeds is an example to Christians.[9]

[1] Chap. 255 (*Obres*, vi, p. 269). [2] Chap. 315 (*Obres*, viii, p. 9).

[3] Chap. 77, *passim* (*Obres*, iii, pp. 98–103). The last clause is expressed somewhat unexpectedly, thus: "Blessed be Thy justice, O Lord, that torments more severely Catholics who die in sin than infidels who die with good intention" (p. 101). For Lull's sternness toward Christians who embrace Moslem beliefs, see chap. 242 (*Obres*, vi, pp. 145–6).

[4] *E.g.* chap. 83 (*Obres*, iii, p. 130), chap. 85 (iii, p. 141).

[5] Chap. 226 (*Obres*, v, pp. 477–8). [6] Chap. 349 (*Obres*, viii, p. 416).

[7] Chap. 341 (*Obres*, viii, p. 315). [8] Chap. 77 (*Obres*, iii, p. 102).

[9] Chap. 226 (*Obres*, v, p. 478).

It is important to notice that the primary reason for which Lull blames the unbelievers is because they refuse to examine for themselves the religion in which they have been born. They scorn the Catholic Faith because they love the "usages and habits" of their own religion, especially its "sensual customs." "Through the great love," for example, "which the Saracens have in this world for women, they believe that in the next world they shall have women likewise," and will have nothing to do with a religion that exalts God so greatly as to "discredit the belief that in Paradise there shall be glory of eating, or of women, or of aught else save of God alone."[1] So, although God has given them intellects, they will not use them—not even so much as for the consideration of those "necessary reasons" by which Lull believes that such doctrines as the Trinity of God can be proved. True, to Lull himself, and to his fellow-Christians, little reasoning, if any, on such a matter is necessary, for both "the attributes of God and His creatures give significance of the perfection of His Trinity." But those who have no desire to realize this can hardly be expected to do so, and only such a desire will enlighten their minds to this extent.[2] If the desire is not put within their nature, some other means must be found to enable them to use their understanding. They deny God's Trinity because they "use their imaginative powers too much and their reason too little."[3] They seek the truth "sensually" and "according to the course of nature." They must learn to seek it "intellectually," with "intellectual and spiritual eyes," using "the mirror of the understanding," "according to the course of nature increate."[4] They will believe "nothing that their imagination cannot imagine" and they "boast that they can understand all that God's power can work."[5] They are established so firmly in their convictions that they reject even the possibility that these may be imperfect. "They refuse

[1] Chap. 240 (*Obres,* vi, p. 129).
[2] Chaps. 77, 317 (*Obres,* iii, p. 98 ; viii, p. 32).
[3] Chap. 77 (*Obres,* iii, p. 99).
[4] Chaps. 174, 181 (*Obres,* v, pp. 51, 123).
[5] Chap. 77 (*Obres,* iii, p. 100).

to incline the memory, understanding and will of their souls towards possibility, but they affirm impossibility. . . . And it is clear, Lord, that those who affirm it to be impossible that Thou hast taken flesh cannot have understanding of Thy Incarnation. . . . Wherefore we must first cause them to allow its possibility, that thereby they may become seekers and finders of truth." [1]

It seems curious to hear a religious teacher blame unbelievers for "loving faith rather than reasons or arguments" [2]; for "destroying their souls intellectually," [3] and "preventing their understanding from following its own nature," [4] rather than for being of little faith and requiring signs and wonders in order to believe. The latter would seem to have been the commoner failing of those who have refused to accept Christianity from the time of Christ's life on earth until to-day. But, in Lull's opinion, the infidels of his time were chiefly to blame because they would not accept the "necessary" or incontrovertible arguments already mentioned which he and others were only too ready to put before them. His whole system, as we shall presently see, was built up on logical, almost mathematical proof: it has even been claimed that his belief in the understanding and its power amounts to a heresy.[5] Here, it is sufficient to say that in the *Book of Contemplation* he insists on the parts played both by faith and by understanding. "True belief," in his view, "is formed of a mortified understanding and a true remembrance and will." [6] "By faith and by necessary reasons" the faculties of the soul are united,[7] and the soul believes the mysteries of the Faith.[8] They are like the two feet of a man who is walking in the way of truth: neither foot alone will effectively (*ordonadament*) carry his body.[9] There are some things which the Christian cannot understand, and must believe, without the aid of reason, to be true.[10] There are others which

[1] Chap. 229 (*Obres*, vi, p. 33).
[2] Chap. 77 (*Obres*, iii, p. 99).
[3] Chap. 259 (*Obres*, vi, p. 303).
[4] *Ibid.*
[5] See pp. 403–5 below.
[6] Chap. 350 (*Obres*, viii, p. 428).
[7] *Ibid.*
[8] *E.g.*, chap. 248 (*Obres*, vi, p. 196).
[9] Chap. 288 (*Obres*, vii, p. 189).
[10] *Ibid.* (p. 190).

due use of the reason will make plainer: it is pure indolence to accept these in blind faith without enquiring into them: to whom much is given, of him will much be required, whether in intellect or in money.[1]

But a continual insistence upon this fact does not amount to an undue exaltation of the understanding. On the contrary, those who by reasoning attain the truth must also attain it by love, which, like faith, is of a higher quality than understanding. As Lull himself puts it:

> Faith is exalted in this world above understanding, for man can love God the more readily by faith than he can know Him through understanding; and faith believes in God without mean, while understanding cannot soar upward to Him till demonstration has been made of other things. . . . And through faith thou shalt understand in the world to come that which now thou canst not.[2]

And the fact that there are truths in Christianity which faith alone can apprehend sets it higher than other religions which have in them less of mystery:

> Since in the law [*i.e.* religion] of the Christians the memory and the will are more occupied with faith than in any other law, because there are more things therein that the understanding cannot understand by necessary reasons, it is signified thereby that the law of the Christians is better than any other and its rewards are greater.[3]

Comparatively little is said in the *Book of Contemplation* against the distinctive beliefs of the Moslems: for the most part, Lull is here content that the war shall be fought on the territory of Christianity. The principal Moslem ideas to which he develops his objections are those on Paradise: he introduces imaginary Saracens—one Maymó and his wives Fátima and Axa—to illustrate his arguments that in Paradise there can be no time, or place, generation, nourishment of the body, physical corruption or various other conditions of this world.[4] From his repeated returns to the subject,[5] it is clear that in the

[1] Chap. 350 (*Obres*, viii, p. 428).
[2] *D.P.*, chap. 52 (*Obres*, i, pp. 90–1).
[3] Chap. 302 (*Obres*, vii, p. 346).
[4] Chap. 311, *passim*.
[5] The chief are in the latter part of the book: *e.g.* chaps, 341, 343, 347 (*Obres*, viii, pp. 316, 332–3, 391).

Christian and Moslem conceptions of Paradise he finds expressed typical and essential differences between the two religions—the one so largely ruled by the senses, the other a religion of the spirit.

To such an extent is he concerned with the Moslems that he urges little against the Jews, attacking principally their habits of life and their rejection of Christ's claims.[1] From time to time he alludes, but only in passing, to other unbelievers, of whom he may already have had some personal experience in his travels : " Tartars, heretics,[2] idolaters and many other sects which adore the sun and beasts and serpents, and do to these the reverence which they should do to Thy Deity, O Lord, and to Thy Humanity." [3] He spends much less space in denouncing these than in affirming the superiority of Christianity to every other religion whatsoever. Some of the reasons which he gives for this allegation are curious. Christianity is the best religion because Christian clergy are more numerous, wise, devout and honourable than the exponents of other religions [4] ; because Christians keep their holy-days more " nobly " than Jews and Moslems [5] ; and because the " law " of the Christian " loves and honours and praises . . . and calls upon the Saints in Paradise more than does any other law soever." [6] Lull is on more generally trodden ground when he lauds Christianity for its infinite trust in God's care and its belief in His power being above nature,[7] and when he shows that, while Jew and Moslem as well as Christian acknowledge God's goodness, the Christian faith best shows that goodness in perfection.[8]

How does Ramon propose, in the *Book of Contemplation*, to deal with infidels—for we may be sure that his treatment of the subject is not merely academic ? At

[1] *E.g.* chaps. 278, 283 (*Obres*, vii, pp. 85, 139).
[2] *Cf.* here chap. 316 (*Obres*, viii, p. 22).
[3] Chap. 278 (*Obres*, vii, pp. 87–8) ; *cf.* chap. 287 (vii, p. 177).
[4] Chap. 110 (*Obres*, iv, p. 46) ; *cf.* vi, pp. 220–1 and p. 138, below.
[5] Chap. 257 (*Obres*, vi, pp. 282–3).
[6] Chap. 279 (*Obres*, vii, p. 101).
[7] Chap. 77 (*Obres*, iii, p. 100).
[8] *Cf.* chap. 186, where this point is made, and the arguments which illustrate it are developed at length, and also chap. 217 (*Obres*, v, p. 411).

this stage in his career, he has still no desire for wars or crusades of arms,[1] "wherein men are wounded, taken captive and killed" and "princedoms, domains and riches are squandered and laid waste." [2] Such wars must cease and give place to peaceful evangelization :

> Since the Christians are not at peace with the Saracens, O Lord, they dare not hold discussions upon the faith with them when they are among them. But were they at peace together, they could dispute with each other peacefully concerning the faith, and then it would be possible for the Christians to direct and enlighten the Saracens in the way of truth, through the grace of the Holy Spirit and the true reasons that are signified in the perfection of Thy attributes.[3]

If many infidels reject all argument, and adopt a *non possumus* attitude towards it, there are many more—and no doubt Ramon had met both kinds in Mallorca—who "follow arguments and love proofs" [4] and are therefore easily approachable. To these, as also to the rest, the faithful are bound to go and expound the Christian religion,[5] "disputing with them and bringing them to see the truth by long demonstrations continuously made with true and necessary reasons," [6] and reproving them, both for their obstinacy and blindness, and for their blasphemies against Christianity.[7]

Why, asks Lull, do not more Christians obey their Lord's last command ? "Since Thou, O Lord, art ever ready to aid . . . how can any Christian fear to preach our holy faith to the infidels ?" [8] "How can a Catholic fear to dispute with an unbeliever ? For as Thou didst cast out from Thy glory the error and falsehood of devils

[1] In one place (chap. 309, *Obres*, vii, p. 419) he appears to be commending the Crusades as a means of recovering "the Holy Sepulchre in Jerusalem and all the other places which the Saracens and infidels possess." But place against this the quotation from chap. 112 cited above (p. 31) and chap. 288 (*Obres*, vii, p. 186) where Lull holds up for imitation the Apostles' method of converting the world "not by the sword, but by preaching."

[2] Chap. 204 (*Obres*, v, p. 316).

[3] *Ibid.* (p. 317).

[4] Chap. 77 (*Obres*, iii, pp. 99–100).

[5] *Ibid.* (p. 103).

[6] Chap. 278 (*Obres*, vii, p. 87).

[7] Chap. 283 (*Obres*, vii, p. 139 ; *cf.* also p. 175).

[8] Chap. 83 (*Obres*, iii, p. 131).

. . . it is a light thing for Thee to confound the false opinions and the errors of unbelievers."[1] Such timid Christians who hesitate to join battle with the enemy have lost the perfect trust which they should have in God's aid and power.[2]

There is no lion, O Lord, how wrathful soever he be and how fierce, that cannot be conquered and slain by ten men if they unite well together. Wherefore, since Thou dost Thyself aid the happy Christian who strives for Thy truth against his enemy, what affright can he have at the wrath and the threats that he meets in unbelievers, since he knows that upon his side he has Thee ?[3]

They have not the sacred example of Christ,[4] or His precept, ever before them. Nor have they the love, either of God or of their neighbour,[5] which should move them to go and preach to men "who are of one species, O Christ, with Thy Humanity and with Thee."[6] Often they have not far to go : the infidels are at their very doors—nay, in the houses which they themselves have let to them—yet they will not so much as protest when they blaspheme.[7] Often, too, they actually hinder the conversion of Jews and Saracens by refusing to help and to receive as their brothers those who are already converted. "Many Jews would become Christians if they had the wherewithal to live, and likewise many Saracens, if the Christians did them not dishonour."[8]

Yet the conversion of the Moslem world is of the first importance ; for, on the one hand, if God will but break the hard heart of the Saracen, he will find himself nearer to Christianity than he has realized[9] ; and, on the other, "once the Saracens were converted, it would be a light thing to convert the rest of the world."[10] So it is

[1] Chap. 83 (*Obres*, iii, p. 131). [2] *Ibid.* (p. 132).
[3] Chap. 85 (*Obres*, iii, p. 140).
[4] Chap. 146 (*Obres*, iv, pp. 278–9).
[5] Chap. 278 (*Obres*, vii, pp. 86–7).
[6] Chaps. 301, 307 (*Obres*, vii, pp. 337, 395).
[7] Chap. 287 (*Obres*, vii, p. 175).
[8] Chap. 346 (*Obres*, viii, p. 374). This opinion appears in *D.P.*, chap. 83, in an extended form, and also, more briefly, elsewhere in Lull's writings.
[9] See p. 67, n. 6, above.
[10] Chap. 346 (*Obres*, viii, pp. 379–80).

the duty of all, from "the Pope and the princes" downwards,[1] to send messengers to Moslems everywhere who shall argue with them "vigorously and valiantly," even if the parishes have to be short of priests in consequence. One must cry more loudly, is Lull's argument, to those that are far off (*i.e.* from God) than to those that are near.[2] Were the good-will present, these things would soon be put into effect, for the "letters and language"[3] of the infidels would quickly be learned by those who now would preach in that language if they knew it,[4] and the courage and endurance of the Christian missionary in face of violence and privation would furnish a new argument for the superiority of his religion over all others.[5]

Again and again Ramon urges these things, which are continually borne upon him, for "daily I hear the speech of heretics and infidels among the unbelieving men that are in our midst, and hardly anyone do I hear reprove them."[6] And now and then his voice takes the note of passion, and we detect the faint premonitions of an eloquence that is to grow greater and graver alike as years go on :

> Do Catholics indeed know the truth, and the errors wherein the infidels live, and have they no regard or care to show them the way of truth, as if indeed they knew not the truth of their own religion or the falseness of the religion of the unbelievers?
>
> Ah, my Lord and my God ! If it should be Thy pleasure for Thy servant to go through streets and squares, to cities and lonely houses, crying aloud Thy truth and the falseness of the unrighteous, and fearing neither hunger nor thirst nor death, then indeed would Thy servant have knowledge that he would be remembered in the mercy of his Lord God.[7]

[1] Chap. 346 (*Obres*, viii, p. 374). *Cf.* vii, p. 178 ; viii, pp. 372, 547, 549. On p. 547 (chap. 360), Lull makes the suggestion, to which he returns in later books, that a permanent yearly sum should be set aside in perpetuity for missionary work and that "cardinals should be assigned to each province of infidels" with an income sufficient for evangelization work in their provinces.

[2] Chap. 125 (*Obres*, iv, p. 150).

[3] Chap. 287 (*Obres*, vii, p. 178). In chap. 346 (*Obres*, viii, p. 370) Lull expresses the hope that the "Holy Father the Pope and his companions" will take in hand the teaching of languages to missionaries.

[4] Chap. 224 (*Obres*, v, pp. 464–5).

[5] Chap. 288 (*Obres*, vii, p. 193).

[6] Chap. 125 (*Obres*, iv, p. 150).

[7] Chap. 25 (*Obres*, ii, pp. 125–6).

Both with regard to style and to argument, the *Book of Contemplation* shows a maturity unusual in the first work of an unpractised writer. Lull has no *juvenilia* : indeed, he is rather disappointingly mature. In so far as his argument is concerned, this is not surprising. When a man of over thirty has been suddenly converted from a life of luxury and vice to one of self-denial and devotion, his ideas and habits are, not unnaturally, within ten years from his conversion, fixed and set. We find, in effect, precisely the same strictures in this book upon kings who refuse access to their subjects, *joglars* who sing lewd songs and women who paint their faces and dress extravagantly, as we find in books written ten, twenty and even thirty years later. The very phrasing is in some places almost identical. It is more surprising to find how great a proportion of what is of permanent value in Ramon's thought is contained in the *Book of Contemplation*. The command of theology and philosophy, in one who had started, a few years before, from zero, and had, in that same period, mastered Arabic (to say nothing of other subjects) to the point of being able to write a book of a million words in it is as astonishing as the logical progression shown in a first work of that length, the rapid development of important theses, the mastery of the author over his task—including the control of his digressions—from its beginning to its end. Ramon was to add to his knowledge,—principally in the natural sciences, and less markedly in comparative religion—and to incorporate his acquisitions in later books. But what he added in the course of forty or more years seems of small account in comparison with the broad and solid foundation that he laid in ten.

Most surprising of all in the *Book of Contemplation* is the maturity of Lull's style. This is for the most part clear and easy, seldom for long involved and never incomprehensible. Repetitions of phrase there are many : the worst fault of the book, indeed, is a frequent verbal heaviness, which might generally without much difficulty have been avoided. The use made of simile and metaphor, though it varies in extent, is, on the whole, considerable. Tracts of argument there are, indeed, unlighted by a single image, perhaps even by a single vivid phrase. But, on the other hand, many pages, especially in the distinction upon love, lend themselves readily to visualization. It is true that a number of the images most frequently called up are conventional (though not necessarily conventionally treated). A fair proportion come from the Gospels : the tree and its fruit, the shepherd and his flock, the winnowing of the wheat, the secret growth of a seed, and a number more. Others are familiar in all allegorical writing : the vessel filled with liquid, the river flowing into the sea, the relations between kings, knights and common people, the force of the sun's rays, the light of the sun compared with other lights. A few are ominously mathematical and deal with angles, triangles and circles. An interesting group of images, collected from various parts of the book, shows that Ramon was paying some attention to natural science. Such are the figures of the "stone seeking its centre," so finely used by St. Augustine, the testing of metals, the balance, the magnet, the mariner's compass, and—a simile queerly applied—the chemical composition of ink.

Most of these images occur too frequently for the places of their occurrence to be here specified, but there are two which are far more common than any others, and give the impression of being used as often as the rest put together. One of these, familiar to all readers of the mystics, is that of fire, under very many of its principal aspects, such as its qualities and appearance, its action on wood and other materials, and its comparison and reactions with water. The second is the image of the mirror, inspired in the first place, conceivably, by St. Paul [1] and St. James,[2] but also, in all probability, by Lull's own conception, already referred to,[3] of the crucifix as the mirror of his soul.

Ah, Jesus Christ my Lord ! Praised be Thou and blessed be all that is Thine ; for Thou hast set before our bodily eyes the

[1] 1 Cor. xiii, 12. [2] James i, 23. [3] See p. 24, above.

mirror of the holy Cross, that it may be a mirror to our souls, which shall be moved thereby to meditate upon the grievous trials and the painful death which were suffered and sustained by Thy righteous Human Nature.[1]

In the main, Lull's use of figures is apt. He scarcely ever, as in his later books, relates " examples " or parables, and his similes are usually brief. Here and there, indeed, they are weak, as when God's knowledge and ours are compared to oil and the water on which it floats,[2] or when Christ's persecution by the Jews between His trial and His death is likened to " the blowing of the leaves of a tree by the wind whithersoever it lists."[3] But more commonly they are applied at least adequately, and not a few of them are easily recalled to the memory. That of the author, for example, comparing himself, in the prologue to his enormous work, with " a mariner who is lost in the ocean, and has hope, O Lord, in Thee that Thou wilt draw him therefrom with joy."[4] The lightning, flashing in all directions, and searching vainly for an infinite God.[5] The rays of the sun, lighting up a dark and muddy path, yet receiving no contamination from it.[6] The child with his tame bird, which he loves so much that he squeezes it with his caresses almost to death.[7] The man who goes to sleep and dreams that he is clothed in white or in crimson, only to awaken and find himself naked.[8] These few examples are sufficient to show that Lull had already learned much that was to stand him in good stead as a writer.

If we compare this estimate of Lull's style with what is said hereafter of the books of his late middle age and decline, we shall discover that there is little to find fault with in these that is not already present in the *Book of Contemplation*. Its *longueurs*, its heaviness, its repetitions never entirely disappear. Its good things, of course, become better, but not so much better as we might reasonably expect.

[1] Chap. 150 (*Obres*, iv, p. 303).
[2] Chap. 19 (*Obres*, ii, p. 94).
[3] Chap. 90 (*Obres*, iii, p. 167).
[4] Prologue (*Obres*, ii, p. 5).
[5] Chap. 4 (*Obres*, ii, p. 19).
[6] Chap. 195 (*Obres*, v, p. 239).
[7] Chap. 290 (*Obres*, vii, p. 214).
[8] Chap. 345 (*Obres*, viii, p. 364).

It is the magnitude and the variety of the *Book of Contemplation*, rather than its style, that have caused Catalan writers to surpass one another in eulogy of it, and even to lose themselves in hyperbole. To the old Lullists it was the "Contemplador major," and it is somewhat in this spirit that modern Lullists have regarded it also. It is the "obra màxima lulliana," for example, to En Mateu Obrador: "l'obra capdal, verament magna, de Ramón Lull." [1] Dr. Torras i Bages, in a work too little known, describes it as "the masterpiece of the Beatus and the greatest work in the whole of Catalan literature," [2]—a bold claim indeed. Menéndez y Pelayo, the great Castilian scholar, is no less impressed by its magnitude, but realizes that magnitude does not always imply greatness. To him the work is an "enorme enciclopedia ascética." [3]

For ourselves we incline for once to the Castilian point of view rather than to that of Ramon's own countrymen. Clearly, the *Book of Contemplation* is the eldest brother of all Lull's other works, and from the very beginning of his career sets a definitive seal upon his genius. Were twentieth-century methods, arguments and conceptions those of the Middle Ages, it is possible that we might think of it as the first Lullists did, or Joan Bonlabi in the sixteenth century, or even Obrador and his contemporaries,—as resembling, that is to say, in the firmament of Lull's many works, "the sun among the stars." [4] As it is, much of it has been outgrown by modern thought, and even apart from this it contains too little of what is destined to be immortal in the writings of Ramon the Lover. Let us think of some of the elements that are absent from it. Excepting only the rigidly allegorical stories of the three damsels and the hermit, near the end of Book V,[5] it is entirely lacking in that narrative element which diversified so many of Lull's later polemical books and gave Catalonia and Europe one masterpiece of early fiction. It is almost entirely without

[1] *Obres*, ii, p. vii; *cf.* also p. xvii.
[2] *Op. cit.*, p. 226.
[3] Cf. *Obres*, ii, p. vii.
[4] *Obres*, ii, p. vii.
[5] Chaps. 355–6 (*Obres*, viii, pp. 483–506).

poetry: that lovely flower which in the later works can be plucked so freely has hardly begun to bud in this. It has little eloquence or passion—and we are to find much of both in Lull before long. It is quite devoid of humour—yet even that is not absent from Lull's temperament, though we could hardly expect it to reach its full flowering here. All these great gaps were soon to be filled, most of them very worthily: it seems unwise to heap excessive praise upon a work which is so shortly to be followed by others no less remarkable.

Yet Dr. Torras i Bages did well to focus his readers' attention upon it, reminding them, at the time when he first wrote, that it was preserved in no accessible Catalan edition. "He who knows not the *Book of Contemplation* knows not the Beat Ramon Lull"[1] was his bold assertion, and, unlike some such claims, it is a true one. Though there are other of Ramon's works which throw upon their author a light more revealing, this book is undoubtedly an illuminating commentary alike upon his life and his temperament, upon his erudition and his literary art. Further, its sheer length, its extreme variety, its comparative equality, its mastery both of subject and expression combine to make it a wonderful achievement. It may not in literal truth "comprehend well-nigh all the knowledge of its epoch," but it is certainly "an immense canvas whereon is depicted the marvellous harmony of the relations between existence create and increate, of nature finite and infinite, of Divine attributes and human faculties, of the hierarchies of heaven and the estates of men in the world, of society civil and religious, of spirit and matter, . . . a brilliant panorama of the universe seen through the glass of luminous contemplation."[2] Bold, indeed, is the comparison of it with the *Divine Comedy*,[3] and, on the merits of the two works, unjustified, but at least there are analogies between the two upon different planes. Let us sum up the qualities of the *Book of Contemplation* in the words of another Catalan writer—a poet who can bring to the study of it much that the work itself lacks,

[1] *Op. cit.*, p. 229. [2] *Op. cit.*, pp. 226–7.
[3] *Op. cit.*, p. 229.

and who is overawed less by its length than by its amazing diversity :

It is a work as full of illumination as of effort, of loftiness and of humility, of ascent and descent alike. It is not a work that climbs upward by slow degrees, but rather a living staircase, with angels ascending and descending upon it. It is no spiritual ladder, like the work of St. John Climacus . . . but a succession of swift and powerful flights like those of the marine eagle that can so often be seen at Miramar, now soaring upward towards the dazzling sun, now, as it were, falling—so swift is its descent—into the ocean.[1] . . . Even so, ever and anon, does Ramon mount up with wings to the ineffable heights, then downward sweeps to the depths of his own heart,—nay, to his own mind which has been dwelling in a vale of darkness.[2]

" A work of gladness and boldness " [3] it is, in short, " a mingling of fervour and fear," [4] a *gran contemplador*, as it was well named long ago after its author, for it is the work of a " great contemplator " indeed.

[1] The writer is surely thinking of the sensitive verses of Rosselló (*Revista luliana*, vol. i, pp. 322–330) :

De la montanya esquerpa a l'ombra gegantina
que'l sol ponent allarga pel pla d'immensa mar,
com águila marina
que esguarda l'ona blava entre'l brancám d'alzina,
pera llançars'hi sopte, aguayta Miramar.

[2] Riber, *Vida i actes*, etc., pp. 63–4. [3] *Ibid.*

[4] *L.A.A.*, 82 (*Bl.*, p. 424).

CHAPTER IV

The *Book of the Gentile and the three wise men*. Argument. Ramon Lull on Moslem beliefs. Weaknesses and merits of the book. Stylistic qualities. Sources and their treatment. Popularity.

At first sight, Ramon Lull appears to refer in the *Book of Contemplation* to no less than three of his other works, the inference from which fact would naturally be that these were all published before it. But two titles out of the three clearly refer to the same book and are mentioned in the last chapter of all: "Let a man have recourse to the *Book of the Gentile*," runs the reference, "which is called the *Book of Questions and Enquiries*." [1] And the third title, that of a *Book of Reasons concerning the three laws*, which is described very early in the *Book of Contemplation*,[2] is never again heard of in Lullian history. As to the first two titles, the former is not mentioned earlier in the book, and the latter occurs twice [3]: it is reasonable, then, to suppose that the *Book of the Gentile* was written during Ramon's nine years in Mallorca and its present title decided upon by him shortly before the *Book of Contemplation* was completed. Or it may have been only sketched before the larger work was finished,

[1] *L.C.*, chap. 366, ii (*Obres*, viii, p. 636).

[2] *L.C.*, chap. 11 (*Obres*, ii, p. 56). The reference suggests that the book is by another writer: "By this book has Thy servant had knowledge that Thy Divine Substance is in three Persons; and has known and been certified of the truth of the fourteen articles, and that the law of the Christians is true, and better than other laws." But there are quite a number of instances of Ramon's referring to his books as if they were written by some other person. See next note.

[3] The earlier reference (*L.C.*, chap. 77: *Obres*, iii, p. 98) seems to mean that the *Book of Questions and Enquiries* was by someone else also. The second reference (*L.C.*, chap. 188; *Obres*, v, p. 184) makes it clear that it is his own. Further, the description which he gives of it prepares us for the statement that it is the *Book of the Gentile* under another title. *Cf.* p. 39, n. 5, above.

and written or re-written directly afterwards, in the period of relief after so great mental strain.[1] As to the third title, it describes the *Book of the Gentile* so aptly that it is generally taken as being an earlier name for it still.[2] All things considered, it seems very likely that a book written at long intervals, during the composition of a much larger one, might have three successive titles, and the similarity of the references to all three may be taken as putting the presumption beyond doubt.

Like others of Ramon Lull's early works, the *Book of the Gentile and the three wise men* bears no indication of date, and contains no references which can fairly be considered as internal evidence amplifying the suppositions just recorded. Another mark of early date is the depreciatory manner in which the book refers to its author, a habit which Ramon soon outgrew. Here, in the prologue, he is described as " guilty, mean, poor, sinful, despised by men and unworthy for my name to be written in this book or in any other." [3] His name does not, in fact, appear in it at all.

The framework of the book shows at once that Lull was seriously attempting allegory as a means of conveying instruction. A certain heathen philosopher (the " Gentile " of the story), who " had no knowledge of God, neither believed in resurrection, nor supposed that there was aught beyond death," is sad at the thought of his approaching end, and, to beguile his sadness, sets off upon a journey. He encounters a typically allegorical forest, a place of wondrous beauty, full of trees bearing the choicest flowers and fruits, and the home of the rarest birds and four-footed animals. But the more beauty he finds here, the greater is his dismay at " the thought of death and the annihilation of his being." So he wanders from one place to another, in the deepest depression.[4]

It chances that at about this time three sages—a Jew,

[1] As I incline to the latter supposition, chiefly for stylistic reasons (see pp. 97–9 below) I date the book 1272–3.

[2] This is the view of Obrador among others. See *Obres*, ii, pp. xx, 373.

[3] Pròlech, *Obras*, i, p. 4. (The Catalan text of the work is in *Obras*, i, the Latin text in Salz., vol. ii.)

[4] *Ibid.* (p. 5).

a Christian and a Saracen—are leaving an unnamed city in company. Deeply immersed in conversation regarding their respective beliefs, they arrive in due course at a spring, which waters five trees, the significance and properties of which are explained to them by a fair damsel named Intelligencia.[1] The first tree has one-and-twenty flowers, "signifying God, and His essential uncreated virtues"[2]—or, more exactly, certain twofold combinations of them. The second tree, with nine-and-forty flowers, represents combinations of these same seven virtues with the "seven virtues created."[3] The nine-and-forty flowers of the third tree consist of the Divine virtues compounded with the seven deadly sins; those of the fourth tree are one-and-twenty combinations of the seven created virtues; while those of the fifth again are nine-and-forty, "wherein are written the seven principal created virtues and the seven deadly sins." By "the knowledge of these trees"—that is, by a consideration in turn of the themes which compose each "flower" and the two "conditions" postulated of each tree[4]—

man may comfort the disconsolate and ease the trials of those that suffer. And by these trees temptations may be mortified and the soul cleansed of guilt and sins. And by the utility thereof, and the fruit that may be plucked therefrom, man flees from eternal torment and comes to everlasting rest.[5]

So saying, the lady Intelligencia leaves the sages, and they begin to discuss what she has said. "Ah, God!" cries one of them, "would that by the virtue of these trees all men might be led to embrace one law and one belief! That there were no rancour or ill-will among them! That even as there is one God alone, all the nations might be united into one, and for ever hold one faith, giving glory and praise to our Lord God! Seems

[1] Pròlech (*Obras*, i, p. 8).

[2] *Viz.* goodness, greatness, eternity, power, wisdom, love, perfection.

[3] *Viz.* faith, hope, charity, justice, prudence, fortitude, temperance.

[4] *E.g.* that the greatest nobility, in Essence, virtues and works, must be attributed to God at all times; that virtues created and uncreated cannot be contrary to each other; that virtues and vices cannot agree; and the like.

[5] Pròlech (*Obras*, i, p. 10).

it not good to you," he continues, "that we all should seat ourselves beneath these trees, beside this fair spring, and hold discussion as to that which we believe, according to the manner which is signified by the flowers and the trees?" The others agree, but at that moment they see the Gentile coming towards them: "a great beard he had, and long hair, and he walked as one that was weary and thin and pale, by reason of the travail of his thoughts and his long journey." He halts by the spring to refresh himself and rest, is saluted by the sages and describes to them his state of mind.[1]

When the Gentile had heard the greeting of the three wise men, and had seen the five trees, and read that which was on the flowers, and taken note of the strange appearance of the three wise men, and the strangeness of their clothing, then fell he to thinking, and marvelled greatly at the words which he heard and likewise at that which he saw.

"Fair friend," said one of the wise men to him, "Whence comest thou, and what is thy name? Thou seemest to me for some cause sorely troubled and disconsolate. How ailest thou? And wherefore hast thou come to this place? And is there naught wherein we may comfort and aid thee? Let us know thy mind."

Then he answered and said that he came from distant lands, and was a Gentile, and went through that forest as one that was out of his mind; and that chance had led him thither. And he described to them the pain and grief whereto he had been brought. "And when ye greeted me," he said, "praying God, Who created the world and will raise the dead, to grant me His aid, then did I greatly marvel at your greeting, for never before have I heard of the God of Whom ye speak, neither at any time have I heard of resurrection. Could one but make plain and show to me by convincing reasons the significance of resurrection, then would the pain and sorrow of my soul be cast out from it."

"How, fair friend!" said one of the three wise men. "Believest thou not then in God, neither hast hope of resurrection?"

"Alack, sir, nay," answered the Gentile, "and if ye can show me aught whereby my soul may have knowledge of resurrection, I pray you to do so. For know the truth, that the grievous pain which is mine comes from this, that I see death approaching, and I think not that after death aught exists."[2]

[1] Pròlech (*Obras*, i, pp. 11–12).

[2] *Obras*, i, pp. 13–14.

The sages conceive pity and love for their heathen acquaintance and resolve to prove to him " that God is, and that in Him are goodness, greatness, eternity, power, wisdom, love and perfection."[1] These truths they purpose to expound by means of the flowers on the five trees, in the way described by the lady, but more briefly; and after a courteous wrangle as to who shall speak first, a question which the Gentile decides for them, the argument starts on its way. The first book, " On God and Resurrection," takes the seven Divine attributes mentioned, and, considering them " by two and two " —a favourite proceeding of Ramon's in exposition—demonstrates the probability that God exists and that life continues after death. The " second tree " is then introduced, and each of the seven attributes is considered with one of seven created virtues, leading to a like result. The " third tree " appears—and the seven attributes are considered with the seven deadly sins ; the " fourth tree" —and the virtues are taken two by two ; the " fifth tree" —and in each of its seven sections a virtue is paired with a vice.[2]

During the greater part of the first book, the sage is allowed to expound without interruption. On one occasion, the Gentile enquires " if beasts and birds will rise again," and is told that they will not," because they have neither reason nor free will, and, if they rose again, God would act contrarily to His justice and wisdom."[3] Again, he asks if in God there is hope, and learns that neither faith nor hope can be in God, because they imply imperfection of knowledge ; " and if they were [in God] there would be no concord between perfection and . . . the virtues of the first tree, and that is impossible."[4] His questions, however, are few, and at the end of the exposition his mind is illumined and he accepts what he has been told (as converts of Ramon's fictions always do) without demur, reproaching himself for not having done so before.[5] When his reproaches are over, he " perceives

[1] *Obras*, i, p. 14. See n. 2, p. 84 above.
[2] *Ibid.*, pp. 17–62.
[3] *Ibid.*, p. 26.
[4] *Ibid.*, pp. 43–4.
[5] *Ibid.*, p. 45.

that his soul is delivered from the torments and the sorrow wherewith his unbelief and error have so long and sorely tried him." [1]

So the Gentile kneeled upon the ground, and raised his hands to the heavens, together with his eyes, which were in weeping and in tears, and he adored God with fervour of heart, and said: "Blessed be the glorious God, the mighty Lord and Father of all that is! I thank Thee, Lord, that Thou hast been pleased to remember this man that is a sinner, who was at the gate of everlasting and infernal destruction. I adore Thee, O Lord, I bless Thy name, and I beg Thy forgiveness. . . ." [2]

Thus far, Lull's apologetics have been more picturesque than potent, for he has dealt with hardly any of a sceptic's real difficulties, merely setting before an imaginary sceptic considerations of an evidential nature and portraying him as capitulating unintelligently. As has already been suggested, Ramon never in his life quite lost the tendency to make evil or untruth collapse on its initial contact with good, and the psychology of his romances suffers correspondingly. In this book, however, he may be forgiven for his departure from probability, since it is only after the Gentile's initial conversion that the main part of the argument begins. Once the first ecstasy of joy has passed, the unfortunate man remembers his parents and kinsfolk who have died in unbelief, and have presumably lost God's glory. Turning brusquely on his mentors, he enquires of them why they have no pity on those who, like himself, have never heard of God, and so cannot serve Him:

And ye, whom God has honoured so highly above other people, why go ye not forth to honour Him among the nations that do Him dishonour, neither loving Him, nor knowing Him, nor obeying Him, nor hoping in Him, nor fearing His lofty dominion? I adjure you, sirs, by God, that ye go out into those distant lands and preach therein, and likewise that ye instruct me how I may serve and honour God with all my might.[3]

Then comes the crucial point of the narrative, for

[1] *Obras*, i, p. 58. [2] *Ibid.*, p. 59. [3] *Ibid.*, p. 60.

the only answer which the sages make is to beg the Gentile, each in turn, to accept his particular belief.

"How!" said the Gentile. "Have ye then not all one selfsame belief and law?" "Nay," they replied, "that have we not, for the beliefs and the laws which we hold are divers. . . ." "And which of you," said the Gentile, "has the worthiest law, and which of your laws is true?" Each of the three wise men made answer, praising his own belief, and attacking that of the others, and they had great strife together.[1]

When the Gentile hears that, though each of the sages believes in God and in future bliss, each reserves the bliss for those who think like himself, his distress is greater than ever. "Alas, sirs!" he cries. "Now have ye plunged me into sorrow and distress yet greater than those which I had aforetime! For then at least I had no fear of suffering, after my death, infinite torments. But now ye tell me that, if I walk not in the way of truth, there are tortures prepared for me to torment my soul after death eternally."[2] In his despair he can only beg the wise men to argue their beliefs before him, and he will pray God to direct him to choose rightly which to adopt as his own. So the book settles down to be a "Book of reasons concerning the three laws," the reasons being compared according to the same artificial method as before of the flowers and the trees. "He who can best make concordance between the articles of his faith and the flowers and conditions of the trees, that one of us will give thereby significance and demonstration that his belief is better than that of the rest of us."[3]

The Jew, who begins, expounds eight articles of his religion,—that God is one, and the Creator of the world; that He gave the Jewish law to Moses; that He will send a Messiah to deliver His people; that all will rise from the dead, be judged, and go either to Heaven or to Hell. The Gentile now asks more questions, most of them very much to the point,—no doubt the same that Ramon himself had been asked by those with whom he argued. Did the good God create evil? What did

[1] *Obras*, i, p. 60. [2] *Ibid.*, p. 61. [3] *Ibid.*, p. 62.

God do before the Creation? How could everything be made from nothing? How can finite and temporal sin merit infinite and eternal punishment?[1] The answers to most of these questions are brief and insufficient, but the Gentile (as before) accepts them. Only on the subject of Paradise is his curiosity less easily satisfied. Are there human relationships there? Is there, either in Heaven or in Hell, hunger and thirst? If not, wherein consists the punishment of Hell? Do the blessed remember this world? And each other? And the merits of their good works? And if not, what can they know of God's justice?[2]

The different schools of thought among the Jews are touched on but lightly, and that almost solely in regard of the life to come.[3] The Jew's case is sympathetically put, and his position is only once or twice looked at askance by his hearer.[4]

The Christian next expounds the tenets of his faith, after a short period spent in devotion, in the order following:

> He said that the articles of his law were fourteen, whereof there are seven that pertain to the Divine nature, and seven that pertain to the human nature of Jesus Christ. They that pertain to the Divine nature are these: That there is one God, Father, Son and Holy Spirit, Creator, Redeemer and Glorifier. They that pertain to the humanity of Jesus Christ are these: That Jesus Christ was conceived of the Holy Spirit, born of a virgin, crucified and dead, that He descended into Hell, rose again, ascended into Heaven, and will come again to judge the good and the evil on the Day of Judgment.[5]

The Christian exposition, though half as long again as that of the Jew, is not, as might be expected, a discussion rather than an exposition. The Gentile confines himself

[1] *Obras*, i, pp. 71, 81, 82, 121. [2] *Ibid.*, pp. 118–9.
[3] *Ibid.*, pp. 100 ff.
[4] E.g. *Obras*, i, pp. 94–5, 99. The Gentile surmises from the history of the Jews that they "are in some sin, wherein ye know not that ye are," and he has no wish, by embracing the Jewish faith, to be compelled to suffer the Jewish "bondage."
[5] *Obras*, i, p. 128.

to occasional questions, and is as well satisfied as ever with the answers.[1] On two points only he requires more information : the nature of the Holy Trinity (a subject developed at some length) and the Incarnation of Our Lord : here for a few pages we have genuine conversation. The Christian, it would seem, is prepared to explain anything : how the Blessed Trinity can be One and yet Three, why the three Persons are Father, Son and Holy Spirit, in what manner the Son was begotten of the Father, what is implied in the procession of the Holy Spirit, why the procession is not from the Father alone but from Father and Son, and so on. There is no hint that all these questions are not as easily soluble as a problem in mathematics, no suggestion that the nature and attributes of the Godhead are not susceptible of being completely understood. "If it were not as thou sayest," runs a typical answer, "the above-mentioned totality would not have concordance with the flowers of the trees, and there would be a perfection contrary to the flowers, and this is impossible."[2] The trees solve every question that can be asked, and in the sense which the author desires. The formulæ, no doubt, are unexceptionable, but not so the steps by which they are arrived at.

In one respect the nature of the Christian's discourse differs markedly from the Jew's : he several times refers to the beliefs of his companions in their relation to his own. He shows, for example, how both Jews and Saracens misinterpret the Christian belief in the Trinity[3] ; how the Saracens fail to understand what is implied in the death of Christ[4] ; how "among the people of the Jews and the Saracens there are fewer religious, fewer martyrs, fewer men that give alms and fewer that forsake the world for God, than there are among the Christians."[5] This, and a certain strain of appeal in the Christian's final words to the Gentile,[6] are the only suggestions of proselytizing in the chapters thus far considered. The reader feels less, as a rule, that Lull is teaching the Christian

[1] E.g. *Obras*, i, pp. 133, 138, 147, 151.
[2] *Obras*, i, p. 163.
[3] *Ibid.*, pp. 165, 189–90 ; *cf.* p. 233.
[4] *Ibid.*, p. 206.
[5] *Ibid.*, p. 225.
[6] *Ibid.*, pp. 229–30.

verities than that he is trying to hold the balance between the three sages.

The account of the Saracen's exposition is prefaced by a detailed description of the preparations which he makes before giving it. "He went to the spring, washed his hands and his face, his ears, nose and mouth, and afterwards his feet and certain other parts of his person, to give significance of original sin and purity of heart." Then he prostrated himself "with his head on the ground, and kneeled three times, placing his head on the ground and kissing the earth," before "raising his heart and his hands and his eyes to the heavens," and invoking Allah in the opening words of the Korân: "In the name of God, the merciful One that showeth mercy, to Whom be given praise, for He is Lord of the world. Him I adore and in Him I trust, for it is He that leadeth us in the right path." [1]

This invocation is followed by many other prayers, after which the Saracen puts forward the plan of his discourse.

> He said to the Gentile that the articles of his law are twelve, to wit: There is one God. He is the Creator. Mahomet is His prophet. The Korân is a law given by God. After death, every man will be questioned in his tomb by an angel, as to whether Mahomet is the messenger of God.[2] All kings will die, except God. There will be a resurrection. The prayer of Mahomet will be heard on the Day of Judgment. On that day we shall render an account to God. Merits and faults will be weighed. [All men] will pass along the road [to Paradise and Hell].[3] There exist both Paradise and Hell.[4]

As will be seen, these articles embody some of the most characteristic of Moslem beliefs, which are described as fully as the customs mentioned in the prologue. As in

[1] *Obras*, i, pp. 231–2. The passage (known as "Al-Fâtihat" or introduction to the Korân) is slightly abridged, and the last words are not exact. No doubt Lull was quoting from memory.

[2] This phrase does not fully express the sense of the article in question. See *Obras*, i, pp. 247–52.

[3] This also is not quite an exact description of the belief expounded. See *Obras*, i, pp. 276–82.

[4] *Obras*, i, p. 232.

the *Book of Contemplation*,[1] Lull makes much of Moslem ideas on Paradise, and of their materialism, on which, as we have seen, he lays great emphasis, evidently considering it to be one of the most vulnerable characteristics of the Saracen's creed. From the Korân itself[2] come the descriptions of Al Jannat, the happy mansion of Paradise, of the " viands of divers kinds, the fairest of garments, wondrous palaces, fair chambers, numerous beds, many and beauteous women with whom men will have corporal pleasure and delight."[3]

> The palaces and chambers shall be of gold and silver and precious stones,—that is to say, of rubies and emeralds and sapphires and pearls, and other stones like to them. . . . In these palaces will be much cloth of gold and silver and silk wherewith they shall be adorned ; and there shall be many beds and rugs and carpets of gold and silver and silk ; and many women of wondrous beauty, right nobly dressed and very pleasant to behold. . . . And there shall be many fountains and rivers and trees bearing leaf, flower and fruit, and casting welcome shade.[4]

But Lull does not omit to present the spiritual with the material :

> " We believe that there will be two manners of glory in Paradise," said the Saracen. " The one is spiritual glory and the other physical. The spiritual glory is to see God, and to love and contemplate Him. This glory will be ours in Paradise, and, as our prophet Mahomet says in his Proverbs, the men that are in Paradise will see God in the morning and in the evening."[5]

[1] See p. 71, above. [2] Cf. *Obras*, i, p. 241, n. 5.

[3] *Obras*, i, p. 241. *Cf.* the descriptions in the Korân (trans. G. Sale, London, 1927) of the life of the blessed : "They shall repose on couches, adorned with gold and precious stones. . . . There shall receive them beauteous damsels . . . having fine black eyes. . . . Youths . . . shall attend them with . . . flowing wine. . . . The pious shall be lodged in a place of security . . . among gardens and fountains . . . near a flowing water . . . amidst fruits in abundance" (Chaps. 44, 55, 56, *passim* : *ed. cit.*, pp. 481, 513–20.)

[4] *Obras*, i, p. 283. (See also preceding note.) This passage concerns the sense of sight only. There are other passages, not less sensuous, on hearing, smell, taste and touch (pp. 284–9). *Cf.* pp. 286–7 : " To give great physical pleasure to man in Paradise, God has created many fair damsels and virgins. . . . In Paradise, man shall lie with the women who in this life have been his," etc.

[5] *Obras*, i, p. 282.

On this and similar matters Lull speaks with knowledge. Oriental scholars remark upon the exactness of his statements; and, so far as we are aware, the correctness of none of his descriptions, either of the customs or of the beliefs of Islam, has been questioned. It would seem that, in addition to reproducing the arguments of those who had debated with him, he had consulted "the Korân . . . and the Proverbs of Mahomet, and the glosses of those who have expounded the Korân and the Proverbs."[1] We may even hazard the supposition that he had become so deeply immersed in the sacred books of Islam during his years of study that he found little difficulty in writing of them from memory. For he shows no sign of having consulted them closely, or copied from them word for word, yet wherever his citations are tested they prove to be exact in substance, though not in letter.

Into a number of subjects he enters with some fulness: the Moslem's belief in the Korân[2]; the questions on the faith which will be put to the dead in their tombs by the black angels Monkir and Nakir[3]; the resurrection, when the rain will be white as milk, and, at the trump of the angel Israfil, "all living creatures shall spring up like grass" and "shake the earth from their heads"[4]; the events of the Day of Judgment, when Mahomet will plead with God for men after all other prophets, from Adam to Jesus, have refused to do so[5]; the sinlessness of Mahomet after his call to be God's prophet[6]; the passing of such as shall be saved over the path or bridge of Al-Sirat, below which is Hell:

> That path shall be as slender as a hair or as the blade of a sword; and some shall pass over it as swiftly as lightning, others as a man that runs, others as a child that crawls, each according to his merits; and he that merits not glory shall fall from that bridge into Hell.[7]

Obviously these dogmas are less susceptible of

[1] *Obras*, i, p. 288. [2] *Ibid.*, pp. 242 ff. [3] *Ibid.*, pp. 247 ff.
[4] *Ibid.*, pp. 257–9. [5] *Ibid.*, pp. 259–63. [6] *Ibid.*, p. 264.
[7] *Ibid.*, p. 277. It will be seen from these references that Lull's Saracen goes some way beyond what the Korân directly teaches, and that Lull knew a good deal therefore about Moslem tradition.

"proof" by the "flowers" of the five trees than those which were expounded by the Jew and the Christian. No doubt, in describing them in such detail, Ramon intended this to be realized, and the puerility of Mohammedan traditions to be contrasted with the nobility of the Christian creed. Less attempt is made by the Saracen to use the "trees,"—he relies rather on categorical assertion. And the Gentile is now inclined to be restive. He understands the five trees and is quick to show his knowledge. As a result, there is occasionally in this part of the work some real discussion; once there is a prompt interposition by the Christian sage[1]; frequently the Gentile questions the Saracen's statements in a tone of confidence which indicates that he has been convinced, or at least notably influenced, by the Christian. Except in the first two sections of the book, the Jew is forgotten, and what we have becomes essentially a contrast between Christianity and Islam. Indeed, it may not be too much to assert that in a few passages the voice of the Gentile is the voice of Lull himself, who, in his earliest discussions with the Mallorcan Saracens, would reply to his adversaries by means of queries, at first timid, then quickly increasing in assurance. Sometimes, in fact, after a short but sharp argument, it is no longer the sage who has the last word, but his pupil:

"If angels and the souls of saints, that merit life and not death, do die," said the Gentile, "then is the perfection of God contrary to justice and goodness . . . by the which is signified that that which thou sayest is not truth."

"Thy argument would be true," answered the Saracen, "if God gave not life again to angels and men's souls. But since all will return to life, and God will make them to live for ever, therefore will He do them no wrong in death; but He would wrong Himself if He used not His virtues in the creatures to bring them to greater nobility and perfection."

Then said the Gentile: "Death is the sundering of soul and body. If the angels have no bodies, how can they die?"

"The angels will die," answered the Saracen, "in that they will come to naught; in this sense it is said that they will die."

[1] *Obras*, i, p. 233.

"Then," replied the Gentile, "will God be opposed to that which befits being; for, since the angels are good, and serve God, they merit having being; and, if they are to be naught, the virtues of God accord with not-being against being, and this is impossible." [1]

Sometimes, without contradicting his teacher categorically, he turns the weakest of his arguments against him:

"Since Mahomet is honoured so greatly in the world, and by so many people, it follows that in him justice accords with the charity of God; for were this not so, then would God not suffer him to be honoured as he is, and, if He suffered it, wrong and honour would accord with charity, against charity and honour and justice, which is impossible. Whence it follows that, by reason of the honour wherewith Mahomet is honoured by God, Mahomet is a prophet."

"From that which thou sayest," answered the Gentile, "it follows that Jesus Christ, Who is so greatly honoured in this world, is God; and that His apostles, and the other martyrs, who are so greatly honoured likewise, died in the way of truth. For, if God suffered not the dead that died in falsehood to be honoured in this world, then that which is said of Christ would of necessity be truth; and, if this were so, then thy law would not be true, neither would Mahomet be worthy of honour nor a prophet." [2]

At the end of his discourse, however, the Saracen is allowed to have the final word: so much the author's sense of fairness could not forbid him.

"Thou hast heard and understood my words, O Gentile, and the proofs which I have given of the articles of our law; and thou hast heard what bliss there is in Paradise, which shall be thine for ever and eternally if thou believe in our law which is given of God." And, when the sage had thus spoken, he closed his book, and ended his words, and saluted the two sages according to his custom.[3]

The conclusion of the whole matter is of interest. The Gentile first recites each of the three lessons which have been taught him, whereupon the sages are all mightily pleased, and exclaim that they have certainly not spoken to one "without heart or ears." [4] Next, all

[1] *Obras*, i, pp. 253–4.
[2] *Ibid.*, pp. 240–1.
[3] *Ibid.*, p. 289.
[4] *Ibid.*, p. 290.

semblance of reality having by now departed from the allegory, the Gentile recites a lengthy prayer, in which, in words by no means devoid of beauty, he converses with each of the virtues and vices by name, and at the end begs God to show him mercy, without, however, making it clear which of the three faiths he has embraced.

His prayer over, he " washes his hands and face in the fair spring, by reason of the tears that he has shed," and wipes them on a white *capso* that he keeps for wiping his eyes when he has given indulgence to his grief.[1] Then, still silent as to his choice of a religion, he begins to bless God, the sages, and the place of his meeting with them, announcing finally that he will discuss the three religions further with two fellow-heathen whom he sees approaching.[2] So he takes leave of the sages, after many " embraces and kisses and much weeping and many tears," [3] and each tells him that he is convinced he will choose his own particular religion, and no other.

When the Gentile has departed, they begin to realize that by comparison with him they appear in none too favourable a light.

> Said one of the three wise men : " If this Gentile, who for so long has been in error, has conceived so great devotion and fervour in giving praise to God, saying that to praise God he would not fear to suffer grievous trials, nor even death, in howsoever dreadful shape it came, how much greater devotion and fervour in praising the name of God should be ours who for so long have had knowledge of God, the more so because God has loaded us with blessings and honours, the which He has given us and gives us daily. And furthermore we ought to dispute among ourselves and see which of us is in the truth, and which in error. And even as we have one God, one Creator, and one Lord, let us have one faith, one law, one religion, and one manner of loving and honouring God. Let us love and help one another, and between us let there be no difference or contrariety of faith or customs. . . ." [4]

They decide, therefore, not to be content with the expositions of their own beliefs which they have already given, but to dispute with each other in due form,

[1] *Obras*, i, p. 299.
[2] *Ibid.*, p. 300.
[3] *Ibid.*
[4] *Ibid.*, pp. 301–2.

according to the "flowers" and the "trees," to see if they can themselves find the truth.

Each of the two wise men found that which was said by the third very pleasing, and they made ordinance concerning the place and hour of the disputation, and the manner thereof; and they resolved that when they should all have reached one faith, and agreed thereupon, they would go throughout the world giving praise and glory to the name of our Lord God. So each of the three wise men departed to his house.[1]

It will be evident to all readers how different in every way is the *Book of the Gentile* from the *Book of Contemplation*. It might well have been written as a recreation, or as a partial relief from the longer and far more exacting treatise.[2] Not that it is anything but serious and earnest from beginning to end: the relief would be rather in its artistic qualities—such as they are—in its brevity, its concern with persons as well as ideas, and its embodiment of its author's own experiences.

In respect of its argument, the *Book of the Gentile* has two weaknesses. On the first of these—its artificiality, and its preoccupation with "trees" and "flowers,"—there is little need to dwell, so obvious is it. More hesitatingly, one admits weakness in its most likeable characteristic—an excessive tolerance, and an unwillingness, not only to score points, but to fight out any argument whatever. Except in the Mohammedan section, the reader feels that he never gets to grips with an unbeliever in the flesh at all, and even there, the discussion invariably stops short with the collapse of the Saracen, as complete as is that of the Gentile in the earlier sections.

At the same time, this weakness adds to the attractiveness of the *Book of the Gentile*, and its unfailing equanimity and fairness (which some may think unnatural in characters who would send each other so lightly to Hell)

[1] *Obras*, i, p. 304.
[2] See p. 83, above. The conclusion of the book in the Latin text (Mayence edition) describes it as having been derived from the *Ars Magna*, and succeeding writers have repeated and amplified this statement. But see p. 100, n. 3, below.

make us realize very forcibly the reasonableness with which, whether in his books or in his disputations, Lull approached his task of converting the unbeliever. From a superficial perusal of the work, the reader would hardly know which side is taken by its author. One would expect a Christian polemist to make his Christian sage speak last, refute the arguments of the rest and end with an indisputable triumph. But no: by a happy idea of the Gentile, the order in which the sages discourse is that of the antiquity of their respective religions. The Christian is given neither the advantage of the initial attack, nor that of the final word, but the weakest position of the three—the second. If it be thought that the purely artistic reason alleged in the fiction for this arrangement is the real one, the presumption cannot be disproved; but a more likely explanation is that the author wished each of the three faiths to stand on its own merits, so that the reader might choose for himself in a fair and unbiassed manner. And this, unless he is too much influenced by the arguments of Lull's own experience embodied in Book IV, he undoubtedly may.

In general, it can be said that the arguments of each sage are set forth in similar fashion, with the same scrupulous care. There is no heat, no eloquence, no emotion. The sages had no need, when taking leave of each other in "right friendly and pleasant fashion," to "crave pardon each of the rest, if he had said concerning the laws of the others any wrong word" (*vilana paraula*).[1] There is not a *vilana paraula* in the book, and hardly a weakness in argument on any one side which is not balanced by a weakness in each of the others. The final task which Ramon sets his sages is perhaps an impossible one, but at least they approach it in a spirit which deserves success.[2]

[1] *Obras*, i, p. 303.

[2] Menéndez y Pelayo (*Orígenes de la novela*, i, p. lxxvii) tries to explain away the indefiniteness of the conclusion of the book lest any should accuse Lull of being a vague theist—an unlikely eventuality. He calls the conclusion an "inocente artificio literario para llamar la atención sobre otros libros suyos, que son indispensable complemento de éste." But in actual fact Lull does not, at the end of the *Gentile*, mention any other of his books, which he

From a literary point of view, the *Book of the Gentile* is somewhat inferior to the *Book of Contemplation*, a finding which confirms the suspicion that it was written as a relief from the longer treatise. It has, perhaps, rather fewer repetitions, and weighs less heavily upon the reader, for, after all, it is technically nothing more than the report of a debate. It is as clear, too, and as easily comprehensible as are those parts of the *Book of Contemplation* which, as to their subject-matter, are of equal difficulty. But it maintains an undiversified level of mediocrity. Its sentences tend to formlessness, and are too often a wearying concatenation of co-ordinate clauses, relieved only by a welcome but very occasional: *E sabs per que?* in Ramon's later manner. In such a lifeless treatise, every staccato note is a relief.

The fiction of the book starts promisingly; it provides the first example of Lull's allegorically framed homilies, and, with the exception of one passage, already noted, in the *Book of Contemplation*, it embodies his first known attempt at narrative. But, though suggestive of better things to come, it soon proves to be in itself the merest convention. There is no characterization in the book, and, after the prologue is over, hardly any description, illustration or use of metaphor. The figures of speech which it employs can, in the total, be counted on the fingers of one hand.[1]

It is thought by some that the *Book of the Gentile* was imitated from an Arabic original which is no longer extant.[2] The prologue certainly gives colour to this supposition. "According to the manner of the Arabic book 'Of the Gentile,'" it says, "I would strive with all my powers, trusting in the aid of the Most High, to seek out a new manner and new arguments whereby those that have strayed may be set in the way to glory

was never loth to do when he thought well. I should prefer to explain the conclusion in either of the ways suggested in the text above.

[1] See *Obras*, i, pp. 153, 174, 191, 238.

[2] There was a "Gentilis in arabico" at the Lullian School in Barcelona in 1466. This may have been either the original or a translation (Alòs: *Los catálogos*, etc, p. 54).

which has no end." [1] At the end of the book, however, we read that it is "newly translated," [2] without further details ; and, considering that it is contemporary with a book which was written first in Arabic and translated afterwards into Catalan by its author, we shall probably be right in assuming that this is also its own history.[3]

Few of Lull's later works had such a vogue as the *Book of the Gentile*. It was translated into French : part of this version was re-published as lately as 1831.[4] The Latin version has already been alluded to, and there is a fifteenth-century edition in Arabic which is probably a re-handling of the book's original form. A Castilian translation, by Gonzalo Sánchez de Uceda, was made as early as 1378. A Hebrew translation is mentioned by some writers, and not at all improbably existed, since the matter of the book would be of no less interest to Jews and to those who were endeavouring to convert them than to missionaries among the Mohammedans. It is clear, in any case, that the book received a warm welcome in the world's literatures. Thus, at the end of his nine years' seclusion, Ramon had two successful works to his credit—one which was to be read chiefly in Catalonia and another which was to travel farther abroad. By both of them, though not perhaps chiefly so, he is likely to be remembered still for many generations.

[1] Pròlech : *Obras*, i, pp. 3–4. [2] *Obras*, i, p. 304.

[3] The matter is slightly complicated by the Latin reading (for "per la honor del qual noueylament es transladat") : "et propter cujus honorem noviter est editus et extractus." The Mayence edition adds to these words—an evident gloss by one who desired to interpret them in his own way—". . . ab Arte compendiosa inveniendi veritatem." I think myself that this is simply a mistake, for I do not believe the *Art* was written till later, but, whatever the explanation of the phrase may be, it does not seem likely to upset the hypothesis put forward in the text above.

Menéndez y Pelayo hazards the influence upon this book of the *Cuzari* (or *Hozari*) of Judá Leví (Yehuda ha-Levi,) with which (*Orígenes de la novela*, i, p. lxxiv) he compares it. The plans of the two works are similar and the works of Yehuda ha-Levi must have been at the height of their popularity in Catalonia and Languedoc in Lull's day. This, in the present state of our knowledge, is as much as can be said with any certainty. On the *Cuzari*, which was written in Arabic and translated into Hebrew in the twelfth century, see Schlössinger and Broydé on Yehuda ha-Levi in *Jewish Encyclopaedia*, vol. vii, and the English translation (entitled *Judah Hallevi's Kitab al-Khazari*) published in London, 1905.

[4] See Rogent i Duràn, *Bibliografia*, etc. p. 365.

CHAPTER V

1274–5

The retirement to Mount Randa. The Divine illumination: historical and legendary accounts. The *mata escrita*. Visit to La Real. Composition of the *Art General* or *Ars Magna*. Other works of this period. Return to Mount Randa. Legend of the heavenly shepherd.

It must not be supposed that, because during these nine years Ramon Lull wrote so steadily and so abundantly, he found complete satisfaction in the exacting work of a writer. Though he had small faith at this time in the possibilities of warlike crusades, he would hardly have been a man, still less a one-time courtier, if his pulse had not quickened at the thrilling appeal of his sovereign and former master on behalf of the crusade of St. Louis.[1] And there met him temptations to leave his studies more insistent still. His preaching experiences in Palma fanned the flame of his desire to devote himself entirely to the work of a missionary. Memories of his travels abroad inspired him with zeal to go into all the world. Again and again, during those first weary years of study, and during the hardly less tedious period in which he was writing his great work in Arabic and translating it into the vernacular, his ardent and active spirit had sighed for Africa or Palestine, where he might prove with the spoken word the efficacy of all that he was writing. "Ah, Lord," he cries, when but one-third of his *Book of Contemplation* is completed,

So great desire has Thy servant to give Thee praise, that by night and by day he toils and struggles as best he may to bring to an end this *Book of Contemplation*; and then, when once it is completed, he will go and shed both blood and tears for love of Thee in

[1] See p. 44, above.

that Holy Land wherein Thou didst shed Thy precious blood and tears of pity. . . . Till this book be ended, Thy servant and Thy lover (*benvolent*) may not go to the land of the Saracens to give praise to Thy glorious name. . . . Wherefore I pray Thee to aid Thy servant, . . . that he may speedily go and suffer martyrdom for Thy love, if it be Thy will that he be found worthy thereof.[1]

Now at last, in the early days of 1274, not only is the *Book of Contemplation* completed, but the *Book of the Gentile* has been revised and published also. Yet there is no question any longer, it appears, of a missionary journey to be undertaken across the seas. What can be the reason for this change of plan? Some hidden instinct, perhaps, tells Ramon that he needs a season of refreshing before the life of a wandering teacher which he so much desires can begin; or perhaps he is fully conscious that the development of his intellect has been starving the growth of the spirit. There are signs in the *Book of Contemplation* that the desire for a life of prayer has haunted him as much as the yearning for the work of a preacher. "Love makes me to desire to live for long as a hermit," he exclaims, "in contemplation of Thy goodness and of the vileness of this world by means of this book which now I make."[2] And again, at a later stage in his task: "When will come that day wherein I may renounce [the possession of all worldly goods] and in the mountains compose and make prayers . . . in great number and of much perfection?"[3] Now that his studies were over, the two ideals which he had envisaged for so long strove in him for the mastery and the ideal of the solitary prevailed. He was free to seek refreshment where he would, and, by going far from the world of temporal cares, to throw off those family ties, of which, however formally he might renounce them, he could never in practice be entirely rid for so long as he remained

[1] *L.C.*, chap. 131 (*Obres*, iv, pp. 187–8). For similar sentiments, *cf.* chap. 136 (*Obres*, iv, pp. 216–7).

[2] *L.C.*, chap. 136 (*Obres*, iv, p. 217). *Cf.* his comparison in chap. 151 (iv, p. 310) of the life of a hermit with the recollected life which he himself was at that time leading, though in the world.

[3] *L.C.*, chap. 315 (*Obres*, viii, p. 11).

at home. This road he chose. Obedient to the summons of the contemplative life, he left his house and his books behind him and went up into a mountain to pray.

There is one spot in Mallorca above all others which suggests itself as a retreat for the would-be hermit. Seen from the entrance to Palma Bay, or from one of the sunlit terraces of its western shore, the view of the twin heights of Mount Randa is unforgettable. A long, level stretch of low hills runs down to the southern extremity of the island. And of that level stretch one thing alone breaks the monotony: a huge saddle-like mountain, dominating both the ridge of which it forms a part and the surrounding plain—gray, stern and silent, forbidding perhaps to some, yet appealing in the midst of beauty so much more tender; inviting approach, but repelling the merely curious.[1]

Standing on the western shore of the Bay, one may look out, as Ramon must often have done, upon the mountain which was to be for him "the mountain of the Beloved."[2] And one may ask oneself what it is that from afar gives Randa its aspect of desolation. It must surely be the monotonous level of the horizon on either side as far as the eye can reach. There is nothing suggestive of loneliness, for example, in the view from the Riera of the north-western Sierra behind the city of Palma. The peaks of the Sierra are obviously higher, but there are many of them. Randa stands apart, alone.

So felt "the said reverend master" of the contemporary biography, as he "went up into a mountain called Randa, the which mountain was no great way from his

[1] Costa i Llobera, in his poem "La Mata Escrita de Randa," has seized the spirit of the place perfectly: the long even lines of his verse call up the view of it from afar:

> Sobre 'l pla de Mallorca 'l Puig de Randa
> eleva 'l gran planell de sa miranda,
> com un enorme, primitiu altar.
> Lluny dels gegants ombrívols de la serra,
> ell que les boyres y la neu desterra,
> vers l'Africa a lo lluny sembla mirar.

[2] *L.A.A.*, No. 103 (*Bl.*, p. 427).

house,[1] to the end that he might the better pray to Our Lord and serve Him."[2] It is not hard to picture him, with worldly encumbrances laid aside, setting out on foot, not of course along the straight, tedious high road of to-day, planted on either hand with almond-groves, but by some more primitive track through country less developed but no less beautiful. These were "the verdant paths of feeling, imagination, understanding and will" which the Lover took as he "went in search of his Beloved":[3] the mountain of the Beloved was in view all the way, and he could fix his gaze upon the object of his journey. Through what was soon to be the town of Lluchmayor he would pass, near the battlefield on which a future Mallorcan king was to be slain, or alternatively he might have taken the road leading through Algaida, past possessions which according to tradition were his own.[4]

Far beyond the last village of the plain[5] would begin the ascent of the mountain. A steep path, stony and hard even to-day, leads upwards to the depression between the two summits. Save for the magnificent views of the Mediterranean which meet the climber, the scenery is not inviting. Boulders are strewn about the path. Shrubs and weeds grow plentifully, but little else. Whether seen from near or from afar, in short, Randa comes as close to austerity and desolation as any spot that can be found upon this fertile island. Was it of the rough climb upwards that Ramon thought when he wrote:

> Pensively the Lover trod the paths of his Beloved. Now he stumbled and fell among the thorns; but they were to him as flowers, and as a bed of love.[6]

At last the heights were reached, and Ramon could

[1] Custurer (pp. 491, 498) suggests that by the "house" from which Randa was "not far" is meant a house on the estate in those parts which is supposed to have belonged to Lull's family. There seems no need, however, to suppose this.

[2] *V.C.*, iii. Cf. *V.B.R.L.*, ii (*Life*, pp. 12, 55).

[3] *L.A.A.* No. 314 (*Bl.*, p. 460).

[4] See p. 6, n. 1, above.

[5] For the village of Randa, which now stands at its foot, did not then exist: there might have been a *masia* or farm-house there, but not more.

[6] *L.A.A.*, No. 36 (*Bl.*, p. 416).

look out upon the vast plain all around him, upon the ocean which lay to north, to east and to south, and upon the picturesque western Sierra. He was alone, and no longer lonely, as he had been in the haunts of men.[1] He was free to contemplate his Beloved : understanding might for a time cease to wander and join with will and memory in its efforts to compass the bliss of Union. No doubt the new recluse sought guidance as to his future, the guidance which comes without noise of words, the inspiration which is breathed more readily in the illimitable spaces of solitude than in the bustle of life in the world. In the seclusion of a cave on Mount Randa he found inspiration and guidance both.

Precisely what happened to him there it is impossible with any certainty to say. The earliest testimony on record states simply that on the eighth day of his retirement, or perhaps earlier,[2] " as he was engaged in contemplation, with his eyes turned towards the heavens, there came to him in an instant a certain Divine illumination which gave him the form and order wherein to write the books [3] that he had in mind against the errors of the infidels, whereat (he) was greatly rejoiced and with many tears gave hearty thanks to Our Lord." [4]

That statement is not an extravagant one, and we may without difficulty believe in its literal truth, the more so as not only does Lull himself bear witness to it,[5] but his worst enemy, the inquisitor Eymeric,[6] declares (*c.* 1376)

[1] *L.A.A.*, No. 47 (*Bl.*, p. 418).

[2] For the phrase used (*V.C.*, iii) " com hagués estat aquí quasi per viij dies " is ambiguous. Cf. *V.B.R.L.*, ii : " cum jam stetisset non plene per octo dies " (*Life*, pp. 12, 55).

[3] *V.B.R.L.* has, as earlier, the singular (" librum, de quo supra dicitur contra errores infidelium " : *Life*, p. 55).

[4] *V.C.*, iii (*Life*, p. 12). *V.B.R.L.* has only the variant recorded in the preceding note. Bouvelles follows closely : " Perseverans ergo plurimus diebus in oratione, non modo in editionem libri unius lumen obtinuit, sed repente tota mente illustratus a Domino. . . ."

[5] Pasqual, i, pp. 130–2. See also *Desconort*, viii,

> Encara us dic que port una *Art general*
> que novament és dada per do espirital . . . (*cf.* xxxv) :

and *Disputatio Eremitae et Raymundi* : " Cogito de quadam Arte Generali, quam Deus mihi ostendit in quodam monte." *Cf.* also Custurer, pp. 498–9.

[6] See pp. 7, 377, n. 2.

that Lullists everywhere believe in the direct inspiration of their hero.[1] Other testimony of about the same date confirms the unanimity of this primitive tradition,[2] which probably embodies the simple if wonderful truth.

The later biographers, in the desire to exalt their subject, exaggerate and embroider this early testimony till it is hardly recognizable. Cornejo writes of an ecstasy, "lasting for several hours," at the end of which time "God had granted him the gift of the infused science, together with that of tongues," and of an appearance of Christ which filled Ramon's cave with a fragrance still perceptible yearly on the festival of St. Paul ![3] According to Seguí,[4] Ramon was plunged into the depths of depression, and would neither eat, nor drink, nor look upon the light of day. Then God visited him, bestowed upon him the grace of contemplation, and unfolded to him His plans for the conversion of the heathen. Corporeal visions of Christ followed. Once He appeared as a seraph and commanded Ramon to write the book afterwards known as the *Art General*. On another occasion, the vision of Him threw his servant into a three days' trance. Again,[5] an angel appeared at a moment when he was in a state of tears and despondency, took from him the manuscript of the completed *Art*,[6] kissed it, encouraged its author, assured him of its potency, and prophesied to him its success. These embroideries can all quite safely be rejected.

Preferable to them, as a rule, artistically, though hardly, if at all, more credible, are the legends, often significant as well as beautiful, which Mallorcan tradition commonly associates with the Beat Ramon's seclusion in Randa. The modern inscription at the entrance to the cave enshrines one of them :

[1] It is true that he adds the words : "putatur fuisse Diabolus, non Christus." See pp. 377–8, below.

[2] Pasqual, i, pp. 129–30.

[3] He describes it as being "like the quintessence of various aromas, and of divers flowers, with every kind of perfume."

[4] Seguí, chap. ii, fols. 3v, 4r.

[5] Seguí, chap. iii, fol. 8v.

[6] It was not, of course, written till later. (See p. 109, below.) But as the angel is in shepherd's dress, the legend is evidently a gloss on that related of the second sojourn on Mount Randa (p. 113, below).

This is the place to which the blessed Ramon Lull retired that he might pray to God. As he was in lofty contemplation, there appeared to him Jesus crucified, Who disappeared as Ramon embraced Him, leaving the Cross in his arms.

A variant of this traditional appearance to Ramon of Christ crucified is frequently depicted in old woodcuts : this version represents him as exclaiming 'O, Bonitas !' and stretching out his hands towards the Figure. A third story is that Ramon perceived a dense cloud set between God and his heart. Though he tried again and again, he was powerless to penetrate it. Then at last he saw the cloud pierced and dispersed by the sun. Perhaps the source of this tradition is to be found in one of Lull's own allegorical writings, of which it may well be an adaptation.

Love shone through the cloud which had come between the Lover and the Beloved, and made it to be as bright and resplendent as is the moon by night, as the day-star at dawn, as the sun at mid-day, and as the understanding in the will ; and through that bright cloud the Lover and the Beloved held converse.[1]

The pilgrim to Randa may carry away with him—too many, alas ! have done so—a tangible remembrance of yet another legend of Ramon's life there. As he walks along the sunny terrace, spangled with many-hued summer flowers, which leads to the cave from the present monastery, his attention may be struck by a small lentiscus (*mata*) which grows freely all around, and, though apparently similar to the usual lentiscus of Mallorca, is in reality distinct.[2] The curious markings of the leaves of this plant, known locally as the *mata escrita*, are attributed by tradition to a miracle. One night, the story goes, Ramon kept vigil by a lentiscus bush and passed the hours of sleep in contemplation. In the morning he found that the leaves of the bush were engraven with characters of the Hebrew, Arabic, Chaldaean and many other alphabets, the occurrence

[1] *L.A.A.*, No. 123 (*Bl.*, p. 430).
[2] Cf. *Estudis Franciscans*, vol. xxi, p. 460.

denoting the various languages in which his *Art* was to be taught to the heathen.[1] To-day the ingenuity of popular devotion has carried on the legend one stage farther. The credulous stranger will be shown leaves of the *mata* of which the markings are said to perpetuate Ramon's own name, and be invited to exclaim at the miraculous nature of what, with the greatest good-will, he may find difficulty in believing.

We well remember our own earliest visit to Randa. It had been a perfect spring day, and, from the summit of the hill the unrivalled Pisgah-views of unexplored country beneath and blue Mediterranean beyond were an eloquent commentary on the pilgrim's song which hails Randa as " mount of vision." Directly below, in a cleft, lay the village, with its tall church tower, while other villages—mere clusters of brown and white houses—could be seen dotted over the plain. No less lovely than that expanse of sunlit fertility was the prospect of the eastern downs and the sparkling sea : Mallorca had put on glorious apparel. But when the hour came to descend, black storm-clouds gathered in force, the purple of the surrounding mountains deepened to a sombre hue, and the misty plain at the foot of the hill was transformed into a dark and threatening ocean.

Did the world beneath him look like that to Ramon Lull, we may wonder, when he came down from the mount of transfiguration, from the reward of a ten-years' labour, to face the gigantic, self-imposed task which lay before him ? That he felt it to be gigantic—overwhelming—we cannot doubt. A life's work worth the performing, envisaged completely, looked at squarely by a level-headed man, can rarely seem otherwise. But, whatever was the nature of his illumination by God, he had learned more in his cave than merely the manner in which he was to write a book. He had learned to read a book—to interpret the book of nature, " the trembling of the leaves (which) signifies obedience, and the scent

[1] *Cf.* Pasqual : *Vindiciae*, i, pp. 63–4 (*cf.* p. 92). Avinyó : *Història del lulisme*, pp. 476–8. Some writers refer this story to Ramon's second visit to Randa, but most follow Pasqual, who places it here.

of the flowers, suffering and adversity."[1] He had learned that a day upon Mount Randa, if his Beloved called him there, could be of greater profit than years spent among his books at home: that "the infused science comes from the will, devotion and prayer," while "acquired science comes from study and understanding."[2] He had learned, indeed, more than he yet knew, for his potentialities for good had been enlarged and increased —nay, his very self had undergone a transformation. Years afterwards, he summed up his experiences on the mount of vision in words which describe it more truly than the embroideries of hagiographers:

Memory and Will set forth together, and climbed into the mountain of the Beloved, that Understanding might be exalted and love for the Beloved increased.[3]

From Randa, without losing any time, Lull went, not to his house in Palma (for he was in no frame of mind for the resumption of family relationships) but to the monastery of La Real,[4] that he might quickly get to work upon some of the books which he had now learned how to write.[5] The first of these,[6] and, in his own mind, the chief, was the famous *Ars Magna* or *Art Major*, to which he afterwards referred by the name of *Art General*.[7]

[1] *L.A.A.*, No. 58 (*Bl.*, p. 420). [2] *L.A.A.*, No. 241 (*Bl.*, p. 448).

[3] *L.A.A.*, No. 103 (*Bl.*, p. 427). *Cf.* the fourth verse of the *goigs* in praise of the Beat Ramon composed for the sixth centenary of his martyrdom in 1915:

O Randa, muntanya amada,
muntanya de visió,
on la pensa és exalçada,
on és doblada l'amô:
l'enyorança encara et dura
del asceta il·luminat.

[4] Mn. Galmés (*Vida*, p. 37) says that the *Ars Magna* was written by Lull "a La Real i a ca seva, anant i venint." The evidence which he gives me for this statement is *L.C.*, chaps. 138, 151, 315, 316 (*Obres*, iv, pp. 227, 310; viii, 11, 14) but I do not find it convincing. *Cf.* Pasqual, *Vindiciae*, i, p. 85.

[5] E encontinent, devallant de la dita muntanya, anà s en prestament al monastir de la Reyal per ço que pus aptament posqués ordonar los dits libres. (*V.C.*, iii: *Life*, pp. 12–13, 55.) *V.B.R.L.* still reads "librum." On La Real, see Custurer, p. 499, n. 64.

[6] Some writers affirm the priority of *L.C.* But see note 5, p. 45, above.

[7] *V.C.*, iii, *V.B.R.L.*, ii. It is also referred to in various places as the *Ars compendiosa inveniendi veritatem* ("Art d'atrobar veritat" or "Art of finding truth"). For the Latin text, see Salz., vol. i.

A mere glance at this work, which has come down to us in Latin, will show how far removed are its methods from those of modern science. It can only be described adequately with the aid of its own illustrative diagrams, but fortunately there is no necessity nowadays to master it, since modern interest in Ramon has little or nothing to do with his encyclopaedism or his scientific method.

The treatise is divided into three distinctions, of which the first expounds seven figures, designated by the letters A, S, T, V, X, Y, Z, and applies each of them to six others, R, E, I, N, C, G. The figure A will give the reader an idea of the complicated nature of the work: it stands for God, Who is represented by a point at the centre of a circle the circumference of which is divided into sixteen compartments, numbered B to R, each standing for one attribute of the Deity—goodness, greatness, eternity, wisdom, power, etc. By considering these sixteen attributes two at a time Lull forms one hundred and twenty permutations of the first figure: BC (goodness is great), BD (goodness is eternal); and so on. The second figure, S, is the soul, the circumference of a circle at the centre of which are superposed four squares of different colours, and which is divided also into sixteen compartments. By means of this diagram are studied the psychic faculties and their different acts with relation to an object. Similar are the divisions of the remaining figures: T, objects of knowledge; V, virtues and vices; X, predestination; Y, truth; Z, falsehood; R, ignorance; E, merit; and so on.

The second and third distinctions are concerned with the application of these figures to typical questions of theology, metaphysic, morals and even natural science, which they are supposed to solve. Any handful of them, gathered at random, will show how Lull's method verged on rationalism, and, even more clearly, how he had absorbed the scholastic ideals of his day. Thus, in the second distinction, he asks why God gives the Body of Christ to the faithful under the form of bread, and not under that of a stone, answering his own question by the statement that the nature of Christ's humanity accords better with bread than with stone. In the third distinction, he solves by his "Art" questions on the immanence of God, the nature of the soul and the problem of good and evil, together with others which surprise us by their variety. Ethics and natural science, as well as theology and philosophy, are represented among them, and we are confirmed in the supposition that all these subjects formed part of the self-planned nine-years' curriculum. "Which is better," runs one question—"the celibacy of the religious life, or marriage?" "Whence come snow and ice?" "What is thunder?" "How are the wind and the clouds engendered?" "Of which is there more in the universe—good or evil?" "Do devils commit sin?"

We smile; but we are forced into admiration as we consider the extent of the book, its orderliness, its use of the imagination and the reasoning power it displays. It is a true "art," a genuine "method," not a mere mechanical device, as one might suppose from Hegel's description of it as a "thinking machine" or Renan's ironic reference to its "magic circles." That the art was not effective is a fault as much of its author's time as of its author, for because in some respects Ramon was in advance of his age it is hardly reasonable to demand that he should be so in everything. Perhaps the early history, which will presently be outlined, of the Lullian cult and the Lullian University of Mallorca, comprises as complete a defence of the *Ars Magna* as even Ramon himself could have desired.

His *magnum opus* completed—for it must not be forgotten that such it always was to its author—Ramon turned his attention to some other projected works which were to be, as it were, offshoots of it,[1] and would minister "to the capacity of unlettered men," who could not master the *Art*. Precisely what these books were is

[1] *V.C.*, iii (*Life*, p. 13), quoted in the text, makes this clear. *V.B.R.L.*, ii (*Life*, p. 55) is rather more detailed: "sub qua Arte postea plures, ut infra sequitur, fecit libros, in eisdem multa generalia principia et magis specialia, secundum capacitatem simplicium, prout experientia eum jam docuerat, explicando."

uncertain, but probably one of them was the *Lectura*, or popular application of the same figures, called after the *Ars Magna*, by one or other of its names, and known also as *Ars Universalis*.[1] Some writers assign to this period the *Book of Demonstrations*,[2] which is mentioned again in the next chapter, and some also place there a group of smaller treatises, known to be of early date, but assignable to no year in particular. These are the *Elementary Principles* of theology, philosophy, law and medicine,[3] the *Book of the Angels* [4] and the *Book of Chaos*.[5] The last is a quite exceptionally fantastic production. It first discusses the essence of chaos, its four intrinsic qualities of "igneity, aereity, aqueity and terreity." Next come its three degrees: the first an imperfectly defined elemental state, which influences the second, that of initial creation, and the third, or subsequent creation. The necessity for these three degrees is discussed, after which are examined certain supposed attributes of chaos, and syllogistic reasonings from the conclusions reached in the foregoing discussion carry fantasy into the realm of complete absurdity. The book is of some interest, however, historically, as further evidence of Ramon's early pre-occupation with natural science, and one modern critic has based upon it his view that Lull was, in the broadest sense of the word, an alchemist.[6]

At the end of some months of labour, Lull returned for a while to the solitude and peace of Randa, primarily

[1] *H.L.F.*, No. 2 (pp. 79–80. *Cf.* No. 132: pp. 293–4).

[2] *Libre de demonstracions*, known in its Latin form (Salz., vol. ii) as *Liber mirandarum demonstrationum*, and apparently impossible to date with certainty. It is strongly personal and fervent in character, but adds nothing to our knowledge of Lull (*H.L.F.*, No. 10, pp. 107–112; Rubió y Lluch, *Sumari*, etc., p. 293; Longpré, col. 1096).

[3] *Liber principiorum theologiae, . . . philosophiae, . . . juris, . . . medicinae* (these are all in Salz., vol, i. Cf. *H.L.F.*, Nos. 3–6, pp. 81–90). Of the last, there is a MS. at Corpus Christi College, Oxford.

[4] *Liber de Angelis* (*H.L.F.*, No. 240, p. 336). Assigned by Pasqual (ii, p. 333), for no discoverable reason, to the year 1275. It figures in the catalogue of 1311 as one of the earliest of Lull's works. Apparently he himself believed in its value, as he translated it from its original Catalan into Latin as late as 1307.

[5] *Liber Chaos* (Salz., vol. iii: *H.L.F.*, No. 15, pp. 124–7).

[6] Torras i Bages, pp. 222–4 (*cf.* p. 406, n. 2, below).

to found a hermitage "wherein he remained for the space of four months, beseeching Our Lord by day and by night that that *Art* which he had compiled might lead to His honour and to the profit of the holy Catholic faith, and that it would please Him to cause it to prosper." [1] The successor of that hermitage to-day is the Franciscan house of Cura, which has recently been re-founded after vicissitudes of which some part will be described in a later chapter.[2] Of the hermitage in which Ramon lived we know nothing, nor of his manner of life there, unless indeed it be the life which he himself depicted in his *Blanquerna*, and which is generally thought to resemble more closely his later life at Miramar.[3] The reasons for this second retirement, however, are easy enough to divine. He had found illumination once: he now sought it again. His book—his great *Art*—had been written: he desired now to consider in solitude how best it could be interpreted to the world. His active life was about to begin: he must spend a brief time on the mount of transfiguration before descending once more, and this time once for all, to the turbulent crowds in the plain.

One legend only has clung to this second period of Ramon's life on Mount Randa, but it is of great antiquity, differs little in the various authorities who relate it, and is singularly suggestive and understandable. We reproduce it, as it stands, in the simple language of the contemporary biography:

It came to pass one day that he met a shepherd, a youth exceeding pleasant and comely of feature, who, in a single hour, related to him as many and as singular things concerning the Divine Essence, and the Heavens, and especially concerning the angelic nature, as a great man of science could have expounded in two days. And when the said shepherd saw the books which the said reverend master had compiled (*ordonats*), he kneeled upon the ground and kissed them, and said, with tears, that there would follow therefrom much good in the Church of God. Then he blessed the said reverend master, making over him the sign of the

[1] *V.C.*, iii, *V.B.R.L.*, ii (*Life*, pp. 13, 56).
[2] See pp. 399–400, below. [3] See pp. 134–5, below.

Cross,[1] as though he were a great prophet. And he left him ; and the said reverend master remained in a state of amazement (*tot esbalait*), for it seemed to him that he had never before seen this shepherd, nor even so much as heard of him.[2]

For centuries after Ramon's death, there was to be a Lullian School on Mount Randa, with pretentious instruction in the *Ars Magna* and "Lullian science." Later yet, under august auspices, a grammar school was to be founded there, and, though this has long since disappeared, the Franciscans have a little school there still. Many, then, have taught on Mount Randa, but the first teacher was an unknown Shepherd.

[1] *V.B.R.L.*, ii: signans caput et totum corpus ejus signaculo sanctae Crucis. . . . (*Life*, p. 56).

[2] *V.C.* iii (*Life*, pp. 13–14). Costa i Llobera has retold the story in verse in his poem "La Mata Escrita de Randa" (p. 103, n. 1 above).

CHAPTER VI

1275–1277

Ramon Lull visits Prince James of Mallorca at Montpellier. Works of this period: *Book of the Order of Chivalry* and *Doctrine for Boys*. Foundation of a missionary college at Miramar. History of the college. Works probably written at Miramar. *Book of the Holy Spirit*, *Complaint of Our Lady Saint Mary*, *Hours of Our Lady Saint Mary*.

THE public life of Ramon Lull may be said to have begun, almost immediately after his return from the hermitage of Randa, with the arrival of a command from Prince James to visit him at Montpellier,[1] where, before the death of his father, he habitually resided. The most likely time at which to place this command is the latter half of the year 1274.[2] On June 21 of that year, the Conqueror, a few days after arriving at Montpellier from the Council of Lyons, had appointed his younger heir as his lieutenant in the city and barony of that name, "desiring him to have the same power as we ourselves," —a popular appointment, it would appear, for Prince James was greatly loved.[3] Some sixteen months later (October 4, 1275), the Prince was married, at Perpignan, to Esclarmonde, sister of Roger-Bernard, Count of Foix, nearly ten years having passed since the rupture of the

[1] *V.C.*, iii, *V.B.R.L.*, ii (*Life*, pp. 14, 56–7).

[2] Assuming, as seems most probable, that the suicide of the slave took place not later than the beginning of 1274, this would give Ramon at least six months at La Real, as well as the four months and eight days or more on Mount Randa, and still it would be possible for him to have crossed to the mainland before the end of the same year. Critics who think six months insufficient for the writing of so many works should consider that Ramon was composing his *Art* under strong inspiration and also that he was writing with great rapidity for a large part of his very long life.

[3] Miret i Sans, *Itinerari*, p. 503; Aigrefeuille, vol. i, p. 143: *cf.* Devic et Vaissette, vol. ix, p. 42.

negotiations with Savoy.[1] Everything points to Ramon's visit as taking place between these two events, probably nearer the first than the second.

It was some years—perhaps six or seven—since James and Ramon had met in Mallorca, and in the interval James had " heard it said " that Ramon had " written certain books " [2] which he was not unnaturally curious to see. No doubt the Prince's interest in Ramon's history, and the pleasure with which he had greeted him on his last visit to Mallorca, had not been entirely untainted by disapproval. The best of men are apt to be suspicious of sudden conversions, and James, if no worse than royal personages of his day, was certainly no better. Had Ramon told him anything in Mallorca about his projected treatise on Contemplation, which in 1268 he would hardly yet have begun to write ? If we may judge from his character, with its combination of diffidence and common sense, he probably had not. In any case, all that he could have said would be of a vague and general nature, and the Prince might be forgiven if he doubted whether the projects would come to fruition. But now all was different. Reports had reached Montpellier—having lost nothing, we may be sure, upon the journey—of Lull's supernatural experiences on Mount Randa, of the publication of an enormous and most learned work written in Catalan and in Arabic, and of the composition of an " Art " of some kind by which all the heathen could be converted and which was said to be infallible. Beneath such rumours, even were they exaggerated, there must of necessity be an important basis of truth. Here was something definite for James to seize upon : he would see those books, and he would find out unfailingly if their writer were really inspired or no.

So Ramon crossed the Mediterranean, and made his way by slow stages to Montpellier, a city with which he must have been familiar from boyhood, and in which,

[1] Devic et Vaissette, vol. ix, p. 48 ; Dameto, bk. iii, p. 1123.

[2] *V.C.*, iii, *V.B.R.L.* goes farther : " quosdam libros bonos " (*Life*, pp. 14, 56–7).

as it proved, he was to write more than one of his best-known compositions. For a student of men and manners, as he had already shown himself to be, few cities in Western Europe could have held so much attraction. Ambitious and wealthy, it was the centre of a vast and ever-growing trade and the scene of a perpetual fair, at which all kinds of merchandise were bought and sold. Through its three ports of Aiguesmortes, Maguelonne and Lattes, it sent goods to Europe, Asia and Africa,—fruits and vegetables, cheese, wine and oil, salted meat, leather cloths and the scarlet dyes for which it was everywhere famous. It enjoyed commercial privileges in Venice, Sicily, Rhodes, Antioch and Jerusalem. It shared in all the benefits of the Conqueror's commercial treaties with Africa. In many respects it rivalled the great port of Marseilles. And, as one consequence of so much activity, Christians of every creed, from two continents, mingled in its streets and squares with Jews, Mohammedans and adherents of stranger cults than these. "Merchants of Italy, Egypt, Palestine, Greece, Gaul, Spain and England," wrote the Rabbi Benjamin of Tudela in his *Itinerary*, "men of all languages can be seen there together with the Genoese and Pisans." [1]

Even apart from this particular attractiveness, Montpellier was a favoured city to live in. Since 1204, it had been an Aragonese possession, and was to remain in the Conqueror's family till James III of Mallorca ceded it, in 1349, to France. Its isolation won it a certain degree of independence ; besides, it was in any case a favourite with James I and his descendants, and, save at infrequent intervals, basked pleasantly in the sunshine of their grace. Its citizens figure freely in the partition-roll of Mallorca, and again and again we read of the Conqueror or his son conferring upon it some favour, or of being received in it with acclamation. So if Ramon learned early to love Montpellier no less than the "City of Mallorca," his birthplace, he may well have learned it at court.

[1] *Cit.* Germain : *Histoire du commerce de Montpellier.* Montpellier, 1861, vol. i, pp. 4–5.

Again, he had affinities with the city because of its ecclesiastical and academic importance. Although its university was not to be founded for some years, it had had schools of law and medicine for more than a century, and, at the time of which we are writing, degrees of medicine and civil law were established in them, and instruction was given in many other subjects. The Pope had considered Montpellier of sufficient importance to be the seat of the General Council of 1274, although, in the end, for want of sufficient accommodation, this was held in Lyons. Activity among the religious orders in Montpellier was great at this period ; Dominicans and Franciscans especially were strong ; many new churches were built there ; and, if true religious progress did not keep pace with external ecclesiastical prosperity,[1] a man of Ramon's profession and character was not likely to stay any the less willingly in a city where, for that very reason, he might serve God the better.[2]

Arrived at Montpellier, Ramon laid his works before his royal patron, who at once " caused the said books to be examined by a master in theology, who was a friar minor,[3] and especially the meditations which he had compiled for every day of the year, each chapter being divided into thirty paragraphs." [4] The Franciscan selected as censor, who is said to have been Fra Bertran Berengari, a well-known theologian,[5] not only approved of the books but presented a report full of " great admiration and respect." [6] It is said that the *Ars Magna* impressed him less than the *Book of Contemplation*,[7]—a

[1] Germain, *op. cit.*, vol. ii, pp. 45–63.

[2] Devic et Vaissette, *passim* ; Germain, *op. cit.*, vol. i, *passim*, vol. ii, pp. 1–63.

[3] Although, in fact, James' inclinations, like his father's, were in general rather towards the Dominicans than the Franciscans. *Cf.* Dameto, bk. iii, pp. 546–7.

[4] *V.C.*, iii (*Life*, p. 14).

[5] " Frater Bertrandus Berengarii olim sacrae Theologiae Professor apud Montem pessulanum ": Wadding, 1287, § 14 (vol. v, p. 164). *Cf.* Pasqual, *Vindiciae*, i, p. 113.

[6] *Ibid.* *V.B.R.L.* has " quas meditationes philosophia et devotione Catholica plenas non sine admiratione reperit frater ille" (*Life*, p. 57).

[7] This seems to be only an inference from the special mention accorded to *L.C.* in the contemporary biography.

fact from which one would like to infer that he appreciated the quality and diversity of Ramon's literary gifts. A more likely explanation, however, is that it was the extraordinary length, scope, and orderliness of the latter book which surprised him. For one reason or another, his verdict has been confirmed by posterity.

The favour shown to Lull and his books by the future king encouraged him to write others. One of these may perhaps have been a further application of the *Ars Magna*,[1] another the *Book of Definitions and Questions*,[2] and a third the *Book of Demonstrations*, the date of which is unknown.[3] The last-named, closely related with the *Ars Magna*,[4] is a treatise of some interest on the conversion of the heathen. The first of its four books discusses the possibility of a comprehension of the articles of the faith being reached; the remaining books put forward proofs in turn for the existence of God, for the Trinity and for the Incarnation. As conditions for the proper use of this treatise, Lull postulates the reader's honest intention to praise and serve God, an open mind as to the truth or falsehood of the author's claims, a desire to attribute to God the greatest possible nobility, and a knowledge of what exactly is meant by the term "understanding." It should be added that the chief reason for dating the book in this period is that, according to the contemporary biography, the *Ars demonstrativa*, which we know to have been written in Montpellier some seven years later, was

[1] So it is usually said, but see n. 4, below.

[2] Which was certainly written before 1275, as it is mentioned in *D.P.*, chap. 73. For a long time it was thought to be yet another name for the *Libre del Gentil* (*cf.* p. 82, above), but the Catalan MS. has now been found in the Ambrosian Library, Milan. See also *H.L.F.*, No. 138, p. 296.

[3] Pasqual (ii, p. 333) also assigns to the year 1275 the Catalan *Book of Prayers and Contemplations of the Mind* ("Libre de oracions e contemplacions de l enteniment en Deu"), but this seems to be only a guess. *H.L.F.* (No.147, p. 300) adds (incorrectly) that no MSS. are extant of this work, and that no mention of it is discoverable in the early catalogues of Lull's writings,—which would make its genuineness almost as hypothetical as its date. There are, however, two extant MSS. and a Valencian version (by Joan Bonlabi, 1521). *Cf.* Longpré, col. 1103; Rogent i Duràn, *Bibliografía, etc.*, pp. 68–71.

[4] Cf. *V.B.R.L.*, ii (*Life*, p. 57): "Fecit Raymundus *sub praedicta Arte sibi data in Monte* . . . librum unum . . . etc." The title is *Liber Demonstrationum, qui est una Brancha Artis Compendiosae Inveniendi Veritatem.*

written now,[1] and that the author of that biography, usually fairly correct, should have confused two similarly entitled works seems very possible.[2]

Two other works can with tolerable certainty be dated in the years 1274–5, the probability being in favour of the latter year of the two.[3] The first is the *Book of the Order of Chivalry*; the second, the *Doctrine for Boys* ('Doctrina Pueril').

The date of the first is partly fixed by its mention in the second as having been already written. Attempts have been made to explain away this reference, but its terms seem, for Lull, quite unusually definite.[4] The second must have been written before 1276, since an event of that year which will shortly be described had clearly at that time not happened [5]—again an unmistakably definite indication. The various critics, therefore, who have dated the *Book of the Order of Chivalry* between 1276 and 1286 [6] are definitely proved to be wrong. How long before the earlier date it was written cannot be even guessed from external evidence, and internal evidence is conflicting. For while, on the one

[1] *V.C.*, iii (*Life*, p. 15). The *Ars demonstrativa* is mentioned but not described: a brief description is added of a *lectura* which was written upon it. (See p. 155, below.) *V.B.R.L.* (*Life*, p. 57) reads similarly.

[2] Another reason worth noticing is Lull's description of himself in *Liber Demonstrationum* as "quidam homo culpabilis, pauper, miser, cum modico intellectu, vilipendus a gentibus, indignus, quod suum nomen sit scriptum in hoc libro nec in altro." There is hardly an example to be found of such complete self-abasement anywhere in Lull's works after 1277.

[3] Because it is difficult to see how into the year 1274 could have been crowded more than we are forced already to attribute to it.

[4] "The beginning of chivalry was to maintain justice, as we have already said (*segons que ja avem parlat*) in the *Book of the Order of Chivalry*" (*D.P.*, chap. 81: *Obres*, i, pp. 150–1).

[5] *I.e.* the founding of Miramar. Cf. *D.P.*, chap. 83 (*Obres*, i, p. 155): "There is none who will found monasteries which shall be established for the learning of divers languages, or who will send friars [into heathen lands] to preach the word of God."

[6] Rosselló (*Obras rimadas*, p. 48) puts it at 1276–1286. Aguiló (see the title-page of his edition) supposes it to have been written at Miramar. *H.L.F.* (No. 258, pp. 362–7) considers the question to be quite open. Obrador (*Obres*, i, pp. 464–5) is suspicious (rather needlessly, I think) of the reference given in note 4 above, but accepts it with caution, though also commenting approvingly upon Pasqual's pure guess that *L.O.C.* was not written till James II's *corts* of 1276. This would bring *L.O.C.* very near to *D.P.* if we accept the reference in the latter book.

hand, it might be supposed to be the work of Lull the recent convert, the style of its prologue suggests some degree of maturity. Unless the prologue was written after the rest of the book, it could hardly be one of the earliest works of the author.[1]

The *Book of the Order of Chivalry* is a much briefer work than the *Doctrine for Boys*, and is divided into seven chapters, "in significance of the seven planets which . . . govern and order the terrestrial bodies." [2] Never rising, either in style or in interest, to as high a plane as does the chapter on chivalry in the *Book of Contemplation*,[3] never approaching it in realism or in fervour, it represents on the whole a decline from the standard already set up by Ramon himself, though to be sure it had a considerable success, and influenced writers as notable as the Castilian Juan Manuel,[4] and Johanot Martorell, author of the Catalan classic *Tirant lo Blanc*.[5] Its fiction, like that of the *Book of the Gentile*, starts promisingly, but its interest is illusory, both interest and fiction ending with the prologue and the rest of the book depending upon them not at all. The style of the book is more monotonous than that of the *Book of the Gentile*, its only merit being

[1] Another suggestion of early date is in the prologue to *D.P.* (*Obres*, i, pp. 3–4) where Lull declares that his name is unworthy to be written in the book, as in *L.C.* and elsewhere (see pp. 49–50 and 120, n. 2, above). Though not extreme, this self-depreciation occurs almost exclusively in the early works.

On the other hand, *D.P.* refers to *Liber Demonstrationum* and *Ars Inveniendi Veritatem*, as well as to *L.C.* and the *Libre de Definicions e Questions* referred to above. It is impossible, therefore, to place it earlier than the end of 1274.

[2] Pasqual (i, p. 254) believed it to have been written for, and at the command of, James II of Mallorca, but this seems to me a mere guess.

[3] *L.C.*, chap. 112 (*Obres*, ii, pp. 57–63).

[4] The general influence of Ramon Lull on Juan Manuel, which is not extensive, is briefly discussed by Menéndez y Pelayo (in *Orígenes de la Novela*, i, pp. lxxxvi–lxxxviii) and the two men are strikingly contrasted.

[5] See L. Nicolau d'Olwer: "Sobre les fonts catalanes del *Tirant lo Blanc*" (*Revista de bibliografia catalana*, Any v, 1907, pp. 5–37), who gives some striking parallels between this work of Lull's (chiefly the early part of it) and *Tirant lo Blanc*, chaps. i–iv, xxvii–xxxii). Previously Marian Aguiló (in his edition of *L.O.C.*, Barcelona, 1879) had noted resemblances, without examining them closely, and Menéndez y Pelayo (*Orígenes de la Novela*, i, p. ccliv) describes the first part of *Tirant* as "calcada, puede decirse que servilmente," on Lull's treatise.

that of straightforwardness. There is hardly a figure of speech in the entire treatise.[1]

The prologue, however, it will be agreed, shows some advance in descriptive power, which augurs well for Lull's future writings. A noble and prudent knight, towards the end of his days, elects to retire to a hermitage, and chooses a solitary spot " in a great wood, abounding in streams and fruitful trees." One autumn day, a squire passes by a spring, " right fair and clear," where the hermit-knight is wont to come daily to pray. The knight, who is " very old, with a long beard and hair and garments in tatters with age," takes up a book when he sees the squire coming—a natural touch—and greets him on his approach.[2]

They " sit down on the fair grass, the one beside the other," and the knight, " knowing that the squire, to show him deference, will not speak first," asks him whence he comes and learns that he is bound for the court of a far-famed king, where he hopes to receive knighthood. On hearing this, the knight " sighs deeply and is plunged into cogitation," remembering his own past exploits. Naturally enough, the squire asks him the nature of his thoughts, and, when he learns that his companion has been for so long a knight, begs him to tell him all he can of the " rule and order of chivalry."

" Fair friend ! " said the knight, " the rule and order of chivalry may be found in this book, wherein I sometimes read, that it may cause me to remember the favour and grace which have been shown me by God in this world, because I honoured and upheld the order of chivalry as best I might." . . .

So he gave him the book, and, when he had read it . . . he remained for a moment in thought, and said : " Ah, Lord God ! Blessed be Thou, Who hast brought me into this place at this time, that I may have knowledge of chivalry, the which thing I have for long desired, without knowing either the nobility of the order or the honour wherein God has brought all that are therein." [3]

[1] Unless we count illustrations as trite as those on pp. 221, 224 (in *Obres*, vol. i) there is absolutely none.

[2] *L.O.C.*, Pròlech (*Obres*, i, p. 205).

[3] *Ibid.* (pp. 206–7).

The book is, of course, by implication, Ramon Lull's, and the hermit-knight presents it to the squire, since his own days are but few, that he may make it known at court. He also, rather pathetically, begs him to return that way when he has received knighthood, and to recount to him all that has happened. But the squire never does so, or thus at least it would appear, for no word is heard of him more. And the reader, who was beginning to find both characters attractive—considerably more so than the Gentile and the three wise men—is disappointed.

The most interesting part of the remainder of the *Order of Chivalry* is the first chapter,[1] which describes, in a somewhat idealistic fashion, the origins of chivalry. The second chapter, dealing with the office and duties of knighthood, repeats to some extent the chapter of the *Book of Contemplation* referred to. We then learn how a squire should be examined before being dubbed knight, and the preliminaries of the ceremony itself : the accounts given suggest the essential connection between knighthood and religion, a connection which in the *Book of Contemplation* is underlined in another way.

The symbolism in the knight's armour—as detailed as that in the vestments of a priest—is of interest to those who have small knowledge of such things, but the detailing of it would have seemed trite in Lull's day. The chapter following this, on the " customs that belong to a knight," is particularly banal, consisting largely of a discourse, and quite an uninspired one, on the seven deadly sins. The final chapter, on the honour that should be done to a knight, is brief.[2]

That the *Order of Chivalry* was popular in Lull's own day is sufficiently proved by the number of translations made from it into other languages. Besides the Latin

[1] Or " part " (*Obres*, i, pp. 208–11).

[2] It ends (*Obres*, i, p. 247) : " We have to treat of a book of the Order of Clergy. . . ." Of this book, which presumably was begun soon after *L.O.C.*, and probably planned on similar lines, nothing is known, nor does it figure in the catalogue of 1311. It is most probably the Catalan original, now lost, of the *Liber Clericorum*, which was written in Latin as late as 1308 (p. 335, below. Cf. *Obres*, vol. i, pp. 295–386) and Rogent i Duràn : *Bibliografia, etc.*, pp. 22–23.

text, there are at least ten extant manuscripts of French versions, as well as two printed editions published in 1504 and 1505. Many English readers will be acquainted with Caxton's *Book of the Ordre of Chyualrey*, made from a French version of this book and printed about 1484. The *Buke of the Order of Knychthede*, translated from Lull's treatise into Scots, by Sir Gilbert Hay (1456), and greatly enlarged in the process, is not so generally known.[1] Evidently Lull's *Order of Chivalry*—short, informatory and picturesque—was found a convenient and attractive original for those who wished to write upon chivalry, and for whom Ramon's name had a meaning, which it would not improbably have for their public also.

The *Doctrine for Boys* was written for Lull's own son Dominic, to whom he frequently refers in it and to whom it is addressed,[2] though not by name. The boy would not have been more than seventeen at the time—probably he was rather less—and the pre-occupation of his father with his choice of a profession [3] and eventual marriage [4] confirms our conclusions as to the book's approximate date. It was not written solely, though primarily, for young Dominic, or at least not for Dominic while young. "Pray for thy wife," says one chapter, "and for thy children, if thou hast any": [5] other chapters deal with education, in the widest sense, showing that the book is a manual for the parent and the teacher, as well as for the child.

Its early pages call for no detailed description. They draw upon the Bible rather more than Lull's earlier

[1] An account of these versions will be found in an edition of Caxton's translation edited by Alfred T. P. Byles for the Early English Text Society (London, 1926). The introduction to this edition also compares Lull's original point by point with these versions, and gives a brief biography of Lull, which contains a few errors.

[2] *D.P.*, Pròlech (*Obres*, i, pp. 3–4). Most of the paragraphs of the work are addressed to "my son," as those of *L.C.* are addressed to God.

[3] *E.g.* in the Prologue, and at the end of chap. 12, among other places (*Obres*, i, pp. 3–4, 28).

[4] E.g. *D.P.*, chap. 28 (*Obres*, i, p. 51). There is no suggestion in the book that the boy was contemplating marriage at the time it was written.

[5] *D.P.*, chap. 84 (*Obres*, i, p. 158).

works, and treat of the fourteen articles of the faith, the ten commandments, the seven sacraments, the seven gifts of the Holy Spirit[1] and the seven beatitudes.[2] Following them are others on the seven joys of Our Lady (there is nothing on the seven dolours[3]), the seven virtues and the seven deadly sins. The next five chapters, on the "three laws," are of great interest. That on Mahomet especially, which is surely the work of Lull the preacher, recalls the *Book of the Gentile*.[4] We next pass to secular instruction, two chapters being considered sufficient to explain the nature of the seven liberal arts of grammar, logic, rhetoric, geometry, arithmetic, music and astronomy. Theology and law claim a chapter each, and a curious chapter on natural science shows that Lull has not lost interest in this subject. A description of the science of medicine serves to convey some homely counsels on health, after which a chapter on the mechanical arts—certain handiworks and trades—leads up to a discussion of the more exalted offices to which the reader of the book may be called : the office of the prince, the higher one of the cleric, and the highest of all, that of the religious. Before leaving the subject of vocation, Lull interpolates a chapter on the theme of missionary work,[5] which sums up the ideas expressed in his *Book of Contemplation* ; already, in a passage which shows that, for all his erudition, he knew how to appeal to youth, he had held up the flaming ideal of martyrdom :

Why wouldst thou not die for Jesus Christ? Because death makes thee to fear. Because thou hadst rather be in this world than the next. Wherefore, wert thou Jesus Christ, thou hadst never died, nor hadst willed to die. . . .

What thing is this, that the lord will die for his vassal, and the vassal will not die for his lord? Or wherefore do the knights of this world die for their lords in battle? Have thou no fear of

[1] Inspired rather by Isaiah xi, 2 (the gift of piety being added) than by Galatians v, 22–3, as might have been expected.

[2] This section is treated rather more freely than is customary.

[3] This omission was soon to be remedied. See pp. 139–40, below.

[4] As early as chap. 5 (*Obres*, i, p. 13) he had warned his son against the sensuous Moslem conception of Paradise.

[5] *D.P.*, chap. 83.

death, for is it not the gate to the life wherein dwell the saints in glory?[1]

From this place to its close, the *Doctrine for Boys* becomes somewhat miscellaneous in its arrangement of subjects. Chapters on the body and the soul, life and death, are followed by others on temptation, vainglory, the feeding and education of children, the inculcation of good habits, the four elements, fate and fortune, the Antichrist, the so-called seven ages of the world—one hardly knows what to expect next. The book is certainly a compendium of varied knowledge.

The chapters of greatest interest are those in which Lull describes the bringing-up of children.[2] There could hardly be a more puritanical childhood than that advocated by this mediaeval Catholic. A boy should never be allowed to see and desire fine clothes, to hear "vanities, idle words, romances and songs," or to smell perfumes such as musk and amber. In girls and women, "to paint and colour the features" is an abomination. A child's first food is to be milk; only when he can "run and play" is he to have "bread if he so desire"; meat is to be given but sparingly, and fruit and sweet things hardly ever. "Wine that is over-strong," we are told, "destroys the natural heat and the understanding, and shortens life," while "strong sauces inflame the humours and destroy the brain." Precautions must be taken no less against the overclothing of children than against overfeeding them. Nature, in short, is the best mother, and "that which she loses in the children of the rich, she gains in the children of the poor." The sons of poor men are protected by their very poverty from many of the temptations which assail the rich.[3]

In the training of the mind, it is important to set noble ideals before children, and to speak little of vice

[1] *D.P.*, chap. 8 (*Obres*, i, p. 21).

[2] These are studied by Luis Pastre, *art. cit.*, who rightly says that *D.P.* is the most reliable of Lull's works for the educationist to study. It is hard to know how far Lull is speaking for himself in *Blanquerna* and *Felix*.

[3] *D.P.*, chaps. 61, 91, 93, *passim*. Cf. *Blanquerna*, chap. ii (*Bl.*, pp. 37–40).

and sin ; to accustom them at a very early age to love God and Divine worship ; to allow no children, or other persons, of ill education, to enter the home. It is noteworthy that the child is to be fully and rigidly instructed in doctrine, and other matters concerning his beliefs, before anything is said to him of morality,[1] and that, just as ascetic habits are inculcated in him from his earliest years, so ascetic ideals are held up to him as he grows older—in order that he may follow them if he feels called so to do, and in any case may admire and reverence them. Not only is the life of the evangelist described with something nearer to emotion than we have yet found in Lull, but the mystical life is glanced at, as embodying a nobler ideal—that of the " infused science "—than the " acquired science " of the theologian. " The contemplative life is nearer to God and farther from sin than is the active life," [2] but, like the missionary and would-be martyr, the contemplative must court self-denial.

Apart from its somewhat faulty progression, the *Doctrine for Boys* is well adapted to its didactic purpose. With but few exceptions, its chapters are short, its paragraphs are short, and its sentences are short. This brevity, most marked, very properly, in the earliest chapters, is a striking contrast to the occasional, and sometimes more than occasional, wordiness of all Lull's earlier writings. Further, there is a charm about the *Doctrine* which makes it pleasant reading. The terse, maxim-like form of all the instructions, the staccato sentences, the briskness with which the author passes from one theme to another combine, to convey this effect, with a further quality : the attractive use, not of elaborate figures of speech, but of the homely illustrations of the skilful preacher. There is no allegory, and no use of anecdote, but the images rise easily enough to the mind to make one regret their rapid withdrawal, and desire more of them :

[1] To this observation it might, however, be objected that the book is not well arranged, and can hardly have been intended for continuous study from beginning to end ; that it is not, for example, until chap. 84 that the boy is instructed in such an elementary matter as saying his prayers.

[2] *D.P.*, chap. 87. *Cf.* p. 102, above.

Whensoe'er, O son, thou seest a fair young woman, poorly clothed, and of honest mien, bearing a fair child, clothed poorly likewise, in her arms, think thou upon the Nativity of the Son of God, Who lay poorly clothed in the arms of our Lady Saint Mary.[1]

Beloved son, if thy mother has great delight in looking upon thee, who art mortal, and hast come from naught, and knowest not if thou be called to the glory of Heaven or the pains of Hell, how much greater will be thy joy when thou shalt see God, the Father and the Lord of all things ! [2]

As much flesh is infested by many worms, even so do many envious men and evil-speakers gather round the man that is avaricious. And knowest thou why ? Because they would have the riches that are his, whereof he makes no utility, either for himself or for others.[3]

Beloved son, when thou seest the rivers and great torrents, whereof the water rushes downwards over the rocks, consider thou how many are the sinners and the unbelievers who fall daily into the mouth of the dragon of Hell. Then mayest thou think how great would be thy fear if thou wert on a lofty bank and didst fall thence into the mouth of a dragon aflame with fire.[4]

Ramon must have written both rapidly and constantly to complete so many books in so short a time—a habit which he later developed unbelievably. A more important result, however, attended his summons to Montpellier than the accomplishment of any of these writings. In the summer of 1276 came the news that King James the Conqueror, now in his sixty-ninth year, had been taken seriously ill at Xátiva, where he was attempting to quell a revolt among the Valencian Saracens. In Valencia he died at midnight on July 26–7 of that year, leaving his principal possessions—Catalonia, Valencia and Aragon—to the elder of his legitimate sons, Peter, and Mallorca, with Cerdagne, Roussillon and Montpellier, to James.

No doubt Ramon had been opening his heart to the future King of Mallorca during the months spent at his side in Montpellier. Only thus can be explained the

[1] *D.P.*, chap. 7 (*Obres*, i, p. 18).
[2] *D.P.*, chap. 42 (*Obres*, i, p. 74).
[3] *D.P.*, chap. 62 (*Obres*, i, p. 110).
[4] *D.P.*, chap. 99 (*Obres*, i, p. 194).

rapid fruition of his plans for the establishment of missionary colleges. For one of the first acts of James II after his accession was to found such a college at Miramar, in Mallorca. Thirteen friars—a number symbolical of Christ and the Apostles—were to live in it, and to devote themselves especially to the study of Arabic, their maintenance being provided by a yearly sum, paid by the King, of five hundred florins of gold.[1]

This signal success, perhaps not wholly expected, raised Ramon's single-minded enthusiasm to fever-heat and marked the first great climax of joy in his life. Other successes his fervour was to win him, but none besides this, perhaps, did he welcome with the almost boyish ardour of one who sees a door slowly opening that will lead to the accomplishment of ideals, most of which, alas ! he was never to see realized. He lauded his sovereign's munificence in verse :

> The Minorites from near and far,
> Remembering God's blessed Son,
> Who calls us to a holy war,
> And bids us work with Him as one,
> Have made the house of Miramar,
> By fair Mallorca's king begun,
> The Moors to save,
> For whom our God great things has done
> Their souls to have.[2]

And he dwelt upon it in his prose fictions :

There was a clerk in that synod who came from an isle beyond the sea, the which is called Mallorca ; and he said to the Bishop, in the presence of all, that that isle belonged to a noble and learned king, the which King of Mallorca is called James. That king is a man of noble customs, and has much devotion as to the manner wherein Jesus Christ may be honoured by preaching among the unbelievers ; and to this end he has ordained that thirteen friars

[1] *V.C.*, iii, *V.B.R.L.*, ii (*Life*, pp. 15, 57–8). The mention of the florin, a coin which did not exist in Catalonia till long after this time, suggests that the author of the contemporary biography may have been French. *Cf.* Sollier, *Acta*, chap. 10, and p. 336, n. 5, below.

[2] *Blanquerna*, chap. 100 (*Bl.*, p. 530). For the original, see *Obres*, ix, pp. 493–5. Pasqual (i, pp. 225–7) cites the verses in an execrable Castilian paraphrase.

minor shall study Arabic in a monastery called Miramar, established and set apart in a fitting place, and he himself has provided for their needs ; and when they shall have learned the Arabic tongue, they will be able to go, by leave of their General, to honour the Fruit of Our Lady, and in His honour suffer hunger and thirst, heat and cold, fears and torture and death. And this establishment, he said, has been made in perpetuity.[1]

No less than twenty-three years later, in the beautiful and pathetic *Song of Ramon*,[2] he recalls the high hopes with which this opportunity, truly heaven-sent, inspired him :

To Francis' sons, by deed new-seal'd,
Miramar's slopes the monks did yield,
That truth to Moors may be reveal'd.
Twixt vineyard fair and fennel-field
God's conquering love broke down my shield :
Then tears and sighs my sore wounds heal'd.

* * * * *

A science I have found that's new,
Whereby comes knowledge of the true,
And falsehood's followers grow few.
Infidels now their creeds will rue—
Tartar and Saracen and Jew—
For God therewith did me imbue.[3]

[1] *Blanquerna*, chap. 65 (*Bl.*, pp. 256–7).

[2] See p. 289, below, and n. 3 on the date of the poem.

[3] *Cant de Ramon*, iii, vi. The translation preserves the metre and rime-scheme, but the original is simpler in expression than can be conveyed in English :

Lo monestir de Miramar
fiu a frares Menors donar
per sarraïns a preïcar.
Enfre la vinya e el fenollar
amor me pres, fé'm Déus amar,
enfre sospirs e plors estar.

* * * *

Novell saber hai atrobat,
pot-n'hom conèixer veritat
e destruir la falsetat :
sarraïns seran batejat,
tartres, jueus e mant orat,
per lo saber que Déus m'ha dat.

The last two lines of the former stanza seem to me to refer to some spiritual crisis of which nothing is now known, but which clearly took place at Miramar. The striking evocation (l. 4) of the countryside will not be lost on those who visit the locality (*cf.* Riber, *Vida i actes*, pp. 48–49).

We can imagine the fervour with which one who, after so many years, could write in this strain would dedicate himself anew to the service of God his Redeemer, and resolve that Miramar should be only the first, and perhaps the least, of many such missionary foundations, though to him always the dearest. Perhaps he saw in King James' generosity a Divine call to carry on the work of the saintly Ramon de Penyafort, who had died, full of years, at Epiphanytide, 1275, and whose efforts to convert the heathen might be expected to bear greater fruit now that apparently the Crusades were over. Certainly the younger Ramon had by this time done all in his power to fit himself for his missionary career. While still in Montpellier he had cut himself off finally from worldly cares, for his wife, who for some three years had attempted with small success to manage her own possessions, found herself obliged at last to ask a kinsman named Galcerán, who was in holy orders, to accept appointment as her legal administrator.[1] This appointment, dated March 13, 1276,[2] freed Ramon, both legally and morally, from the irksome duties which had so heavily oppressed him while he was writing the *Book of Contemplation*. He returned, about this same time, to Mallorca,[3] and for a year or more threw himself wholly into the work of the foundation of Miramar.

It was not till the end of 1276 that James received from Pope John XXI, who had recently succeeded to the

[1] The document making the appointment is to be found in Pasqual, i. pp. 212–3, and also in Rubió y Lluch, *Documents, etc.*, i, pp. 3–4. The opening lines are very explicit as to the cause of the petition of Ramon's wife:

"Certum est et manifestum quod Blanca uxor Raymundi Lulli venit ante presentiam nostri Petri de Calidis bajuli asserens et denuntians eidem bajulo, quod Raymundus Lulli eius maritus est in tantum factus contemplativus, quod circa administrationem bonorum suorum temporalium non intendit: quare suplicando petiit a nobis, cum sua intersit pro se et filiis suis et dicti Raymundi Lulli communibus, quatenus daremus curatorem bonis dicti Raymundi Lulli, qui ipsa bona regat, gubernet, tueatur et defendat et salva faciat."

[2] So Pasqual, but it is not certain that the document (Rubió y Lluch: *Documents, etc.*, i, pp. 3–4) is dated after the old style. The year might therefore be 1275.

[3] Pasqual (i, p. 214) believes him to have been there for at least a short time before the appointment of P. Galcerán.

See of Peter, the formal bull approving his project,[1] and couched in terms flattering both to himself and to his late father, a king in whom and in whose ancestors "shone the zeal of devotion and faith." But, as Ramon stayed at Miramar only till a few months later, it may be assumed that his work there was already far advanced when news of the papal blessing reached him ; the language of the bull, too, suggests that the teaching of the friars might have begun. The deed of transfer had been signed by the King on October 15, less than three months after his father's death, and five weeks after his own coronation (September 12). And as we have documentary evidence that James was in Mallorca in the March preceding[2] it seems likely (especially if Ramon was there also)[3] that provisional arrangements at least were made then. It may even be that James' finding himself still in Mallorca in July explains his probable absence from the Conqueror's deathbed.[4]

For natural advantages, few better spots in the whole of Mallorca could have been chosen for the monastery than Miramar. The land belonged to Ramon's friends

[1] The document (Rubió y Lluch : *Documents, etc.*, ii, (i, pp. 4–5) ; Pasqual, i, pp. 222–4) is dated from Viterbo on November 16, 1276. The essential part of it runs : ". . . Statuisti et etiam ordinasti, ut in insula Majoricensi, ad te jure hereditaria pertinente, in loco, qui dicitur Daya in parrochia Sancti Bartholomaei Vallis de Musa, monasterium sive locus religiosus de tuis bonis propriis constituatur, in quo tredecim fratres ordinis Minorum, qui juxta ordinationem et institutionem provintialis ministri continuè in arabico studeant, et commorentur, ut tandem instructi competenter in illo, ad terras paganorum se conferant, animarum profectibus intendentes . . ."

The date of the bull ("xvi Calendas Decembris") is accepted by many authorities. Mut, Quadrado and others, however, read "Octobris," because of the form of address ("Nobili viro Jacobo, nato clarae memoriae Regis Aragonum") which they take to imply that the Pope had not heard of James' accession. This reading would bring the date back almost to that of the Pope's own election, and seems, besides, quite an unnecessary emendation. Bihl (p. 340) proposes to make the date October 17 and quotes Stapfer: *Papst Johannes XXI, Eine Monographie*, Münster-i.-W, 1898, p. 101, n. 2 ; Longpré (col. 1078) also reads October 17.

[2] See Pasqual, i, pp. 211–2, Av., p. 131. The latter has a useful chapter on Miramar (pp. 131–40).

[3] See p. 131, n. 3, above.

[4] All the accounts quote the Conqueror's last words to Peter, but none mentions any exhortation to James. Tourtoulon (bk. iv, chap. 5) goes as far as to say that the younger son set out for Valencia, but no more.

of La Real, who exchanged it for some property of the King's.[1] As its name denotes,[2] it is in full view of the sea, lying on the north-western slopes of the Sierra, in all but the most fertile part of the island. To-day the fennel of Ramon's song is more in evidence than the vine, which has practically disappeared from the locality, but wide sweeps of silver-grey olive groves set off the azure sea, and above the grounds which once belonged to the monastery dark overhanging pines lend grandeur to what without them might seem a too effeminate beauty. The contrast between the ascetic hermit, oppressed by unescapable responsibility and the unknown future, and the successful founder light-heartedly lauding his benefactor is not more striking than that between the austerity and bareness of Randa and the fair prospect of Miramar glimpsed from the grey wooded heights above it on a day when a sunset spreading gloriously over the ocean encourages the illusion that the scene is too wonderful to be real.

Ramon himself, who read in the book of nature with as much avidity as in any other, can hardly have failed to dwell musingly upon this contrast. Away yonder, out of sight, lay Randa, far beyond the city of his birth, " austere as the life that he led there, rising like his own Divine inspiration above level plains as vast as his own projects." Now for a time life was pleasanter : instead of the sombre, parched lentiscus there was the lustrous evergreen oak ; woods and running water took the place of slopes that were sullen and treeless ; the peaceful companionship of gardens succeeded the mountain top's isolation. " Even the sea was different. For yonder, on Mount Randa, its monotonous waves washed the southern shores, leading him times without number to lament the blindness of the infidels who dwelt beyond it, in Africa and the East. Here, on the west of the island, not only was it more splendid and more brilliant, but it

[1] Pasqual, i, pp. 216–8 ; Av., pp. 132–3. The fact is referred to in *Cant de Ramon*, iii (p. 130, above).

[2] The name, it will be noted, does not occur in the papal bull, and was probably given to the college at its foundation, since which time it has clung to the district. It is first found in a document of 1279 (Pasqual, i, p. 220).

seemed to bear him towards the continent of Christian Europe, and with him his prayers for the conversion of the world." [1]

It is not hard to picture the busy yet restful life which, for a short space of time at least, Ramon led in these idyllic surroundings. He has left no description of his work in the college with the friars—whose very names are unknown—but there can be little doubt that it was mainly work of supervision, since he remained at Miramar for so brief a period, conceiving his own true sphere to be a wider one than the little obscure monastery by the silver and blue sea. There is no record of his having himself taught the friars, though it is hard to imagine his not doing so. He may well, in the main, have lived for the most part the life of a contemplative, writing steadily, watching the development of the college, advising those who taught in it, and inspiring both teachers and disciples with his own ideals. This assumption accords admirably with the tradition that Ramon's picture of his hero Blanquerna in his hermitage is autobiographical even to its details. If it be so, he would rise daily at midnight, opening "the windows of his cell, that he might behold the heavens and the stars, and begin his prayer as devoutly as he might, to the end that his whole soul should be with God." [2] After Matins and Mass, at which both Blanquerna and his companion, a deacon, assisted,

> Blanquerna left the church, and took recreation in his soul from the work which his body had done, and he looked upon the mountains and the plains [3] that he might have recreation therein.
>
> So soon as Blanquerna felt himself refreshed, he betook himself again straightway to prayer and contemplation, or read in the books of Divine Scripture, and in the *Book of Contemplation*, and thus he remained until the hour of terce. After this they said terce, sext and none, and after terce the deacon went away to prepare for Blanquerna certain herbs and vegetables. Blanquerna likewise

[1] After J. M. Quadrado: *Recuerdos de Miramar, passim.*

[2] *Blanquerna*, chap. 98 (*Bl.*, p. 407).

[3] This phrase would be applicable to Randa rather than to Miramar. See p. 113, above.

laboured in the garden, or at some other business, that he might not become slothful, and that his body might have the greater health, and between sext and none he went to dine. After he had dined, he went back alone to the church to give thanks therein to God. When he had ended his prayer, he remained yet an hour, and went to take recreation in the garden, and by the fountain, and visited all those places wherein he could best make glad his soul. After this he slept, to the end that he might the better endure the labours of the night.[1]

Lastly, when vespers and compline are over, and the sun has set, Blanquerna mounts "the high ground . . . above his cell" (Miramar, like Blanquerna's hermitage, is on the hillside) [2]

and remained in prayer until prime, gazing upon the heavens and the stars with tearful eyes and devotion of heart, and meditating upon the honours of God and upon the sins which men commit in this world against Him. In such great affection and fervour was Blanquerna in his contemplation, from the set of sun even until prime, that when he had lain down and fallen asleep, he thought that he was with God even as he had made his prayer.[3]

We may give here, in a few words, the subsequent history of Miramar. Its life was not a long one, and it is not known ever to have sent out any missionaries, though the natural presumption is that it did so. The loss by King James, in 1285, of his Mallorcan dominions harmed it but little, for his conqueror and nephew, Alfonso III of Aragon, was anxious to continue the endowment, and indeed engaged himself to increase it and to complete the unfinished college buildings. This promise was confirmed in 1292, by his brother and successor, James II of Aragon,[4] but, soon after, some disaster supervened, the nature of which is unknown, with the result that Miramar was abandoned.[5]

[1] *Blanquerna*, chap. 98 (*Bl.*, pp. 407–8).

[2] The traditional Randa hermitage, on the other hand, is on the very summit of the hill, so this phrase would hardly be applicable to Randa.

[3] *Blanquerna*, chap. 98 (*Bl.*, p. 408).

[4] It should be noted here, to prevent subsequent confusion, that from 1291 to 1311 there were two James II's in Spain—James II of Aragon and James II of Mallorca, his uncle.

[5] See *Desconort*, lv, and p. 264, below.

It was never re-founded, even when in 1298 the usurper James II was effectively dispossessed of Mallorca in favour of the former king, James II his uncle. Either Lull's munificent benefactor was now too poor, or he had too much to think of : perhaps he had even lost interest in his own foundation. On March 19, 1301, the buildings were made over to the former owners of the estate, the Cistercian monks of La Real, with the obligation to maintain in them two priests of their order, who, on certain appointed days, would say masses for his soul and for the souls of his ancestors. Miramar itself remained a royal possession, passing from James II of Mallorca to his son Sancho, and thence to James III and his brother Ferdinand, after which it came again, with the rest of the island, into the hands of the kings of Aragon. Religious instruction was long given there ; in 1395, for example, we hear of two priests teaching "Lullian science"; later came two Hieronymite hermits; in 1443, Dominicans. After this date the buildings had sundry occupants, notably a "reverend Francisco Prats," who composed poems to Ramon Lull's memory : in 1485, again, we learn that the first printing in Mallorca was done here. Gradually, after this, the place suffered longer and longer spells of abandonment. In 1811, being still Crown property, it was alienated by decree of the Cortes of Cádiz. The last and most pleasing stage in its history remains to be told in another chapter.[1]

For the moment, ere we take up again the crowded story of Ramon's activities and wanderings, let us pause to consider the nobility of the ideal which he set himself, and this first crest of its accomplishment at that moment of his life which was perhaps the most purely beautiful, save for the sublime moment which was also that of his death. If the spectacle of knights taking the cross with St. Louis is a noble one, how much nobler is that of the apostolic band of friars, unknown to posterity, preparing to meet a subtler enemy than the Saracen with the arms of peaceful warfare, and putting on the panoply of God. "Considered thus, the foundation of a school of Oriental

[1] See pp. 398–9, below.

languages, which in other circumstances might be a trite enough idea, becomes an idea wholly sublime, raising its author at once to lofty heights." [1]

There seems some reason for assigning to the year or years spent in Miramar the composition, in Latin, of the *Book of the Holy Spirit*,[2] which, though very much shorter, is reminiscent in its general plan of the *Book of the Gentile and the three wise men*.[3] Two sages, one of the Greek and one of the Roman obedience, meet on a certain Whit Sunday near a spring, where the Lady Intelligencia, whose palfrey is drinking there, shows them a "tree," the ten flowers of which are the "conditions" by which may be solved the principal problem accounting for the separation of East and West, that of the procession of the Holy Spirit.[4]

While they are talking together, there comes up a Saracen, who for a long time has been desirous of Christian baptism and has recently been to Constantinople to obtain it. But on his arrival there he has witnessed in a church a dispute on the *Filioque* clause and other points

[1] From a dialect sermon by Juan Maura, celebrating the sixth centenary of Miramar (January 21, 1877), and reprinted in *Homenage al Beato Raimundo Lull*, etc., Palma, 1877, pp. 159–60. The relevant lines are:

"Si és hermos veure aquells valents crusats defensar ab sa sanch de sas venas sa seua patria, sa seua civilisació y sas seuas creencias, y reconquistar pam a pam sa terra usurpada; si axó, dich, és hermós, ho es molt més veure sa noble figura de Ramon Lull axecantse majestuosa demunt tants de guerrers y conquistadors per emprende cuantre els Arabes una crusada desconeguda, ab sas armes de sa ciencia y de sa fe. Axi considerada sa fundació de un colegi de llenguas orientals, que en altras circunstancias no sería més que un pensament vulgar, es un pensament grandiós, una idea sublime que coloca a n'es seu autor a una gran altura."

[2] Salz., Vol. ii. As in most of his other early works, Lull denounces himself in this, as "homo pauper culpabilis, cujus nomen non dignatur scribere in hoc libello." The book mentions the *Ars Magna* and the *Gentil* as already written. The usual dates assigned to it are 1276–8, though some suppose it to have been written at Montpellier in 1275. Both with regard to this work and those next treated, there is some uncertainty. It must be remembered that there is a sentimental tendency for Mallorcan writers to place as many of Lull's books as possible at Miramar, when nothing certain is known about their composition, and Pasqual in particular succumbs easily to this temptation. Cf. *H.L.F.*, No. 8 (pp. 100–2).

[3] Cf. *Bl.*, chap. 86 (pp. 365–6), where both works are mentioned.

[4] *Liber de Sancto Spiritu*, Prologue (Salz., ii, p. 1).

of contention ; in consequence, being an intelligent man, he has deferred baptism, and is now on his way to Rome to hear the Roman arguments at their fountain-head, and to decide for himself which party is in the right.

In the presence of the Saracen, the two sages discuss the questions which separate their communions, characteristically drawing lots in the first place to decide which of them shall begin. The effectiveness, and even the relevance, of their arguments varies considerably. The Greek, for example, maintains that that which is most credible and understandable is most predicable ; and as the procession from Father and Son is more difficult, both to believe and to understand, than procession from the Father alone, it therefore follows that the Holy Spirit proceeds from the Father only. The Latin sage replies that the belief of his communion is the more predicable, because it gives the greater honour to Father, Son and Holy Spirit, all Three.[1]

This alone is possibly rather startling, but when the sages, not content with arguing from theology, reason also from the relative virtues and manners of life of their clergy, all semblance of logic vanishes. The Eastern sage claims that, because the Greek clergy have not the wealth of the Latin clergy, they are therefore nearer the contemplative life than the active, and this is the better life of the two . . . " whence it is demonstrated that the Holy Spirit proceeds from the Father only." This and similar contentions are disputed by the Latin, who argues that, because the Western clergy exceed the Eastern in number, have more princes and prelates, greater liberty, greater power, more clergy and religious, greater honour and greater learning, the doctrines which they teach must be true, the more so as Rome belongs to the Latins and not to the Greeks, and Rome has always been at the head of Christendom.[2]

In the end, the sages take leave of the Saracen, who decides to stay for a day where he is and think over all that he has heard from them. They for their part pro-

[1] *L.S.S.*, Pt. I, chap. 10 (Salz., ii, p. 5).
[2] *L.S.S.*, Pt. I, chap. 9 ; Pt. II, chap. 9 (Salz., ii, pp. 5, 9–10).

pose to spend their whole lives in arguing these questions publicly in the hope of reaching an agreement.[1] The natural comment of the unprejudiced reader is that they should first revise their arguments. Were it re-published to-day, the *Book of the Holy Spirit* would be interpreted as a not very skilful satire on our unhappy divisions. It is probable that Lull did not choose his characters' debating points without some such satirical intention, for, as we shall see, he never tired of lamenting disunion. But from what we know of his general attitude as shown in his other works, and from the equal irrelevance of many of the arguments on both sides, it seems certain that his principal aim was to demonstrate the superiority of the Western Church over the Eastern—though, as in the *Book of the Gentile*, he is always fair and courteous, and never attempts to follow up an advantage unfairly.

It would seem to be at Miramar also, or possibly elsewhere in Mallorca, in the years 1275–6, that Lull wrote the first in order of those of his poetical works which have come down to us.[2] The *Complaint of Our Lady Saint Mary,*[3] consisting of thirty-two rimed stanzas written in alexandrines—a French epic metre—is precisely the type of poem that a one-time courtier in the Middle Ages might be expected to write on first attempting religious verse. The subject was a common one and many verses were written upon it in France, Catalonia,[4] and other Latin countries.[5] Our Lady is addressed much as though she were the heroine of a chivalric romance, but idealized as

> The damsel gentle and sweet who is the lady of love.[6]

[1] *L.S.S.*, Pt. II, chap. 10 (Salz., ii, p. 10).

[2] There is no definite evidence of date. See Pasqual, i, p. 255, and Ramon Llull, *Poesies*, ed. Ramon d'Alòs, p. 154.

[3] *Plant de Nostra Dona Santa Maria.* The title in some MSS. is a longer one, viz.: *De la Passió de Jesucrist e lo Desconort que hac Nostra Dona de son Fill.* Cf. *H.L.F.*, No. 92, p. 263.

[4] For some Catalan examples, see *Poesies, ed. cit.*, p. 154.

[5] See Wechssler: *Die romanischen Marienklagen*, Halle, 1893, who gives a general Romance bibliography.

[6] La douça donzella qui és dona d'amors. For this idea, cf. *Blanquerna*, chap. 64 (dialogue between a knight and an abbot).

The incidents of the Passion are described, from the betrayal by Judas to the commendation of Our Lady to St. John, and the completed lament is then offered "to great and to small" (*los grans e los menors*) in words which bear testimony to Ramon's missionary zeal :

> Humbly would I present it to small as well as great,
> That on Our Lady's sorrows they oft may meditate.
> Alas ! If once she sorrowed in Heaven's high estate,
> More deeply yet must grieve her this world degenerate.
> Her blessed Son's dishonour'd by noble and preláte
> Who will not go to Syria, His love to celebrate.
> To thee, O Queen and Virgin, this lay I dedicate.[1]

The *Hours of Our Lady Saint Mary* anticipates, both by its title and by its content, a similar work in prose which was written by Lull about fourteen years later and will be described in its proper place.[2] The poem has seven main divisions, corresponding respectively to the seven canonical hours, and each division contains seven twelve-lined octosyllabic stanzas, riming in couplets. Various minor points suggest that this and the last composition are of approximately the same date,[3] but again there is no clear indication. As to the merit of the *Hours*, little can be said that is flattering : Ramon's verse style, like that of many hymn-writers (the poem was written "to be sung to the tune of hymns") was facile but not distinguished, and the poem is lively rather than eloquent, with a tendency to the aphoristic which became more pronounced in the author's verse as he grew older. The subject-matter of the *Hours* has little to do with the Blessed Virgin, except that she is mentioned in each stanza, the author's aim being rather to unite devotion

[1]
> Lo dó als uns e als altres per ço que les llangors
> membren de Nostra Dona, e la gran deshonors
> que és faita a son Fill per prelats e senyors,
> car en la Terra Santa no fan dire llausors.
> E si Nostra Dona el cel hagués dolors
> car tan pauc honram son Fill, ara l'hagra majors.
> A vós, Verge reïna, coman est xant d'amors.

Elsewhere in this stanza Ramon mentions himself by name.

[2] See pp. 228–31, below.

[3] Principally the title, the stanza, and reminiscences of the poetry of the troubadours. *Cf.* Pasqual, i, p. 256 ; *H.L.F.*, No. 94 (p. 264).

with general teaching upon the Faith. The section for Matins is concerned with the nature and properties of the Godhead ; that for Prime, with Jesus Christ ; for Terce, with the gifts of the Spirit ; for Sext and None, with the seven virtues and the seven deadly sins respectively ; for Vespers, with the seven sacraments ; and for Compline, with a variety of other subjects. It may be permissible to quote a single attractive stanza, from the final section, as a specimen of Lull's early art in verse at something like its best. It is hardly below the average level of such verse in other countries in Lull's day, though it was not for his poems that he was to take a high place in the history of literature :

When I behold earth, heaven and sea,
And hear the birds sing merrily,
Pluck flowers and smell their perfume sweet,
Taste all delightful kinds of meat,
Touch finest cloth, wood polishèd,
Thrice-precious gold and ruby red,
Then feels my heart for Heaven's high Queen
Love that is unsurpass'd, I ween.
With her I speak, to her I pray :
My body and soul are hers alway.
To her with faltering voice I cry :
" Thou seest me, Lady : thine am I." [1]

[1] Quant veig la terra e la mar,
Lo cel, e aug aucells cantar,
E sent de las flors lur odor,
E de las viandas sabor,
E toch drap, fust, aur e rubis,
Per la dona de paradis
Ab la qual parle en pregan ;
Quant l arma e l cors li coman,
Adonchs sent al cor tal douçor
Que hanc no la sentí major,
E dich a la Verge ploran :
" Veus me dona'n vostre coman."
(*Obras Rimadas*, p. 172.)

CHAPTER VII

1277–1285

Ramon Lull's first visit to Rome. Death of Pope John XXI. Unknown period of Lull's life (1277–1282): conflicting theories. Visit to Perpignan: *The Sin of Adam*. Sojourn in Montpellier: *Ars demonstrativa*; *Book of the first and second intentions*.

At more than one point in the life of Ramon Lull, there occur incidents which, though mainly by chance, recall to us the life of St. Francis of Assisi, whose influence had already touched him, and whose follower he was in time to become. It will be remembered with what high hopes Francis first journeyed to the court of Innocent III, and how he dreamed of a great tree which inclined its branches towards him, while he himself became so tall that he could reach them with the greatest ease. This confidence may or may not have been reflected in Ramon as he journeyed to Rome in the spring of 1277: from our knowledge of his optimistic temperament and of his successes during the past few years, we should judge that it was. Certainly the blighting of Francis' hopes and dreams by Innocent has its parallel in the disillusionment which came to Ramon at Rome—and that not once but many times.

The object of Ramon's first visit to Rome, says the contemporary biography, was "to obtain of the Holy Father and of the Cardinals that throughout the world should be founded monasteries wherein should be studied divers languages, to the end that unbelievers should be converted."[1] The experiment of Miramar was to be

[1] *V.C.* iii (*Life*, pp. 15–16; cf. *V.B.R.L.*: *Life*, p. 58). Some idea of the nature of these proposals to the Pope may be obtained from *Blanquerna*, chaps. 80, 100 (*Bl.*, pp. 325, 530) where similar suggestions are made and Miramar is definitely mentioned as the model on which future foundations should be based.

repeated, in short, upon a larger scale. It was an ambitious proposal, and could hardly have been expected to bear fruit immediately. As it happened, the proposal could not then be made. When Ramon arrived at the Papal court, he found that John XXI had just died,[1] and his successor had not been elected. This experience, which he was afterwards to reproduce in one of his romances,[2] decided him to postpone his plans, and to undertake fresh activities.

Precisely how he was occupied between 1277 and 1282 we do not know. The contemporary biography sends him to Paris and presents him as teaching where once he had meant to study, expounding his *Ars Magna* and winning support for his methods and ideals in a place more important than the restricted spheres of Montpellier and Mallorca, and more accessible than the court of Rome.[3] But it is clear from other evidence [4] that the contemporary life (which scorns dates throughout) omits a period of nine years, and that Lull crowded many and varied experiences into the time that elapsed between the death of John XXI and his own sojourn in Paris.

Let us try to reconstruct the events of this shadowy epoch in the light of such evidence as we have. It is probable that, when Ramon left Miramar for Rome, he had some reason to hope that his journey would not be unfruitful. For one thing, John XXI had already given his blessing to one of his long-dreamed-of colleges. For another, although he had not long been Pope, enough was known of him to show that he was a man after Lull's own heart. He was a student—and that not only in theology and philosophy, but also in the sciences, especially in medicine, and (it was even whispered) in

[1] *V.B.R.L.* has: " Invenit Papam tunc recenter mortuum, scilicet dominum Honorium IV Papam " (*Life*, p. 58). *Cf.* Custurer, p. 503 and pp. 200–2, below. If *V.B.R.L.* is correct (as Longpré, col. 1079, believes), this would imply a gap in its narrative of eleven years (1276–1287), but I think it has merely confused two names. Others (Pasqual, Rosselló, Avinyó, etc.) read Martin IV for Honorius IV: this I consider the least likely assumption of the three. See Pasqual, *Vindiciae*, i, p. 165, for the argument.

[2] *Blanquerna*, chap. 77 (*Bl.*, p. 309).

[3] *V.C.*, iii, *V.B.R.L.* ii (*Life*, pp. 16, 58).

[4] See Pasqual, i, pp. 262–310, *passim*, and p. 259, below.

occult lore. Then, for all the shortness of his reign, he had been able to give manifest proof of his overmastering zeal for missions. A synod held at Constantinople had acknowledged his primacy and the Byzantine Emperor and his son had embraced the Roman obedience. This was an inspiring event, coming so soon after the Council of Lyons, held in 1274, which had largely been concerned with the healing of the schism of the East. The Pope followed it up by sending ambassadors to France, Sicily, Aragon and England to inquire if they would consider a new crusade. The answers were that they would not —they were all too deeply engrossed with home politics. But an unexpected happening counterbalanced that disappointment. The Khan of Tartary, Abaga, who had promised such help as he could give to the crusade of 1269, and had also sent messengers to the Pope desiring to ally himself with any crusade that might be formed in the future, asked now that he might be granted some Christian missionaries. Before this could be accomplished, John XXI met with a sudden and tragic death; his successor, Nicholas III, sent in 1278, under the leadership of one Gerard de Prato, five Franciscans who were to preach first in Persia and then in China. Of these events, and of the obstacles which the missionary friars encountered in Persia, there are echoes in Lull's *Blanquerna*.[1]

Did Ramon stay in Italy until the election of Nicholas III in November 1277? Did he lay his projects before the new Pope before leaving? Had he even some hand in the sending of the missionaries to the Khan? In spite of the interest in this adventure which his book reveals, the probability seems to lie in the negative.[2] If Ramon had remained at the Papal

[1] Chap. 80 (*Obres*, ix, p. 302: *Bl.*, pp. 330–1); *cf.* chap. 87.

[2] Pasqual's contention that he left Rome in the spring of 1278 (i, pp. 271–2) seems to be based, like the pages which follow it, on a typical piece of subjective interpretation, of the kind to which he is so greatly inclined. P. Longpré (col. 1078) thinks that the reference (*Obres*, ix, p. 302) to the events of 1278 proves Lull to have been at Rome at that time, whereas to me it only seems to prove his interest in the matter. If *V.C.*, *V.B.R.L.*, really refer (*Life*, pp. 16, 58) to the death of John XXI, their suggestion that Ramon left Rome soon after his arrival there is another argument of some weight.

court for so long as to discover of what mettle Pope Nicholas was made, it is unlikely that he would have left so soon for what appears to have been little less than a world tour of preaching and exploration.

Where he went we cannot with certainty say. It is generally thought that he travelled first to Germany, and in some way met the prudent and upright emperor Rudolf of Habsburg, who at that time had just repaired a serious breach between the Empire and the Papacy, and may well have been, as is generally believed, the model of the attractively presented but rather more other-worldly emperor in *Blanquerna*.[1] Tradition credits Ramon with making subsequent visits to countries as far apart as Abyssinia, Egypt, Palestine, Turkey, Greece, Morocco, Andalucia—and even England![2] The evidence in favour of this tradition is very slight.[3] Two of his books, written soon after his return from whatever countries he visited, may best be relied upon to confirm or refute it: these are *Blanquerna* (*c.* 1283) and *Felix* (*c.* 1286).

Blanquerna certainly embodies much experience of travel, though not necessarily, of course, experience gained at first hand. Its concluding chapters describe distant countries—Barbary, Abyssinia, Tartary, Turkey, Georgia—and others the identities of which can only be guessed at, but which are referred to in terms not proving, but strongly suggesting, personal observation.

> . . . A southern land which lies within the regions of the desert. . . . In that land there were many kings and princes who adored idols and likewise adored the sun and the stars and the birds and the beasts. The people of that land are very many, and they are black, and have no law [*i.e.* religion].[4]

[1] He first appears in chap. 48, and for some time takes a prominent part in the narrative. He is also brought with great effect into its epilogue.

[2] This is repeated by Pasqual (i, pp. 270–1). That Lull ever visited England is a myth closely connected with that which makes him an alchemist (see pp. 405–7 below).

[3] Some of Lull's biographers draw the most extravagant conclusions from such evidence as there is. All that I personally consider relevant is brought together in the text below.

[4] Chap. 84 (*Bl.*, p. 357).

. . . One of the messengers of the Cardinal journeyed southwards, and found a caravan of six thousand camels, laden with salt, leaving a town by name Tibalbert, and going to that country wherein is the source of the river Damiata. . . . These men are all black, and adore idols, and they are men of genial temper, who hold justice very dear, and slay every man whom they discover in falsehood, and hold all that they have in common. In that land is an island in the middle of a great lake ; and on that island there lives a dragon to whom the people of that land do sacrifice, adoring it as a god.[1]

. . . Northward, beyond the mountains . . . there was one land, Gotlandia by name, where at the end of every five years there appeared a white bear, as a sign that that year there would be an abundance of fish, whereon these people live. There was another land wherein by enchantment the trees were made to speak. Another land is there, near to Bohemia,[2] where there is a hoopoe in a wood, and if any man cuts a branch from a tree in that wood, straightway come lightning and thunder from the heavens and set in peril of death every man who is in that wood. In another land every man thinks that he has a god in his field, and another in his stable, and another in his garden. In another land, near to Dacia,[3] are men who live on naught save the beasts which they hunt . . . and when they have killed one of them they remain in that place till they have eaten it, and then seek another.[4]

From these and similar passages Mn. Galmés has deduced a complete itinerary for Lull's travels, concluding that he went northwards from Rome, through the countries of Guirlanda and Bocinia, returning by Dacia, Turkey and Ultramar (Palestine), continuing southwards by way of Abyssinia from Tibalbert to the source of the river that waters Damiata, until at length he reached Barbary.[5]

[1] Chap. 88 (*Bl.*, p. 374).

[2] Most versions here have " Bocinia," and " Girlanda " for " Gotlandia " above (cf. *Obres*, ix, p. 343).

[3] For " prés Dacia," some critics would read " prés d'Asia," which suggests the neighbourhood of Russia.

[4] Chap. 88 (*Bl.*, pp. 374–5).

[5] *Obres*, ix, p. xvi. A student of the evidence may think these deductions somewhat bold, but the interpretation is a conservative one compared (for example) with that of Pasqual, who sends him from Rome, through Germany and Russia, to Turkey, Greece and Arabia ; thence by way of Egypt and Barbary to Morocco ; thence by boat to England ; and finally back to Christian Spain by way of Granada and Portugal (i, pp. 270–1).

The evidence of *Felix* is less striking than that of *Blanquerna*, though Pasqual considers it to be of some importance.[1] Three references are all that can be given, and at least two of these are vague in the extreme. The first [2] merely remarks that "a pilgrim was at prayer in Jerusalem, and, remembering the Passion of Jesus Christ, had very great fervour and desire to die for His love." The second [3] is rather more detailed, but has nothing that can fairly be described as local colour: a pilgrim is again in Jerusalem, "marvels greatly at the negligence of the Christians" who allow the Saracens to hold it, and, entering a mosque where he sees honour being paid to Mahomet, marvels still more because "the Christians are not diligent in preaching to unbelievers and showing them the way of truth." The third reference is to the Tartars, but, as will be seen, it compares very unfavourably with the references quoted from *Blanquerna:*

A holy man visited the Tartars and many other idolaters who lived near them. That holy man regarded and considered the works which they did, and marvelled when he saw them do such dishonour to God,—namely, when some set up as God idols of gold and silver, others the sun, others the moon, others beasts and birds, and after divers manners made strange gods.[4]

The nature of these passages does not, to our mind, make it possible to deduce from *Felix* anything whatever about Lull's travels.

Various other references, however, put beyond doubt the fact that Lull travelled widely during these five years, though they give but little idea of where he went. In 1299 he confesses to having "undertaken many great tasks and traversed a great part of the world" [5]; it would seem that before that year he had been in Ethiopia, and

[1] Pasqual, i, pp. 268–9, 296, 303–4.
[2] *Felix*, bk. viii, chap. 17 (*Obras*, iiib, pp. 66–7).
[3] *Felix*, bk. viii, chap. 29 (*Obras*, iiib, pp. 126–7).
[4] *Felix*, bk. viii, chap. 59 (*Obras*, iiib, pp. 274–5).
[5] *Cant de Ramon*, viii:

. . . hai trop gran fait emperat.
Gran res hai del món cercat.

possibly in Morocco and England.[1] In 1305 he records in the *Liber de fine* that a "certain man," who by the context is shown to have been undoubtedly himself, gave up all that he had, and, because of the evil state of the world, went over the whole earth seeking how best this could be remedied.[2] The same book, in terms which distinctly suggest that the author knew Tartary, describes the intellectual and spiritual poverty of the Tartars, and the reported desire of their emperor for Christian baptism.[3] Lull also writes, possibly from personal acquaintance, of Turkey, Ceuta and several parts of Andalucia,[4] and says clearly that he has been in Jerusalem.[5] Our knowledge of Ramon's life between 1283 and 1305 is so complete, as will later be seen, that no place can be found for more than a very small part of these extensive travels at a time other than in the years 1277–1282. Hence, though he could hardly have visited all the places to which his biographers have sent him, and it is also difficult to believe that he did not for part of the time return to Miramar,[6] it seems certain that the conclusions drawn from the works quoted have their basis in fact.[7]

In 1282, returning to ground familiar to him, Ramon stayed for a while in Perpignan, where he found that his

[1] *De nova et compendiosa geometria* (1299), *cit.* Pasqual, i, p. 269. See p. 289 n. below. The latter part of the reference is not very definite. Pasqual also brings forward a reference from *De Praedicatione* (1304), which merely says that the author was for a long time in countries beyond the sea and in Saracen lands: this is surely quite inconclusive.

[2] Prologue. See p. 316, below.

[3] *De Fine*, ed. Palma, 1665, p. 52: Ego vere fui in partibus ultra-marinis, et audivi, quod Cassanus Imperator Tartarorum pluries dicebat, quod volebat de fide Christianorum esse certus, quoniam si de ipsa haberet certitudinem, ipse se faceret Christianum, et faceret, quod tota sua militia esset omnimode baptizata, et quia certitudinem non habuit, factus fuit cum tota sua militia Sarracenus: et sic in Dei Ecclesia contritio magnam habet materiam, et subjectum, ad corda eorundem remordendum.

[4] See p. 318 below. I do not myself find this piece of evidence in the least convincing.

[5] See p. 318 below. It is fairly certain that this is a genuinely personal reference, but it may be founded on Ramon's visit to Jerusalem soon after his conversion. Longpré (col. 1079) does not take this into consideration.

[6] Sollier: *Acta Sanctorum*, p. 645; Bihl, p. 331, Keicher, p. 24.

[7] Cf., throughout this paragraph, Pasqual, i, pp. 293 ff.

old pupil, James II of Mallorca, was in residence. All had not gone smoothly with the young king since his parting from Lull some six years earlier. After the Mallorcan ceremonies of the September following his accession, he had made a tour of his newly acquired dominions on the mainland, in order to receive the assurance of his subjects' allegiance. Chroniclers and historians all record that he was welcomed everywhere, and especially at Montpellier, where, besides confirming the city's privileges, he removed certain of its grievances,[1] and where the inhabitants were so enthusiastic that they fell on their knees to do him homage.[2] But he was not to be allowed to live peaceably on his inheritance, as he desired.

His brother Peter had been from boyhood as pugnacious and eager for aggrandisement as he himself was complacent and generous. More than once during their father's reign this had become apparent to his subjects. In 1271, for instance, on the death of the Count of Toulouse, Peter had made serious and elaborate preparations to take possession of his domains by force ; nor would he desist from his attempt, even when his father forbade him to make it, until the prohibition was extended to his followers.[3] No wonder, then, that James the Conqueror, before his death, had some misgivings as to the results of his imprudent partition of his kingdom, and " knowing how uncertain was the loyalty and friendship between the two brothers " and " how few were the signs of their love," [4] charged Peter straitly, when on his death-bed, to respect his brother's inheritance.[5]

Nothing could have been clearer than the Conqueror's admonition. Yet he had been dead very few months when Peter began openly to complain because Montpellier, that border-state at once strategically valuable and commercially prosperous, had not been left to him. Once his coronation at Saragossa (November 11, 1276)

[1] Aigrefeuille, bk. vi, p. 148.
[2] Lecoy de la Marche, i, p. 153.
[3] Zurita, bk. iii, chap. 75 ; Devic et Vaissette, ix, pp. 2–3.
[4] Zurita, bk. iii, chap. 101.
[5] *Chronicle*, etc., dlxiii (*ed. cit.*, ii, p. 673).

was over,[1] he began to plan how the disadvantage at which he was placed might, at least in part, be corrected, and, soon afterwards, he took the bold step of demanding openly that James should acknowledge his overlordship and do him homage for his inheritance. The brothers met—more than once, it would seem—at Perpignan and Montpellier, and Peter made an unsuccessful attempt to win over James' brother-in-law, the Count of Foix, to his purposes.[2] The only result of this, however, was the conclusion, between the Count and King James, of an offensive and defensive alliance for five years against King Peter (May 10, 1278).[3]

But, when it came to actual resistance, the younger brother could do little. His territories were scattered and his forces far weaker than his brother's. For various reasons, appeal to the Pope was impracticable, while the powerful king of France was disinclined to interfere in what was purely a family quarrel.[4] In the end, by sheer compulsion, he consented to Peter's demands, and at Perpignan, on January 20, 1279,[5] he acknowledged himself to be his brother's vassal.[6]

Humiliated by his defeat, and (if we may judge by subsequent happenings) burning for revenge, James crossed to Mallorca, where the formalities of homage had to be gone through also. A council was held in the Church of St. Eulalia, Palma, and one authority records that among those present was a Ramon Lull whom he wrongly takes to be the venerable father of our Ramon.[7] On December 10, 1279, delegates were elected who were to pledge Mallorca's homage to King Peter. Rather

[1] His brother James was apparently present at this (Devic et Vaissette, ix, p. 51).

[2] Zurita, bk. iv., chap. 7, and elsewhere.

[3] Lecoy de la Marche, i, p. 155.

[4] *Ibid.*, p. 154.

[5] Different authorities give the date as January 19, 20 and 21 : the second seems the most probable.

[6] A full account of the terms of surrender is given in Lecoy de la Marche, i, p. 157. *Cf.* Zurita, bk. iv, chap. 7.

[7] Dameto : bk. iii, p. 462. He asserts that the "Ramon Lull" mentioned was our Ramon's father, and adds that, in 1295, "el mismo, u otro de su nombre, fué jurado de la ciudad y reino" (bk. iii, p. 820). But see p. 11, above, which appears to contradict this statement directly.

more than a year later (February 18, 1281) the guarantees demanded were duly given in the Franciscan convent of Valencia, in which city the king of Aragon was staying.[1]

Almost immediately after this, the ambitious Peter's attention was distracted from his home politics by the opportunity of expansion in Africa, an offer being made him by the nephew of the king of Tunis to obtain for him the city of Constantine if he might himself hold it as his vassal. Accordingly, Peter set sail for Africa in June, and remained abroad until, early in August 1282, he received a deputation offering him the crown of Sicily.[2] But all this time James appears to have been in Mallorca, and to have stayed there until very early in 1282, when he returned to Perpignan.[3] It was probably at the beginning of that year that Ramon Lull also arrived there, before the terrible news of the Sicilian Vespers (March 30) reached the Mallorcan king and there followed the events (too numerous to be detailed here) which led up to Peter's acceptance of Sicily. Alternatively, it might have been late in the same year, for James neither accompanied the expedition to Africa, nor went later to Sicily. On September 4 Peter was crowned King of Sicily at Palermo, and soon afterwards we find James bidding a gallant farewell to his sister-in-law, Queen Constance, "leading her horse by the bridle" and "lifting her into a beautiful boat from the ship," [4] when she set sail to join her husband.

Amid such exciting events James found time to talk with Ramon, and it will be supposed that the conversation ran on the adventures of the one abroad and the disappointments of the other at home—the ambition of Peter, against whom, as a youth, Ramon may most probably have taken James' part in the schoolroom, and possibly the way in which James hoped to gain his revenge, a way which, when realized, brought him, in the end, disaster.

If the two discussed such subjects, there is no trace of the discussions in Ramon's writings, which place on

[1] Dameto: bk. iii, p. 463.
[2] Muntaner, chap. 54.
[3] Pasqual, i, p. 229.
[4] Muntaner, chap. 95.

record an entirely different kind of conversation, very typical in its way of the thirteenth century. In an atmosphere of massacres, dethronements, conquests, expeditions and struggles for power, the King of Mallorca and his former seneschal sat down and discussed the sin of our first father! The King, it appears, was perplexed as to why Adam should ever have been permitted by God to sin, and why He does not do away both with sin and with punishment and bring all men to glory.[1] Ramon hereupon offered to explain this, which he did in a hundred octosyllabic couplets of uninspiring verse called *The Sin of Adam* (*Lo Peccat de N'Adam*).[2]

James remained for some time in Perpignan, or at least made that city his headquarters. He was there when he joined forces with his brother-in-law Philip III of France against his brother Peter, and it was from there that he fled after the latter had made him a prisoner. Perpignan, indeed, was the centre of that international yet domestic drama, for it was occupied by the French soon afterwards, and it witnessed both the defeat and the death of Philip, a few weeks before that of Peter, in the October of 1285.[3]

[1]
Un senyor rey que bé enten,
Se maravella molt sovén,
Que Deus qui es bô en quant es
No fallís en neguna res,
Quant fé a Adam lo mandament
Qu' el fruit no menjás, éll scient
Que Adam faría lo peccat
D' ont mant hom seria dampnat . . .

These are the opening lines of the poem (*Obras rimadas*, p. 179).

[2] Pasqual (*Vindiciae*, i, pp. 140–1) makes Lull write a book on the conquest of the Holy Land while he is at Perpignan, citing *Desconort*, lv, as sufficient evidence, which it certainly is not. There seems no reason to suppose that he wrote any such book at this time. The reference in *Desconort* is much more probably to one of the two " Petitions " which Ramon addressed to Celestine V and Boniface VIII (pp. 252-6 below).

[3] For a full description of the struggle, which it would be irrelevant to give here, see: Muntaner (especially chap. 119), Dameto (bk. iii, *passim*), Zurita (bk. iv, chaps. 56 ff.), Devic et Vaissette (ix, chaps. 49 ff.), Lecoy de la Marche (bks. ii, iii, *passim*), Aigrefeuille, bk. vi. Dameto supports James against Peter; Zurita, like Desclot (chaps. 134 ff.), is less fond of James; Muntaner blames Philip for deceiving James, and says that all the French kings have been deceivers, " down to this day."

Meanwhile, early in 1283, Lull passed to the neighbouring city of Montpellier, a place in which he was not only very much at home [1] but able to write easily and with success. Now that he had returned from his travels, his business was to arouse interest, far and wide, in his projects for the propagation of the faith. At Whitsuntide, 1283, a Chapter-General of Dominicans was to be held at Montpellier. Ramon had several links with this order: St. Ramon de Penyafort had belonged to it; James the Conqueror had befriended it; in reconquered Mallorca it had flourished greatly; he had named his own son after its founder. Naturally enough, when he heard of the forthcoming event, he saw in it an excellent and ready opportunity for the publicity he needed.

The most conservative critic can hardly fail to see Ramon himself in the "layman" of a fictitious narrative which he wrote a few months after the Chapter and which runs as follows:

> In a town which is named Montpellier . . . there was a great Chapter General of Preachers. In this Chapter were assembled bishops and other prelates and friars of all Christian lands, and they read letters in the Chapter concerning divers things, and recounted the deaths of friars from all Christian lands who had died that year. After these words there rose a layman who was the advocate of the unbelievers when they embrace the holy Catholic faith, and he said in the presence of all that if mention were made of the deaths of the friars whose souls live in Paradise, how much the more should remembrance be made of the deaths of the unbelievers who die in the sin of ignorance, and lose eternal life, and die in everlasting fire. And he begged that instruction should be given to them through the which these words should be fulfilled in them,—namely, that Jesus Christ has taken away the sin of the world through His Incarnation and Passion.[2]

In the story, the layman's plea is so well received that in "all chapters general of religious brothers, memorial (is ordered to) be made of the unbelievers who have died in the sin of ignorance." [3] But the facts seem rather to have been that the Dominicans received Ramon badly.

[1] See pp. 116-8, above. [2] *Blanquerna*, chap. 90 (*Bl.*, pp. 383-4).
[3] *Ibid.* (p. 384).

They certainly appear to have thought little of his *Art*,[1] and, as to his projects, they must have been at best but lukewarm. For, in some verses of this date, Ramon, after extolling the fervour of the Franciscans, demands suddenly :

> But what see we the Preachers do
> That love so much to serve Our Lord ? [2]

and classes the Order of the Preachers with

> Bishops, that great possessions hoard,
> Prelates, that prize this world below,
> Kings, sleeping with unbuckled sword
> In sloth so base.[3]

He was not to reverse his judgment in the future.

In Montpellier Ramon stayed for at least two years, and settled down to write with some vigour. First of all, he composed, in Latin, the *Ars demonstrativa*,[4] and lectured publicly upon it—no doubt in the monasteries or schools of the city, which had not yet its university. This new work aims at inventing, by a combination of metaphysic and logic, an art by which all sciences shall be demonstrable, universally and incontrovertibly. It does not enumerate the principles of any one science, but teaches the method of finding those common to each, assuming an acquaintance of the student with the terms in which it is expressed.

This *Art* was particularly favoured by Lullists of a later day, though for us it has no greater significance than the *Ars Magna*. Its method involves the same algebraical, semi-mechanical syllogizing, made more facile—one can hardly say " made easier "—by the construction of metal circles, and the superposition of these

[1] See p. 236, below.

[2] *Blanquerna*, chap. 100 (*Bl.*, p. 530). For the word *servir* (" serve ") some MSS. read *fruir* (" enjoy "), which makes the question an even sterner one.

[3] *Ibid.*

[4] See p. 119, above, Salz., vol. iii, *H.L.F.*, No. 13 (pp. 118–23), Longpré, col. 1092, and *V.C.*, iii, *V.B.R.L.*, ii (*Life*, pp. 15, 57). Some authorities date this book as early as 1282 : it must certainly have been completed soon after Lull's arrival at Montpellier. There is only one Catalan MS. at Mayence.

one upon another. Those who give themselves to such studies as these with assiduity, says Lull, will find themselves constructing syllogisms almost without knowing it, even in their sleep.

We can no more describe the *Ars demonstrativa* in full than the *Ars Magna*, so complicated are its workings, but we can give some examples of the questions, profound and puerile both, which the study of it is supposed to solve. For at the end of the book are a large number of questions with solutions worked out algebraically. The applications made by the author are principally theological, though other classes of application are included. "Could God be God if He could sin?" reminds one of the *Ars Magna*. "Does the Divine will love all that the Divine wisdom knows?" is another typical question. "Does Divine mercy suffer when Divine justice punishes the sinner?" puts a problem not infrequently debated, in a slightly different form, to-day. "Was free will ordained with intention to damnation or salvation?" shows an attitude curiously twisted and warped, to modern ideas. "Do the devils desire to die?" "How do the angels speak?" are two further questions which approach the fantastic. "Is it allowable to kill an infidel without first attempting to convert him?": this, for the Middle Ages, was a practical matter of the first importance. Then we come to scientific questions: "Does fire convey heat to dampness or to the object which is damp?" And to social problems, some only of which have survived the intervening centuries between Lull's day and ours: "Have the poor any right in the possessions of the rich?" "Is a poor man more capable of giving testimony than a rich woman?"[1]

Together with this *Art*, Ramon composed an *Introductorium* to it,[2] a *Compendium* of it,[3] a *Lectura* upon its figures,[4] which may all be passed over, as well as a *Book*

[1] Salz., iii, pp. 52–112.

[2] Also known as *Ars Notatoria*, but more usually as the *Introductorium Artis Demonstrativae* (cf. *H.L.F.*, No. 12, pp. 114–8).

[3] *Compendium seu commentum Artis Demonstrativae*, Salz., vol. iii (cf. *H.L.F.*, No. 16, pp. 127–8; Longpré, col. 1093).

[4] Salz., vol. iii (cf. *H.L.F.*, No. 14; pp. 123–4; Longpré, col. 1093).

of Propositions [1] based upon it, the nature of which can easily be imagined, and some *Introductory Rules* to its practice, in Catalan verse.[2] At Montpellier, too, during this stay there, he wrote an *Art of finding the particulars in the universals* [3] and the better known *Book of the first and second intentions* (*c.* 1283).[4]

This last is a second treatise composed by Ramon for his son Dominic. Eight years had passed since he had written for him the *Doctrine for Boys*, and the youth had now reached full manhood. This new book was composed, as it seems, in the hope that he might follow in his father's steps, and, having "newly gone into the world," [5] would not fail to serve God there. The first and principal intention of man, as Lull has already taught in his *Book of Contemplation*,[6] is the disinterested love of God ; the secondary intention (that of gain and material prosperity) is often put in place of the first by those who love God only for the sake of reward and fear Him lest He should send them to Hell. All creation, according to this book, follows the intention for which it was created, with the single exception of man, who has not been true to it. In particular, Mahomet has led a portion of mankind from the first to the second intention by inculcating false and materialistic ideals of religion.[7]

After discoursing upon intention in general, Lull goes on to write, in each of the four remaining divisions of the book, of God, of the Creation, of the Incarnation, and

[1] Cf. *H.L.F.*, No. 18 (pp. 130–3) ; Longpré, col. 1093. We might also place here the *Liber exponens figuram elementalem Artis Demonstrativae* (or *Liber de gradatione elementorum*) published in Salz., vol. iv (*H.L.F.*, No. 19, pp. 133–4).

[2] Most readers will agree with the latest editor of Lull's verse in describing the *Regles introductòries* as "obra didàctica gens interessant" (*Poesies*, p. 11), but Torras i Bages (p. 215) thinks its "entrada de gran majestat." For the Latin version, *cf.* Salz., vol. iv, and *H.L.F.*, No. 20 (p. 134).

[3] Salz., vol. iii; cf. *H.L.F.*, No. 17 (pp. 128–30).

[4] *Liber de prima et secunda intentione* : Salz., vol. vi. The Catalan text, which is extant, was probably the original ; cf. *H.L.F.*, No. 46, pp. 217–9 (*Obras*, vol. i, pp. 307–80).

[5] "Lo meu fill, que natura me fa amable, e qui noueylament ve en lo mon" (*Obras*, i, p. 310).

[6] *Obras*, i, pp. 311–4 ; cf. (*e.g.*) *Obres*, ii, p. 4 and pp. 52, 55, above.

[7] *Obras*, i, p. 316 ; Salz., vi, p. 4.

(at greatest length) of temptation and prayer.[1] The first of these divisions describes the nature of intention in the Godhead, and that which we ourselves should have towards God ; the second and third describe the intention of God in creating and redeeming the world ; the fourth is more practical, being divided into thirty sections, on the virtues, deadly sins, ordinances of the Church, and estates of men in the world. A short and uninteresting homily to Dominic ends the book.

Both style and argument are well suited to a young man of Dominic's age and character. Just as the style is more advanced than the maxim-like style of the *Doctrine for Boys*, so the arguments (of the earlier sections at least) no longer suggest the dogmatic writer of text-books but aim at provoking thought. At the same time, the treatise is almost entirely without distinction, and the descriptions of prelate, clerk, prince and knight compare but poorly with the animated pictures of the same types in the *Book of Contemplation*. Ramon was perhaps over-productive during this pleasant sojourn in Montpellier.

For works of all kinds, as will be seen, were issuing from the pen of this ready writer. Only to an enthusiast for his cause could so great industry have been easy. Wars and rumours of wars were all around, and, before Ramon left the city, his old master, King James, had been dispossessed of that fair island which was his former seneschal's birthplace and home. The usurper was not, as it chanced, King Peter ; for, as the elder brother was about to inflict exemplary punishment upon the younger for his rebellion, he had been taken ill with a fever and died (November 11, 1285). "He would have been another Alexander in the world," adds his admirer, Muntaner, "if he had only lived ten years longer." [2] But an Alexander of similar temperament succeeded him in his son Alfonso, whom on his death-bed he had bidden take vengeance for him. And it was Alfonso who, while his father was still alive, sailed for Mallorca, invested

[1] Cf. *Obras*, i, p. 316 and Salz., vi, p. 2 ("De divisione hujus Libri").
[2] *Op. cit.*, chap. 146.

Palma, and took it almost immediately, entering it but a week and a day after his succession to the throne of Aragon.[1] So James, unable to cope with his nephew, had perforce to return to Roussillon, where he solaced himself by nibbling spasmodically at the Catalonian frontier.[2]

Amid distractions so grievous as these, we repeat, and in a country so troubled with dissensions, some men might have found it difficult to write. But Ramon's sorrow for his former lord and sovereign, loyal Mallorcan though he was, could not compare with his long-pledged devotion to Lady Valour. His heart surely fixed where true joys are to be found, he wrote for the first time—but not for the last—at a speed so amazing that we can scarcely credit it. The full extent of his industry, indeed, has not yet been indicated. For over and above this prose and verse, these works of such length and intricacy,[3] he composed what many think his masterpiece, the "Romance of Evast and Blanquerna," published together with two opuscules, *The Book of the Lover and the Beloved* and *The Art of Contemplation*, and known, to all who know Lull himself, as *Blanquerna*.

[1] Accounts of Alfonso's campaign differ considerably. The most judicious examination of the facts is perhaps that of Lecoy de la Marche, i. pp. 286 ff.

[2] Aigrefeuille, bk. vi, p. 152.

[3] To the works mentioned above must be added the *Començaments de medicina* (or *Ars compendiosa medicinae*), extant both in Latin and Catalan (Longpré, col. 1107), which probably dates from the concluding months of Lull's stay at Montpellier (*i.e.* early in 1285). *H.L.F.*, No. 84, p. 258.

CHAPTER VIII

Blanquerna (*c.* 1283). Uncertainty as to its exact date. Outline of its narrative. As a whole, Lull's greatest literary achievement. Its faults largely the faults of its epoch. Its merits of characterization, construction and style. The Franciscan spirit in *Blanquerna*. Its portrayal of the social and political life of its time. Its insistence on missionary effort. *The Book of the Lover and the Beloved* and *The Art of Contemplation*: two short works for contemplatives.

THE date of *Blanquerna* is not certainly known, though it can be determined by internal evidence fairly closely. Since it is mentioned at the conclusion of the *Doctrine for Boys* as about to be written,[1] it seems probable that it was begun soon after that work was ended, perhaps at Miramar, perhaps in those years following the visit to Rome which we have tried with doubtful success to account for. If indeed Lull travelled far and wide until 1282, he would have taken up his pen again on settling at Montpellier, and his first task would naturally be to finish this romance. About such travels, as we have seen, there is much in its later chapters, both the nature and position of which may be considered confirmatory evidence for this opinion.

"In a town which is named Montpellier," says Chapter 90, "in the which was written this *Book of Evast and Blanquerna*, there was a great Chapter General of Preachers."[2] Now this must almost necessarily refer to the Chapter-General of Whitsuntide, 1283,[3] and, as the quotation is made nearly at the end of the romance,[4]

[1] *Obres*, i, p. 199: "Wherefore I shall now cease, and we shall treat of the *Book of Evast and Blanquerna*." For the most part, critics have either missed this reference or disregarded it for no good reason.

[2] *Bl.*, p. 383.

[3] See p. 153, above.

[4] If the two opuscules at the end of *Blanquerna* were written before the main narrative (see pp. 178-9 below), Chapter 90 would be very near the end of *Blanquerna* indeed.

it is not unreasonable to date the book in that year. If an earlier reference[1] is, as has been suggested, to a Chapter-General held at Bologna in 1285, then the early part or the middle of that year may more probably be the correct date. But the mention of either Chapter (especially of the latter) might well be a coincidence, for Blanquerna's renunciation of the Papacy is a striking but certainly a fortuitous anticipation of the *gran rifiuto* of St. Celestine in 1294,—a fact which may serve to remind us that such chances do happen in literature.[2] However, the certainty that after 1283–5 Lull did not again reside in Montpellier[3] until 1303, by which time Miramar, so proudly mentioned, and that more than once, in the romance,[4] was brought to ruin (*afollat*),[5] makes it essential to date *Blanquerna* between the two earliest of these years. Some may prefer to take 1283 as the actual date, and some 1284 : all we can say with certainty is that everything points to the epoch, and nothing, except somewhat vaguely, to either year.[6]

The romance is a long one, and being, unlike others of Lull's more important works, available in English, need only be described in such brief outline as is necessary to make a criticism of it intelligible. Blanquerna, the hero, is the son of devout and wealthy parents, Evast and

[1] *Viz.*: in chap. 86 (*Bl.*, p. 367) : "The Cardinal . . . went also to Bologna, where there was to be a general chapter of the Preachers."

[2] Though Gottron (*Franziskanische Studien*, Münster, 1924, vol. xi, p. 220) would place the fifth book of *Blanquerna* for this reason in 1295–6.

[3] Except for periods (in 1287-8, 1289-90 : see pp. 223-33 below) so brief that it would hardly have been possible, even for him, to have written a romance in the time.

[4] *Bl.*, pp. 256, 325, 530.

[5] *Desconort*, lv (*Poesies*, p. 104) ; *cf.* p. 135, above.

[6] Mn. Galmés (*Obres*, ix, p. xiv) thinks the reference in chap. 92 (*Bl.*, p. 388), to a king who complains to the Pope on being disinherited by another king, is to James II's deposition by his nephew in November 1285, but the reference is so vague that it seems to me less likely to be historical at all than any other of those cited (*cf.* Pasqual, *Vindiciae*, i, p. 147). What *is* certain is that, when chapter 65 was written, James II of Mallorca was reigning, for he is referred to by name as king (*Bl.*, p. 256) and the monastery of Miramar as being in existence. All that I should deduce from these two references, therefore, is that *Blanquerna* was nearly finished (at least) by 1285, which we know with tolerable certainty already. (It will be seen from a comparison of this note with *Bl.*, p. 19, that I have now slightly modified my views on this matter.)

Aloma, who "for much time and long" have lived together without children.[1] He is brought up with great care,[2] his parents' intention being to embrace the religious life once he is of age, and leave to him the management of their possessions. But, when they propose this to him, they find to their dismay that he has decided to lead the life of a hermit and would fain take leave of them immediately. Aloma, with a woman's quick wit, bethinks her of a friend's daughter, Natana, who may be able perhaps to dissuade him from his purpose and win his heart. But the only result of a carefully arranged interview between Blanquerna and Natana is that the girl becomes enamoured of the religious life and enters a convent, whither her mother, after a period of rebellion against the daughter's wishes, follows her. Blanquerna, too, takes a pathetic leave of his parents, and departs, whereupon they decide to sell their estates (as Blanquerna's creator had done), endow a hospital, and appoint as its chaplain and administrator "a monk who was a priest, an old man, of good life and a native of other parts." [3] This done, they set themselves to wait upon the patients, and live from day to day by "begging for the love of God." Seven episodes in their new life follow, each illustrating the mortification of one of the seven deadly sins, and the first book (of the five [4] which make up the whole) concludes with an account of their eventual deaths.

The second book contains a long description—in places a slightly tedious one—of Natana's life in her convent, of which she is eventually made abbess. After

[1] See p. 9, above.

[2] Chaps. 2, 3. Here as well as in *D.P.* (pp. 124–8, above) we find some of Lull's numerous and (for his day) progressive ideas on the upbringing of children.

[3] In connection with the appointment of an administrator for Lull's own possessions (see p. 131, above), it is interesting to read (*Bl.*, p. 78) that "Aloma proposed to Evast that they should make some man overseer who was of their own kindred. But Evast said that this was not wise, because kinsfolk are wont to have overmuch pleasure in possessions commended to them, and think and plan how they may be made the heirs." Was this Lull's own experience?

[4] The five books, as the reader of this biography may by now be able to guess, symbolize "the five Wounds which our Lord God Jesus Christ received upon the Tree of the True Cross" (*Bl.*, p. 29).

rising to this exalted position, she makes "ordinance concerning the five corporal senses"—to each of which is assigned a chapter,—and episodes succeed these which deal with the seven virtues, with the three "faculties of the soul," and with watchfulness and prayer.

It is a relief to read that "now we must needs return to Blanquerna,"[1] whom we find in one of Lull's typical forests, "through the strangeness and solitariness of (which) place, and the heavens and the stars, his soul was highly exalted in the contemplation of God."[2] A magical forest it is indeed, and a forest of allegory, for in it is "a fair palace right nobly builded,"[3] inhabited by ten ancient men of venerable mien, who prove to be——a delightful conception!—none other than the Ten Commandments:

> Blanquerna entered a great and beautiful hall wherein . . . were ten chairs of gold and ivory fairly carven, in the which sat the ten commandments in estate of great honour. Right nobly were they clad in silks and gold; great beards had they, and long hair, and in appearance were as aged men. Each one held upon his knees a book, and wept and bewailed very bitterly.[4]

Blanquerna marvels at their grief, and, learning from each in turn how they are "daily disobeyed" by men, can scarcely refrain from weeping also. After they have blessed him and given him leave to depart, he continues his journey "with cheerful spirit," seeking a place in the forest where he may build his cell.

> At the hour of none, when he had said his office, he sat down near to a fountain, and ate one of the seven loaves which he carried with him. When he had eaten, and had drunk from the water of the fountain, he gave thanks to God and continued upon his journey. As he went through the forest, he saw lions and bears and wolves and wild boars and many other evil beasts; and because he was all alone and unaccustomed to seeing such beasts he had fear and was affrighted in his mind. But Hope and Fortitude recalled to him the power of God, and Charity and Justice strengthened his mind, and he fell to prayer, and gave thanks to God, because He had given

[1] *Bl.*, p. 154. [2] *Bl.*, p. 155. [3] *Ibid.* [4] *Bl.*, p. 156.

him such company, whereby he remembered His power, and was enabled to trust in His hope.[1]

Blanquerna's next adventure is with "two ladies, right nobly dressed and very pleasant to look upon," [2] who turn out to be Faith and Truth, with their sister Devotion, and with their brother Understanding, an aged man "garbed in crimson samite, whereby is signified the Passion of the Son of God." [3] Further episodes lead up to the meeting with the *joglar* whose "office" is to extol true worth, and with the emperor[4] who passes them, lance in hand, and afterwards journeys with them to the marble-walled palace of the Lady Valour.[5] The description of their first encounter is most striking:

The emperor . . . related to them both how that in the chase he had pursued a wild boar for so long that he had become parted from his companions. . . . He asked the jester (*joglar*) and Blanquerna if they could give him aught to eat; for hunger constrained him greatly, because two days had passed in the which he had neither eaten nor drunk.

"Lord!" said Blanquerna: "Hard by is a fountain where thou mayest drink the pure water and eat of the fresh grass which grows around it." The emperor answered, saying that without eating he could not drink, and that it was not his custom to eat grass; but that he thought soon to die if he found not some thing to eat of a kind whereto he was accustomed.

Blanquerna led the emperor to the fountain, and they sat all three upon the fresh green grass near by. Blanquerna drew out the three loaves that remained to him, and together they brake their fast and dined.[6]

When at length the three companions part, the emperor has resolved to spend the rest of his days in the service of God and his fellow-men, and Blanquerna becomes more than ever intent upon finding a place for his hermitage. But, after many adventures, including the slaying of a wolf and the rescuing of a maiden from her seducer, he meets an "evil and unruly" knight, Sir Narpan, whom,

[1] *Bl.*, p. 161. [2] *Ibid.* [3] *Bl.*, pp. 164–5.
[4] See p. 145, above. [5] See p. 32, above. [6] *Bl.*, p. 177.

after several unsuccessful attempts, he succeeds in converting. Together they enter a monastery : we lose sight of Narpan, but Blanquerna mounts by successive stages to the dignity of abbot, and a number of chapters, by no means devoid of interest, describe his experiences as a monk. The second part of the work concludes with the " Book of *Ave Maria*," each chapter of which illustrates a clause of the *Ave Maria* by an incident in Blanquerna's rule.

In Book III, the abbot is elected to an unnamed episcopal see, and we learn how he orders and reforms his diocese according to the principles of the eight Beatitudes. Next he becomes Pope, and takes in hand the conversion, reformation and sanctification of the whole world, naming each of his fifteen cardinals after one clause of the *Gloria in Excelsis Deo* :

> " Let the first part be assigned to me " [he says], " because through the dignity of my office I am the first among you. To each of you Cardinals let there likewise be given a part according to the antiquity and dignity of his office, and let each part follow the other according to its order ; and let each part be an office which each one of you shall hold himself bound to honour and maintain in the Court, that Jesus Christ may be honoured in the Court, and that through it He may be honoured in all countries of the world." [1]

Book IV describes the work of these cardinals at some length, and in doing so inveighs against various abuses, political and social, of Lull's day.

For many years Blanquerna holds the papacy, but he has never forgotten " the desire which he had had aforetime to lead the life of a hermit," [2] and there comes a day when he begs of his cardinals leave to renounce his high office, and, alone in some solitary place, to " be the servant and contemplator of God." [3] With great grief they allow him to leave them and he takes up his abode " upon a high mountain wherein was the church of a hermitage, near to a fountain." [4] There his life is described in detail, in words already in part quoted.[5] The fifth and

[1] *Bl.*, p. 320. [2] *Bl.*, p. 402. [3] *Bl.*, p. 403.
[4] *Bl.*, p. 404. [5] *Bl.*, pp. 407–9. See pp. 134–5, above.

last book of *Blanquerna* consists mainly of two opuscules supposed to have been written by the hermit, and called the *Book of the Lover and the Beloved* and the *Art of Contemplation*. After this there remains but one single chapter, in which we come upon the emperor, who has now forsaken the world and is seeking Blanquerna's hermitage :

> Blanquerna ! Who can show thy cell ?
> Where art thou gone ?
> Fain would I be where thou dost dwell
> With God alone ! [1]

A bishop, hearing these words, points out to him the direction he is to take, and thus, abruptly, in the most approved " modern " fashion, the romance ends.

Let it be said at once that, looking at Ramon's prose writings from the standpoint of to-day, we see *Blanquerna* as representing the highest point of his achievement. " Over and over," says the twentieth-century reader, " it is worth the whole *Ars Magna* and its appalling mechanism." [2] Gone are the encyclopaedic mania, the artificiality of construction, the insensitive formalism and the semi-rationalistic arguments which mar so much of Ramon's other work, both early and late. Instead of the reasoner, we have here the dreamer, the mystic, the poet. The obsession of " arts " is removed from him, and true art, of which Ramon was always capable, comes in to take its place. Such questions of serious import as are discussed in the book enter it only in a highly poetized form, with the result that, to our age at least, Ramon is never more convincing, unless it be in some of the most eloquent of his verses. " Filled to overflowing with the beauty of the Infinite, dazzled (*enlluernat*) with the light that never fails, afire with love uncreated, he built his book alike with care and love, and with the deep conviction that the language and the manner of it were factors of the first importance in revealing and making known the beauty of the Beloved, to the end that

[1] *Bl.*, p. 530.
[2] A. E. Waite, in *Occult Review*, London, August 1926, p. 99.

from such knowledge there might issue a burning, overpowering love." [1]

That there are faults in the narrative of *Blanquerna* we can freely admit : they are faults which belong, not to an individual insensibility to art, but to the stage of extreme childhood beyond which prose fiction had not at this time passed. The interest is unequally spread over the whole work : the colloquies of Evast and Aloma tend to become tedious ; the life of Natana in the convent intrigues us as little as does her character ; and if there ever were seven deadly virtues they are the virtues which she inculcates in the sisters. It is only with the second half of the second book that the story ceases to halt, and that, even when its pace is slow, the reader becomes content to dally in its company.

Nor are the characters always drawn convincingly. The good ones, when they meet the bad ones, have an effect upon them which is altogether too instantaneous for the contact to seem in the least natural. This is a trait which we have already found in Lull's less purely artistic writings. It is nowhere more noticeable than here. Sir Narpan may for a time resist Blanquerna, Nastasia may put up a show of fight against her forbiddingly ascetic daughter—but the reader knows at once that they will eventually capitulate, and therefore has small interest in the struggle. Blanquerna, like Evast before him, goes through his unreal world, a Midas of morality, transforming all the bold, bad men he touches, and by a painless and therefore fictitious process making them as good as gold. Where any character proves recalcitrant to the treatment—the cellarer, for instance, the archdeacon and the chamberlain—he is punished by being left undeveloped and undefined, no character at all, but a lay figure.

Yet such defects are few and of small importance by comparison with the book's many merits. That it can be translated, literally and in its entirety, into English, and read with delight, six centuries and a half after it was

[1] From Mn. Galmés' *proemi* to his edition of the romance in Catalan (*Obres*, ix, p. vii).

written, is sufficient commendation. Indeed, we do it less than justice if we fail to realize how little of the prose fiction in Europe is not posterior to it. "It is a century older than Froissart's *Chronicles*, Chaucer's *Canterbury Tales* and Wyclif's translation of the Bible, and a full two centuries than Caxton, Malory and Commines. Two hundred and fifty years separate it from the masterpiece of Rabelais, which occasionally resembles it in minor detail. In Spain, Lull is roughly contemporary with Alfonso the Wise and Juan Manuel, but was older than almost all the men who are commonly spoken of as the founders of Spanish (*i.e.* Castilian) prose."[1] Even in Italy, where genius flowered early, though Dante was almost Lull's contemporary, Boccaccio and Petrarch were not born till about the time of his death.

These facts once realized, *Blanquerna* becomes a masterpiece, not only of Catalan literature, but of European, and its intrinsic merits stand out the more strikingly by reason of its early date. In fairness to Ramon we may consider its successes in characterization first. Blanquerna, who fails to interest us as a youth, captures our regard entirely, once he has left his parents and his adventures have fairly begun. He is not above being tempted, and that sorely—witness the episode of the rescued maiden[2]—and, in spite of the dizzy heights to which he rises, one feels that his individuality is never lost. His progress from triumph to triumph is as regular and as rapid as that of any giant-slaying hero of chivalry, but as the end of the book shows, he has an inner sanctuary of the soul, which fleetingly, from one time to another, we are allowed to see.

Even more skilfully and movingly presented than Blanquerna is Aloma his mother,—a woman of unusual strength both of character and of affection, quick to see an advantage in debate, shrewd enough to consult her obstinate husband only when her decision is already taken, eloquent when love or grief moves her to words, and intensely appealing when even her resource and persuasiveness are reduced to impotence. Never does

[1] *Bl.*, pp. 20–1. [2] *Bl.*, pp. 192–6.

Ramon's art rise to greater heights than in her laments to the Blessed Virgin over Blanquerna's departure :

I have had but one son and he it is whom thy Son takes from me. In peril of evil men and of wild beasts He makes him to go ; alone He will make him to be all the days of his life ; raw herbs he will eat ; his clothing will be but his skin, and his locks, and the air around him. Do thou look down and see how fair is my son Blanquerna in his person and in his mind : think thou how sun and wind and nakedness will darken him and destroy the beauty of his features. When he is cold, who will give him warmth ? When he is sick, who will tend him ? When he hungers, who will give him to eat ? If he fears, who will strengthen him ? If thou aidedst not my son, even without my prayers, where would be thy pity and thy mercy ? Let the grief that I have for my son, as I behold him going to his death, in affliction and penance, alone in the forest, I know not whither, call to thy mind the grief that thou hadst for thy Son when thou sawest Him done to death and crucified.[1]

Lull's other successful characters are nearly all allegorical. The Ten Commandments, to whom even hardened reviewers (of the English version of *Blanquerna*) lost their hearts, are not less real than the shadowy monks and canons who move across Ramon's ample stage and are at once lost to view. The Lady Valour, Faith and Truth, Understanding, and Devotion can all be clearly visualized. Sir Little-care-I and Sir What-will-men-say are shown to us only once,[2] but we recognize them immediately, and welcome them, when at a later date they reappear in *Felix*.[3] A few other persons, too, have the life and warmth of human beings : the nameless bishop, for example, who anticipates Blanquerna in resigning his see to devote himself to contemplation, and, of course, Ramon the Fool, who is meant to be Lull himself :

There came into the Court a man with shaven head and clothed in the garb of a fool. In the one hand he carried a sparrowhawk, and in the other hand a cord to which was tied a dog which he led. This man greeted the Lord Pope and the Cardinals and all the

[1] *Bl.*, p. 74. See pp. 139–41, above. [2] *Bl.*, p. 392.
[3] See p. 210, below.

Court on behalf of the Lord Emperor, and he spake these words: "I am Ramon the Fool, and I come to this Court by the commandment of the Emperor that I may exercise my profession and seek my companions." When he had spoken these words, he gave the sparrowhawk food, and afterwards made it come to his hand two or three times. After this he struck and beat the sparrowhawk with the cord to the which his dog was tied, and again he cried to it that it should come to his hand; but the sparrowhawk, because the Fool had struck it and put it from him, escaped and flew out of the palace of the Pope, and became wild. When Ramon the Fool had lost his sparrowhawk, he struck the dog very severely two or three times; and, whensoever he called it, the dog returned willingly to him.[1]

As skilful as the portrayal of the best of the characters in *Blanquerna* is the narration of the "examples," anecdotes and fables with which the book is studded. Many of the episodes, it is true, which are alleged to have actually taken place, bear the most obvious signs of having been invented, even when they are vividly told. The avowedly fictitious incidents, on the other hand, related by the characters are, as a rule, well presented. Most of them, directly or indirectly, are Oriental, and, as in some of his later books, Lull appears to have culled them himself from Arabic sources. The fables of the wolf's penance,[2] the parrot and the monkeys,[3] and the pine, the fig and the date [4] are cases in point. Each story is told clearly, with no waste of words, and equally brief and pointed is each moral. When the narration is at fault, it is generally through excess of brevity, though the contrast of this with the leisurely trend of the main story is rarely unwelcome.

The style of *Blanquerna*, as a whole, is simplicity itself. Every trace of pedantry and learning has disappeared from Lull's manner, every one of those tendencies to heaviness which in earlier books we have had occasion to notice, every suggestion, however slight, of obscurity. It has been called the style of a wandering friar, but in its

[1] *Bl.*, pp. 317–18. [2] *Bl.*, pp. 197–8.
[3] *Bl.*, p. 198. (Reproduced later in *B.B.*, pp. 80–1.)
[4] *Bl.*, pp. 218–19.

simplicity and directness, which often make a lack of verisimilitude seem almost natural, it is rather the style of a child. Who, in reading *Blanquerna*, ever thinks of the encyclopaedist and the philosopher at all? Except in the opuscules appended to it, all the doctrine it contains is simply and naively expounded, most of it by means of anecdote told and picture painted by one who now appears before us plainly as a poet.[1]

Although Ramon had not yet turned from the order of St. Dominic towards that of St. Francis, no one will fail to recognize in *Blanquerna* the true Franciscan spirit which shines through the book from its beginning to its end. The ideal of poverty is extolled, from the account of Evast's wedding in the first chapter, to that of the emperor's renunciation of his possessions in the last. That beautiful phrase, "the poor of Jesus Christ," rings in the ears: "bread of alms," Ramon would say with St. Francis, "is food of angels." Yet the striking story of the Canon of Poverty and the wealthy burgess,[2] which may well be based upon fact, shows that poverty of spirit is set, and rightly so, above the mere abandonment of material wealth. It will be remembered also, in this connection, how the cellarer is reproved by Blanquerna for his attention to the inner man in preparing for a journey.[3] But the author is equally severe in his condemnation of superficial asceticism, especially when it is accompanied by covetousness and lack of charity.[4]

The duty of holy joy is taught by the example of Blanquerna's disciple in the monastery[5]: the same spirit, which enables a priest or a religious, as clearly as any other man, to see life whole, is extolled in the incidents relating to the Canon of Persecution, who enters the taverns, and drinks and dances with those who frequent them,[6] and the Cardinal of "Benedicimus Te," who rides through the city "to see if he can hear any man blessing God" and converts a "ribald man," and through him

[1] Seguí (*cit.* Pasqual, i, 316) tells us that Philip II of Spain (who certainly had a good choice of literary masterpieces) carried this book about with him and read it constantly on certain of his journeys.

[2] *Bl.*, pp. 274–5. [3] *Bl.*, p. 220. [4] *Bl.*, p. 223.

[5] *Bl.*, pp. 216–18. [6] *Bl.*, pp. 299–301.

others, by making him his friend.[1] It might be said that this spirit, in one form or another, dominates the last three sections of the book. For it is intimately connected with the spirit of the preacher and evangelizer, which is everywhere manifest, nor is it in any way contrary to the community spirit, which Lull seems to wish might be extended to other spheres than the monastery.[2]

Another notable characteristic of *Blanquerna* is the light thrown by it, and the stress laid, upon the social and political life of this time. Although the place of Blanquerna's birth is described only as "a certain city," enough is said to prove that it is as a rule the Catalonia, Aragon, and, most of all, Languedoc of Ramon's close personal knowledge that he depicts. Montpellier is mentioned more than once, and it is clear [3] that Blanquerna's monastery is thought of as being near that city, and probable that the Bishop whom he succeeds is of the same diocese.[4] It is the people of Languedoc with whom we mix in these pages. And we use the word "mix" deliberately. There is no longer a procession, a pageant, of mediaeval characters, as in the more imperfect art of the *Book of Contemplation*. We no longer walk round a museum and see them in glass cases, duly catalogued and labelled. Individual characters may not always be well developed, but the whole crowded stage, with its continually changing figures, is for ever alive with movement. The personages may be quaint, unnatural, fantastic, but we accept them—and that is the true test—as we accept the quaint and unnatural figures of some modern fantasy. If they will not fit into our own world, we are willing to go and live for a time in theirs. The discerning mind can penetrate the unreality and extract the truth. It is then that the real Languedoc emerges. "The reader finds that he has strayed by some happy chance into the mediaeval *plaça* of a Levantine city, swarming with a miscellaneous

[1] *Bl.*, pp. 349–50. [2] See (*e.g.*) *Bl.*, pp. 321–2, 379.

[3] *I.e.* from the beginning of chap. 56 (*Bl.*, p. 213).

[4] He is referred to merely as "the Bishop," from which so much would be inferred.

multitude of mendicants and merchants, of *joglars* and light women, of bishops and religious,—and, above all the confusion, rises the Cathedral, lifting up its spires to heaven."[1] It is a real *plaça* in which we meet them; a real Cathedral in the background. The Pope who is so highly extolled is a typical Pope of Ramon's day, and it is the actual court and government of James II that comes in for not inconsiderable criticism.

In this brief survey of an extensive book, no attempt will be made to do more than indicate some of Lull's most constant themes. Among them are a number on which he has already delivered himself, such as the frequency with which women "dye their eyebrows and their hair, daub colours on their faces, and adorn their garments,"[2] a subject which the new *genre* allows him to treat with more flexibility and picturesqueness than was possible in the *Book of Contemplation*:

> The Cardinal of Adoramus Te saw a lady who followed the procession, the which lady was richly adorned with gold and silver and precious stones, and her face shone with the colours which she had placed thereon, even as images shine when man has placed varnish upon them. The Cardinal kneeled before the lady and made as though he would adore her, saying that she was like to an idol, and that for this reason he kneeled to her. Great was the shame of that lady and of all the others that were with her. When the Pope had ended the procession and had sung Mass, he desired to know for what reason the Cardinal had disturbed the procession and had kneeled before the lady. . . . [Then] he made establishment that no woman that was dressed and adorned after the manner of idols should witness his procession nor be in any church wherein he sang Mass.[3]

Other themes already treated are the love of all kinds of men for "great place,"[4] the wrongs done by princes to the Church,[5] the undue wealth of certain of the clergy,[6] and the inaccessibility of those in authority.[7] This is not the last place, as will be seen, where he decries these

[1] Riber: *Vida i actes*, p. 95.
[2] *Bl.*, p. 158; *cf.* pp. 284, 294–5, 391, etc., etc.
[3] *Bl.*, pp. 358–9.
[4] E.g. *Bl.*, pp. 231, 347, 393; *cf.* 402 ff.
[5] E.g. *Bl.*, p. 278.
[6] E.g. *Bl.*, pp. 221, 385 ff.
[7] E.g. *Bl.*, pp. 289–90, 382.

abuses.[1] Themes which have been less common in his work, up to the present, are legal injustices, to which, under this form or that, he devotes a good deal of space —the prevalence of bribery, the harsh treatment of debtors, the scarcity of advocates, the penalizing of the poor, and the like abuses.[2] Other common vices treated are drunkenness and ribaldry (which, as we have noticed, he attacks in a somewhat sympathetic spirit),[3] cheating in business,[4] and the tolerance of brothels on the public roads at the entrances of cities.[5] Most of these abuses are only illustrations of a truth enunciated in the final chapter of the book :

> Scarce any man fulfils the final intent for the which all offices were in the first place ordained ; for the office of clerk was founded first upon a good intent, and the same is true of . . . every other office ; but now have we come to a time wherein a man fulfils not so much as he might the intention for the which the offices and sciences were made. And for this cause the world is in error and strife, and God is neither known nor loved nor obeyed by those that are bound to love and know and obey and serve Him.[6]

For this reason, Blanquerna gives as a penance to the *joglar* who visits him the task of going " throughout the world, crying out and singing first of one office and then of another, and making known the intent for the which were made in the beginning the office of *joglar* and all other offices." [7]

The obligations which Ramon lays upon others are not dissimilar. Though the first three books of his romance are concerned mainly with the sanctification of the faithful, and the fifth deals with the life of contemplation, he manages in all of them to say not a little about the main subject of the fourth—the conversion of unbelievers.

> How many boast that, if occasion came,
> Right gladly they would die by sword or flame !
> But oh ! how few will go on God's Crusade,
> For when they think on Death they are dismayed ! [8]

[1] Cf. *B.B.*, pp. 56–7.
[2] See *Bl.*, pp. 291–2, 381–8.
[3] *Bl.*, p. 349.
[4] *Bl.*, pp. 301–2.
[5] *Bl.*, p. 283 ; cf. *B.B.*, p. 45.
[6] *Bl.*, p. 527 ; *cf.* pp. 156–7, above.
[7] *Bl.*, p. 527.
[8] *Bl.*, p. 300.

Ramon's ever-present sympathy with Jews and Saracens,[1] and his admiration of the noble qualities in their religions[2] are gathered up into a vast yearning, and an irrepressible tenderness for those that "daily through ignorance journey towards the fire that is everlasting."[3] At all costs, more labourers must be found for so ample a harvest.[4] The Bishop Blanquerna, unable to journey to foreign lands, goes every Sabbath to the local synagogue, "to preach and hold discussion with the Jews, to the end that they might become Christians."[5] As Pope, he sends to heathen countries envoys of various kinds, much as Nicholas III had done in actual fact.[6] These envoys will learn the languages of the heathen, "preach to them by example and custom, and by metaphor and similitude,"[7] and convert them. Further, such languages are to be taught in Christian monasteries, as is done at Miramar,[8] and heathen teachers are to be employed if necessary. On another occasion the Pope orders a bishop to receive fifty Tartars and ten friars, and lodge them together that each group may learn the other's language[9]: thirty of the Tartars are converted, and are thereupon sent back to their country with five friars, where they convert the great Khan.[10] Yet again, we read that "two messengers from the king of India came to the Pope, beseeching him to give them students to learn their language,"[11] a request which is at once granted. In the main, Lull still advocates peaceful rather than warlike methods,[12] and is obsessed by the language problem, even discussing the experimental adoption of Latin as a universal language for one city in every province.[13] But he is not now averse to the use of force as well as argument,[14] looks with favour upon the military orders if they use their peculiar advantages to

[1] Cf. *Bl.*, pp. 352–3, 365, where he examines the complaints which they make of Christians.

[2] E.g. *Bl.*, pp. 285, 394.

[3] *Bl.*, p. 281.

[4] See *Bl.*, pp. 161–8, *passim*, 305, 306, etc., etc.

[5] *Bl.*, p. 296; *cf.* pp. 296 ff., below.

[6] See p. 144, above.

[7] *Bl.*, p. 375. For similar ordinances, see pp. 311, 357, 360.

[8] *Bl.*, p. 325.

[9] *Bl.*, pp. 328–9.

[10] *Bl.*, pp. 330–1.

[11] *Bl.*, p. 400.

[12] E.g. *Bl.*, pp. 323, 366–7.

[13] *Bl.*, p. 396.

[14] *Cf.* (e.g.) *Bl.*, p. 330.

the best purpose,[1] and of course laments that " that place is in captivity wherein [Christ] was conceived and born and crucified, for the Saracens hold it in their power." [2] He does not hesitate, in the character of his hero, to admonish the Holy Father straitly upon all these subjects. " The Pope with his companions could order the whole world if he so desired . . . and great sin is to be attributed to the Pope if he use not his power in ordering the world." [3] The Pope of the story, it must be added, goes rather crudely to work : one would hardly have thought that his methods of dividing the world into twelve parts,[4] of pacifying all who are at strife by means of costly presents,[5] and of compelling unbelievers who are subjects of Christian princes to learn Latin and the Scriptures,[6] would have emanated from a mind in many respects so practical as Lull's. Many other of his proposals are both progressive and far-seeing.

Of the two opuscules which form part of *Blanquerna*, the *Art of Contemplation*, though from every standpoint the less important, is much more closely connected with the principal narrative than is the *Book of the Lover and the Beloved*.[7] Blanquerna the hermit desires " to make by art a Book of Contemplation," which may lead him " to have devotion in his heart, and in his eyes weeping and tears, and make his will and understanding the higher rise to the contemplation of God in His honours and His wonders." [8] Not only are Blanquerna's experiences during his contemplation described in detail several times in the course of the book,[9] but he is never once lost sight of from the first chapter to the last, and there are also striking reminiscences of the romance in the chapters on the *Ave Maria* and on the Commandments.[10]

The thirteen chapters of the *Art of Contemplation* comprise a descriptive introduction, and one chapter on each

[1] *Bl.*, p. 327.
[2] *Bl.*, p. 282 ; *cf.* p. 334.
[3] *Bl.*, p. 314 ; *cf.* also p. 360.
[4] *Bl.*, pp. 373–4, and elsewhere.
[5] *Bl.*, p. 333.
[6] *Bl.*, p. 326.
[7] For a comparison and contrast between the two, see *A.C.*, pp. 1–4.
[8] *A.C.*, Prologue (*Bl.*, p. 469).
[9] E.g. *A.C.*, chaps. 1, 5, 8, *passim*.
[10] *A.C.*, chaps. 8, 9.

of "twelve parts, namely these: Divine Virtues, Essence, Unity, Trinity, Incarnation, *Pater Noster*, *Ave Maria*, Commandments, *Miserere mei Deus*, Sacraments, Virtues, Vices."[1] The "art" of the book (in the Lullian sense) consists in the contemplation of the Divine virtues in relation to each other, and then with relation to the other parts of the book. The virtues may be contemplated "in divers manners, one of which is to contemplate one with another, or one with two or three or more. A second manner is that whereby man may contemplate these virtues in their relation with Essence or Unity or Trinity or Incarnation. Another manner is that whereby with these virtues is contemplated Essence or Unity or Trinity or Incarnation. Another manner is in the words of the *Pater Noster* and the *Ave Maria*, etc. A man may contemplate God and His works with all the sixteen virtues or with any of them, according as he would make his contemplation long or short, and as the matter of the contemplation befits certain virtues rather than others."[2]

No adequate treatment of so vast a devotional plan could be contained within the limits of thirteen short chapters. Lull makes it quite clear that he aims only at giving some brief idea of the method which he recommends, and he further warns his readers that the book is meant to be suggestive and to contain indications of method for their individual guidance. It is not to be supposed, that is to say, that either devotion or profit of any kind will necessarily result from the mere perusal of the book, even if this be undertaken with thought and prayer. It is a manual for practice. Due attention is given to the external conditions of its use,[3] and that it is meant to be used is made abundantly clear:

And when [Blanquerna] had ended his prayer, he wrote down the substance of his contemplation, and afterwards read that which he had written; but in his reading he had less of devotion than in his contemplation. Wherefore less devout contemplation is to be had in reading this book than in contemplating the arguments set forth therein; for in contemplation the soul soars higher in

[1] *A.C.*, Prologue (*Bl.*, p. 469). [2] *A.C.*, Prologue (*Bl.*, pp. 469–70).
[3] *A.C.*, Prologue (*Bl.*, p. 470).

remembrance, understanding and love of the Divine Essence, than in reading the matter of its contemplation. And devotion accords better with contemplation than with writing.[1]

It is for the reader, or the exercitant in Lull's method, to say how far this method is of value to him. To Blanquerna—which means, doubtless, to the author himself—it was helpful. "Because he followed an Art in his contemplation, did Blanquerna so abound in the contemplation of his Beloved that his eyes were ever in tears and his soul was filled with devotion, contrition and love."[2] It is only in appearance that it is a purely intellectual treatise. For those who follow its directions, understanding, will and memory all play their parts, and the mingling of affective language with intellectual imparts, even to the mere perusal of the book, considerable variety. With its more complicated and forbidding chapters may be compared such passages as the simple and beautifully phrased prayer which closes the chapter on Unity, the eloquence of which, in the original Catalan, depends largely upon its quasi-Oriental use of prose-rime[3] and the subtlety of its prose-rhythm. Many other passages in the book reinforce this beauty, and relate the *Art of Contemplation* rather with *Blanquerna*, to which it belongs, than with the other *Arts*, to which those who have not read them might suppose it to be similar.

Intimately allied with *Blanquerna*, however, both in structure and in detail, the *Art of Contemplation* is related to Lull's scientific works by the rigidity of its insistence upon method, and to his life and those of his works which reflect it most clearly by its references to the ideals of evangelization. Here, as elsewhere, Ramon is never for long a pure contemplative. A number of the practical theological problems discussed in others of his works are referred to briefly here: the eternal doom of unbelievers,[4] the implications of sin,[5] the stumbling-blocks

[1] *A.C.*, chap. 3 (*Bl.*, p. 485); *cf.* the concluding words of the opuscule.
[2] *A.C.*, chap. 2 (*Bl.*, p. 480).
[3] *A.C.*, chap. 4 (*Bl.*, pp. 487–8); cf. *Bl.*, p. 183 n.
[4] *A.C.*, chap. 12 (*Bl.*, p. 522; *cf.* pp. 479, 496).
[5] *A.C.*, chap. 6 (*Bl.*, p. 494).

to belief in the Real Presence of Christ in the Sacrament of the Altar.[1] The occupation of the Holy Land by infidels is not forgotten by one who was ere long to be an ardent preacher of crusades.[2] And the goal of the contemplative life which he preaches is represented, not—in this work—as a mystical union with God, but as the infusion of grace whereby he may be enabled to bring others to a knowledge and love of Him :

> Wherefore, since this is so, to Thee, O Love, O Virtue, O Truth, I bind and submit myself all the days of my life, that I may honour Thy graces, and proclaim to unbelievers, and to Christians who have lost their devotion, the truth of Thy virtue and Thy truth and Thy love.[3]

We have kept until last a description of the *Book of the Lover and the Beloved*, which, though in the complete *Blanquerna* it precedes the *Art of Contemplation*, is most fitly treated here. For it represents the climax of the romance, and, according to modern ideas, of the whole of Lull's literary work also. Since Lullian studies in Mallorca and elsewhere have taken renewed life and a more modern orientation, this opuscule, small as it is, has come to be regarded as the central piece of Ramon's work, as the book which brings us nearest to the source of his inspiration and activity, as the earnest of his literary immortality.

Though the theory seems incapable of proof,[4] we have ourselves little doubt that the book was written, at least in part, some time before *Blanquerna*, in all probability at Miramar or in some other place of retirement, and incorporated with the narrative as an afterthought. In the oldest extant catalogue of Lullian writings, indeed—that of 1311—the book appears as a work separate from *Blanquerna*[5] and the distinction was maintained in

[1] *A.C.*, chaps. 7, 11.

[2] *A.C.*, chap. 6 (*Bl.*, p. 495).

[3] *A.C.*, chap. 2 (*Bl.*, p. 477).

[4] Mn. Galmés (*Obres*, ix, pp. xv–xvi) uses arguments which, to say the least, are bold, by which he seeks to prove more than, to my thinking, is possible in the present state of our knowledge. Lull's use of the words *amic* and *amat*, for example, at the end of *L.C.*, can hardly be said to be of any value as an argument.

[5] *Liber Brachernae ; Liber Amici et Amati.*

various early editions. The connection between the two works is very slight ; no characters or events of the novel are alluded to in the *Book of the Lover and the Beloved*, as they are in the *Art of Contemplation*[1] ; nor is there any reference to it, direct or indirect, throughout. The careful reader's irresistible conclusion will be something like this. In writing Chapter 98 of *Blanquerna*—that is to say, the last chapter but two—Ramon has penned a very vivid and detailed description of a contemplative's idealized retreat, based probably on his own experiences in Miramar and Randa. By a natural transition, his thoughts turn to the little book which he has himself made, probably for his own devotional use,[2] in such a retreat. He therefore includes it, by the easy device of representing it as the work of Blanquerna, and makes it his ninety-ninth chapter. But he has already written another opuscule—the *Art of Contemplation*—which he probably intended to be used in a similar way[3] : this he now adds as a final chapter. And now, some kind of epilogue to the neglected and almost forgotten narrative being necessary, one further addition is made. The present hundredth chapter is written, and the two opuscules are combined in one enormous Chapter 99.

Two fairly definite statements are made in *Blanquerna* as to the origin of the *Book of the Lover and the Beloved*, which may well be considered as truth and no part of the fiction. First, we are told that it is indebted, probably for its manner rather than for its matter,[4] to Moslem

[1] Other works of Lull's are referred to in *L.A.A.*, 143, 287 (*Bl.*, pp. 432, 455) ; it may be noted that, if by *Elements* is meant a "Liber principiorum" (see p. 112 above), they are all known to have been written before 1276.

[2] See p. 180, below.

[3] *Bl.*, pp. 469–70.

[4] For Lull merely purposes to make his book "according to the *manner* of the Sufis" : there is no suggestion of indebtedness beyond this (*Bl.*, p. 410). The reference in chap. 88 of *Blanquerna* (*Bl.*, pp. 375–6) is obviously not intended to be taken as fact, for it describes the *Book of the Lover and the Beloved* as having been *translated* from a Moslem work, which, from the nature of it, is impossible ; nor does the description of it tally exactly with the book's content. It seems possible that the book as we have it was modelled on another book of the same or a similar name in Arabic, no longer known. Probst's study, "L'amour mystique," derives the opuscule from Franciscan sources and the *Song of Songs*, and interprets the passage referred to above as a "fiction littéraire destinée à corser l'intérêt du traité mystique, auprès de Chrétiens nouveaux ou

sources. Blanquerna remembers a Saracen telling him of " certain men called Sufis " who have " words of love and brief examples which give to men great devotion ; and these are words which demand exposition, and by the exposition thereof the understanding soars aloft, and the will likewise soars, and is increased in devotion."[1] Secondly, the book is quite clearly described as being the outcome of contemplation. Blanquerna is asked by a hermit in Rome to make a kind of " rule for hermits " —something is meant, no doubt, like García de Cisneros' *Spiritual Exercises* of two centuries later. He agrees, but is unable to begin ; so he resolves to " give himself fervently to the adoration and contemplation of God, to the end that in prayer God should show him the manner wherein he should make the book and likewise the matter of it." His soul rises " to the supreme height of its strength in contemplation," he is " carried away in spirit," and it " comes to his will " that he should write a book of rather a different kind from that which he has been asked to write.[2] Then, as a prologue to the opuscule, comes a short statement of how it was composed :

Blanquerna was in prayer, and considered the manner wherein to contemplate God and His virtues, and when he had ended his prayer he wrote down the manner wherein he had contemplated God : and this he did daily, and brought new arguments to his prayer, to the end that after many and divers manners he should compose the *Book of the Lover and the Beloved*, and that these manners should be brief, and that in a short space of time the soul should learn to reflect in many ways. And with the blessing of God Blanquerna began the book, the which book he divided into as many verses as there are days in the year, and each verse suffices for the contemplation of God in one day, according to the art of the *Book of Contemplation*.[3]

Three *dramatis personae* (if the phrase be allowable) walk through the garden of which the flowers are the

anciens, ou même d'infidèles qu'il voulait convertir, par l'attrait d'une imitation d'un Orient fabuleux" (p. 322). Of *L.A.A.* as a whole he says: "Lull emploie sans doute parfois des formes, des expressions orientales, mais le fond n'a jamais rien de particulièrement musulman."

[1] *Bl.*, p. 410. [2] *Bl.*, pp. 409–10.

[3] *L.A.A.*, Prologue (*Bl.*, p. 411).

"words of love and brief examples" of this book: the Beloved, the Lover and Love.

The Beloved, according to the author himself, is God.[1] The God of Christianity, let it be understood—Three in One, One in Three [2]—"the sovereign and eternal Good," One "infinite in greatness and power and wisdom and love and perfection," [3] a God Who is both immanent and transcendent,[4] Creator [5] and Redeemer [6] of mankind: above all—and most frequently of all—a God most worthy of love, Who can be, wills to be and is sought and found by man, through beauty, through goodness and through truth.[7]

> "O Beloved," said the Lover, "I come to Thee and I walk in Thee, for Thou dost call me." [8]
>
> "Thou, O my Beloved! art so great a Whole, that Thou canst abound, and be wholly of each one who gives himself to Thee." [9]

Again, the Beloved is represented, more particularly, as the Lord Jesus Christ, named, in that one Name, both God and Man.[10] Little is said of His childhood" and nothing further of His life on earth, teaching or example. He comes before us as the Redeemer and the Sacrifice for our sin,[12] and this that He may be held up as the supreme object of our love.[13] There is no dwelling on the physical aspect of the Passion: the Cross is spoken of as a "Place," [14] and the shedding of blood is idealized into the wearing of crimson garments,[15] just as the act of Incarnation is described as Christ's coming "in the vesture of His Lover." [16] If the descriptive references to the Passion be examined one by one, it will be found that they are almost all symbolical.

In Himself, and in Christ Jesus, God the Beloved

[1] *Bl.*, p. 410.
[2] See p. 184, n. 3, below.
[3] *L.A.A.*, 37; *cf.* 39, 69, 83, 178, 202, 205, 250, 263, 265, 267, 269, 305, 308, 310.
[4] *L.A.A.*, 24, 40, 219, 304, 332.
[5] *L.A.A.*, 271, 272, 284, 304, 317, 322.
[6] See p. 184, n. 3, below.
[7] *L.A.A.*, 43, 211, 288, 311, 328, 354.
[8] *L.A.A.*, 297.
[9] *L.A.A.*, 68.
[10] *L.A.A.*, 321; *cf.* 328.
[11] *L.A.A.*, 15 is the sole reference, and that only a passing one.
[12] *L.A.A.*, 101, 153, 276, 313.
[13] *L.A.A.*, 135.
[14] *L.A.A.*, 67.
[15] *L.A.A.*, 262; *cf.* 91.
[16] *L.A.A.*, 30.

Father loves man with an "infinite and eternal love, perfect and complete."[1] He is "true and free, merciful and just with His lover."[2] "Mercy and pity . . . are essentially in His Will, without change soever"[3]; between His mercy and His love there is no distinction.[4] All who love Him He makes to abound in love,[5] arming them for their battles,[6] rescuing them in peril,[7] tending them in sickness,[8] healing their wounds,[9] but grieving not for the grief and the trials which come to them with the healing, for these are His gifts and they but bring them nearer Him.[10]

> "Tormented was I by love, O Beloved, until I cried that Thou wast present in my torments; and then did love ease my griefs, and Thou as a guerdon didst increase my love, and love doubled my torments."[11]

The Lover, again in Lull's own words, is "a faithful and devout Christian"[12]: "longsuffering, patient, humble, fearful, diligent, trustful."[13] As we shall presently show, he is a contemplative, though there are many traits in his character which are applicable to the most varied types of Christian. He has been called by God to a life of self-denial and devotion.[14] He is ascetic as well as mystic,[15] seeking his Beloved by paths that are perilous and long,[16] wearying his body, casting away his wealth and leaving the joys of this world.[17] He is completely weaned from temporal delights,[18] his joy being to serve God,[19] and his grief to see men neglect and offend Him.[20] He desires to live, while his Beloved wills, so that

[1] *L.A.A.*, 111; *cf.* 115, 214.
[2] *L.A.A.*, 33; *cf.* 97, 203.
[3] *L.A.A.*, 161; *cf.* 151, 191, 309, 316.
[4] *L.A.A.*, 166.
[5] *L.A.A.*, 3, 6, 214.
[6] *L.A.A.*, 133.
[7] *L.A.A.*, 303.
[8] *L.A.A.*, 23.
[9] *L.A.A.*, 244.
[10] *L.A.A.*, 31, 51, 95, 106, 166, 191, 217, 230; *cf.* 239.
[11] *L.A.A.*, 109.
[12] *Bl.*, p. 410. A possibly exceptional use of the word is discussed briefly in *Bl.*, p. 415, n. 1. It is also used occasionally of a Christian who is not faithful (e.g. *L.A.A.*, 144).
[13] *L.A.A.*, 33; *cf.* 238, 279.
[14] *L.A.A.*, 35, 297.
[15] *L.A.A.*, 144, 149, 339, 346.
[16] *L.A.A.*, 2, 11, 36, 112, 113, 212, 314, 329.
[17] *L.A.A.*, 12.
[18] *L.A.A.*, 8, 9, 338.
[19] *L.A.A.*, 6, 31.
[20] *L.A.A.*, 4, 34, 99, 130, 201, 248, 253.

he may serve Him upon earth[1]; when he dies, he desires to die as a martyr.[2]

Less clearly defined than the Lover and the Beloved is the figure of Love, which appears to represent the love of either, or to be a synthetic allegorization of the loves of each. Love and the Lover go apart together, to commune of the Beloved.[3] When the Lover is in rapture, Love swoons[4]; when he forgets the Beloved, Love falls sick,[5] or vanishes and cannot be found[6]; when he sleeps, Love dies, but revives when he awakens.[7] Again, Love falls sick and is tended by the Lover, with patience, perseverance, obedience and hope.[8] This is the love which is " born of remembrance," " lives on understanding," and " dies through forgetfulness."[9] Elsewhere, however, Love is a more powerful and transcendent personality. He is seen dowering a lover with noble gifts[10]; he gives the Lover grievous trials to bear[11] and imprisons his whole being,—body, mind and soul[12]; and yet he comes to him to " nurture and direct " his life, so that at his death he may be able to vanquish his mortal enemies.[13] He is sent for to be present at his death.[14] Elsewhere, again, Love is more purely abstract, and is conceived independently of any other personage. He is the enemy of indifference (*desamor*) :

> Love and Indifference met in a garden, where the Lover and the Beloved were talking in secret. And Love asked Indifference for what intent he had come to that place. " That the Lover may cease to love," he replied, " and the Beloved to be honoured." The words of Indifference were greatly displeasing to the Beloved and the Lover, and their love was increased, that it might vanquish and destroy Indifference.[15]

It is this Love that does battle with Truth against Falsehood,[16] and that gives himself to whom he will—that

[1] *L.A.A.*, 52, 80, 176, 281, 322.
[2] *L.A.A.*, 5, 309; *cf.* 254, 255, 359.
[3] *L.A.A.*, 89.
[4] *Ibid.*
[5] *L.A.A.*, 208.
[6] *L.A.A.*, 210.
[7] *L.A.A.*, 240; *cf.* 17.
[8] *L.A.A.*, 245.
[9] *L.A.A.*, 138; *cf.* 224.
[10] *L.A.A.*, 110.
[11] *L.A.A.*, 223; *cf.* 232, 346.
[12] *L.A.A.*, 113–4, 168; *cf.* 300.
[13] *L.A.A.*, 207.
[14] *L.A.A.*, 112.
[15] *L.A.A.*, 163; *cf.* 199.
[16] *L.A.A.*, 192.

is, to those who desire him, for he refuses to constrain free will. And this is the Love that stands between Lover and Beloved, so that "the Lover cannot reach the Beloved unless he pass through Love." [1]

Although these three personages play a very large part in the *Book of the Lover and the Beloved*, the foregoing description of them neither defines its scope nor is in any way suggestive of its beauties. It touches upon a great variety of subjects which have been treated by Lull more fully in his earlier writings. Comparatively few of the paragraphs are philosophical or speculative,[2] and even these hardly ever descend to the puerilities of scholasticism. Nor is much more attention given to Christian doctrine: Lull cannot refrain from preaching the Trinity and the Incarnation by parable and symbolism as well as by precept, since these beliefs are set by him in the forefront of his fight against Islam.[3] But no other dogmas are stressed: the Blessed Virgin is mentioned but twice,[4] the Sacrament of the Altar not at all. There are chance references to the beliefs and practices of the Moors,[5] to ecclesiastical abuses,[6] to the religious life [7] and to astrology.[8] Apart from these, and the main subject of the book, the principal, if not the only theme dealt with is missionary effort and enterprise, references to which have already been made in this chapter [9] and are far too numerous to quote in detail. One striking paragraph may, however, be cited, which illustrates quite exceptionally well the general character of the book, its absence of preoccupation with dogma, and its insistence on love, contemplation and evangelization:

[1] *L.A.A.*, 258, 259; *cf.* 260.

[2] Most of these will be found among the last hundred paragraphs of the book: in *B.L.B.* some of them have been omitted.

[3] For the Trinity, see *L.A.A.*, 261, 266, 269, 270, 302, 306, 307, 362, and the second paragraph of *Bl.*, p. 533. For the Incarnation, see *L.A.A.*, 153, 273, and the references of notes 10 to 16 of page 181 above.

[4] *L.A.A.*, 15, 327.

[5] *L.A.A.*, 154, 285, 286.

[6] *L.A.A.*, 292; *cf.* the last complete paragraph of *Bl.*, p. 535.

[7] *Bl.*, p. 532, § 2. This paragraph, and that of the next note, are not found in all the versions of *L.A.A.*

[8] *Bl.*, p. 534, § 4.

[9] See p. 182, n. 20, p. 183, nn. 1–2, above.

> "Say, O Fool [*sc.* of love]! What is Religion?" He answered: "Purity of thought, and longing for death, whereby the Beloved may be honoured, and renouncing the world, that naught may hinder me from contemplating Him and speaking truth concerning His honours." [1]

Turning now to the main theme of the book—the relations between Lover and Beloved—we find that they are, in the strictest sense of the word, profoundly mystical. This quality, together with the finely sensitive and poetic expression which interprets it, is undoubtedly responsible for the strong appeal which the *Book of the Lover and the Beloved* has made to many of widely differing creeds.

The ideal of the book is the life of Union, in which "Lover and Beloved are so straitly united in the Beloved that they are one actuality in Essence." [2] There is no suggestion of annihilation, or loss of personality, but we can trace a progression in mystical experience from the point where the Lover is asked: "How long wilt thou be with thy Beloved?" and can answer: "For as long as my thoughts remain on Him," [3] to a degree of higher aspiration:

> Said the Lover to his Beloved: "Thou art all, and through all, and in all, and with all. I would give Thee all of myself that I may have all of Thee, and Thou all of me." The Beloved answered: "Thou canst not have Me wholly unless thou art wholly Mine." And the Lover said: "Let me be wholly Thine and be Thou wholly mine." [4]

And thence to a state which must represent at least the threshold of the Unitive Life:

> Whether Lover and Beloved are near or far is all one; for their love mingles as water mingles with wine. They are linked as heat with light; they agree and are united as Essence and Being.[5]

The force which impels the Lover to seek this Union is disinterested, selfless love.[6] Within and without, behind him and before him, is his love.[7] It is not so

[1] *L.A.A.*, 359.
[2] *L.A.A.*, 211.
[3] *L.A.A.*, 25.
[4] *L.A.A.*, 68.
[5] *L.A.A.*, 50.
[6] Cf. *Bl.*, p. 534, § 1.
[7] *L.A.A.*, 358.

much, however, this impulse towards Union which is a distinctly mystical trait, as the method which the Lover pursues to attain his goal. In the *Art of Contemplation*, as we saw above,[1] the contemplation is described as being unspeakably greater than the art. And the path which the Lover takes to his Beloved's abode is not that of Lullian science, nor even of the "acquired science" of theology, but the more direct way of the infused science which comes from "the will, devotion and prayer."[2]

All the best-known experiences of the mystic, as well as the stages which lead to the life of Union, are touched on, though sometimes but lightly, in the *Book of the Lover and the Beloved*. In the Purgative Way, the contemplative longs to flee to the Beloved, but he is held, enchained and tormented[3]; his eyes shed tears, his body undergoes inflictions and endures fasts[4]; but though his trials are doubled, his love is doubled with them.[5] In the Illuminative Way, he experiences "that light whereby the Beloved reveals Himself to His lovers"[6] and calls upon all that love to light their lanterns at his heart.[7] He has now reached the stage where he can sing of the Beloved and of his newly-found joy in Him,[8] and where his soul has no longer to labour, but can lie passively for a time and be attentive to God's workings within it.[9] When Deity and Humanity open the doors and the Lover goes in to the Beloved,[10] he is already perhaps in St. Teresa's sixth mansion; for he has been experiencing the *vistas de esposos*,[11] and enjoying periods of intimate communion with his Beloved. This is that communion which needs no "noise of words" to establish it:

The Lover and the Beloved met, and the Beloved said to the Lover: "Thou needest not to speak to Me. Sign to Me only

[1] See p. 176, above. [2] *L.A.A.*, 241. [3] *L.A.A.*, 168.
[4] *L.A.A.*, 234. [5] *L.A.A.*, 9. [6] *L.A.A.*, 206.
[7] *L.A.A.*, 173. [8] *L.A.A.*, 185.
[9] *L.A.A.*, 28, 29, 31, 278, 288.
[10] *L.A.A.*, 43; *cf.* St. Teresa, *Moradas*, vii, chap. 2, and my *Studies of the Spanish Mystics*, i, p. 194.
[11] *Moradas*, vi; *Studies*, etc., i, pp. 184 ff.

with thine eyes,—for they are words to My heart,—that I may give thee that which thou dost ask."[1]

Like most of the greatest mystics, Ramon says little of the supernatural favours which God has granted him, nor are rapture and ecstasy given a great place in his little classic. He does, however, make several references to such experiences and to spiritual states closely connected with them. Both contemplatives and readers of mystical literature will recognize the state of the "pensive" lover who is "rejoicing in his Beloved" and is insensible to outer things,[2] and that of the lover "singing of his Beloved," as he goes through a city, "as one that was a fool."[3]

Many miscellaneous references mirror different aspects of the mystic's life. He contemplates the Passion and Death[4] and the sacred Humanity[5] of his Redeemer; he strives with God in the mystical strife of love[6]; he endeavours to avoid the perils of overmuch thought and speech[7]; above all, he tastes the intimacies of solitude.[8] Most of the metaphors common to mystical writers occur: the cloud between Lover and Beloved through which they hold converse[9]; the ladder by which the contemplative mounts from earth to heaven[10]; the ocean of love, without port or shore, in which the Lover perishes.[11]

On the psychological side, while the working of the powers of the soul is described poetically[12] and not fully, there are some indications at least of Ramon's actual experiences. We read of the will being in union, the understanding being stilled, and only the memory having power to act[13]; of the failure of memory and understanding to reach God,[14] while both the understanding with the will,[15] and the memory with the will,[16] are able to

[1] *L.A.A.*, 29. [2] *L.A.A.*, 357. [3] *L.A.A.*, 54.
[4] *L.A.A.*, 276. [5] *L.A.A.*, 332. [6] *L.A.A.*, 20, 118.
[7] *L.A.A.*, 142, 159, 208. [8] See p. 189, n. 1, below.
[9] *L.A.A.*, 123. [10] *L.A.A.*, 288, 328. [11] *L.A.A.*, 235.
[12] Or even dramatically, as also, very markedly, in *A.C.*, and elsewhere. See *L.A.A.*, 18, 19, 127.
[13] *L.A.A.*, 54, 227. [14] *L.A.A.*, 92.
[15] *L.A.A.*, 314. [16] *L.A.A.*, 103; *cf.* 128.

do so ; of another attempt made by the understanding alone[1] ; of the contrast between the workings of will and understanding[2] ; of the concentration of all three faculties upon God[3] ; and of the ideal state in which all three are together in union.[4] Some of these references, it is true, admit of more than one interpretation, so that scientifically they are of less value than a similar number would be in other writers ; nevertheless, their interest is considerable.

It remains to add that the *Book of the Lover and the Beloved* not only gives some insight into the mystical life, but also demonstrates how completely the mystic reverses life's common values. Lull makes no pretence of despising the active : indeed, no sooner has he soared to the heights of contemplation than the Beloved leads him down again to the world, where, in fact, he lived so ardently and died so nobly.[5] Nor does he despise the creatures, who are to be loved, he says, for their Artificer's sake,[6] to be valued as a ladder leading from earth to heaven,[7] and even to be prized for their symbolic and allegorical uses.[8] But both the world and life in the world have different meanings for the lover and for the worldling. What, to the lover, is happiness ? " It is sorrow borne for Love." [9] What is loneliness ? It is the companionship of many people.[10] What is dishonour ? It is forgetting the Beloved.[11] Who is rich ? " He that loves truth." [12] To the Lover there is no distinction, such as the world makes, between joy and sorrow, pleasure and pain.[13] Fear is unknown, for so long as his heart is fixed upon God.[14] Night, which men use for sleep, is given him for meditation.[15] Solitude, which men shun, means for him the truest companion-

[1] *L.A.A.*, 139 ; *cf.* 184.

[2] *L.A.A.*, 348 ; *cf.* 19 and the comment upon this paragraph by Professor Edmund Gardner in *Modern Language Review*, 1924, vol. xix, p. 247.

[3] *L.A.A.*, 169 ; *cf.* 189, 220, 335, 364.

[4] *L.A.A.*, 131.

[5] *L.A.A.*, 56.

[6] *Bl.*, p. 533, § 1 ; p. 532, § 3.

[7] *L.A.A.*, 328.

[8] *L.A.A.*, 40, 338.

[9] *L.A.A.*, 65.

[10] *L.A.A.*, 46, 47.

[11] *L.A.A.*, 108 ; *cf.* 289.

[12] *Bl.*, p. 532, § 4.

[13] This theme recurs continually, and is indeed one of the master-themes of the book ; *L.A.A.* 196 is a typical example.

[14] *L.A.A.*, 119, 121, and *passim.*

[15] *L.A.A.*, 147.

ship.[1] Death, which men dread, is to him but one of the gates to the Beloved's city.[2] All these things, and many more which the book expounds, are to the world paradoxes, and they are gathered up into one pregnant paragraph which describes first the outward manifestation, and then the sublime view-point, of the hidden life :

> "Say, O Fool! What meanest thou by a marvel?" He answered : "It is a marvel to love things absent more than things present ; and to love things visible and things corruptible more than things invisible and incorruptible." [3]

On the poetry of the *Book of the Lover and the Beloved* there is no need to dwell, so completely does it expound itself to every reader. Here, as in other respects, Lull's powers were at their height when he wrote this book. The vividness of his parables,—begun, continued and ended in four or five lines—is not more remarkable than the simplicity of the purely devotional passages which kindle with poetry as well as with love. At their best, these paragraphs are inimitable and unforgettable : some few of them will assuredly take rank in English with gems of mystical poetry of the finest water.

Nowhere in all his work is Lull more sensitive than here to the wonders of Nature : the *Book of Contemplation*, in this regard, is by comparison dumb. Many will say that, both here and elsewhere, Ramon never again reached such heights. While he produced nothing as sublime, or as sustained in its sublimity, as St. Francis' great "triumph song of oneness," he is yet so conscious of the Divine immanence in Nature that at times he seems to be writing a poetical commentary on this very theme. He is in the direct line of those mystics who have found their Creator at once in the shining of the stars, in the flowering of His fields, and in His ways with men : in him St. Basil, St. Hilary and St. Augustine find an echo, as well as St. Francis. So in this little classic we watch with him the turbulent stream,[4] the majesty of the

[1] *L.A.A.*, 46, 47, 234, 246, 357.
[2] *L.A.A.*, 342 ; *cf.* 60.
[3] *L.A.A.*, 83.
[4] *L.A.A.*, 4.

lightning,[1] the swift gathering of the waves of the sea,[2] the sunlit clouds shining as brightly as the daystar or the moon,[3] the eclipse in the heavens which brings darkness over all the earth.[4] We are warmed by the splendour of the sun,[5] watch it go down and withdraw its brightness,[6] walk in gardens or fruitful orchards,[7] drink of their cool, clear springs,[8] and rest in their grateful shade.[9] We hear the singing of the birds at dawn in garden and forest,[10] but we hear them also as we tramp over hill, valley and plain,[11] along rough and thorny paths,[12] both long and short,[13] climbing up into the mountain (expressive phrase !),[14] and, from the heights, descending not only to the plains but to the depth of precipices.[15] Not sight alone but every sense we possess is evoked by this nature-lover and poet.[16] We listen to the breeze stirring the faintly trembling leaves[17]; we catch the faintly borne perfume of flowers.[18] And whither does this sensitiveness, this keen delight in the visible world lead us ? To the Divine Nature, is the answer. As one of Lull's own countrymen has sung, of this very work :

> La floreta del prat de rica flayre,
> el cantador aucell,
> el riuet saltador, l'alè del ayre,
> tot, tot li parla d'Ell.[19]

During the centuries which have intervened between Lull's day and our own, a misguided enthusiasm for

[1] *L.A.A.*, 38. [2] *Ibid.* [3] *L.A.A.*, 123.
[4] *L.A.A.*, 206. [5] *L.A.A.*, 6. [6] *L.A.A.*, 304.
[7] *L.A.A.*, 27, 163. [8] *L.A.A.*, 22, 283. [9] *L.A.A.*, 47.
[10] *L.A.A.*, 16, 26–7, 41, 58, 116. [11] *L.A.A.*, 34, 113.
[12] *L.A.A.*, 36, 346. [13] *L.A.A.*, 70. [14] *L.A.A.*, 103.
[15] *L.A.A.*, 56.
[16] I exclude from this enumeration the purely conventional forests, "fair springs," "tall trees," where we expect to meet hermits, sages and fair ladies in this as well as in Lull's other works, and also conventional metaphors of planting, watering, harvesting, etc.
[17] *L.A.A.*, 58. [18] *L.A.A.*, 58.
[19]
> The sweetly scented meadow flower,
> The gaily dancing stream,
> The singing bird, the air's soft breath :
> All speak to him of Him.

(Jordi Canadell : "L'Amich del Aymat." In *Revista luliana*, ii, p. 207.)

exposition has led to many unfortunate attempts being made to " explain " Lull's masterpiece to the simple,[1] attempts both fantastic and prosaic, which too often have explained away the poetry of the book as well as its devotion. From these commentators, the beautiful bird-passages, with their riddling images, have suffered most. Fortunately, in these modern days, the efforts of critics have been directed more and more towards the presentation of a text which shall be as nearly as possible the primitive text of Lull, and the presentation of it without commentary, so that it may give its own message. And in this message, as we shall presently show, lies the most characteristic quality of the Lullism of the twentieth century.

[1] See Obrador's edition of *L.A.A.* (Palma, 1904), pp. 22–3.

CHAPTER IX

1285–1286

Ramon Lull returns to Rome. Death of Martin IV and election of Honorius IV. *The Hundred Names of God*, written in Rome. *The Book of the Tartar and the Christian*. Lull leaves Rome for Paris: his stay there and relations with Philip the Fair.

In March 1285 Ramon turned Romewards once more, and this time his visit was attended with greater success than it had ever been in the past. Its beginnings, nevertheless, were not auspicious, for no sooner had he arrived at Rome than the mischance of eight years earlier[1] was repeated: the news reached him that Martin IV, another of the French popes who might have favoured his plans, had just died (March 28) at Perugia.

On hearing this, Ramon left Rome, attended a second Chapter-General of the Dominicans, held at Bologna that Whitsuntide,[2] and then returned to Rome to seek an interview with the new Pope, Honorius IV, which was granted. If he had left the Holy City immediately on hearing of Martin's death, anticipating a long interregnum, he could hardly have been more mistaken. Only four days elapsed before Honorius was elected—one of the speediest elections in the Papal history. In this Pope, Ramon had at last one who believed both in his plans and in his abilities to translate them into action,—one who, further, was himself a man of action. The annals of Spondanus give some idea of one direction which his activity took:

In the first year of his pontificate, the said Honorius, desiring very ardently the propagation of the Christian faith, by means of

[1] See p. 143, above. [2] See p. 160, above.

the conversion of the Saracens and the reduction of the schismatics of the East, required that the study of Arabic and of the other languages of the heathen should be established at Paris . . . and, to this end, he sent letters to Jean Cholet, Cardinal of Saint Cecilia and Apostolic legate in France. For the foundation of these colleges and the conversion of the Saracens there worked with ceaseless industry and the greatest eagerness the Catalan Ramon Lull, of whom we have made mention above, and who, in this cause, made difficult and perilous journeys in Italy, France and Africa.[1]

There are other traditions concerning the influence which Ramon had upon Honorius—none of them, however, so well attested as this. It is said, for example, that the Pope established a school of heathen languages at Rome ; that he definitely set up the Miramar college as a model for this school and others ; that the disbanding of the so-called religious order of the Apostles by the Pope's command in 1286 was due to Ramon's denunciations of them[2] ; and so on. The only deduction which we may safely draw from these traditions is that Ramon had a certain influence with the Pope, a fact which in itself is important.

In Rome, during this same year 1285, Lull wrote another work in verse, the *Hundred Names of God*, a series of one hundred rimed poems, each of ten three-lined stanzas, and each describing one attribute of the Deity. It is addressed to the Pope and his Cardinals, with a prayer that they will cause it to be put into Latin, since he, Ramon, is "ignorant of grammar."[3] A passage from

[1] *Annales*, 1285, *cit.* Pasqual, *Vindiciae*, i, chap. 17, pp. 165–6.

[2] Ramon certainly refers to this order with veiled disapproval in *Blanquerna* (chap. 76, *Bl.*, p. 306) and more sternly (perhaps a significant fact) in *Felix*, written in 1286, just before the order was disbanded (*Felix*, bk. viii, chap. 13 ; *Obras*, iiib, p. 49 ; *cf.* iiia, p. 168).

[3] This confession (from the prose introduction to the book) might seem to prove that Lull knew no Latin. But this view, though it has been seriously put forward, is quite untenable. Since he lectured for a year in the University of Paris soon after this date, and since, further, he uses a number of Latin words in this very poem, we conclude that his ignorance was merely comparative, and was confined to an inability to turn his native Catalan into elegant Latin verse, or even into a prose comparable with that of the Korân which he cites. There is no reasonable doubt that a number of his works earlier in date than 1285, and already described, were written originally in Latin, and one who in middle life could master so difficult a language as literary Arabic

the prologue describing the source of the basic idea of the book is so characteristic as to deserve quotation :

Since the Saracens believe that they have proof that their law is given them by God in that the Korân is so wonderful a writing that—as they say—none can make another like to it, therefore I, Ramon, unworthy as I am, would strive with the aid of God to make this book, in the which there is better material than in the Korân. . . . In that book the Saracens say that there are ninety and nine names of God, and that he who knows the hundredth Name will know all things. Wherefore I make this book of the Hundred Names of God ; and, since it follows not that I know all things, I do it to reprove their false opinion.[1]

Apart from the polemical motive for writing the book, Ramon seems to have thought of it as having an intrinsic " virtue," which commentators have described as " talismanic " and attributed to Arabic influence.[2] He intended his hundred " psalms "—for so he terms them—to be sung in church, " as the Saracens sing the Korân in their mosques," a brief *laor* appended to each having a relation to it similar to that of the *Gloria Patri* and the Psalms of David. The book is also of value, continues the introduction, " for contemplating and knowing God and for proving the Christian faith, . . . for consolation and delight and for preaching." In reality, any value it may have had under the last three heads has long since disappeared.[3] It seldom reaches a higher level than one of monotonous didacticism, in which

would surely not fail to learn so easy and so necessary a one as Latin. Proofs that he knew it at a later date than this abound. See S. Bové : " Ramon Llull y la lengua latina," in *Boletín de la Real Academia de Buenas Letras de Barcelona*, vol. viii, pp. 65–88, Rubió y Lluch, *art. cit.*, pp. 285–6, and Rubió y Balaguer : " La Lògica del Gazzali posada en rims per En Ramón Lull," in *Anuari de l'Institut d'Estudis Catalans*, 1913–14, pp. 317–18. Further references, and a sane commentary on the point at issue, will be found in Longpré, col. 1112.

[1] From the same introduction (*Obras rimadas*, p. 201). On the question of the ninety-nine names, see *Journal of the Royal Asiatic Society*, New Series, vol. xii, pp. 1–70.

[2] See, *e.g.*, J. Ribera in *Homenaje a Menéndez y Pelayo*, 1899, ii, pp. 211–12. Lull himself writes : " As God has placed virtue in words, stones and grass, how much more has He placed in His names."

[3] An interesting study of the sources and significance of this work will be found in R. Otto, *art. cit.*, pp. 515–23.

its verse-form has little meaning[1]: all Lull's commentators seem for once to agree, in calling it dull.[2] From this dulness its principal deviation is into the sententious, where, it must be admitted, the short lines to which Lull generally limits himself aid him to write pithy, maxim-like stanzas,[3] and the shortness of these stanzas themselves makes discursiveness difficult. Yet there is little beauty or interest in these maxims, unless it is where an unexpected quaintness adds point to their trite moralizing :

In dungeon foul of sin imprisonèd to be
Is evil plight indeed, for never man is free :
God keep us from that same, through His great clemency.[4]

Somewhat rarely, the personal note is sounded,—a note of melancholy, as a rule, such as we have seldom found in Lull's writings up to the present. There are so many abuses in the world ; God is so little loved ; Christ is so unfaithfully preached.[5] And Ramon is sad because of it :

Ofttimes for sorrow tears I shed,
For few are the men that I have led
To preach God's grace to souls that are dead.[6]

[1] Cf., *e.g.*, ii (O Essencia), iii (O Unitat), lxxxii (O Movent), xciii (O Intenció Principal).

[2] Mn. Riber among them ; though he characteristically instils some of his own poetry into his severe criticism of the *Cent Noms de Deu* (see *Vida i Actes*, p. 100).

[3] Some of these may be compared with the maxims of the *Libre de Proverbis*, written eleven years later ; *cf.* p. 273, below.

[4] lxxxiii (*Obras rimadas*, p. 285) :

Estar pres en carçre de mal e peccat
Es presó mala e sens nulla libertat ;
D'aytal presó nos guard Deus per la sua pietat.

[5] Cf. *Obras rimadas*, pp. 237, 244, 250, 281.

[6] lxxv (*Obras rimadas*, p. 277) :

Tristicia 'm fa sovén plorar,
Car no puch molts homens concordar
Que als infaels vagen Deus mostrar.

Occasionally these passages take on a more resolute tone :

Aquell que volria procurar
En la Terra Sancta a recobrar,
No deuria tròp dormir ne sajornar.

(xciv : *Obras rimadas*, p. 296.)

One or two of these personal laments are the lines best worth reading in the book, for in them is reflected the character of that faithful and true lover of God which Ramon is and will be to Christian readers for all time. Some of his simplest stanzas, apart from these, are his most appealing, whether he is repeating his childlike creed-litany of the Name of Jesus,[1] or expressing in his own words the fundamental truths of the Gospel[2]:

God, Who art our most loyal Friend,
In all the ideals that love can blend
Thou art our All, Thou art our End.

* * * * *

A Friend for His mighty love is He:
His pardon and grace are full and free:
In our hearts He would fain for ever be.

* * * * *

Dearer than wealth untold is the love
Of lover below and Beloved above
When charity deep their hearts doth move.[3]

or whether, most rarely of all, he fringes the territory of the mystic:

To those who in contemplation live
The sight of Himself our God will give,
And this is love's high prerogative.

* * * * *

[1] xxxiii: O Jesús (*Obras rimadas*, p. 235).
[2] *Cf.* lxxi (p. 273): O Servit, and lxxxvii (p. 289): O Amich.
[3] Deus, qui ets Amich molt leyal!
Tu est tot lo nostre cabal
En tot ço que amor val.

* * * * *

Es Deus Amich car vòl amar,
E vòl donar e perdonar,
E vòl en cor de home estar.

* * * * *

Amistat d amich e d amat
Val mays que tot l aur monedat
Com se aman ab gran caritat.

He that sees God with the soul's clear sight
Has tasted of glory infinite :
No more can he stray in sin's dark night.[1]

To the years spent in Rome, where the conversion of the Tartars, so greatly hoped for at the time, was a continual subject of discussion, belongs the *Book of the Tartar and the Christian*, also called *Book on the psalm "Quicunque vult,"* which we have in Latin.[2] This is another of Lull's narrative works which embodies a debate on theological subjects. A rather attractively presented Tartar has for a long time been anxious about his soul, and would have sought counsel from some religious teacher had not thoughts of his wives, children, and home, and of the material losses which might follow his conversion, impeded him. The death of a certain knight who is a close friend of his leads him to think seriously about the future life. " Hic, qui prius fuerat potens, possidens multa," he reflects, " modo factus est impotens, nihil habens." [3] So he goes for advice to a Jewish teacher, learns from him of the Jewish faith and is only repelled by it. The same result follows a consultation with a Saracen, whereupon the Tartar visits a Christian hermit,[4] hoping in his beliefs to find satisfaction. But here he meets with the worst fortune of all, for the hermit refuses to enter into any discussion. " If you will be led into the way of truth," he says, " follow the Christian religion, for the truth has been given us by Christ Jesus, Very God and Very Man, Who died for our redemption and salvation." [5]

" What ! " cries the Tartar. " Do the Christians believe that God became man, and died ? "

[1] xcvi : O Invisible (p. 298).

Segons natura de cogitar
Se pot Deus veer en l amar,
En lo qual lo fa honrat estar.

* * * * *

Veer Deus ab vista espiritual
Es veer que mays que altre val,
E qui mays guarda hom de tot mal.

[2] Salz., vol. iv : *H.L.F.*, No. 23 (pp. 144–8).

[3] Salz., vol. iv, pp. 1–2. [4] *Ibid.*, pp. 2–4. [5] *Ibid.*, p. 4.

"They do," replies the hermit. And, in due order, he recites to him the articles of his creed.

"And how can all this be?"

"Ah, as to that," returns the man of God, "I cannot say. I can only take it on trust."

By this time night is coming on, and the Tartar, in despair of discovering a religion acceptable to him, remains at the hermitage. On the next day, he proposes to return early to his own city, but first watches his host saying Mass, and at the moment of the elevation, his curiosity being thoroughly aroused, interrupts him. For the moment, naturally, his questions are unheeded, but, after the service is over, he is enlightened,—or, more correctly from his own point of view, is plunged into greater darkness than before.

"We pay no attention to aught else," the hermit tells him, "when we are engaged in the most holy Sacrifice of the Body of Christ. It was His Body that was in my hands."

The Tartar, of course, is stupefied, as well he may be. "I wondered before," he says, "but now I am more vehemently amazed. That bread which was in your hands was God and man? Clearly, your faith is meaningless." [1]

Then the poor Art-less hermit bethinks him of a comrade more learned than himself.

"Go to the hermit Blanquerna," he advises him. "Blanquerna will explain." [2]

Needless to say, Blanquerna does so, and to the Tartar's complete satisfaction. When did Blanquerna ever fail? It is on a Sunday, at about the hour of prime, that the Tartar comes upon the super-hermit, who is reciting the *Quicunque vult* and vesting for Mass. At the end of the service, the enquirer lays bare his difficulties: the idea that God is a Father, that He has a Son Who can die, or Who can continually become bread at the simple words of a hermit. He recounts what has happened to him, whereupon Blanquerna reassures him. The Christian faith *can* be understood, he asserts. And he gives him the *Quicunque vult* to read! [3]

[1] Salz., vol. iv, p. 4. [2] *Ibid.*, pp. 4–5. [3] *Ibid.*, p. 5.

The initial effect of the reading is to make confusion, if this be possible, still worse confounded. But no sooner has the Tartar read the words through than Blanquerna begins to explain them. There are thirty-five verses in the hymn, and each is expounded in its turn, frequently at no great length, by means of "metaphoras sumptas a vegetativo, sensitivo et intellectivo in conjuncto."[1] After this exposition, Blanquerna adds another on the mystery of the Eucharist and the Tartar begins to feel "the grace of the Holy Spirit coming to him." Can Blanquerna explain it all in any other way? Yes: "per metaphoras sumptas ab Angelis et a corporibus supracelestibus."[2] But at this moment—and we must suspect no irony!—the honest enquirer finds himself suddenly and completely convinced. Grace has supplied faith to one whom understanding has prepared to receive it. "Blessed be the Lord God Almighty," cries the Tartar, "and blessed be all His works, and blessed be the time and place wherein I found Blanquerna!"

There follows a long and noble prayer which the convert offers to God,[3] after which he asks for baptism and is instructed to go and seek it of the Pope. "And, once baptized," adds the hermit, "return home, and preach the faith of Christ, and fear not death, but suffer and labour, as Christ suffered and laboured, for the good of all men."[4]

The Tartar duly arrives at Rome and the Pope grants his desire. At his own request he is given the name of Largus.

"And why hast thou chosen such a name?" the Pope enquires, when the rite is over.

"Because God was so bountiful (*tam largus*) to men in sending His Son to earth," is the reply, "that I desire to perpetuate His bounty. Nam propono me *largiri* morti ex amore illius, qui pro me fecit illud idem."[5]

So the Pope blesses him and offers him any legitimate favour that he may care to ask. In reply he begs that a book which Blanquerna gave him, containing an account

[1] Salz., vol. iv, p. 26. [2] *Ibid.* [3] *Ibid.*, pp. 26–8.
[4] *Ibid.* [5] *Ibid.*, p. 29.

of their conversations together, may be translated into many languages, in order that the heathen may know what the Christians really believe, and not be misled, as he himself was.

The request granted, Largus takes leave of the Pope. And, as he goes, some of the dignitaries standing by drive home one of Ramon's pet teachings. "Would that the Pope would send more of such messengers over all the earth!" exclaims one. While another cries: "Would that a great Prince might be found to lead a new crusade, and to lay down his arms only when no infidels are left to oppose the Catholic faith!"[1] Ramon is becoming converted to the use of force, it would appear: he has already moved some way from his original position.[2] But, although the question of these alternative methods is now taken up, the book—which has been an interesting and highly characteristic one, short and never diffuse—peters out in an inconclusive discussion.

When Ramon left Rome, probably in the spring of 1286, it was to go to the important and influential University of Paris, with the active goodwill of Honorius, and possibly even at his suggestion. A letter[3] from the Pope to "Nicholas [de Nonancuria], Chancellor of Paris" had preceded him, in which the writer, "ad exemplum pontificum Innocenti IV, Alexandri IV, Clementis IV et Gregorii X,"[4] urges that instruction in Oriental languages be provided for missionary students in the University.[5] In all probability Ramon bore further letters from Honorius, recommending him to the courtesy

[1] Salz., vol. iv, p. 30. [2] See p. 30, above.

[3] Denifle et Chatelain: *Chartularium Universitatis Parisiensis*, Paris, 1889, ff., i, pp. 638–9 (No. 527). The letter is dated Jan. 23, 1286.

[4] Cf. *ibid.*, i, p. 212 (No. 180), reproducing a similar letter from Innocent IV which asks for provision in the theological faculty to be made for ten scholars skilled in Oriental languages, and p. 372 (No. 324) reproducing a letter from Alexander IV.

[5] "ut clerici, in Arabica lingua et in ceteris partium Orientalium linguis eruditi, qui Parisius mittebantur, pro necessariorum defectu ab incepto studio desistere non cogantur."

of the Chancellor and desiring for him freedom and encouragement to expound his projects and doctrines.[1]

On examining the accounts of Ramon's sojourn in Paris, we are brought face to face with statements apparently contradictory. The contemporary Catalan biographer relates that "when he was at Paris, he lectured publicly in the school of Master Britolt, Chancellor of the said University. And when he had been there for some time and had seen the manner of the University he went to Montpellier."[2] The Latin Life adds that, at the behest of the Chancellor, Ramon lectured in Paris on his *Art General*.[3] Seguí, following a well-established tradition, relates that forty experts were instructed by the Chancellor to examine the *Art*, and that they concurred in approving it,[4] with the result that its author lectured in the University for about a year, receiving the title of "Master," which in fact he uses on occasion from that time forward to describe himself in his own writings.[5]

The "Master Britolt" here mentioned is none other than the somewhat notorious Berthauld de St. Denis,[6] whose dictatorial and autocratic rule involved the University in such continual tumult that he had in the end to be sent to Rheims as Archdeacon, whence he was promoted shortly afterwards to the bishopric of Orleans.[7] A fine, if vehement orator, and a learned and intrepid theologian, Berthauld was nevertheless unfitted to govern a university at a time when theological feeling ran so high. It may have been the dissatisfaction of Ramon

[1] Longpré (col. 1080), who follows *V.B.R.L.* in its reference (*Life*, p. 58) to the death of Honorius IV, suggests that it was the hearing that this letter of Jan. 23, 1286 had been sent which brought Lull to Rome.

[2] *V.C.* iv. (*Life*, p. 17); cf. *Life*, pp. 16, 58, and pp. 142-3 above.

[3] *V.B.R.L.*, ii (*Life*, p. 58): "Veniens ergo Raymundus Parisios tempore Cancellarii Bertholdi, legit in aula sua Commentarium Artis Generalis de speciali praecepto praedicti Cancellarii, perlectoque Parisiis illo Commentario, ac ibidem viso numero scholarium, rediit ad Montem Pessulanum . . . etc."

[4] *Cf.* p. 343, below. Is this tradition due to a confusion with the event there recorded?

[5] *Cf.* Longpré, cols. 1077–8, for another suggestion as to this.

[6] *Chartularium*, etc., ii, pp. 23, 43–6, 47–8, 66–7, 70, 97, 120.

[7] *Chartularium*, etc., Letters of Aug. 6, 1290, Oct. 15, 1290, Nov. 16, 1295. Apparently Berthauld persisted in exercising various of the Chancellor's duties after his promotion and Boniface VIII had to intervene.

with the "manner of the University" which decided him to leave it.[1] It is difficult, however, to accept the authority of the contemporary biography here, for Berthauld did not succeed to the Chancellorship till the very end of 1288, holding it until August 1295. The earlier of these two dates is certainly correct, being based upon irrefragable documentary evidence.[2]

Not many of Lull's biographers have known or taken account of this fact,[3] and those who have done so have assumed the contemporary Life to be correct and dated Ramon's sojourn in Paris as beginning later than 1287.[4] This chronology has the advantage of making it possible to justify the reference of the Latin biography to the death of Honorius IV [5]; but a study of the activities of Ramon between 1287 and 1295, as outlined in the following pages, will show that no possible time can be found for the Parisian visit and lectures during the Chancellorship of Berthauld, and the only reasonable conclusion is therefore that the contemporary Life is mistaken in its reference to him. This supposition is the less unlikely since the passage in question occurs at a place where the biography is very faulty,[6] and it does not preclude the possibility that Ramon did meet and have intercourse with Berthauld at this time, though the latter could not then have been Chancellor.

[1] Though I hardly think that this is implied by either *V.C.* or *V.B.R.L.*; *cf.* Pasqual, *Vindiciae*, i, p. 170. Wadding (*Annal.*, 1287, *cit.* Pasqual, i, p. 371) states that Lull's teaching was badly received at Paris, but Pasqual considers him biassed.

[2] *Chartularium*, etc., Letters 550–1, directly disproving *H.L.F.*, p. 14, which dates Berthauld's chancellorship from 1287 at latest, and possibly from as early as 1285. Letter 550 is written by Honorius to Nicholas de Nonancuria on Dec. 1, 1288, and styles him Chancellor. The following letter is written on Dec. 31, 1288, to Berthauld as Chancellor.

[3] *Cf.* Av., p. 270; Riber, *Vida i Actes*, p. 103; Galmés, p. 52.

[4] *Cf.* Keicher, p. 25: "Daher machte er sich auf den Weg nach Paris, wo er frühestens in Dezember 1288 eintraf." But, even if *V.C.*, *V.B.R.L.*, be correct, he might have arrived in Paris before Berthauld succeeded Nicholas; the only essential would be that he should have been there during his chancellorship.

[5] Cf. *Life*, pp. 16 n., 58. If Ramon had not left Rome before the end of 1288 he might easily have arrived there after Honorius' death, which occurred on April 3, 1287. But I repeat that I cannot fit *V.B.R.L.* into any possible chronological table.

[6] *Cf.* p. 143 n. 1 above.

Two other of Lull's activities in Paris during this period are known to us. It is at least highly probable that he attended yet another Chapter-General of the Dominican Order which was held at Paris in Whitsuntide, 1286, and pleaded his cause once more.[1] It may be presumed that his appeal was entirely without success, for, from this time onward, we find him attending Chapters, not of the Dominicans, but of the Franciscans. "Ah, Understanding and Will!" he had written not long before, "Cry out and awaken the watchdogs that sleep, forgetting my Beloved. . . . And, Memory, forget not the dishonour which is done to my Beloved by those whom He has so greatly honoured."[2] The "watchdogs of the Lord" were to be separated yet farther from Ramon before long, and, later still, were to avenge themselves upon his memory.

A more auspicious visit—for he could have had few expectations from the Preachers—would have been that to Philip the Fair, King of France, who had succeeded his father, Philip III, in 1285, and whose mother was the sister of the disinherited James of Mallorca. In all probability, James himself was at the French court just then, France being the most appropriate refuge for him after his exploits with its late king against the recently deceased Peter. With a royal introduction, and the known favour shown to Ramon by Pope Honorius, Philip could hardly refuse to see him, and one author at least is bold enough to ascribe to Ramon's importunity the supposed foundation by the King of a missionary college in Navarre which was afterwards transferred to Cambrai.[3] But this would seem doubtful, both from lack of corroborative evidence and because European affairs were exceedingly disturbed, the Sicilian question having in no way been settled, as we shall presently see, by Peter's

[1] Pasqual, *Vindiciae*, i, p. 171, and *Desconort*, xiv (p. 259 below). This would make the third of the three Dominican Chapters mentioned in the latter reference, the others being those of Montpellier, 1283, and Bologna, 1285 (pp. 153, 192 above).

[2] *L.A.A.*, 127 (*Bl.*, p. 430). The reference is, of course, to the *Domini canes*.

[3] Vernon, *cit*. Av., p. 246.

deathbed renunciation of the island-kingdom to the Pope. A fourteenth-century miniature represents Ramon at Philip's court, presenting three of his books to a lady who is probably the Queen or the Queen-Mother.[1] No suggestion of any interest on her son's part is conveyed by the picture, and Ramon himself, in a clearly autobiographical passage, written about 1286, is suspiciously silent about the result of his interviews with Philip :

> A man who for a long time had laboured for the utility of the Roman Church came to Paris and said (*dix*) [2] to the King of France and to the University of Paris that there should be established in Paris monasteries, wherein should be learned the languages of those that are unbelievers ; and that into these languages should be translated the *Ars demonstrativa* ; and that with that *Ars demonstrativa* men should go to the Tartars and preach to them and show it to them ; and that there should be Tartars at Paris who should learn our writing and language before returning with this knowledge to their own country. All these things, and many besides, were brought by that man before the King and the University of Paris, and he desired likewise their confirmation by the Pope and their establishment in perpetuity.[3]

From what is not added to these words, as well as from absence of all testimony to the contrary, it would appear that Ramon obtained little from King Philip except good wishes.

[1] See Jordi Rubió : "El Breviculum, etc.," p. 88 and Fig. 18.

[2] *Cf.* pp. 279-80 below.

[3] *Felix*, bk. viii, chap. 46 (*Obras*, iiib., pp. 210–11). It will be observed that it is still the conversion of the Tartars (rather than the Moors) which is uppermost in Ramon's mind.

CHAPTER X

1286–1287

Works written in Paris. *Felix, or the Book of Marvels* (1286). Argument of the book. *Felix* compared with *Blanquerna,* to its disadvantage. The autobiographical element in *Felix.* Special interest of its seventh part, the *Book of the Beasts.*

Of the three or four works which Ramon wrote during his stay in Paris only one still enjoys any reputation. A book of which the title promises the reader " visions of delight " (*Libre de plasent visió*) is clearly mentioned by Ramon himself[1] as having been written about this time, but nothing unfortunately is known of its whereabouts, or (apart from what he tells us here) of its nature. His *Book of the fourteen articles*[2] is an attempt to prove the Christian faith from a position differing slightly from any which he had taken hitherto : he connects the fourteen articles with the fourteen Divine dignities, and endeavours to show that to deny the former is in effect to deny the latter.[3] *The Dispute between a Believer and an Unbeliever*[4] puts forward the commonest objections which infidels have raised to the Faith, together with solutions to them. " Ramon, unworthy servant of God,"

[1] See *Felix,* bk. viii, chap. 14 (*Obras,* iiib, pp. 52–3), and Rosselló's note in *Obras,* iiia, p. vii. Apparently Bonlabi knew it (see Prologue of his translation (1521) of *Blanquerna*).

[2] *Liber de quatuordecim articulis sacrosanctae romanae catholicae fidei:* Salz., vol. ii ; *H.L.F.,* No. 11 (pp. 113–14).

[3] He returns in this book to his former custom of self-depreciation, referring to himself in the Prologue (Salz., ii, p. 1) as " culpabilis et peccator et multum inops scientia et meritis ac caeteris rebus." This would of itself suggest an early date, but other internal evidence puts it later. Pasqual (*Vindiciae,* i, p. 161) dates it from Montpellier in 1283. There is no external evidence.

[4] *Disputatio fidelis et infidelis,* Salz., vol. iv (cf. *H.L.F.,* No. 24, pp. 148–52).

presents the book to the University of Paris in his self-conferred character of "procurator of the unbelievers,"[1] begging the authorities to examine it, correct its errors if it contains any, and afterwards present it to such preachers as he hopes they will send out to convert the world. This work, therefore, seems to be closely connected with Ramon's petitions to the King and the University. We do not know if it was ever used.

The glowing terms in which Ramon writes of the University suggest that, far from disapproving of or being discouraged by anything that he has found in it, he has considerable expectations from its authorities. To it, he says, the whole world looks for enlightenment in the way of truth,[2] and from it men shall go in great numbers to convert heathen philosophers, so that in the end the entire human race shall owe its knowledge and love of God to the illumination which comes from Paris.[3]

Neither in plan nor in content is the book very remarkable. A Catholic explains his religious beliefs to an infidel, and the infidel opposes to them his own views, that they may see which are the stronger and the better grounded. The eight sections deal in turn with the existence and nature of God, the Trinity and the Incarnation, the Sacraments, the beginning of the world, the resurrection, and the problems of predestination and free will.[4]

The one outstanding work which Ramon produced during this sojourn in Paris[5] is his fantastic romance entitled *Felix, or the Book of Marvels*.[6] The importance of this is comparable both in nature and in degree with that of Lull's other great romance, *Blanquerna*, and, since it is less accessible to English readers, it must of necessity

[1] Cf. *Blanquerna*, Chap. 61 (*Bl.*, pp. 236–37).

[2] . . . a qua totus orbis terrarum se exspectat illuminari in viam veritatis (Salz., iv, p. 1).

[3] . . . ita quod lux supremae scientiae et honestatis vitae Parisiis edita illuminet mundum universum ad cognitionem et dilectionem Dei (Salz., iv, p. 1).

[4] *H.L.F.* (*loc. cit.*) gives the infidel's views on the first of these points at some length, but passes lightly over the remainder of the discussion, so that the proportion is lost in this summary.

[5] *Obras*, iiia, p. vii.

[6] See note 2 to *Obras*, iiia, p. vii.

be described in more detail. The prologue divides the book into ten parts—dealing in order with God, Angels, Elements, Heavens, Plants, Metals, Beasts, Man, Paradise, Hell—and introduces us to the fictitious author, a man living abroad, who "wept and lamented because God has so few in this world who love and praise and serve Him." This man has a son named Felix, whom he sends on a journey round the world that he may learn to marvel at the wonders that he sees. The boy "asks what he understands not and sets down what he learns"[1]; on his return, father and son make this romance together.

The first book, "Of God," describes Felix' opening adventures. He meets a fair shepherdess guarding her flock in a wild forest and trusting in God to protect her from all harm. He has hardly left her when she is attacked and killed by a wolf, and he begins to doubt God's providence—nay, the very existence of a God—since one who trusts in Him is left to perish. A hermit, by demonstration, anecdote and object-lesson, restores his faith, and afterwards, at his request, instructs him as to the nature of the Godhead, the Unity of God, the Holy Trinity and the Creation, pointing out, in so doing, the importance of exercising the understanding as well as of having faith. At the conclusion of this instruction, which is enlivened by occasional dialogue, Felix leaves the hermit and continues his travels, meeting with a woman in great sorrow who is going to seek consolation of Blanquerna, "a very holy man and one of great wisdom, who . . . with words of God comforts those that are sad and counsels those that are in doubt concerning things which they understand not."[2] They journey to him together, and discover him "beneath a fair tree, with a book wherein was much learning of theology and philosophy wherewith he contemplated the King of Glory."[3] Needless to say, he is able at once to console the woman, who thereupon disappears from the story, leaving Felix sitting at Blanquerna's feet and being instructed upon the Incarnation, the Passion, original

[1] "Del Pròlech" (*Obras*, iiia, pp. 3–4).

[2] Bk. i, chap. 7 (*Obras*, iiia, p. 45).

[3] *Ibid.*, p. 47.

sin, the Blessed Virgin, the prophets and the apostles, and being given much incidental information which is too miscellaneous to be summarized briefly. After this, Felix leaves Blanquerna and the first book ends.

For a whole day Felix journeys, "and finds nothing at which to marvel,"[1] when he espies a tiny church where there is an altar of St. Michael, and another hermit, who is reading Lull's *Book of the Angels*. He salutes the hermit, and a reference to "a painting, above the church door, of a winged man with balances in his hand"[2] is sufficient to plunge the two into a discussion upon the angelic world, which, however, is comparatively brief and enters into none of the subtleties which intrigue Lull elsewhere. The third book, on the Heavens, opens with the description of a storm by which Felix is overtaken before he finds refuge with a shepherd in a cave. Fond as he is of putting such meetings to profit, it seems at first unlikely that the shepherd will teach him a great deal:

> Felix saluted the shepherd, who returned his greetings courteously, and Felix remained near the shepherd and waited for him to speak. For a long time they remained together, and neither spake a word, so that Felix marvelled greatly that the shepherd said naught and was so thoughtful.[3]

Eventually, however, the ice is broken, and the shepherd discourses upon the empyrean and the firmament, and proves to be more of a philosopher than he had appeared. The storm being now over, the shepherd and Felix go out together, and walk on until their ways diverge, after which Felix comes upon a professional philosopher who is giving lessons upon the four elements to a select class consisting of a royal prince and a number of young nobles. He joins in the lesson, and learns a great deal of useful mediaeval "philosophy" upon the subjects of lightning, thunder, clouds, rain and wind, the text-books used being, strange to say, Lull's own *Book of Chaos*, *Book of the Articles*, and *Book of the Gentile*. After another lesson, on the four seasons, Felix and the

[1] Bk. ii, chap. 1 (*Obras*, iiia, p. 85).
[2] *Ibid.*, p. 86. [3] *Ibid.*, pp. 97–8.

philosopher accompany the pupils into an orchard, where the prince's brother, who is learning knightly accomplishments, comes to practise them with his master and some companions. An incident staged by their father, the King, teaches Felix the superiority of the study of philosophy to the practice of horsemanship and arms,[1] and he leaves the court "praising and blessing God."[2]

We thus come to the fifth book, "Of Plants." After leaving the tutor and his pupils, Felix meets a squire whose master has forsaken him in order to take up the study of plant life "and contemplate God therein according to the art and manner of philosophy and theology, the which art is written in the *Book of the Articles*, and ordered according to the *Ars demonstrativa*."[3] Finding the master, and being anxious to learn of him, Felix accompanies him in his scientific expeditions, but though he is taught some interesting lessons, these are concerned rather with moral philosophy than with nature.

The sixth book, "Of Metals," continues Felix' conversation with the squire's late master, which turns upon the nature of metals, the moral and spiritual lessons to be learned of them, the qualities, more particularly, of silver, iron and loadstone, and the nature of alchemy.[4]

The seventh book, "Of Beasts," which forms within *Felix* a whole as complete as does the *Book of the Lover and the Beloved* within *Blanquerna*, will be considered at the end of this chapter. The eighth book, by far the longest of all, deals with man. For a long time our hero's experiences have been unusually barren of marvels, and it is with some relief that he at length scents another adventure :

There were some sheep in a meadow whereinto a wolf had entered who was killing these sheep and devouring them. Near that meadow was a shepherd's hut, and the shepherd was lying in his bed, and would not rise therefrom, by reason of the evil weather,

[1] Bk. iv, *passim*. [2] Bk. v, chap. 1 (*Obras*, iiia, p. 133).
[3] *Ibid.*, p. 136.
[4] This chapter (bk. vi, chap. 4) "De la Alquimia" (*Obras*, iiia, pp. 163–6) may be compared with pp. 405–7 below.

the cold and the rain. Near that place where the shepherd lay, a dog was fighting with another wolf; and it barked loudly, that the shepherd might awake and help it against the wolf with whom it fought, and against the wolf that was killing the sheep. Great marvel had Felix at the sloth and cowardice of that shepherd, who would help neither the dog nor the sheep.[1]

Needless to say, Felix sternly reproves the shepherd, who treats him with scorn, and the incident is turned into a parable:

Those Christians who dwell near to the infidels are calling loudly, that pope and holy men may rise up and destroy the errors which are contrary to the holy Christian faith. Great pity and grief have I because the wolf is slaying the sheep, and the dog fights bravely, but none aids him.[2]

Felix walks on, and meditates upon the nature of man—a creature of such strange contradictions, who can do so much that is good, yet so much also that is bad. To the reader's delight, he meets two characters mentioned, only too briefly, in *Blanquerna*: Sir Little-care-I and Sir What-will-men-say. They are engaged in a dispute so violent that they fail to return his greetings.

"In all the world," said the one, "there is naught so pleasing as the honour and good repute of men. . . . It is to gain honour that fair garments are made, and men desire fair houses, fine palfreys, rich harness, much money and many servants. For honour men bestow gifts and invitations in great number, and for honour they risk their lives in battles and assaults and many things like to these." On the other side spake Little-care-I and said: "To God alone, and to none other, belongs honour, for God alone is of Himself, and all else has come from naught, and, if God upheld it not, to naught it would return. And if any man has honour, he must hold it ever with intention to honour God."[3]

All three walk along together while this discussion continues, until they come to the gate of a city, whereupon Sir What-will-men-say insists upon donning the crimson hose and elegant shoes that he has brought, and even

[1] Bk. viii, Prohemi (*Obras*, iiib, pp. 1–2).
[2] *Ibid.*, p. 2.
[3] *Ibid.*, pp. 3–4.

upon changing his garments lest any should fail to take notice of him. His companions reply that, since nobody knows them, it matters little if they go unshod, and they refuse to wait for him. "Proudly and with great ostentation" he walks alone through the main street of the city, but the only attention he receives is from two merry youths, who mock him and endeavour to pull off his fine garments. Enraged, he draws his knife upon them ; a quarrel ensues, and both he and one of the boys are slain. One of the most promising characters in the book having thus been disposed of, Felix and Little-care-I continue their journey in a much sobered mood, and meet with various adventures. Before long, however, a new hermit comes upon the scene and Felix begins his lessons once more.[1]

The new discussion turns upon the nature of man, why he exists, whence he comes, why he has been placed in the world, why he desires children, why he is ill and well, young and old, and why he dies. For the most part it is the hermit who speaks, Felix being content to listen. They pass to the pleasures of remembrance, understanding and will, the pleasures of the five senses, and the nature and prevalence of good and evil : the expositions are now longer and freely diversified with anecdotes. After a chapter devoted to the active and the contemplative life, in which occur several reminiscences of *Blanquerna*, there are instructions on the virtues and their contraries,—on faith and unbelief, hope and despair, charity and cruelty, and the like, and afterwards on contrary states and actions, such as riches and poverty, praise and blame. The illustrative anecdotes, which take up a large proportion of each instruction, gain considerably in verisimilitude, and continually convey the impression of having been adapted from real life. A few lines from one and another will make this clear :

It came to pass that a pilgrim came to a noble king, who was very powerful and had much wealth and many subjects, and he

[1] Bk. viii, Prohemi (*Obras*, iiib, p. 8).

said to him : " Since God has given thee so much in this world, why takest thou not the Holy Land beyond the sea from the Saracens, who hold it to the dishonour of Holy Church, and givest it not to the Christians ? . . ." [1]

" In a city," said the hermit, " there was a hospital which had been ruined by bad administration ; and by reason of the ruin thereof, many of the poor had suffered grievously, and had no beds, and naught to eat, and oftentimes it came to pass that they died of hunger and cold. . . ." [2]

There was a lady, the spouse of a noble count, who went through a certain city upon a pilgrimage to Santiago, and lodged in a hostelry wherein two men were quarrelling over a game, and speaking words of villainy concerning Jesus Christ and Our Lady. . . . [3]

Others are allegorical, though occasionally they drive home topical lessons. Others are mere similitudes, parables and fables.

The chapters on contrary states continue until it would seem that there were no contraries left to expatiate upon. At the end of the fifty-seventh chapter of the eighth book, the instructions change to a series of ascetic homilies on abstinence, conscience, confession, penitence, prayer, almsgiving, temptation, and the like. By this time Felix takes a great part in the conversation, interrupting the hermit with questions, counter-anecdotes and comments. The quality of the instructions diminishes sensibly : they become, for the most part, conventional moral discourses, of no subtlety whatever. As for the tales, which grow more and more numerous—in places they are even strung together by twos and threes—few of them are in the smallest degree realistic : on the contrary, they are pointless, trite and dull, very obviously manufactured for the purpose of conveying a moral. This grows progressively truer as the eighth book proceeds on its way.

For some time before its close, the reader suspects that Ramon has been tiring of his task, though it is hard to say why in that case he continues it so far, since there is

[1] Bk. viii, chap. 27 (*Obras*, iiib, p. 117).
[2] Bk. viii, chap. 29 (*Obras*, iiib, p. 127 ; *cf.* iiib, p. 360).
[3] Bk. viii, chap. 35 (*Obras*, iiib, p. 156).

no discernible reason for giving the book "Of Man" seventy-two chapters. The shortness of the last two books confirms the suspicion. The ninth book, "Of Paradise," though dealing with a subject which interested Lull greatly, consists of only three brief instructions,—on the glory of the angels, and of the body and the soul of man,—and these are given, like those in the tenth book, "Of Hell," by the hermit, no attempt being made to provide Felix with further adventures. One or two of the stories which the hermit tells in these chapters have the ring of truth, or at least of skilful fiction, and are not without colour. Such is that of the cleric who had a "very great love of chastity," but, unfortunately for this love, had also, "a woman in his parish who was very fair," and on whose account he was sorely tempted. He combats the temptation by imagining the pains of Hell:

> He imagined how the bodies of men shall all be white like glowing coals of fire, and they shall be piled up for ever in Hell on top of each other, so that the heaps shall make mountains higher than Mount Canigou; and they shall be for ever in sulphur and boiling water and flame of fire; for all the elements shall join in tormenting the bodies that are in Hell, the which Hell is in the middle of the earth.[1]

Not even these alarming thoughts can cure him, however, especially when this very woman tells him in confession that she has sinned in precisely the way he is tempted. It will be observed that Ramon is becoming more critical of the clergy than he was in the *Book of Contemplation*. The salutary moral of the story lies in the fact that this cleric eventually reformed, not through fear of punishment, but from the love of God.

The conclusion of the book is not quite conventional. Felix at last considers himself "well instructed"—as one can readily believe—and, leaving the hermit, travels on until he reaches an abbey where he offers to stay for a time and relate the marvels he has seen. So delighted are the monks that they insist upon his taking their habit and continuing his way as a member of their order. But,

[1] Bk. x, chap. 3 (*Obras*, iiib, pp. 361–2).

before he can start, he falls ill and dies : the author has apparently forgotten that he made Felix' father compile the book *Of Marvels* on his son's return from his travels ! He is buried beneath the altar, and, in accordance with his dying wish, another monk takes his office and bears this book throughout the world, expounding it and adding to its contents.

It will be realized from what has been written that *Felix* falls considerably below *Blanquerna* in almost every way in which it can be compared with it. Except spasmodically, there is no characterization : the principal persons of the story are merely pegs on which to hang discourses,—even Felix, even Blanquerna (in this book) are nothing but lay figures. So soon as a character is no longer needed, he disappears, and the author does not so much as trouble to explain his disappearance.

But, worse than this, there is no plot-interest whatever in the story : one might even say there is no story. The personality of the hero constitutes only a false and superficial unity. Nobody cares where Felix goes next, what hermit or philosopher comes his way—for they are all " prudent, wise and learned "—or what any one of them tells him when they meet. In fact, we are perfectly indifferent to the book's conclusion, especially as it has grown steadily duller since the climax of its interest has been passed with the death of Sir What-will-men-say, who, might, had he lived, have given the narrative some vivacity.

Other shortcomings of *Felix* are obvious to every reader : its almost complete lack of poetry, its unskilful use of " examples," which are bandied to and fro like tennis-balls, and the unsatisfactory character of the examples themselves. Their only virtue lies in their number, and few critics but those in whom the head is completely under the dominion of the heart will be able to praise them.[1]

[1] I quote Mn. Riber (*Vida abreujada*, p. 31), but only in astonishment at the efficacy of the Midas-touch of his poetical temperament :

Per ventura, cap altra obra lul·líana és, més que el Fèlix, abundosa de

But perhaps most of the reader's disappointment with *Felix* is expressed by saying that he feels in it a loss of power. Its author, he would say, was hardly past his literary prime when he wrote *Blanquerna* : by the time that he finished *Felix* his art is like that of an old man : its vital force is gone. Yet only three years—if indeed as much—lay between these two books, and Lull was to write things in the future not far beneath the level of *Blanquerna.*

How can we explain this failure of power? It is hard to say. The reader may allege in favour of *Felix* that it opens (as it does) very skilfully, that its descriptions are occasionally lifelike, its glimpses of contemporary life realistic, the best of its numerous "examples" of considerable point and interest. If these things are true, the inferiority of the book as a whole is not less so, and one can only account for it by postulating as its causes depression, half-heartedness or overwork, or supposing that at Paris, where Ramon was occupied in matters so much weightier, the mere compilation of a story hardly seemed to him a task worth doing well.

If this be so, the perfunctoriness with which he executed this work may explain another of its curious characteristics. Although he mentions in it most of the causes he has at heart, and refers to several of his earlier writings,[1] he seems to be less preoccupied than usual with his pet ideas,—and this is certainly not because he is over-concerned with the literary aspect of his story. He inveighs against nepotism, bribery, worldliness, hypocrisy and other vices of the time, but with less than

contínua i verdejant esponera. Com en el bosc lul·lià de Miramar les eures s'enfilen als pollancres tremolencs, qui allarguen els braços a les alzines àrides, lligades per l'abraçada espinosa dels romaguers als pins, vestits de tan espessa i llarga cabellera que tapa la menuda vegetació de mil plantes humils, i tot el bosc vibra sordament amb la multitud anònima de les bestioles i amb l'alat exèrcit dels ocells ; així mateix, en el meravellós libre lul·lià, un bell apòleg s'ajunta a una semblança o a una contarella gentil ; un eximpli és al costat d'una al·legoria, i un castell torreja vora una ermita ; i un escuder no és lluny d'un cavaller, ni una noble ciutat d'una abadia opulent i honrada.

[1] Notably the *Book of the Gentile* (*Obras*, iiib, pp. 68, 160, etc.), and *Doctrine for Boys* (*ibid.*, pp. 68, 362) besides those referred to in the text above and the unknown *Book of Pleasant Vision* (*ibid.*, pp. 53–4 ; *cf.* p. 205 above).

his usual vehemence, insistence and effect. He is calm and academic, using them mainly to illustrate his homilies. Similarly, his arguments for a new crusade, and for increased missionary activity, are urged but faintly and, in general, kept in the background. Not that they are the less recognizable by good Lullians for that. The unmistakable atmosphere of *Blanquerna* pervades *Felix* : the world of the heroes of each romance is the world of Divine values, of which we too become members as we test each man that we meet, not according to criteria of wealth or great place but by whether or no he is a servant of the Lady Valour. A passage like this rings true :

> So Felix and the shepherd made to the king the reverence which is fitting to a king, and the king greeted Felix and the shepherd. Then the king said to Felix : " For what reason have ye done me reverence and honour, and how know ye that I am worthy of such honour ? " " Lord," answered Felix, " . . . since thou hast brought up thy sons to honour God, thou art worthy for honour to be done thee."

This is the world in which emperors and jesters go hand in hand, and eat dry bread together like friends—the world of *Blanquerna*.

One less pleasing characteristic of *Felix* must in fairness be referred to here : the preoccupation of its latter part with sins of the flesh. Ramon nowhere fails to reprove unchastity, or glosses over the faults even of priests and bishops under this head : in other words, the composite picture which his books present of mediaeval morality is by no means an agreeable one. But what elsewhere he mentions occasionally, he paints in *Felix* with unusual fulness, nor is his frankness entirely confined to the reproving of sin. References to sex in the book are far too numerous to be specified [1] : were it not that Ramon mentions the subject so lightly and passes from

[1] These are of the kind found (much less frequently) in *Blanquerna*, and show that the subject was commonly and frankly discussed by moralists as by others. See, for typical examples, *Felix* (*Obras*, iiib, pp. 231, 234, 235, 325, 361).

it so easily one would suppose it to have been at the time an obsession with him. The light woman (*folla fembra*) in *Felix* is a type as common as any. A few of the illustrations which the last hermit gives to our hero are so obscene as to be quite unrepeatable, and this, so far as we know, is a thing which, enormous as is the number of Lull's books, can be said of no other of them whatever. One of these stories—that of the woman who stripped herself before the bishop—has an autobiographical value and is referred to above.[1] The curious may study another representative one, which deals with the essential foulness of illicit intercourse[2] : this is equally moral in principle, but, in detail, repulsive to a degree.

While uncritical biographers will freely term *Felix* autobiographical, the cautious reader will be very uncertain how far Ramon refers in it at all to his own experiences. It is possible, but no more, that his are the adventures of "a man who went through the world reproaching princes and prelates because they brought it not to pass that the heathen should come into the way of truth,"[3] or of the "man, poorly clad, who went from court to court observing the conduct of princes and noble barons, that because of it he might praise and bless God."[4] The only passage which can, as we think, be safely taken as an actual experience of Ramon's is one which was partially quoted at the end of the last chapter. "Sir," enquires Felix of one of the hermits, "how may Holy Church be made to grow in the world and the error be diminished which is in those that oppose her?" The hermit answers him by relating what are clearly the arguments with which Ramon went to Philip's court in Paris. "After this manner, son," he adds, "might the Roman faith increase; for, if the Tartars and the inhabitants of Liconia, and the other heathen, are converted, the Saracens will be destroyed; so that, by the way of martyrdom, and through the greatness of charity, the whole world will be converted to Christianity."[5]

[1] *Obras*, iiib, pp. 120–21. See pp. 18-19 above.
[2] *Obras*, iiib, p. 155.
[3] *Obras*, iiib, pp. 221.
[4] *Obras*, iiib, p. 269.
[5] *Obras*, iiib, pp. 210–11.

We shall take up this rather interesting statement of missionary policy in a later chapter.

The criticism passed upon *Felix* in these pages is not intended to apply to its seventh section, the *Book of the Beasts*. Though this is an integral part of the romance as it now stands, and must have been so from the time of the conception of *Felix*, since it fills a necessary place in it, it was in all probability written separately at an earlier date, and is superior to the rest of the *Book of Marvels* in every manner.

A superficial reader acquainted with mediaeval Spanish fiction might be inclined to attribute this superiority to the use made by Lull of the collection of animal tales known in Castilian as *Calila y Dimna*,[1] itself indebted to preceding Oriental collections, as is testified by almost every page of its narrative. From what version of this work Lull borrowed,[2] or whether, with his knowledge of Arabic, he went back to Arabic sources, it is impossible to say, and unnecessary to discuss, in this biography. So much of the borrowed matter is transformed in the re-setting, and so much more of the *Book of the Beasts* is original, that the study of it soon reveals it as in every way Lull's own.

Its borrowings from *Calila y Dimna*, or from the sources of that collection, are, so far as our present knowledge of these sources goes, confined to perhaps a dozen episodes, nearly all of which are examples related by one or other of Lull's animal characters, not incidents in the story itself. The principal exception is in the episode of the bellowing of the ox, which frightens the lion ; the related elements of the character of the lion, the part played by the crafty fox and the slaying of the

[1] I cannot think that there is the slightest doubt of this influence, but *cf.* Longpré, col. 1092.

[2] At the end of *Calila y Dimna,* we read that the book was done into Latin from Arabic, and later turned from Latin into Castilian by the command of Alfonso the Wise (while still *infante*). See *Calila y Dimna,* ed. Solalinde, Madrid, 1917, p. 284. The whole question of the date and transmission of the collection is very complicated, but of secondary importance here. It is sufficiently manifest that Lull might have known *Calila y Dimna* in at least three languages.

ox by the lion are not improbably derived from *Calila y Dimna* also.[1] Of the examples from this source incorporated in the *Book of the Beasts*, the chief are those of the monkey and the drum,[2] the goose and the crab,[3] the lion and the hare,[4] the glow-worm mistaken for a fire,[5] the rat-maiden[6] and the four unfortunates in the pit.[7] The incident of the fox begging the lion to satisfy his hunger by eating her[8] has also a close but not an exact parallel in *Calila y Dimna*,[9] while several further incidents were almost certainly adapted by Ramon from other sources. Such are the outline story (not the details) of the ambassadorship of the ounce and the leopard to the court of the king of men[10]; the experiences of the ox and the horse in man's service[11]; the story of the flea and the louse[12]; and that of the curious woman and the cock,[13] familiar to readers of the Arabian Nights. If this seems a formidable list, it must be made clear in the first place that many of the borrowed elements were common property, and also that they are by no means incorporated as they stand in any of their other known versions. Some of them, such as the ox-narrative, are taken from their context and woven skilfully by Ramon into his plot. Others, such as the story of the rat-maiden, are shortened, and not always improved[14] in the process, as a comparison of the two versions will show. Others, on the contrary,

[1] Cf. *B.B.* pp. 25–8, 35–7, 70–5 with *Calila y Dimna* [*ed. cit.*, henceforth abbreviated *C.D.*], pp. 47, 50–1, 57, 59–60, 103–4. Other and minor elements of this part of the plot may also have been suggested by *C.D. H.L.F.*, pp. 355 ff., discusses some of these.

[2] *B.B.*, p. 27; *C.D.*, pp. 57–8. These two stories are almost identical.

[3] *B.B.*, pp. 30–3; *C.D.*, pp. 66–8.

[4] *B.B.*, pp. 17–18; *C.D.*, pp. 69–70.

[5] *B.B.*, pp. 80–1; *C.D.*, p. 97. As will be seen elsewhere (p. 161), Lull is particularly fond of this anecdote, using it several times.

[6] *B.B.*, p. 15; *C.D.*, pp. 174–5.

[7] *B.B.*, pp. 37–40; *C.D.*, pp. 249–53.

[8] *B.B.*, pp. 72–5.

[9] *C.D.*, pp. 87–8.

[10] *B.B.*, pp. 44 ff.

[11] *B.B.*, pp. 5–7.

[12] *B.B.*, pp. 18–19. At a later date this unsavoury incident was related as having happened at the court of St. Louis.

[13] *B.B.*, pp. 76–9.

[14] So much better is the *C.D.* rat-story than that of *B.B.* that I cannot believe Lull to have adapted the Castilian form of the story: he must certainly have used a briefer or cruder version.

are lengthened or improved beyond recognition. The fox who in *Calila y Dimna* is deceived by the empty drum becomes a monkey. The story of the creatures in the well, though at best a somewhat rambling one, is told with considerably more skill by Lull than by the Castilian compiler. The glowworm story, too, is greatly improved : the group of monkeys is reduced to a single animal,[1] the officious " bird " becomes a parrot, and for the man who reproves it is substituted a crow sitting in the selfsame tree.

Turning to the original part—which is by far the longer part—of Lull's story, we are at once struck by its merits. Let us set aside the anecdotes—original or borrowed, it matters not. They are briefly told, occasionally with effect but more usually without interesting detail. They are in no way essential, however, to the narrative, and it is the plot and characterization of the book, not its embellishments, which remain in the memory.

The story belongs to the well-known " Reynard the Fox " cycle, and the animals are, in the main, given their conventional characteristics, while the conventional ending of the fox's destruction is kept also. Lull's narrative is a brief one, very much more interesting than the verbose, sententious and involved *Calila y Dimna*, well constructed, full of incident, never halting for long and propounding real problems which the reader is eager to solve. The first question which the author raises—whether or no the lion will be elected king—is quickly answered. But the fox's intrigues with the elephant (it will be noticed that, contrary to custom, she is represented as a vixen) at once raises a fresh question as to whether the king will be dethroned, and this is not answered until the end of the book. Throughout the narrative we are kept amused and interested by the clever way in which Dame Reynard substitutes small and timid beasts for large and strong ones in the king's innermost council.

[1] A change almost as effective as the striking contrast between Lull's Dame Reynard and the two jackals Calila and Dimna, the principal characters of the two stories.

And all this time events are succeeding each other so quickly that the main question is hardly remembered except when it is recalled purposely. The finest and most original part of the story is undoubtedly the lion's intrigue with the leopard's mate during her lord's absence on royal business, and the subsequent murder of the aggrieved party. The interview between leopard and weasel,[1] though the characters move on a low plane, strikes a deep note of pathos ; and the narrative of the battle between the leopard and the ounce[2] gives us a climax that, in a story of human beings, would be one of tense excitement. Only less interesting because less original is the description of the ox's disillusionment in the service of man and his subsequent victimization by Dame Reynard. A third episode, the journey and experiences of the lion's ambassadors, would be of greater merit if it did not repeat so much that we find in *Blanquerna* and elsewhere : readers of the *Book of the Beasts* who know nothing of Lull's other works will find it intriguing.

The local colour of the book is, very properly, stripped of many Orientalisms : its monkeys, camels and parrots are not over-frequent and its peculiarly Eastern anecdotes are few. In a beast-story which convention limits so strictly there is not much scope for characterization, but Ramon has made much of his opportunities. An indignation which only the presence of genuine satire robs of its impressiveness is aroused by the king's scurvy treatment of the lion's presents, and we have already commented upon the pathos and tragedy which surround the last appearances of the leopard. But the sympathies of the sensitive reader are reserved, at the end of the book, for two " little people of the lion," the rabbit and the peacock, who, having sworn a forced oath to the fox and the elephant that they will keep their guilty secret, are frightened by a more imposing display of force into betraying it. It is surely a hard heart that does not wish them back again in the royal favour—unless, indeed, they are more secure outside it :

[1] *B.B.*, pp. 61–2. [2] *B.B.*, pp. 66–7.

But when Dame Reynard had made an end of speaking, the king looked at the rabbit and the peacock after a manner that was most terrible, and uttered a great roar, to the end that in the consciences of the rabbit and the peacock the nature of his high office might have greater virtue than the fear which they had of Dame Reynard. And when the lion had uttered a great roar, he commanded the rabbit and the peacock, with great wrath, to tell him the truth ; and they could no longer restrain themselves, but told him all the truth. Then the king, with his own hand, slew Dame Reynard, after the which thing his court returned to its former good estate, and the king made the elephant and the bear and other honoured barons to be of his council, and cast out therefrom the rabbit and the peacock.[1]

Further points of interest in the *Book of the Beasts* deserve brief mention. The quaintness with which animals relate anecdotes of men and women,[2] as in real-life stories men and women do of animals, it has in common with other works of its nature. It goes farther than some in making its personages, especially the wily Dame Reynard, talk religion and cite Scripture for their purpose.[3] On one occasion, and perhaps on two, it refers to its author, recalling what is certainly his experience, long past, with his Saracen slave,[4] and representing "a man poorly clothed, and having a long beard,"[5] as reproving the king of men in the story in the same way as Lull had no doubt more than once reproved kings in the flesh. In both picture and legend the Ramon of 1286 is portrayed as having a *barba florida*, and he generally portrays himself thus from now onward.

We approach *Felix* as a whole, undoubtedly, with high expectation : we leave it with feelings of deep disappointment. The one bright patch in that unexpectedly monotonous work is the *Book of the Beasts*. It would be illuminating could we know its full history : as it is, we can only pass on to what is to come with the feeling that Ramon may yet have in store much that is worth the reading.

[1] *B.B.*, pp. 89–90.
[2] E.g. *B.B.*, pp. 3–4, 22, 23, 24, 73.
[3] E.g. *B.B.*, pp. 9, 33, 41.
[4] *B.B.*, pp. 13–14 ; *cf.* pp. 41-2 above.
[5] *B.B.*, p. 51.

CHAPTER XI

1287–1292

Paris, Montpellier and Rome. The *Book of Saint Mary*. Minor works. Sojourn in Genoa, preparatory to an African mission. Spiritual crisis: problems of interpretation raised by the evidence. Recovery and journey to Tunis. First missionary experiences. Escape from a furious crowd. Return to Europe.

After " some time," as the contemporary biography has it,[1]—probably in the spring of 1287[2]—Ramon left Paris for Montpellier, where he lectured on his *Art*,[3] and wrote another book, entitled the *Art of finding truth*.[4] This was a development of the *Ars demonstrativa*—a concession, according to the contemporary life, being made in it to human frailty[5]: the " concession " consisted in the reduction of the sixteen figures of the earlier *Art* to four, and (which was more important) in the use and

[1] *V.C.*, iv (*Life*, p. 17). [2] See p. 201, above.

[3] *V.B.R.L.*, ii (*Life*, p. 58). *V.C.* is silent here.

[4] *V.C.*, iv, *V.B.R.L.*, ii (*Life*, pp. 17, 58). This is the *Ars inventiva veritatis*, and is not to be confused with the *Ars inveniendi veritatem*, another name for the *Ars Magna* (p. 109, above). For an account of it, see *H.L.F.*, No. 34, pp. 176–83. The first words are: " Ars praesens ab arte demonstrativa descendit." The date 1287 is Pasqual's (*cf.* Alòs: *Los catálogos, etc.*, p. 71 and n.). Longpré (col. 1093), Rogent i Duràn (*Bibliografia, etc.*, p. 52) and others prefer 1289, but I think Pasqual's conjecture is better.

[5] The phrases used (*Life*, pp. 17, 58–9) are curious and almost identical, though *V.B.R.L.* is more explicit than *V.C.*: " aximetex reduí en tots los altres libres les xvj figures a quatre per amor de la fragilitat humana " ; " ponendo in ipso libro, nec non et in omnibus aliis libris, quos ex tunc fecit, quattuor figuras tantum, resecatis seu potius dissimulatis propter fragilitatem humani intellectus, quam fuerat expertus Parisiis, xij figuris ex sedecim, quae prius erant in Arte sua." From these accounts it is clear that the change was a permanent one, and applies to Ramon's later books of the kind. According to Pasqual, however (i, p. 373), both *V.C.* and *V.B.R.L.* have misunderstood the nature of the simplification.

application of the terms of the *Art* themselves instead of the employment of algebraical notation. Though in fact the number of figures used is smaller, the new *Art* seems at first glance equally complicated. In the first figure there are nine principles ; thirty-six permutations of these taken two at a time, making thirty-six compartments ; three triangles (green, red and yellow) representing respectively difference, concordance and contrariety, beginning, mean and end, and majority, equality and minority ; and three concentric circles, in further application of the nine principles, turning upon each other, and giving combinations of threes. This is the least complicated part of the *Art of finding truth*, the subtleties of which become more and more like those of its predecessors. At the conclusion, directions are given for its practice, and by its means are answered questions similar to those already specified.[1]

At Montpellier, probably for the first time, Ramon attended a Chapter-General of Friars Minor, held there at Whitsuntide, 1287.[2] His purpose in being present at this assembly was certainly to put before it projects which had been submitted, without much success, to Chapters of the Dominicans. Possibly his next move was to have been a return to Rome, where he could report the tale of his successes and failures to the sympathetic Honorius, and ask for further aid. But, on April 3, 1287, Honorius died, and it was not until the following February, when his successor, Nicholas IV, had been elected, that Ramon left Montpellier and set out for Rome. He started, no doubt, with a high heart, for Nicholas was a Franciscan—the first of his order to be elected Pope—and might have been expected to do even more than Honorius had done to further his wishes. While

[1] In Montpellier also, and in 1287, Lull wrote the *Quaestiones per Artem Demonstrativam seu Inventivam solubiles*, which deal with all kinds of subjects and are not dissimilar to those already described (pp. 111, 155, above). A fairly complete account of this book is given in *H.L.F.*, pp. 134–40. See also Longpré, col. 1093, but, as to date, *cf.* p. 223 n. 4 above.

[2] Wadding, *Annal*, 1287, *cit.* Pasqual, i, p. 371. *V.C.*, *V.B.R.L.* say nothing of this occurrence, but *Desconort*, xiv (p. 259) confirms its probable correctness.

journeying to Rome, he made a brief halt[1] at Genoa,[2] where he translated his *Art of finding truth* into Arabic.[3] On his arrival at Rome, Nicholas IV, as was to be expected, received him kindly, but was, as it happened, genuinely unable to take steps to assist him. The brief pontificate of Honorius had been only too fully occupied with the Sicilian question. Peter of Aragon's death-bed protestations, already alluded to, had been set aside in favour of his written testament. His eldest son, Alfonso, after wresting Mallorca from his uncle, found himself king also of Aragon, Catalonia and Valencia ; to James, the second son, afterwards James II of Aragon,[4] was bequeathed the stormy legacy of Sicily. Honorius was as uncompromisingly opposed to the rule of James as Martin had been to that of Peter : had excommunication sufficed to cow the Spaniard, the Pope would have immediately won. But, in spite of the worst he could do, Alfonso and James stood firm, so that Nicholas succeeded to an unedifying political controversy which it required all his resource to negotiate. It is true that by May 1289 he had contrived to get the Angevin nominee of the Papacy crowned King of Sicily at Palermo, but this did not greatly help matters, for its chief result was to substitute two kings for a king and an uncrowned pawn, and had not Alfonso been desirous of withdrawing from the quarrel, a solution might have been delayed indefinitely. As it was, a temporary treaty was signed in February 1291, only four months before the untimely death of Alfonso.

Long before this, however, Nicholas had been able to set to work to show his sympathy with practical missionary

[1] *V.B.R.L.* gives this detail : " Venit ad Genuam, ubi non multam moram faciens . . ." (*Life*, p. 59).

[2] Some biographers (*cf.* Av., p. 283) suppose that Lull went to Genoa in 1287 with the intention of embarking for Africa, and decided only after his arrival at Genoa to visit Rome. I know, however, of no evidence in favour of this, except that the contemporary life makes no suggestion that he intended to go from Montpellier to Rome direct : but neither does it suggest that he meant to go to Africa. Since Honorius sent Ramon to Paris, it would be natural for him to return to Rome—whoever the Pope might be—to report progress, and still more so to visit a Franciscan Pope as early as might be.

[3] *V.C.*, iv, *V.B.R.L.*, ii (*Life*, pp. 17, 59) ; *cf.* p. 223, n. 4, above, and the references there given.

[4] See p. 135, n. 4, above.

enterprise. Naturally enough, he was keenly interested in the friars who had been sent out in 1278 to Persia and he had done something to remove the difficulties which they were encountering. Just before his predecessor's death, a request had come from the favourably disposed Khan of Persia that Christian missionaries should be sent to China likewise, where the great Kúblái Khan was reigning. This matter Nicholas took up, so soon as his efforts at king-making were concluded, and sent, as the first missionary to China, the Franciscan John of Monte-corvino, who spent in that country the forty remaining years of his long life. About the same time, the Pope did another thing that had been partly foreshadowed in *Blanquerna*[1] when he divided the revenue of the Holy See into two parts and made over one half to the Cardinals, an act conceived in the true Franciscan spirit.

Lull, who no doubt took note of these doings, was more than disinclined to surrender the hope that Nicholas IV would in the end grant his wishes. So, when he returned to Montpellier in 1289, the Sicilian situation being then at its tensest, it was with the idea of coming back to Rome very shortly. On the way, he attended another Franciscan Chapter at Rieti, between Rome and Perugia, at which was elected a new General, Fra Ramon Gaufredi.[2] Evidently Gaufredi was interested in Lull, whom we now see drawing continually closer to the Franciscans.[3] He probably spent some time examining a number of his works and discussing with him his projects, for, soon after their meeting, he gave him letters for the provinces of Rome, Apulia and Sicily, requesting those who should receive them to afford him leave and opportunity to expound his *Art* in suitable convents.[4] These letters were dated October 26,

[1] *Blanquerna*, chap. 79.

[2] See Wadding, vol. v, pp. 52, 210, 235, 336, 338.

[3] In one of the letters described below, Gaufredi calls him "amicus ordinis et devotus ab antiquo in relevandis fratrum nostrorum inopiis gratiosus et in subsidiis sollicitus et attentus."

[4] See Mut, bk. ii, chap. 4, who gives in full the text of one of the letters. This is also reproduced by Pasqual (i, p. 388 n.) and by Rubió y Lluch (*Documents*, etc., pp. 9–10). For Pasqual's quite justifiable deductions from the letters, see i, pp. 388–91.

1290, from Montpellier, where the two met again, if indeed they did not travel together from Rieti. Lull purposed to use them immediately, to return to Rome, and possibly even to go southwards thence to Sicily: probably he took note that the political situation was slowly clearing, and judged that his cause would be the better served by his acting without delay. So he remained at Montpellier only a little time longer, and as he set out thence once more he must have looked back with satisfaction on the work that he had accomplished in the sympathetic surroundings of his favourite city during the fifteen months that had elapsed since his arrival from the Whitsuntide Chapter at Rieti.

To begin with, he was giving lectures, during the greater part or the whole of this time, in the University of Montpellier, which Nicholas IV had created by a bull of the year 1289, uniting thereby the various schools which already existed there.[1] But, as well as lecturing, Ramon wrote at least four books,[2] each of some interest, and translated another into Latin from Arabic.[3]

Of the original works dated or presumed as coming from Montpellier in 1290, the *Art of loving the good*[4] is assigned to no particular place, but as the author states that it was "invented in the year of the Nativity, 1290, on the vigil of St. Laurence" (August 9), there seems no doubt on this point. It is a disappointing treatise to readers of the *Book of the Lover and the Beloved*. For it

[1] He added faculties of canon law and arts, and brought the faculty of medicine under ecclesiastical authority, thus uniting the faculties of medicine, civil and canon law and arts in one University. See p. 154, above.

[2] For Pasqual's conjecture (i, p. 381) that the *Investigatio generalium mixtionum* (probably the same book as the *Liber de mixtionibus principiorum*; cf. *H.L.F.*, No. 152, p. 302) was written in 1289, either in Montpellier or in Italy, though quite credible, is by no means secure. This book is a metaphysical, not a chemical, treatise despite its title.

[3] The *Compendium logicae Algazelis*, (*H.L.F.*, No. 137, p. 296) written first in Arabic—it is not known when. Salzinger (*cit.* Pasqual, i, p. 383) says that it was also translated from Arabic into Catalan, but I know no clear evidence for this. The Catalan version is described as having been made "de latí en romans." Nor is it certain that the translation into Latin was not made during one of Lull's earlier sojourns in Montpellier (*cf.* Longpré, col. 1104). On all these questions see Rubió i Balaguer: "La Lògica del Gazzali, etc." in *Anuari* etc., 1913–14, pp. 311–54.

[4] *H.L.F.*, No. 39, pp. 197–200; *cf.* No. 249, p. 339.

follows the same syllogistic method as the other "Arts."[1] As Ramon hoped, by means of his evidential writings, to shut up the intellect (*ligare intellectum*) of the infidel to the acceptance of truth, so also he believed it possible to shut up his will to the love of the one true God—the Blessed Trinity—and to lead him to love through knowledge.[2] It may be added that, in the "questions" upon the Art which, in Lull's usual manner, comprise the last of the book's five distinctions, there are many reminiscences of the *Book of the Lover and the Beloved*, and suggestions of a later book, the *Tree of the Philosophy of Love.*

This *Art* was originally written in Catalan, "so that those who know no Latin may have an art and doctrine of love,"[3] and also that those who understand Latin may learn how to write of such matters in the mother tongue. The Catalan original, however, contains a number of Latin words for which Lull makes excuse by alleging the poverty of the vernacular, and the complete work, he says, is shortly to be put into Latin.[4]

The book was also to be turned into Arabic, "to confound the Saracens," for by means of it (says the prologue) Christians will be able to resolve all the objections which the Saracens make to our religion, and to overthrow Islam also. Yet, continues the author, we do not in this *Art* write expressly of the Trinity or the Incarnation, for we do not wish to offend Moslem readers, "neither do we purpose to set this paragraph in the translation which we make of this treatise into Arabic."[5]

More attractive than this new *Art* is the *Book of*

[1] As the Latin version of the Prologue (Salz., vi, p. 1) puts it: "Per [*Artem Amativam Boni*] datur et monstratur Amantia, sicut per *Artem Inventivam* datur et monstratur Scientia, nam quemadmodum Scientia intitulatur sub intellectu, ita Amantia intitulatur sub Voluntate."

[2] "ut artificialiter possimus cognoscere Amantiam per Scientiam et amare Scientiam per Amantiam." (Salz., vi, p. 1.)

[3] *Ars Amativa Boni*, Prologue (Salz., vi, pp. 2–3). There are Catalan MSS. at Paris (Bibliothèque Nationale) and at Munich.

[4] *Ibid.* (Salz., vi, p. 3). There is no suggestion that a translator will be needed: Lull will do it himself.

[5] *Ibid.*

Saint Mary,[1] written about this time in the vernacular; it has, in our view, received overmuch praise from Catalan commentators, who perhaps have been unduly influenced by their sympathy with its subject, which we fully share. From the literary standpoint, it appears to mark a further descent from the standard of *Felix*, and is certainly a long way below *Blanquerna*. Here and there it reminds us of a fiction which forms part of the latter romance,—the "Book of *Ave Maria*." [2] The groundwork, as usual, is allegorical. Two ladies, Lausor ("Praise") and Oració ("Prayer"), are in great distress because, in the cities from which they are travelling, Our Lady and her Son are not honoured by the inhabitants as is their due. "One praises his clothing, another his wine, a third his hawk, his steed and his lance," but few praise Christ and His Mother.[3] As to prayer, "some ask for riches, others for honours, others for health and others for life in this world, and scarce any . . . pray for the life of the world to come." [4] Lamenting thus, they decide to seek consolation for a while in solitude, and, reaching the habitual "fair wood," find another lady, Entenció ("Intention"), tearing her clothes and plucking her hair, in her distress at man's sinfulness. The three make common cause, and have not gone far together when they come upon a hermitage with a chapel dedicated to the Virgin. The hermit proves to be "no lettered man, but a layman," who has little conception of prayer:

> I can but speak of bodily things, and I pray for my ass, and for my cock, and that my dog, who was wounded by a wolf, may be healed, and I pray also for the forgiveness of my sins.[5]

The ladies perceive that he is "a simple man, and that if they were to speak to him subtly concerning Our Lady he would not understand them," [6] but he tells them of a "holy man" whose company will please them better. On further enquiry, they learn that this man (like Ramon

[1] *Libre de Sancta Maria*. The Latin version is entitled *De Laudibus Beatissimae Virginis Mariae*, and is described in *H.L.F.*, No. 81, p. 257. The version here used is the original Catalan.

[2] *Bl.*, pp. 235–66.

[3] Pròlech (*Obres*, x, p. 6).

[4] *Ibid.*, p. 7.

[5] *Ibid.*, p. 11.

[6] *Ibid.*

Lull) was " rich, when in this world, and well endowed with temporal possessions, and learned in many sciences, and he has left the world and given all that he had for the love of God and of Our Lady."[1] They travel on, and find him digging in his garden, at which—having expected to find him lost in Divine contemplation—they are politely surprised, until he explains to them that even a hermit needs some exercise. When he learns who they are, he is only too glad to rest from his gardening to talk with them about holy things, at which point the prologue ends, and with it the narrative part of the treatise.

The thirty chapters of the book (which, it need hardly be said, symbolize the thirty pieces of silver) embody the conversations between the hermit and the three fair ladies. It is in our estimate of these that we must part company from Mn. Riber, who describes them as a " magnífica conversa,"[2] and the entire work as " sweeter than honey and the honeycomb,"[3] as also from Mn. Galmés, to whom it is " the most succulent fruit of Lull's varied productiveness."[4] In our judgment, the prologue is of considerable interest and not devoid of skill, the three ladies being defined with much individuality and the two hermits being drawn and contrasted most pleasingly. This skill in characterization, too, is carried into the main part of the book. Of the three ladies, Prayer is the most impassioned and eloquent ; the Lady Praise is calmer and more dignified, but also more determined, and has most of the initiative of the party ; the Lady Intention, whose function is to relate " examples," is, by comparison with them, somewhat colourless, and there is reason to think that this effect of light and shade is quite intentional.

The conversations themselves, however,—and they form the greater part of the book—are as flat as any in Lull's fictions. The teaching (which frequently has little to do with Our Lady) is conveyed with great prolixity and no distinction of manner. The figures of

[1] Pròlech (*Obres,* x, p. 11).
[2] *Vida i actes*, p. 115.
[3] *Ibid.*
[4] *Obres*, x, p. xiii.

speech are in the main conventional, and contain little poetry. And the anecdotes, which abound, are inexpressibly trite ; one after another of them comes to a dreary end without any point being made at all ; to contrast them with the anecdotes of *Blanquerna* is painful. Many of them, as in *Felix*, turn on the subject of unchastity, and though they are less revolting than those in that romance, the dead level of their dull respectability makes them even more monotonous. Let the anecdote of the " Joglar de Sancta María," [1] for example, be compared with the moving French story of " Le Jongleur de Notre Dame " by any whom the reading of a few pages of the *Book of Saint Mary* fails to convince of its ineptness. Or, to look at the matter from another aspect, let the undoubtedly poetical conceptions of Our Lady as the protection of soldiers and sailors,[2] and as the Dawn,[3] be contrasted with the prosaic surroundings in which the germ of poetry is planted, and the ineffectiveness of its development.

In short, this work accords less with the eulogies of its commentators than with its author's description of it in his prologue. " Questions, definitions, praises, prayers and intentions," he begins, " are the foundations of this book.[4] . . . Subtleties we avoid, in so far as we can, that the book may be comprehended." [5] Undoubtedly, the book is not subtle : even the hermit who was a " simple man " could have understood it. And undoubtedly its various elements are given equitable representation and clearly distinguished the one from the other. Lull has left the domain of literary art in the *Book of Saint Mary*. No doubt it reached its public and was appreciated by them. It seems a pity to try to make it something other than it is.

The *Book of Antichrist* [6] is of no great interest : Lull does not believe, with Arnau de Vilanova, that the time of Antichrist has already come, but merely uses his

[1] Chap. 16 (*Obres*, x, pp. 122–3). [2] Chap. 29 (*Obres*, x, p. 220).
[3] Chap. 30 (*Obres*, x, pp. 222–7). [4] Pròlech (*Obres*, x, p. 3).
[5] *Ibid.*, p. 5.
[6] *H.L.F.*, No. 239, pp. 335–6. This book was probably written originally in Catalan ; the Catalan text is at Munich.

theme as a plea for more determined campaigns against unbelievers. The *Tree of desired philosophy*,[1] though more attractive, is less so than other books in the series of "trees" which Ramon was to write later. It is another of the works written for his son Dominic, of whom he has evidently still great hopes, though, as we learn from a casual reference, he has not seen him for so long that he has not heard if he has profited by the *Book of the first and second intentions*.[2] He represents himself as being alone in an orchard, meditating on God and the state of the world and the scarcity of people who love God and serve Him. There comes to him the idea of writing a simple book, of an allegorical kind, round the figure of a tree, which his son may bear from country to country, giving knowledge thereby of God.[3]

Then follows a similitude, worked out in some detail, and by no means unprofitable for purposes of devotion, for all that a bare description of it may seem of little interest. The tree is planted in memory, understanding and will, and watered by a river which flows from the three sources of faith, hope and charity. From this proceed the four streams of justice, prudence, temperance and courage. The tree is watered ten times, after the manner of the commandments, and it "gives seven times of its fruit," even as the Holy Spirit gives seven gifts.[4]

The last of the books written at Montpellier in 1290,[5] and entitled, rather clumsily, *Questions which were asked by a certain Friar Minor*,[6] does not call for description beyond the remark that the questions are thirty-two in number and of the kind of which examples have already

[1] Salz., vol. vi (cf. *H.L.F.*, No. 42, pp. 205–7). Both Latin and Catalan texts are extant. The translation (if such it is) in Latin given by Salzinger differs considerably from the older Latin version preserved at Paris, Innichen and Cortona (Longpré, cols. 1103–04).

[2] Dist. i, pt. i, c. (Salz., vi, pp. 5–6): "Multum temporis transivit, Fili, quod tibi misi *Librum de Intentione*, et quia longum tempus est, quod te non vidi, ideo nescio, utrum ab illo receperis utilitatem, etc."

[3] Prologue (Salz., vi, pp. 1–2).

[4] Dist. i, pt. i (Salz., vi, p. 2).

[5] So Pasqual thinks, but the book is not dated, and *H.L.F.* (pp. 329–30) gives no credence to the conjecture.

[6] *Quaestiones quas quaesivit quidam frater Minor. H.L.F.*, No. 223, pp. 329–30.

been cited. Another book written at about this time, the *Fount of the Divine Paradise*,[1] is not given in the oldest Lullian catalogues, but all internal evidence points to its genuineness. The "Paradise" of the book is Holy Church, its fount being the Scriptures, and the four rivers which water the Garden and flow from the fount being the four methods of interpreting the Scriptures—historical, allegorical, tropological and mystical.

It would have been late in 1290 when, armed with Gaufredi's letters, Ramon returned to Rome. On his arrival, he again had audience of the Pope, and is said to have presented him with a tract on the conquering of the Holy Land, a subject which, as we are now beginning to see, was occupying him increasingly. Practically nothing is known of the nature of this tract, not even its title,[2] but it was an appropriate gift, for Nicholas, in the midst of his other affairs, was making heroic efforts at the time to organize a new crusade. Unhappily his efforts were to fail, and, close upon the failure, there was to come the crushing news of the fall of Acre in 1291, which closed the rule of the Christians in the East. Then Nicholas may well have remembered the plea in Ramon's tract for the unification of the military orders of the Templars and St. John, the dissensions between which had been partly responsible for the disaster. Alas, that the union had been "easier to hope for than to accomplish."[3] When at last it was too late, Nicholas began to make desperate but unavailing plans to accomplish it, to recover the lost ground by force of arms and to inaugurate councils of war for a new offensive. His

[1] *Fons Paradisi Divinalis*. *Cf.* Pasqual, i, p. 381, *H.L.F.*, No. 237, pp. 334–5, Longpré, col. 1097. Alòs (*Los Catálogos*, p. 74) queries its genuineness, but gives no grounds for doing so.

[2] Pasqual is the source of the information and all that he says is (*Vindiciae*, i, p. 187): "Primo autem Nicolaum IV adivit, eique praesentavit libellum, qui sic incipit: *Deus in virtute tua ostenditur hic, quomodo Terra Sancta recuperari potest*. Modus autem est quod ex omnibus Ordinibus Militaribus fiat unus Ordo qui continuo per mare et terram pugnet contra Saracenos praeter alia, quae ibi praescribit: qui libellus, ut constat in ejus fine, fuit datus Romae summo Pontifici anno 1290." *Cf.* Golubovich, p. 367, *Poesies*, p. 161, and p. 152, n. 2, above.

[3] Philippus Brictius, *cit.* Pasqual, i, pp. 376–7.

activity, however, had little effect, and in the year after the fall of Acre he died.

Meanwhile, Ramon was far away. For all the attention which the Pope may have given, as it seems likely that he did, to his counsels of war, he probably felt that events were too disturbing for his counsels of peace to have effect : much calm deliberation was essential before the experiment of Miramar could be repeated on a large scale throughout Europe, and this was still the project nearest to his heart. So, after a very short period spent at Rome, he abandoned the idea of dallying in Italy with Gaufredi's letters : the moment had come when words should give place to actions.[1] Since some time must elapse before life would be peaceful enough at Rome for his purpose, he would use that time well, return to Genoa, embark for Barbary, and there put some of his theories into practice, preaching and disputing with the heathen according to his own methods, and "proving the holy Incarnation of the Son of God, and the Holy Trinity, which the infidels believe not."[2]

Doubtless, although the Mallorcan preacher had, so far as we know, halted as yet only once in Genoa, it had not been long before he had become known there. When he returned,[3] the news that he was going to Barbary spread quickly. Rumour, it is probable, spoke more freely about him than knowledge. It was known that "Our Lord had inspired him upon a certain mountain,"[4] and the expectation was expressed that "our Lord God would work marvels by his hands."[5] So much was

[1] *V.C.*, iv (*Life*, pp. 17–18) makes his motives quite clear : "Més com en la dita Cort romana posqués poc aprofitar per los grans empaxs que y sentía, delliberà de tornar s en en Génova per ço que de aquí pus facilment posqués passar en Barbaría per preicar." *V.B.R.L.* (*Life*, p. 59) adds : "ad experiendum, utrum ipse saltem solus in aliquo posset proficere apud ipsos, conferendo cum sapientibus eorum, etc."

[2] *V.C.*, iv (*Life*, p. 18). *V.B.R.L.* (*Life*, p. 59) adds : "immo caeci, nos Christianos tres Deos colere, asserunt," and, for "proving" reads "manifestando eisdem secundum Artem sibi datam a Deo."

[3] The usual date given for the return is the spring of 1292, but I see no adequate reason for making it later than the preceding year.

[4] *V.C.*, iv (*Life*, p. 18). *V.B.R.L.* (*Life*, p. 60) supposes what was known to have been a little more detailed.

[5] *V.C.*, iv (*Life*, p. 18) ; cf. *V.B.R.L.*, ii (*Life*, p. 60).

sufficient then, as it is now, to give a man due measure of notoriety or fame.

But Ramon himself, if the contemporary record—as we cannot doubt—speaks truly, was less confident than his admirers upon the eve of his first missionary journey. He had collected his books, and taken his passage on the boat,[1] when there came to him "a mighty temptation."[2] He began to count the cost of this perilous adventure. "His understanding showed him, as clearly as if he saw it, how that, so soon as he reached Barbary, the Moors would neither hear him, nor permit him to dispute or to preach, but would stone him, or at the least condemn him to perpetual imprisonment."[3] It was a prospect dark enough to daunt the heart of any man who felt his life's work still to be before him. Saint Peter himself, the contemporary biographer reminds us, had shown no greater courage.[4] And so shaken was Lull in his faith that he allowed the boat to sail without him, remaining in Genoa in the throes of doubt.[5]

Naturally enough, it was no sooner too late to change his mind than he found himself in the grip of a spiritual reaction.[6] God would surely damn him for this grievous defection from His will. Worse, his sin would cause the people, who had put such trust in him, to lose their faith in God's power. So greatly did these two thoughts torment him that when but a short time had passed he became ill of a malady the nature of which he revealed to none, if indeed he himself understood it.

He came well-nigh to the point of despair, and had such sorrow within his soul that it went as it were from him, and he fell

[1] *V.C.*, iv (*Life*, p. 18). Once again *V.B.R.L.* is more explicit: "Cum ad transfretandum, sicut praetangitur, navigium et alia parata fuissent omnia, omnesque libri sui in navi cum necessariis aliis introducti . . ." (*Life*, p. 60).

[2] ". . . eundem tentatione gravissima subito coepit probare" (*Life*, p. 60).

[3] *V.C.*, iv (*Life*, p. 18); cf. *V.B.R.L.*, ii (*Life*, p. 60).

[4] "De la qual cosa hac gran temor lo dit reverent mestre [*V.B.R.L.*: "timens pelli suae"] axí com se lig de mossènyer Sent Pere" (*Life*, pp. 18, 60).

[5] Both Catalan and Latin chroniclers (*Life*, pp. 19, 60) suggest that his action was due to the "permission" or "inspiration" of God "to Whom at that time he was not pleasing."

[6] Or "contraria temptació" (*V.C.*, iv; *Life*, p. 19).

grievously sick ; in the which sickness he remained for a long time and to none would he reveal the nature thereof.[1]

Doubtless Ramon's illness was a genuine mental disturbance, and, if the curious narrative which we shall quote literally from the contemporary biography be true, there is no need to suppose the visions of which it speaks objective ones.

" The feast of Quinquagesima drew nigh,"[2] runs the biography, " and, sick as he was, he caused himself to be carried to the church of Messer Saint Dominic.[3] When they sang that holy hymn which begins 'Veni, Creator Spiritus,' his understanding soared aloft towards our Lord, Whom with heartfelt tears he entreated that by His great benignity He would pardon him that great defection.[4] When they had set him in a room within the dormitory, the said reverend master continued his lofty prayer. And looking towards the ceiling of the said room, he saw a tiny light, as it were a star, from the which issued a voice which spake to him these words : 'Within this order thou shalt be saved.' "

" So soon as he had heard these words, the said reverend master sent to the monks [begging them] to clothe him with the habit of Messer Saint Dominic,[5] the which thing they dared not do, because the Prior was not there. Now when the said reverend master had returned to his lodging, he remembered how that the Friars Minor had found the *Art* which our Lord had shown him more acceptable than had the Friars Preachers ; wherefore he

[1] *V.C.*, cf. *V.B.R.L.* (*Life*, p. 61) : " . . . tactus est tanto dolore cordis, ut in corpore febricitando gravissime aegrotaverit, sicque Genuae languens diutius, nec alicui causam sui doloris aperiens, fere ad nihilum redactus est."

[2] *V.B.R.L.* (*Life*, p. 62) has " adveniente die sancta festi Pentecostes." This looks very much like a correction of the Catalan version, made for reasons obvious from the context.

[3] It would be natural for him to return to his first love in such a condition of mental disorder.

[4] *V.B.R.L.* (*Life*, p. 62) has : " ingemiscens ait intra se : numquid non Spiritus iste Sanctus me posset salvare ? "

[5] Ramon had no doubt during a considerable period been considering seriously becoming a religious. His disordered mind now seizes on this idea and he tries to carry it out immediately. A normal man would rather concern himself with making amends for his defection.

thought that he would leave the order of Saint Dominic and take the habit of Messer Saint Francis. While he thought upon these things, he saw upon the wall nigh at hand a cord or girdle of [the order of] Messer Saint Francis. And when he had thought thereon for the space of an hour, looking up, he saw that same light which he had seen [when he was with] the Preachers, and heard the same voice, which said to him, almost threateningly : 'And did I not tell thee that only in the order of the Preachers thou wouldst find salvation? Look, then, what thou wilt do.' "

" When the said reverend master had heard this, he reasoned within himself that if he entered not the order of Friars Minor his books would be lost, and that, on the other hand, according to the voice which came from the star, he himself would not be saved if he entered not the order of the Preachers. Thus he was thrown into deep distress, and after long thought he elected rather to be damned himself than to cause the total loss of that *Art* whereby many might be saved. So, notwithstanding the star, he sent presently to the Guardian of the Friars Minor and begged of him the habit of the glorious Messer Saint Francis, which they promised him forthwith as he was near to death." [1]

" Now albeit the said reverend master believed that our Lord would not pardon him, yet he desired not to give an evil example of himself to the people, by dying otherwise than as a true Catholic, but rather to make profession of Christianity. When the priest had brought him the precious Body of Jesus Christ, and, standing before him, desired to deliver it to him, the said reverend master felt that his head was being turned by force to the right hand, and likewise it seemed to him that the precious Body of Jesus Christ passed to the left hand, saying to him these words : 'Thou shalt suffer condign punishment if thou desirest in thy present state to receive Me.' But the said reverend master was firm in his purpose, choosing rather that he himself should be damned than

[1] This need not necessarily have been the case in actual fact, but the Friars were evidently not anxious to risk the results of refusing to humour him.

that his *Art*, whereby many might be saved, should be lost; and when again it seemed to him that his head was being turned to the right hand, our Lord being before him, he flung himself from the bed, and fell, with his face to the ground, at the feet of the priest, and, with this show of devotion [1] afore-mentioned, the said reverend master communicated. 'Oh what a marvellous temptation is this!' says a doctor. 'The patriarch Abraham trusted in our Lord, and against all hope he had hope, and even so did the said master Ramon, choosing rather himself to be damned than that his *Art*, whereby many might be saved, should be lost. Wherefore we may say that he loved his neighbour better than himself.'" [2]

No other episode in Ramon's whole life is related by the contemporary biographer with anything approaching the fulness and intimacy which mark this. The account of it is substantially the same in both Latin and Catalan biographies, and gives us the sole clear glimpse which we may fairly be said to possess into the inner and spiritual life of a man concerning whose external activities we know so much. That it is not authentic there is no reason whatever for believing. Its realism, its detail, and the boldness of its avowals stamp it as a genuine confession. Ramon evidently regarded his defection as St. Peter regarded his denial, and describes it without attempt at palliation. If it be objected that he relates no other of his sins in detail, the reply is that those committed before his conversion he groups together, while as to his subsequent offences against God, there is none so grave that it can be so much as compared with this.

Pasqual and other Lullists of his time rejected this

[1] *V.C.*, ficta devoció; *V.B.R.L.*, devotione ficta. But see Pasqual, ii, p. 25, where a variant reading is given which need not necessarily be correct (cf. *Life*, p. 22, n.).

[2] *V.C.*, iv (*Life*, pp. 19–22). *V.B.R.L.* varies only slightly throughout, but omits the words "says a doctor," and adds "seu potius, ut videtur, divinae probationis dispensatio"; also, after "should be lost," it has: "velut sol nube tectus, dum nihilominus ardens in se, sub quadam suae mentis obumbratione de Deo modo mirabili desperando, Deum et proximum propter Deum infinities plus, quam se ipsum, diligere probatus est, ut evidenter colligitur ex praedictis" (*Life*, p. 65).

narrative completely, arguing in a most uncritical fashion from what they chose to consider its improbability to the spuriousness of the pages which record it.[1] Hardly any writer, and certainly no scholar, would uphold such a view to-day,[2] and we shall not spend time in discussing it, except to remark that only a hagiographical fanatic, fearful lest he should impute to his hero one single weakness or sin, could consider such a narrative as this intrinsically improbable. Ramon was a man, with the failings which the greatest and saintliest men have known and freely acknowledged. And his courage and devotion only shine the more clearly by contrast with his one very human defection.

Some years before he could have related to the anonymous biographer the story reproduced above, Ramon incorporated a part of his experiences, using language highly figured and poetic, but not unrecognizable,

[1] Those interested may consult Pasqual, ii, pp. 18 ff: who presumes to know what the contemporary biographies "meant to say." Of the arguments he uses, that which is generally adduced to-day is Lull's statement in *Desconort*, xii (written probably in 1295):

> . . . Depús que Jesucrist a mi es fo revelat
> en la crots, segons que d'amont vos he contat,
> e en la sua amor mon voler confermat,
> no pequé a scient en null mortal pecat.

Various explanations of this not very serious difficulty are possible: (1) the date of the *Desconort* is not certain (see p. 256, n. 5, below); (2) the third line might refer to this very crisis or to some other event not identical with that to which the first two lines refer; (3) Ramon may have looked upon his defection as occurring after his illness had begun and not therefore as a mortal sin; (4) alternatively he may have considered it as a dispensation of God for His own purposes (cf. *Life*, p. 19, ll. 1–4) though this would not strictly prevent its being a mortal sin; (5) he is writing in character in the *Desconort*, and hence it does not follow that every detail in the passages ascribed to "Ramon" is true of Ramon Lull. The last explanation I consider to be the most likely: Ramon was not writing his autobiography, but a poem, and he wrote of himself somewhat loosely. Nor need we suppose that, when he looked back upon this experience as a whole, it was with unrelieved compunction. He went through a "Dark Night of the Spirit," and at one point it overwhelmed him for a moment. But eventually he emerged from it triumphantly, as the following pages in the text above will show.

[2] I do not lose sight of Mn. Avinyó's unhappy attempt (Av., pp. 283–92) to support Pasqual's theories. It is a pleasure to contrast with them the strictures of Mn. Riber on Pasqual's "resolta gosadía" (*Vida i actes*, pp. 122–3), and Senyor Rubió's frank comment that the attitude of Custurer, Sollier and Pasqual "no sembla prou sincera" (*Revista dels Llibres*, ii, p. 93).

in the *Tree of the Philosophy of Love* (1298).[1] Even more evident is the application of some lines written in Rome only three years after these events, when he had newly taken the habit of St. Francis [2] :

There was a man that was a sinner who greatly prized the vanities of this world, and greatly displeased God in many ways; but God, having willed to deal mercifully with that man, granted him grace, so that he knew his sinfulness and for a long time did all that he could to further the honour of God. It came to pass that this man fell grievously ill, and for a great space of time was in this state,[3] and God, to chasten him severely in this life, allowed the devil to set him in a state of despair, so that he despaired of the mercy of God,[4] remembering his sins, which were great, and reflecting less upon God's mercy than upon His justice; so that, losing that great love for God which he was wont to have, and having no hope, he lost all esteem of himself, and thought each day that he would die by reason of his great sickness, and represented to himself in his imagination the pains of Hell to which he thought himself condemned for ever, and this, so he affirmed, would come to pass more certainly than happens when a man holds in his hand a piece of bread and purposes to eat it.[5]

This is one side of the truth: let the later book tell the rest:

Sick was the Lover by reason of his love, the which love had caused him to be sick through overmuch sighing, weeping and fear. So he said to Love, who was the source of all his love, that he would fain send a message, by a desire, to the Physician of love, begging him to come and heal him and make him whole of his sickness. . . .

[1] See pp. 282–3, below.

[2] The description is clearly of Ramon himself, and, with all we know of his life, we have no knowledge of any other serious illness of his whatever.

[3] The original is emphatic: "Esdevencse que aquell home fon malalt longament e de molt greu malaltía."

[4] "Deus . . . sofferí que l demoni lo posàs en desesperança, en tant que aquell home se desesperà de la misericordia de Deu."

[5] *Arbre de Sciencia*: Arbre exemplifical, iii (*Obres*, xii, pp. 382–3). The narrative continues: "Yet he had some small illumination of hope in Our Lady by reason of a book which he made for love of her, in the which book he praised her greatly." The book is presumably the *Book of Saint Mary*, composed not long before the crisis at Genoa.

In § iv of the "Arbre exemplifical" (*Obres*, xii, pp. 406–7) occurs a not dissimilar *exempli*, which may also be autobiographical, but there is less suggestion that it is and the evidence does not convince me.

The Physician examined the Lover, and took his pulse, and he found that the Lover had need of a medicine which should give him frenzy, that love might cause him to speak as a fool, for they that speak of love in manners most like to those of fools are they that are in truth the sanest. So the Physician compounded a medicine of the roots of the tree of love, that it might be very potent, and gave it to the Lover, bidding him drink it for love of his Beloved.[1]

In the latter of these paragraphs is the poetical account of Ramon's healing, which we shall now tell in prose. While still he lay on his bed of sickness, he heard by chance that there was a galley[2] in the harbour preparing for a journey to Tunis. His soul leaped at the news: here was an opportunity for him to retrieve his honour! Ill as he was, he insisted upon being carried down, with his books, to the harbour, but his friends,[3] quite naturally, would not allow him to set sail.[4] So much trade, however, was done in those days between the busy port of Genoa and the North African cities that no great harm resulted from the delay. A few days later, news was brought to Ramon of a boat[5] that was going to the identical port. This time his determination was stronger; perhaps, too, his health was improving. In any case, he overcame all his friends' objections, embarked upon the boat, though again he had to be carried to it, and urged the sailors to put to sea without delay lest anything might impede his departure.[6]

No sooner was Ramon at sea than the burden of remorse which had weighed upon his soul fell from him, and an overwhelming joy took its place; his mysterious malady left him as mysteriously as it had come, so that within a few days he was as well as he had been in his

[1] *A.F.A.*, pp. 105–6; *T.L.*, pp. 33, 35.

[2] *Galera* (*V.C.*).

[3] *V.C.*: "los seus amics, veents ell estar en tan gran malaltía. . . ." *V.B.R.L.*: "amici sui videntes, eum in mortis janua existentem . . ." (*Life*, pp. 23, 65).

[4] *V.C.*: ". . . forçaren lo de romandre." *V.B.R.L.*: ". . . ipsum etiam invitum de navi (quod multum doluit) extraxerunt" (*loc. cit.*).

[5] *Barca* (*V.C.*). *V.B.R.L.*: "alia navis, quam Genuenses vulgariter barcam vocant" (*loc. cit.*).

[6] *V.C.*, iv (*Life*, pp. 22–3).

life.[1] On landing at Tunis, Ramon at once began his work ; his methods can in no way be better described than in the actual language of the contemporary biography, so full and clear is it.

" They went into the city," begins the biographer, " and the said reverend master began day after day to seek out those that were most learned in the sect of Mahomet, declaring to them how that he had studied the law of the Christians, whose faith and its foundations he knew well ; and now had come there to learn of their sect and belief (*credulitat*) ; and if it were found that this was better than that of the Christians, and they could prove it to him, he would assuredly become a Moor (*per cert ell se faria moro*).

" When many had heard this, all the learned Moors who were in the city of Tunis gathered together, alleging the strongest reasons which they knew or could [find] on behalf of their sect ; and when the said reverend master had answered these [reasons] readily and given satisfaction therein, they were all astonished and confounded, whereupon he began to speak after this manner :

" ' It behoves every man that is wise and learned to maintain that faith and belief that attributes to the Divine Majesty (which each one of you believes and allows) the greatest honour, goodness, power, glory and perfection, and all these things in the greatest equality and concordance. And, further, that faith and belief must be most zealously maintained and exalted which sets the greatest concordance and convenience between our Lord God and His effect. Now, as I understand, from the arguments that have been set before me, all of you, who hold the belief of Mahomet, understand not in the Divine dignities acts proper which are intrinsic and eternal, without which the Divine dignities have been or would be otiose *ab aeterno*.[2] . . . But . . . to postulate of God

[1] " Venc una tan gran leticia en la ànima, que dins molt pocs dies ell fo axí dispost en la sua persona, com may fos estat ; de la qual cosa se maravellaren fortment aquells qui ab ell veníen " (*V.C.*, iv ; *Life*, p. 23 ; cf. *V.B.R.L.*, iii ; *Life*, p. 66).

[2] At this point *V.B.R.L.* develops the argument rather more fully than *V.C.* See *Life*, pp. 67–9.

otiosity *ab aeterno* . . . would be blasphemy, and contrary to the equality and concordance which are in very truth in our Lord God. Wherefore, by this reasoning, the Christians prove that Trinity of Persons is in the Divine Essence, the proof whereof by necessary reasons was, so I heard the other day, revealed to a certain hermit, who received by Divine inspiration an *Art* which proves by reasoning how that in the simplest Divine Essence there is Trinity of Persons. If ye would give ear to these reasons, and to this *Art*, and [consider them] with quietness of mind (*ab pensa reposada*), then would ye perceive clearly, not these things aforementioned only, but likewise how the Second Person [of the Trinity] has united with Himself human nature, and how reasonable it is that in His humanity He should have suffered Passion, through His great mercy, for us that are sinners, through the sin of our first father, to the end that He might bring us at the last to His glory and bliss, for the which we were created.' "[1]

Arguing thus, Ramon apparently met with considerable success, and might have made many converts had not a member of his audience, fearing lest "their sect would come to total extermination and destruction," denounced him to the Caliph, praying that he might be delivered to a "cruel death."[2] The Caliph summoned his council, which decided against Ramon by a majority. A powerful member of the council,[3] however, made an appeal on the preacher's behalf,[4] and this was so far effective as to change the sentence of death to one of banishment.[5] Already Ramon had been imprisoned. As soon as the decree of the council was made known, a band of Moors—whether these were friendly or hostile to him is not clear—dragged him from his cell towards

[1] *V.C.*, iv (*Life*, pp. 23–6).

[2] So *V.C.*, iv ("requerintlo que a cruel mort fes morir lo dit crestià"). *V.B.R.L.* has "juberet truncari" (*Life*, pp. 26, 70).

[3] *V.C.* has "un gran moro"; *V.B.R.L.*, "quidam eorum prudens atque scientificus" (*Life*, pp. 27, 70).

[4] His arguments are given in *V.C.* and *V.B.R.L.* (*Life*, pp. 27, 70).

[5] *V.B.R.L.* adds: "Edictum est a rege, ut penitus lapidaretur, si quomodo amplius reperiretur in patria Tunicensium" (*Life*, p. 70).

a Genoese boat which was lying in the harbour and about to sail. But, during the deliberations of the council, public feeling in the city had been stirred against the foreigner. When he appeared in the streets, showers of stones and a storm of blows fell about him,[1] and probably only the protection of those who were haling him to the boat saved him from being stoned to death then and there.

It might be supposed that Ramon was relieved, if not overjoyed, at his narrow escape from the mob. But he was no longer the man of little faith that he had been at Genoa. All that he could think of, as he was being dragged along the streets to the harbour, "in peril of death, reviled, cursed and plucked by the beard,"[2] with fierce, swarthy faces all around him, was the loss of opportunities which would be entailed by his departure from Tunis. What of these souls, brought by his teaching, through the grace of God, to the point of preparedness for baptism,[3] if he left them to sink once more into their former ignorance? To remain would be to die, yet his departure would be for them death eternal.[4]

The choice was an easier one for him to make than that which had faced him during his mental agony in Genoa, and we may believe that he hesitated not for a moment. Joying and sorrowing,[5] he was brought to the ship and left alone there. His captors, having deposited him, went their ways. The tumult within the city subsided. Men's minds turned to other matters. Then it was that Ramon took advantage of some moment when the boat's crew was engaged. Quietly and secretly

[1] *V.C.*, iv: ". . . Quants foren los colps galtades e pedrades, no s porían recomptar;" cf. *V.B.R.L.*: "Cum ergo extraheretur de carcere, passus est a multis multa opprobria, verbera et aerumnas" (*Life*, pp. 27, 70).

[2] Cf. *Desconort*, li:

> que no sabets com eu soi menyspreat,
> per Déu, tantes vets maldit e blastomat,
> e en perill de mort e per barba tirat,
> e per vertut de Déu pacient són estat?

[3] *V.B.R.L.* (*Life*, p. 71) specifies further: "disposuerat enim viros famosae reputationis et alios quam plurimos ad baptismum."

[4] *V.C.*, iv, *V.B.R.L.*, iv (*Life*, pp. 27–8, 70–1).

[5] *V.C.*, iv: "Alegrava s . . . remembrant la passió del seu Amat; dolía s emperò e no poc. . . ." (*Life*, p. 27).

(*amagadament*) he slipped away, returned to the land,[1] and found a retreat where he could lie in safety until the opportunity came to re-enter the city and resume his preaching.[2] " Wholly on fire with love for God, he feared not to enter once again into the perils of death, if thereby he might bring about the salvation of any soul."[3] But, as he lay there, his eyes were opened to the hopelessness of his project. A redoubled clamour uprose. Some Christian—a merchant, no doubt—was going about the city of Tunis on his business. Unfortunately for him, he resembled the preacher in clothing and gesture, and no sooner did the people catch sight of him than they rushed upon him and would have haled him off and stoned him incontinently had he not had the wit to cry out at the top of his voice (*ab gran veu*) : " I am not Master Ramon."[4] The real Ramon was wise enough to take warning from this event of the inflammable state of the Moors in the city just then.[5] Without more ado,[6] he crept back to his ship, not abandoning by any means the mission which he had hoped to continue in Tunis, but postponing it to a more convenient season.

[1] *V.B.R.L.* says that, as the boat was going, Ramon slipped into another which lay in the harbour : " relicta nave recedente quandam aliam in eodem portu latenter intravit, sperabat enim, si aliquo modo posset venire ad terram absque impedimento impetus bestialis eorum, quod in supradictis opus bonum, quod inceperat, consummaret." (*Life*, p. 71.)

[2] *V.C.*, iv (*Life*, p. 28).

[3] *V.B.R.L.*, iv (*Life*, p. 71).

[4] *V.C.*, iv (*Life*, p. 28).

[5] " E com açò pervengués a sabuda del dit reverent mestre, considerà que allò era misteri divinal e que per consegüent ell no y poría aprofitar en res, llavors tornà en nau e venc s en en Nàpols " (*V.C.*, iv : *Life*, p. 28).

[6] So *V.C.* *V.B.R.L.*, however, has : " remansit itaque Raymundus tribus septimanis, qui videns, se nihil posse ibi pro Christi servitio adimplere, pervenit Neapolim."

CHAPTER XII

1292–1295

Arrival at Naples. The *Book of the five wise men.* The *Affatus.* Election of Celestine V. The *Petition of Ramon.* Boniface VIII succeeds Celestine V: Lull again unsuccessful at Rome. The *Desconort*: its substance, metrical qualities, and spiritual music.

THAT Ramon's first missionary journey to Africa did not end more disastrously is probably attributable largely to the amicable relations that existed between Aragon and Tunis. With all the Moorish states James the Conqueror and his successors thought it well to be on terms of friendship. Their ambitions were not primarily those of Castile: Christian territories lay beyond all their frontiers, and across the sea were the tempting prizes of the Mediterranean. So for generations we read of commercial treaties and political alliances with the kingdoms of Granada, Morocco, Tlemcen, Bugia and Tunis; the last three especially were in close relations with Aragon and the last most so of all. Politically, Tunis was a convenient taking-off ground for an attack on Sicily; commercially, it was the most prosperous trading centre in the north of Africa. Hence both Catalonia and Mallorca had protective treaties with that kingdom; their consuls and other officials lived there in a *funduq* or little colony; their manufacturers were well represented there; and their merchants were always welcome. As we shall later see, the tolerance and the generous treatment accorded to Moslems in Aragon stimulated these friendly relations, and no doubt more religious proselytizing was attempted and achieved on both sides than history has recorded.[1]

[1] On this subject, see Antonio de Capmany: *Memorias históricas sobre la marina, comercio y artes de la antigua ciudad de Barcelona*, Madrid, 1779–92;

Nevertheless, little of it would in the nature of things be done publicly, and, when Ramon left Tunis, he must have realized that he had strained relations with the Moors to such a point as to make an auspicious return there impracticable for a long time to come. The date of his departure is known with some exactness from the fact that he began a new book, while he was still in the port of Tunis,[1] in mid-September 1292, and completed it at Naples on January 13, 1293. This book is the *General Table*,[2] which aims at completing (by demonstrating briefly) the method of the inventive and amative arts, and is wholly concerned with general rules and principles, whence its name. Ramon himself considered it of great value, and made it the basis of several later works.[3] But it is not one of his books on which modern readers desire to dwell, and to them its chief if not its sole interest is chronological.

The boat which took Ramon away from Tunis left him at Naples. Here he stayed for some little time, giving public lectures on his *Art*,[4] preaching to such Moors as were in the city,[5] and writing a number of minor works about which it is necessary to say very little.[6]

A. Giménez Soler: "Episodios de la historia de las relaciones entre la corona de Aragón y Túnez," in *Anuari del Institut d'Estudis Catalans*, 1907, pp. 195–224, and "Documentos de Túnez del Archivo de la Corona de Aragón," *ibid.*, pp. 210–59.

[1] "At sea, in the port of Tunis" is the phrase used; so it is probable that it was begun while he was on the boat and waiting for it to sail.

[2] "Tabula generalis," or "Taula general." The book is generally known under its Latin name, but the Catalan text is probably its original form; *cf.* Salz., vol. v; *H.L.F.*, No. 35, pp. 183–7; Rubió y Lluch, "Sumari, etc." pp. 291–92; Rogent i Duràn, Bibliografía, etc., pp. 51–53.

[3] The *Lectura super Artem inventivam et Tabulam generalem* (see pp. 250, 255 n, below. Salz., vol. v, *H.L.F.*, No. 38, pp. 191–7; Longpré, col. 1093); *Lectura compendiosa Tabulae generalis* (Salz., vol. v, *H.L.F.*, No. 37, pp. 190–1); and *Brevis practica Tabulae generalis*. The last named (sometimes dated January 1299: see Alòs: *Los catálogos*, etc., pp. 61–2) is not to be confused with the similarly entitled work completed at Genoa on February 1, 1304 (cf. *H.L.F.*, pp. 188–90, 294, and p. 311, n. 2, below).

[4] *V.C.*, *V.B.R.L.*, iv (*Life*, pp. 28, 72).

[5] This we learn from the *Lectura* mentioned in the next note.

[6] The "Lectura" for the *Ars inventiva*, published together with that for the *Tabula generalis* (n. 3, above) about 1294–5, may have been begun at this time. See pp. 250, 255, below. A treatise on the "lightness and heaviness of the elements" (*De levitate et ponderositate elementorum*, c. 1293: *H.L.F.*,

One of them, which recalls the *Book of the Gentile*, and the story of Blanquerna and the Tartar, is of considerably more interest than the remainder, for it illustrates admirably the difficulties under which Roman missionaries laboured at the end of the thirteenth century. This is the *Book of the five wise men*.[1]

The sages who figure in it are Latin, Greek, Nestorian, Jacobite and Mohammedan. It must not be forgotten in reading this and similar books that the Nestorian and Jacobite churches, especially the former, were an important factor in the Mongolian problems of the day. Most of the evangelization of Asia, up to the time of John XXI, had been accomplished by Nestorian missionaries, and to their influence was largely due the toleration accorded by Mongols to Christians and even the requests of various Mongol tribes for missionaries to be sent them from Rome. Such successes as the Nestorians had achieved in five or six centuries were multiplied to an incredible extent by the imagination of the Europeans ; few can realize, perhaps, how potent an influence upon the Crusaders was the belief in that Nestorian priest-king, the legendary Prester John, who at any time might appear (so ran the belief) from his unknown domains in Central Asia, and, at the head of a fierce army, lead them to victory. The Jacobites, or Monophysites of Syria, to-day a sect of small importance, had in the twelfth and thirteenth centuries reached the climax of their history. Their titular city of Antioch was an important metropolis ; they had flourishing schools of philosophy, theology and science ; and their hierarchy numbered twenty metropolitans and one hundred bishops. It was not till the last years of the thirteenth century that the schisms and persecutions began which led to their diminution and decay.

But against the laudable activities of these sects there has to be reckoned the harm which was done in the

No. 86, p. 259 ; Longpré, col. 1107), said to have been written at the request of Neapolitan doctors, need not detain us. The *Liber de affatu*, 1294, is considered below (p. 250).

[1] *Liber de quinque sapientibus*, Salz., vol. ii ; cf. *H.L.F.*, No. 9, pp. 102–7. The Catalan MS. is at Munich ; only the Latin text has been published.

sight of the heathen by the importance of their heresies and the differences between their beliefs and those of both Latin and Greek missionaries. This St. Louis had found, scarcely a generation before, when he sent William of Rubruck as an ambassador to the Great Khan, in the mistaken belief that Christianity had already taken root among the Tartar tribes. As the years went on, the danger to Christianity of these unhappy divisions was seen to be growing greater. A toleration was awaiting Islam in these parts no less genuine than that extended to the Christians, and, from the invasion of the Mongols under Jenzig Khan onwards, the peril that the whole of Asia would turn to Mahomet or to Buddha, instead of to Christ, was continually in the thoughts of the most earnest and ardent missionary souls in Christendom. It is precisely this peril that Lull's four Christian sages are discussing when they espy the fifth—a Saracen—in the distance. What will happen now in the Holy Land? Is there any hope whatever of its conquest? Will not the Saracens be more likely to convert the Tartars and subjugate the Eastern Christians? In this case, they will become a greater menace to Christianity than ever.

There is no danger to be feared from the Saracen of the story, it would seem, for, like the Tartar of the earlier book, he is anxious to be converted, having been led through the study of philosophy to doubt the teaching of Islam. But, like the Tartar also, he has been told by a Christian hermit that the Catholic faith is too lofty to be demonstrated to the understanding: it can only be accepted and believed, and, were it not so, there would be no merit in faith. The Saracen, however, who is skilled in philosophy, cannot trust in a possible salvation which is to come through faith unsupported by reason, and he is now in search of someone who will prove the truth of a religion in such a way as to satisfy his intellect.

The four sages, like all sages of Lull's fictions, are eager to convert the Moslem. They propose a lengthy debate, to which the Saracen may listen, on their several forms of Christianity. The results of this debate shall be laid before the highest Christian authorities, in the hope that a general discussion may be decreed on the differences between Rome and the schismatic bodies, in which will be used the *Ars Inventiva* and *Tabula Generalis*. The book, however, is too short to record the whole of the sages' debate, and contains only the exposition of the Latin. This he begins by repudiating the idea that the truth of any religion can be demonstrated in the same way as a mathematical theorem, and passes to contrast the faith of each of his companions with his own. Against the Greek he upholds the *Filioque* clause in the *Quicunque vult* ; against the Nestorian, that there is not in Christ one Person only of the Godhead ; against the Jacobite, that in Christ are both the Divine and the human natures ; and against the Saracen, the fundamental Christian doctrines of the Trinity and the Incarnation.[1]

At the end of the *Five Wise Men* comes an opuscule which is strictly part of it,[2] known as the *Petition of Ramon*, and dated from Naples in 1294 : this will fall into its place in our narrative shortly. Before writing it, Ramon must certainly have completed (on Easter Eve, 1294) the *Affatus* [3] (or *Liber de Affatu seu de sexto sensu*) the Catalan text of which is among the unpublished Lullian manuscripts at Munich. Its aim is to make out the power of speech to be a sixth sense, an idea found also in the *Lectura super Artem Inventivam*, in which book he makes reference to the *Affatus*.[4]

In the summer of 1294 there came to Naples the astounding news of the election to the Papacy of Celestine V. This election had been made in very unusual circumstances. For no less than twenty-seven months after the death of Nicholas IV the throne of St. Peter had been without an occupant. So divided were the Cardinals in their national and political

[1] Salz., ii, pp. 1–4.

[2] For (according to the narrative) the Latin sage retires after the debate to the shade of a tree and thinks how he may draw up the petition which follows to the Pope and Cardinals (Salz., ii, p. 50).

[3] *H.L.F.*, No. 148, p. 300 ; Alòs, *Los Catálogos*, etc., p. 72 ; *cf.* J. Borrás : " Un sesto sentido, el affatus." In *B.S.A.L.*, 1914, pp. 19–26.

[4] Quaestiones, 237–46 : " De Affatu." Salz., v, p. 325 ; *cf.* p. 247, n. 6, above.

allegiances, that it seemed as though the interregnum might continue indefinitely. What paradoxical inspiration led them to unite in calling to the Papacy a frail and emaciated hermit of seventy-nine years of age, to visit his wretched abode in the mountains, and, overruling his pleas of age and of incompetence, to lead him through tens of thousands to his coronation? It was not to be supposed that the reign of such a pope could be anything but short and turbulent. From first to last he was the helpless tool of younger and more ambitious men, both clerical and lay. When at length, from sheer inanition, he laid down his sacred office, and exchanged supreme power for cruel confinement, it was to die after a few short years, to be canonized in 1313 by the Church and to be made notorious by Dante as an example of moral weakness,

> colui
> che fece per viltate il gran rifiuto.[1]

It is not clear why Ramon Lull should have hoped for anything from this hermit-pope. True, Celestine was own brother to Blanquerna,—a contemplative, yet called, as Blanquerna had been, to an active life in the service of the Church; a devout and holy man, beloved of the extreme party of the time known as the Spirituals, and in principle likely enough to sympathize with Ramon the Fool. But by this time Ramon had had experience enough of life to know that sympathy alone would not take him far, and that Rome would be not less troubled under Celestine than under Nicholas. Yet, however we may explain it, he went straight to the Roman court, "to see if he could obtain that which he had desired."[2]

During Celestine V's brief but tumultuous reign of five months, and probably while he was at Naples from

[1] *Inferno*, iii, 58.

[2] *V.C.*, *V.B.R.L.*, v (*Life*, pp. 29, 73). Note the phrase: "Venc lo dit reverent mestre en Roma" ("ivit Raymundus ad curiam Romanam"). Actually Celestine V was elected at Perugia, his consecration took place at Aquila (on the borders of the kingdom of Naples) and he abdicated at Naples itself. It seems unlikely, therefore, that Ramon stayed in Rome for any length, as *V.C.* asserts, if, indeed, he went there at all.

November 13 to December 10, the fervent apostle succeeded in presenting him with two works which between them embodied his desires. The first of these is an allegorical book based upon the *Ars amativa*,[1] thought to have been influenced by the *Roman de la Rose* and entitled *Flowers of Love and Intelligence*[2]; it was sent to Celestine and his "honourable and discreet college," in the hope that they might give heed to the *Petition of Ramon* which accompanied it.[3] The aim of the *Petition* was that God might be known and loved in the world; that of the *Flowers*, "that the lover may know, love and contemplate his Beloved, Who is God, and set his will upon loving Him."[4] Probably the *Petition* was written in some haste, for its theme was taken up four years later, and developed more carefully, in a work of greater importance,[5] as were also the suggestions in it, and in the *Flowers*, of courtly poetry and the songs of troubadours. Both narratives use the similitude of Lover and Beloved. Goodness and Love seize the Lover and imprison him in his Beloved's glory. The Power and the Will of the Beloved command him to go into all the world and sing there His praises. Such language, taken alone, might be considered vague and rhetorical. Read together with the *Petition of Ramon for the Conversion of the Heathen*, it is seen to be expressing in beautiful and symbolic terms the decision of a resolute mind.

This *Petition* appeals to the Pope and his Cardinals to "open the treasury of Holy Church,"[6] that all may

[1] The opening words make it clear that a knowledge of the principles and definitions of the *Ars amativa* is necessary for the understanding of the *Flowers*.

[2] *Flores amoris et intelligentiae* (*H.L.F.*, No. 41, pp. 204–5; Longpré, col. 1104).

[3] *Petitio Raymundi pro conversione infidelium ad Coelestinum V*. Golubovich (pp. 373 ff.) reprints the Latin text, which is also in Salz., vol. vi. The Catalan text is at Munich.

[4] Salz., vi, p. 1.

[5] See pp. 279–87, below.

[6] The quotations in this and the next two paragraphs are from the Latin text of the *Petition* (Salz., vi; pp. 50–1 of *Liber de quinque sapientibus*. I have not the least doubt that it is to this work, or to the similar production presented to Boniface VIII, that Ramon is alluding in *Desconort*, xxiv, 9–12, lv, 12, in spite of Pasqual (*Vindiciae*, i. pp. 140–1), and that the work mentioned in lvi is the same.

partake of her treasures, both temporal and spiritual. Here there is nothing vague about Ramon's desires. "For every Christian there are a hundred or more that are not Christians" but are "journeying towards everlasting fire." Let a tithe of the Church's entire wealth be assigned to crusades and missionary work till the Holy Land is conquered and the world won for Christ. Let one Cardinal be chosen to spend his life searching for the best preachers "in all countries of Christendom"—"holy men, religious and secular alike, who to honour our Lord God would fain suffer death." Let these preachers be taught, among them, all the languages of the world. Let colleges for the learning of foreign tongues be founded in Tartary as well as in Christendom. Let schismatics be recalled to the one fold, for it is they—no doubt the Eastern sects are referred to—who can best convert Moslems and Tartars.

How dreadful it will be, continues the *Petition*, if the entire Mongol world embraces the religion of Saracen or Jew. At present it is not difficult, by means of disputations, to convert them, for the religion they have is rudimentary ("non habent Legem") and they allow our missionaries free access. But how long will this state of things last? "For, if the Tartars set up a religion ('faciunt Legem'), as Mahomet did, either Saracens or Jews will be able to convert them to their religion, and all Christendom will be in dire peril."

Other plans Ramon has to urge, all of which fit in with these. He is entirely won over by now to the project of a great new crusade. The "lands of the infidels," as well as the Holy Land beyond the sea, must be conquered—"et hoc per vim armorum." There should be frequent and definite missions to schismatics to show them "that they are in error and that the Latins are in the way of truth." Letters should be written from Rome to Moslem kings, asking them to send to Rome some of their sages, to be instructed in what Christians really believe. A similar procedure may be applied to schismatics. They and the Saracens alike, in short, will be won over by "necessary reasons" such as "I, Ramon

Lull, unworthy man " have in plenty, and will gladly put forward when required.[1]

The petition ends on a lofty note, with a plea to Pope and Cardinals " to work for the honour of God, Who has so greatly honoured you." The task may indeed be a long one, and beset by many obstacles, but do not men of the world overcome such for the sake of temporal riches ? Too apt are Christian teachers to sit at home while kings and princes light-heartedly engage in costly and perilous campaigns for rewards which are as nothing compared with those of Christ. Too readily do our leaders exclaim that the world will be converted " in God's good time."

" In God's good time " ![2] That is surely to-day. Did not God create men to serve Him ? Did not Jesus Christ and the apostles and martyrs give us an example ? Has there ever been a time when God has not willed to be loved by His people ?

" I would fain say more," ends the *Petition*, " but I fear lest I have said too much. If indeed I have been presumptuous, I crave forgiveness. But most of all I beg that I myself, unworthy as I am, may be sent to convert the Saracens, that I may do honour among them to our Lord and God."[3]

It is to be feared that the presentation of these writings had but little effect on the worn-out hermit-Pope, who, at the end of the year 1294, laid down the heavy burden of the tiara, after a certain amount of not disinterested pressure, but with a ready enough will, there seems no doubt. Ramon was either in Rome at the time,[4] or,

[1] Ego Raymundus Lullus indignus aestimo me multas tales habere secundum aliquem novum modum, quem Deus mihi dedit, ad vincendum omnes illos, qui contra Fidem Catholicam aliquid volunt probare, vel improbare.

[2] Si dicitur, quod omnia ista fient quando Deo placuerit. . . .

[3] . . . ut vobis placeat me indignum primum mittere ad Saracenos ad honorandum inter illos nostrum Dominum Deum.

[4] In Rome, perhaps during 1294, but in what month is not known, Ramon wrote his *Book of the Rational Soul* (*Liber de anima rationali*, Salz., vol. vi, *H.L.F.*, pp. 211–15). In this (according to the prologue) he makes an enquiry into the nature of the soul, " according to the rule of the *General Table*." By this book, he adds, a man may learn to know both himself and God, since the rational soul is the image and similitude of God. (" De fine huius libri "). Pasqual (ii, pp. 61–2) dates this book 1296, because it cites the *Arbor Scientiae*

much more probably, in Naples. Whether he had expected much from Celestine, or whether his real aim in sending him the two books had been to arouse public interest, it is impossible to say. It may be that he had foreseen the approaching end of Celestine's short reign and thought it well to prepare the ground for a future Pope and await developments.

These, unhappily, favoured him little. The able and ambitious Gaetani, who, eleven days after Celestine's abdication, succeeded him as Boniface VIII, was unlikely to have much to say to him, the more so on account of the political crisis to which recent events had led. Elected in Naples, Boniface went to Rome in January 1295 for his coronation on the 25th, and to Rome Lull perseveringly followed him.[1] But there was small hope of any degree of success for years to come. The Sicilian question was stirred up once more, and in the ensuing war both James II of Aragon and his brother Frederic were involved, on opposite sides. Within Italy itself, Florence and Tuscany were in disorder, and there was strife between Genoa and Venice. Even in Rome, Boniface found himself in bitter and deadly conflict with Jacopo and Pietro Colonna, two cardinals belonging to a powerful family which had been successful in ruling, among other popes, the well-intentioned Nicholas IV. And, to crown all, the long struggle between Boniface and Philip the Fair, which was to last through the whole pontificate, had already begun before the Pope succeeded. Hence, if he had been disposed to look with favour upon far-sighted missionary enterprises, and to aid one whose

(1295) and the *Liber de Articulis Fidei* (1296). The date 1294 is given in one of the Latin MSS. of the book itself, but see *H.L.F.*, p. 215, Longpré, col. 1093. I consider the evidence for 1296 (Longpré, col. 1093) strong, but not conclusive.

[1] It seems to have been now that Ramon completed the huge *Lectura super Artem Inventivam et Tabulam Generalem*, also extant in a Catalan MS. entitled *Art de fer e solre questions*, which was probably begun a great deal earlier (see p. 247, above). Its "thousand brief questions" (really 912) include such varied problems as: "Can God annihilate Himself?" "Could the world be what it were if God were not?" and the rather plaintive "When there are so many sermons, why are there so many sinners?" Question 45 refers to Boniface VIII as being Pope. See Rogent i Duràn: *Bibliografía*, etc., pp. 51–2.

language was that of troublesome Aragon and whose interests were sponsored by Philip, it would have been difficult for him, in the circumstances of his pontificate, to do so.

Ramon seems, nevertheless, to have had audience, on a number of occasions, of Boniface VIII, to have presented to him a petition modelled on that already described,[1] and to have pleaded, with more than his usual vehemence,[2] the causes which were so dear to him. Perhaps on that account there was a greater decisiveness than usual about his failure.[3] In the corrupt and intriguing Papal court, his persistence and devotion made him nothing but scornful enemies. Many were the setbacks and the rebuffs that he received, says the contemporary biographer, "but for the honour of our Lord he bore them with all gladness."[4]

Not uniformly so, however, for in that same year (1295)[5] of Boniface's election, Ramon gave vent to the bitterness of his successive disillusionments at the Papal court in what is perhaps the finest work in verse that he ever composed: the *Desconort*[6] ("Disconsolateness"). One

[1] See pp. 251–4, above; *cf. H.L.F.*, No. 253, pp. 341–2, Gottron, p. 19 (*cf.* Dmitrewski, p. 7; Longpré, col. 1109). The text of the *Petitio Raymundi pro conversione infidelium et recuperatione Terrae Sanctae ad Bonifacium VIII* is to be found at Paris and Munich.

[2] *V.C.*, v (*Life*, p. 29) says that he besought the Pope "many times." *V.B.R.L.*, v (*Life*, p. 73) has: "Cui etiam *totis viribus* conatus est supplicare Raymundus, etc."

[3] The omissions of *V.C.* are eloquent, and the passage deserves quotation in the original: "Com hagués estat aquí per algún temps e hagués ordonats aquí alguns libres, succeí papa Bonifaci octau al qual aximetex moltes voltes suplicà lo dit reverent mestre per algunes utilitats de la sancta Fè catòlica. E jatsia sostingués molts enuigs e afanys en seguir la dita cort, emperò per honor de nostre Senyor tot ho portava alegrement" (*cf. Life*, p. 29).

[4] See last note. *V.B.R.L.* emphasizes the persistence of Ramon rather than his longsuffering.

[5] Some MSS. date the poem 1285, but the year generally given (1295) is almost certainly correct, for (1) the "thirty years" of stanza iii support it, (2) the chronology of stanza xiv is only possible of 1295 (*cf.* p. 203 above and *Poesies*, p. 160), (3) stanza li surely refers to the Tunisian experiences of 1292–3, (4) the conversion of the Tartars by the Saracens (stanza lxiii) had hardly begun even as early as 1295. There are also many parallels with the *Petition* to Celestine V (pp. 251–4, above).

[6] I keep the familiar Catalan form of the word rather than the recently introduced 'Desconhort,' and refer to the poem by this name throughout.

passage in which he seems to refer to its composition implies that he wrote it " to alleviate somewhat the grief which he had when he could not accomplish the sacred work (*sant negoci*) of Jesus Christ in the court of Rome." [1] The sub-title of the poem describes it as " made by master Ramon Lull in his old age, when he saw that neither the Pope nor the other lords of the world would put forth a method for (*metre orde en*) the conversion of the heathen, according as he had prayed them at many and divers seasons." [2] Such descriptions prepare one to find in the poem the most personal and passionate outpourings of Ramon's ardent soul.

Some autobiographical passages from the *Desconort*, which consists of sixty-nine twelve-lined stanzas of monorimed alexandrines, have already been quoted in this narrative, and these will not be repeated in the description of the poem which follows. The elegiac tone is prominent from the opening lines :

> No friend can make me glad, how dear so e'er,
> Save Thee alone, for Whom this load I bear
> To bed and board ; nor can I, here or there,
> Find joy in aught that I can see or hear.[3]

Ramon first relates the story of his life, conversion and ideals. For thirty years he has striven in vain to have these ideals translated into action. In the bitterness of his soul he goes into a wood to be alone. There he sees a venerable hermit, with long beard, a staff in his hand, and little clothing on his back beyond a hair-shirt. " Why art thou so sorrowful ? " asks the hermit. Ramon tells him, and meets with long-desired sympathy.

> " Ramon," the hermit said, " thou hast lost what thing ?
> Why seek'st thou not redress from Heav'n's high King,
> Who, if He chastens, comfort too can bring ?

[1] *Arbre de Sciencia*, pròleg. (*Obres*, xi, p. 3) ; *cf.* p. 269, below.

[2] At the end of the poem we read that it was " made in the court of Rome " *Poesies*, p. 112).

[3] E no hai null amic qui negú gauig m'aport,
mas tan solament vós, per què eu lo faix en port
en caent e en llevant e són çai en tal sort
que res no veig ni auig d'on me venga confort.
(i, 9–12.)

They that lose Him their hands will ever wring,
But only they can know no comforting.
So if thou hast no friend to tell this thing,
Show me thy heart and all thy sorrowing." [1]

Some of the failures of these thirty years are recounted to the hermit. Had he some success to report, he would reckon no trials that he had suffered too great. But even his comrades laugh at him.

Lonely am I, abandoned and unsought.
I look men in the face—would tell my thought—
But few are they that heed : the rest say naught,
Then call me fool.[2]

All to whom God has given most honour on earth despise him and his words, as though they were the words of one who " foolishly speaks and nothing does at all." [3] His *Ars magna*, given him by inspiration from Heaven, which can impart knowledge of " all natural things," [4] he holds for lost : " scarce any for it cares." [5] He can never have joy in aught again.

The hermit endeavours to console him. If Ramon has done his utmost, and God has inspired him to do it,

[1] " Ramon ! " dix l'eremità, vós què havets perdut ?
Per què no us consolats en lo rei de salut
qui abasta a tot ço qui per ell és esdevengut ?
Mas aquell qui el perd no pot haver vertut
en ésser consolat, car trop és abatut.
E si vós no havets null amic qui us ajut,
digats-me vostre cor, e què havets haüt.
(vi, 1–7.)

[2] . . . ans són sol abandó
e can los guard en la cara e els vull dir ma rasó
no em volen escoltar, ans dien que fat só
los de més.
(xvi, 7–10.)

[3] com hom qui follament
parla e res no fa.
(vii, 8–9.)

[4] una *Art general*
que novament és dada por do espirital
per qui hom pot saber tota re natural,
segons que enteniment ateny lo sensual.
(viii, 1–4.)

[5] e tenc-la per perduda car quaix a hom no en cal.
(viii, 9.)

then God, when He sees fit, will give the increase and provide many labourers for the harvesting. He himself must be glad and joyful : despondency unfits a man to be God's servant and leads him into deadly sin, even into such a sin as sloth. For a long time Ramon will not listen to these arguments. He can only endeavour to make the hermit realize the extent of his failure :

Wife have I left, children and riches great ;
For thirty years sore trials have been my fate ;
Five times I have been to Court, God's delegate ;
Thrice with the Preachers have I held debate
In Chapters-General, and thrice more of late
In Minors' Chapters : could I enumerate
The trials of one to God's love dedicate,
And all I have said to those of high estate,
Thou would'st not me as idle and slothful rate
But pity one that is disconsolate.[1]

The hermit, however, shows no more sympathy when he hears Ramon's story, but proves to be a Job's comforter, discussing with great frankness his companion's actual and presumed faults, until Ramon exclaims that he has hardly deserved to be spoken of so uncharitably. Hereupon the discussion becomes less personal and the hermit takes up the main cause of Ramon's grief, and suggests, not a remedy, but a reason for it. If the *Art* is neglected and despised, as he asserts, and

[1] Car muller n'hai lleixada, fills e possessiós
e trenta anys n'hai estat en treball e llangors,
e cinc vets a la Cort ab mes messiós (*lit*, at my costs).
n'hai estat, e encara a los Preïcadors
a tres capítols generals, e a los Menors
altres tres generals capítols ; e si vós
sabíets què n'hai dit a reis, e a senyors
ni con hai treballat, no seríets dubtós
en mi que sia estat en est fait pereós,
ans n'hauríets pietat si sots hom piadós.
(xiv, 3–12.)

The five visits to the (Papal) Court would be in 1277, 1285 (twice), 1290, and 1294 ; either the last visit of 1295 is not counted or the two visits of 1285 (more probably) are reckoned as one. The three Dominican Chapters-General would be those of Montpellier (1283), Bologna (1285) and Paris (1286) ; the Franciscan Chapters must be those of Montpellier (1287), Rieti (1289) and Assisi (1295).

read by men as fast
As cat runs that through burning coals has passed,
Then thought no more of.[1]

is not this because the Christian verities cannot be proved by argument? Evidently it is the Tartar's hermit who is speaking, for he alleges the identical reasons by which the Tartar was so much distressed:

That which thou dost ask,
That faith be prov'd by reason is a task
Impossible.[2]
. . . If we could clearly prove our faith,
Merit were lost.[3]
. . . The truth of God being infinite,
Man's understanding reaches not its height;
Much must be hidden from our mortal sight;
Wherefore thine arguments are worthless quite.[4]

Ramon, as befits a "procurator of the unbelievers," protests against this attitude passionately. If the faith cannot be proved, how can Christians be blamed for not teaching it? And do they not justly cry out upon God, if He gives them understanding, and yet expects them to follow a law which runs clean counter to it? He, Ramon, does not claim that man's little mind can comprehend the infinite, but only that sufficient of that infinite is granted to its comprehension to enable a man to be a Christian and to love and serve God.

These considerations lead the hermit to change his

[1] mas com gat que passàs
tost per brases, los lligen, per què a ells no faç
quaix res de mon negoci.
(xxii, 8–10.)

[2] . . . car no par
que sia possíbol la nostra fe provar.
(xxiii, 5–6.)

[3] Ramon, si hom pogués demostrar nostra fe
hom ne perdria mèrit.
(xxv, 1–2.)

[4] . . . encara que l'entendre humà gens no conté
tota la veritat de Déu que infinida es manté
tant, que causa finida tota ella no té;
per què vostra rasó no par que valla re.
(xxv, 8–11.)

attack. He now points out that it is useless to preach to Mahomet's followers, both because of their obstinacy, and of the difficulty of their language. Ramon replies that, as to the first point, experience has shown that Moslem philosophers are becoming restive with the Prophet's teaching, and could be converted with comparative ease :

> If to them men for disputations went
> And proved their faith by force of argument.[1]

As to the learning of Arabic, that is quickly done, and quickly it should be done.

The hermit disagrees :

> Ramon, when world-conversion God shall will,
> His Holy Spirit wisdom shall instil.
> With gifts of tongues His servants He shall fill
> As in the Apostles' days, so shall He still.[2]

" No," says Ramon, " God has ever willed the conversion of the world, giving men liberty to choose between good and evil. If you think that we are without power to convert the heathen, your sin is the greater."[3] But the hermit asserts that he is right. It were better to " retain what has been already won " than to go abroad to heathen lands where so many have met with failure.[4] Let Ramon betake himself to some quiet spot, where he may pass the rest of his life in well-earned tranquillity.[5]

It becomes increasingly clear, as the poem proceeds, that the hermit represents Ramon's lower self. He is rebuked for his suggestion, sternly. " And what of the God-given *Art* ? "[6] enquires Ramon. " Can I allow it,

[1] aquells venrien tost a convertiment
si hom ab ells estava en gran disputament
e la Fe los mostrava per força d'argument ;
e aquells convertits convertirien la gent.
(xxviii, 5–8.)

[2] Ramon, can Déus volrà que el món sia convertit,
adoncs darà los llenguatges per lo Sant Esperit
e convertirà lo món, segons que havets ausit
de Crist e dels Apòstols.
(xxix, 1–4.)

[3] xxx. [4] xxxi, 1–3. [5] xxxiii, 9–12. [6] xxxv, 7.

after all this labour, to be lost? What shall I say to its Giver when He calls me to my last account"?[1] For answer, the hermit begins to attack the *Art*. If it be indeed of value, how is it that it was unknown to olden philosophers? And, if it be of God, why do you repine? In that case, whether you yourself live or die matters little:

> Its virtue can by no device be kill'd
> For all God gives is perfectly fulfill'd.[2]

This point in the discussion seems in one sense to mark the climax of the poem. Hereafter the hermit is less the doubling of Ramon's own personality, and more the individual opposed to his convictions and ideals. Unfortunately, the line of argument which he takes is highly unsympathetic. What God does is just. If He wills that the heathen perish in Hell, we must not on this account be disconsolate.[3] Ramon becomes impatient with such arguments, and, did not courtesy forbid him to do so, would break off the conversation. Instead, he listens while the hermit develops his theory of Divine election. The discussion becomes more acrid.

> Hermit, hadst thou a better education,
> Thou might'st indeed discuss predestination.[4]

cries Ramon. To which the hermit:

> Thou wouldst not pine, wert thou in hope well school'd,
> If the whole world should be unjustly rul'd.[5]

[1] xxxv, 9–12.

[2] xxxvi, 7–9:

> Fas falliment
> con tems que aprés ta mort ella vinga a nient,
> car tot açò que Déus dóna ve a bo compliment.

[3] The couplet (xl, 2–3) is particularly cold-blooded:

> e si met en infern li malvat discreent,
> no devets per tot ço haver desconsolament.

[4] N'ermità, si vós fóssets home qui fos lletrat
mills sabríets parlar d'home predestinat . . .
(xlv, 1–2.)

[5] Ramon, si en vós fos molt gran esperança,
si tot lo món està en molt greu balança,
del seu mal estament no hàgrets malenança.
(xlvi, 1–3.)

They cease at last to argue, both realizing that it is useless to continue, and the hermit, despairing, no doubt, of one whom he holds to be in such error, resumes his task of consolation. Thereupon Ramon, for his part, resumes his plaints, in lines which, in their original, throb with the eloquence of suffering [1] :

> Not greatly, hermit, should a man complain
> If children, lands and wealth are from him ta'en,
> And God be pleased to send his body pain.
> But, if the name of God be had in vain,
> Blasphemed, despised, forgotten, then 'tis plain
> Nor God nor man unmovèd can remain.
> Know'st thou not how for God's sake I have lain
> In grievous plight, waiting but to be slain,
> Pluck'd by the beard and curs'd with vile disdain,
> Yet patiently enduring every bane ?
> How can I any comfort hope to gain
> When, despite all, no nearer comes God's reign ?

Though the hermit cannot appreciate Ramon's arguments, neither can he refrain from sympathizing with his grief. He tries to console him, as before, by pointing out that God, being just, must necessarily reward him for all that he has done for Him, in perfect faith that he has acted well :

> Rejoice thou, then, in that which thou hast done.
> Think not o'ermuch of that thou wouldst have won. . . .
> Be fill'd with fear and love of God alone.[2]

[1] N'ermità, no és molt si hom és desconsolat
en perdre infants, diners e heretat
e en estar malaute pus que a Déus ve de grat ;
mais ¿ qui es pot consolar que Déus sia oblidat,
menyspreat, blastomat e tam fort ignorat
com de tot ço sia Déus fortment despagat ?
Encara ¿ que no sabets com eu soi menyspreat
per Déu, tantes vets maldit e blastomat,
e en perill de mort e per barba tirat,
e per vertut de Déu pacient són estat ?
mas que Déus en lo món sia tam pauc amat
no és hom en lo món que me'n feés conhortat.
(li.)

[2] E alegra't en tu e en ton captener,
e no sies trop forts en ço que vols haver. . . .
e a tu abast Déus per amar e temer.
(lii, 9–12.)

Then Ramon rises for a moment above his sorrows. Reward has not entered his thoughts. His one desire is that God may be glorified and loved by all men everywhere.

> I am not glad
> If there be great reward, nor am I sad
> If there be little.[1]

He outlines the petition which he has presented to the Pope. He has pleaded for the teaching of languages to missionary friars, as was done at Miramar,

> —May he repent who brought that work to naught !—[2]

for the ordaining of a tithe devoted to the recovery of the Holy Places, the holding of debates for the conversion of schismatics, and the unification of the military orders under a "King of the Holy Sepulchre." [3]

The hermit, strange to say, after his indifference to argument, is considerably moved by this recital of Ramon's projects. He muses long upon it, and, at length, finding no flaw in what Ramon proposes, offers to join forces with him, and, with tears and sighs, begs his forgiveness for what has passed :

> "I pray thee, sir, my grievous fault condone.
> Henceforth would I be sad with thee alone.
> Ah, Truth, Devotion, Love ! Say, whither are gone
> The thanks and praise that should to God be done ?"
> Then to the vanquish'd hermit went Ramon,
> Gently he kiss'd him, and they wept as one.[4]

[1] per què eu no són jausent
si hai gran guasardó, ni no estaig dolent
si n'hai pauc. . . . (liii, 4–6.)

[2] —e haja'n conciència qui ho ha afollat !— (lv, 8.)

The pathetic parenthesis of this well-known line is the sole indication that we possess of the nature of the fate of Miramar. It was evidently through the work of one person that the college came to an end : more it is difficult to deduce (see p. 135, above).

[3] . . . e que llur major fos rei del sant muniment. (lvi, 11.)
Cf. pp. 317–19, below.

[4] . . . e volc ésser ab Ramon trist e desconsolat,
e pregava Ramon que li fos perdonat
en plorant, suspirant, e dix : "Ah, veritat,
devoció, caritat !" E vas on és anat
lo grat que a Déu deuria ésser donat ?"
Can Ramon viu l'ermità que ab ell s'era acordat,
adoncs lo va baisar : ensems han molt plorat. (lvii, 6–12.)

This is the quite effective ending of the main portion of the narrative, which, it will be seen, is not remarkable for its verisimilitude. As so often happens in *Blanquerna*, the devil's advocate seems to be converted by little more than the mere contagion of the angels, and the very improbable *dénouement* would certainly appear to support the hermit's theory that conversion is independent of argument and comes through the grace of God alone. We need not follow the hermit in his lamentations at not having learned of the *Art* earlier, nor in his resolve to stay at the Papal Court, as a *joglar*, singing the *Hundred Names of God*, while Ramon returns to the Moors with little expectation of seeing him again on earth. A few words upon the beauty and value of the poem, however, may not be amiss.

Apart from its metrical qualities, which place it high among Ramon's poems, the *Desconort* displays considerable skill in construction, and also offers the interest of its connection with the author's life and personality. As to the former quality, the bold opening, the picturesqueness of the descriptions and the dramatic force of the dialogue strike every reader. But one is too apt to seize upon the biographical parts of the poem and to neglect the remainder of its substance, as though there were nothing in it but repetition of arguments already used elsewhere. On the contrary, the chief psychological interest of the *Desconort* lies in the incorporation in the personality of the hermit of certain of the author's own thoughts and feelings alternately with the remarks of the candid friends and declared opponents whom a practical idealist is never without for long. There is a deeper interest still in the poem considered as a whole, which certainly speaks, as clearly and fully as any document we possess, for Ramon himself. We hear from his own lips, not only the story of his past, but his ideals, his projects, his desires, his beliefs, his doubts, his questionings and his fears, in the proportion—and this is the most important point of all—which they occupied in his own mind at the time.

We may well pause for a moment upon this poem to

picture to ourselves the man who wrote it. Miramar had been built : it had also been abandoned and destroyed. If its founder had been befriended by kings and emperors, kings and emperors had also forsaken him. From his travels over half the known world, a Divine knight-errant, knowing not yet of the martyr's crown which awaited him, still less of his literary immortality, he returned again and again to Rome, the world's centre, where the palace of his ideals, in the phrase of the Portuguese lyrist, stood

> na sua pompa e aerea formosura.[1]

Anthero de Quental might indeed have been thinking of Ramon Lull,

> um cavaleiro andante,
> Por desertos, por sois, por noite escura,
> Paladino do Amor,[2]

when he describes his hero beating upon the door of the palace, which opens only to reveal disillusion:

> Com grandes golpes bato á porta e brado :
> " 'Eu sou o vagamundo, o desherdado,
> Abri-vos, portas d'ouro, ante meus ais ! "
> Abrem-se as portas d'ouro com fragor,
> Mas dentro encontro só, cheo de dôr,
> Silencio e escuridão, e nada mais ! [3]

In such a spirit as that of Quental's knight did Ramon set down the bitter and poignant chronicle of his shattered illusions. Viewed thus, he is a pathetic figure, and is even capable of becoming a tragic one.

[1] *O palacio da ventura*, tr. A. F. G. Bell :
" Majestic . . . in aërial glow of light."

[2] Through fierce sunshine or dark night
I traverse deserts in knight-errantry,
A paladin of love.

[3] Loudly I beat upon the door and cry :
" A vagabond, an outcast here am I,
Open unto my sorrow, golden door ! "
With crash the golden doors fly open wide,
I enter, but grief-stricken find inside
Silence and darkness drear, and nothing more.

But behind all the autobiography in the *Desconort* there is its spiritual music, which plays to the tone-deaf as well as to those who can hear it. One movement succeeds another, each with its characteristic quality. Of one the key is an enthusiasm still youthful in increasing age, an idealism as constant as it is pure. Of another it is discontent, disillusion, melancholy,—and this is the dominant movement which gives the poem its name. Here again it is blind faith, here a robust and reasoned confidence, here the tenderness of Christian charity. It is true that, as Torras i Bages well points out, the poem has nowhere " that quietness and repose of great Christian poetry," that " majesty of peace which we find in Dante, who, even in the horrors of the Inferno discovers . . . that great and sublime immobility which shadows forth eternity."[1] Lull was a lesser man than Dante, but he was a man at all points like ourselves, and from the *Desconort* can be distilled the essence of his humanity. The emotions which throb in it are those that throb in ourselves. The noble spirit which pervades it is the spirit that we would fain make our own. This, indeed, like no other of Ramon's works, is " Raymund Lully's great elixir."

[1] P. 245.

CHAPTER XIII

1295–1298

Ramon Lull professes as a Franciscan tertiary. The *Tree of Science*. Genoa, Montpellier and Paris. The *Tree of the Philosophy of Love*: its poetry, its artificiality, its variety, its fervour. Summary of its argument. Lull's complete immersion in his subject. A book for actives.

ABOUT this time—in all probability at Assisi and shortly before writing the *Desconort*[1]—Ramon appropriately joined "the most tempest-tossed society which the world has ever known,"[2] by professing as a Franciscan tertiary. That he took this step will surprise few who have followed his career up to the present time. We have seen how, in the early days of his apostolate, he was attracted rather to the Dominicans, probably through the influence of James the Conqueror and Ramon de Penyafort: we have seen, too, how he gradually withdrew from them his allegiance. They had rejected his God-given *Art*; his three attendances at their chapters-general had brought them no nearer sympathizing with him; and for many years he had been comparing them disadvantageously with the Friars Minor. There was much in their ideals with which he was peculiarly at one: it is possible to infer from the Genoa narrative that he had for long been inwardly impelled to become one of them. But the ideals of St. Francis triumphed. Since the foundation of Miramar Ramon's heart had warmed increasingly to the

[1] The evidence is that there was a chapter-general of Friars Minor at Assisi in 1295; that Ramon had attended three such chapters (p. 259, above) before writing the *Desconort*; that he is not known to have attended more than two, excluding this; and that, on Michaelmas Day of the same year he began to write the *Arbre de Sciencia*, in which he portrays himself in the habit of a religious.

[2] Paul Sabatier: *Life of St. Francis of Assisi*, London, 1894, p. 222.

Franciscans, by whom his *Art* was being taught. Though we know nothing of his attending their chapters-general earlier than 1287, his experiences at these chapters would appear to have been happy, and he had received fraternal kindness from Gaufredi. In 1289 a bull of Nicholas IV first gave papal recognition to the famous Third Order which has enrolled so many saints in the glorious course of its history. This may well have drawn Ramon's attention to a foundation much in the public eye and completely in accord with his ideals. He was, and remained, a layman, and the Third Order was for laymen, whom it called to a life of discipline and rule, yet to a life not inconsistent with their worldly duties. It may well be that it was at Genoa, or soon after his illness there, that Ramon decided definitely to join the Franciscans, and that he took the first opportunity of doing so on his return from Africa.

During the autumn and winter of 1295 Lull was still in Rome, and was engaged upon the second longest of his works in Catalan which have come down to us : the *Tree of Science*. This is an immense production, filling, in the modern Catalan edition,[1] just thirteen hundred pages, having an analytical index of fifty-six pages and containing a large proportion of didactic matter which in these days can be of interest to very few. No part of it is more attractive than its evidently autobiographical opening, which promises a book of great delight,—a promise unfortunately not fulfilled.

Disconsolate and tearful, Ramon was singing his *Desconort* beneath a great tree, to alleviate somewhat the grief which he had when he could not accomplish in the court of Rome the sacred work (*sant negoci*) of Jesus Christ and the public weal of all Christendom.

And while he was here, disconsolate, in a lovely vale abounding in fair springs and lofty trees, there passed along that vale a monk, who heard Ramon singing. And, as the song was both sorrowful and devout, he followed the voice and came to the place where Ramon was, and judged from his habit and long beard that he was

[1] *Obres*, xi, xii, xiii.

strife between the gold and the emerald in the ring of a king.[1]

When we say that the last section of the book consists of questions and answers related to the subject-matter of those preceding, it must be added that there are over four thousand of these and that they fill considerably more than one-third of the pages of the book. They do not differ greatly from similar questions and answers already cited from other works, and they cannot be said to demand quotation.

The *Tree of Science* being completed, Ramon bears it to the altar of St. Peter's, commends it to " Jesus Christ, to Our Lady, to the angels and to the saints that lie in Rome," and begs the Pope and the Cardinals to take it under their protection.[2] Perhaps the most remarkable thing about this work is the orderliness and calm which pervade it, for all that it was written at a time of mental and spiritual stress. There is hardly a trace in it of the disillusion reflected in its prologue and poured forth with such passion in the *Desconort*. Long before the end is reached, Lull is himself again. Hard work has restored to him his serenity,—and hard work the writing of the *Tree of Science* must have been, for it is wholly intellectual, nor does its length betoken mere prolixity. All might not agree with the author's repeated boast that " in this book we speak of things in abbreviated fashion,"[3] but all would agree that, if regard be had to the conventions of method which he adopted, he repeats himself singularly little.

The *Tree of Science* took Lull just over six months to write, having been begun on Michaelmas Day, 1295, and ended on April 1, 1296. Yet we hear of two more books which were finished in the June following. Evidently Ramon, having found solace for his disconsolateness in writing, continued the treatment successfully.

One of these books, written both in Catalan and in

[1] *Obres*, p. 431.
[2] *Obres*, xiii, p. 515.
[3] *Obres*, xi, p. 243; *cf.* xii, p. 342.

Latin,[1] and completed at Rome on June 23, 1296, is called the *Book of the Articles of the Faith*[2] and is sometimes referred to as the *Apostrophe*.[3] Its aim, the proof of the fourteen articles, is familiar to us; its method, at first sight, is simpler than that of Lull's "Arts," but the same arguments recur. The book establishes the existence of God by means of five propositions, these being the existence of a supreme good, of a being of infinite greatness, of eternity, of infinite power, and of infinite virtue. From this point it goes on to prove the articles in turn.

To the year 1296, too, in all probability, belongs the *Book of Proverbs*, described as having been finished at Rome, and containing over six thousand aphorisms. Lull's idea of[4] the nature of proverbs being both curious and vague, and his skill in writing them not being well represented in this volume, it is unnecessary to examine the *Book of Proverbs* as fully as his later collections of the kind. The first section contains proverbs on the hundred names of God, "concerning which we have already made a book." The second endeavours to give information in proverb form upon the nature of created things, starting with abstract qualities and eventually reaching heat and cold, lightning and thunder, metals (in Chapter 99),

[1] It was originally written in Catalan, and the version which we find in Salz., iv, pp. 1–26, is described as a literal translation into Latin. After this is given a free translation into Latin, which Lull "caused to be made," for what reason is not stated. Cf. *H.L.F.*, No. 27, pp. 162–66, Rogent i Duràn: *Bibliografía*, etc., pp. 30, 39–40, and the dissimilar comments of Longpré, col. 1097.

[2] *Liber de articulis fidei sacrosanctae et salutiferae legis christianae*, sive *Liber Apostrophe* (*H.L.F.*, No. 27, pp. 162–6). Those who date the *Liber de anima rationali* 1296, following its Catalan text, Pasqual and others (see *H.L.F.*, p. 215, and p. 254, above), assign to it the same day of the year as to this book.

[3] From the apostrophe to the Holy Father which the book contains.

[4] Salz., vol. vi; cf. *H.L.F.*, No. 43 (pp. 207–10); Rubió y Balaguer: *Los códices*, etc., p. 328; Alòs: *Los catálogos*, etc., p. 70; Longpré, col. 1108. MSS. in both Catalan (*Libre de proverbis*) and Latin (*Liber proverbiorum*) are extant, and agree in giving the date of composition of these proverbs as 1299. Almost all critics, however, amend this date to 1296. P. Longpré inclines to retain 1299, and assumes a special visit to Rome in October 1299, of which we have no record. This seems very unlikely (*cf.* pp. 296–8 below) but the internal evidence is certainly strong.

and angels (in Chapter 100). The third is concerned wholly with ethical and religious subjects. The first section has one hundred and two chapters, and the second and third have each one hundred : each chapter contains twenty proverbs. The description of the contents indicates that the proverbs are for the most part maxims, ethical propositions, or dogmatic statements. Lull's definition of a proverb is : "Brevis propositio, quae in se continet multam sententiam et scientiam." One or two examples from the first chapter will show what he means by this :

1. Quia Deus est Ens perfectum, suum Nomen est perfectum.
2. Deus et suum Nomen realiter convertuntur.
3. Nomen Dei, quod homo nominat, est similitudo nominis Dei.
4. Nomen Dei, quod est Deus, non est creatura, sed nomen Dei, quod homines nominant, est creatura.[1]

Some time after June 1296, "seeing that from the Holy Father he could obtain nothing,"[2] Ramon decided to return homeward. On the way he made a halt at Genoa,[3] where, according to the contemporary biography, he "compiled certain new books of his *Art*."[4] These must have been published at a later date, for we have no other record of books written in Genoa at this period. From Genoa Ramon went to Montpellier,[5] and here he was able to have some conversation with the dethroned James of Mallorca, who was residing there.

Although it was more than eleven years since Mallorca had been taken from him, and its restitution had long been ordered, Fortune's wheel had not yet turned completely in his favour. His policy of carrying

[1] i, 1–4.

[2] *V.B.R.L.*, v (*Life*, p. 73). *V.C.* (p. 29) has "com veés a la fi que res no obtenía."

[3] Pasqual (ii, p. 70) says that at Genoa he intended to embark again for Africa. I know of no ground for this supposition, except the vague reference in *Desconort*, lxi, 1–4. Pasqual says there is also a reference in the *Arbre de Sciencia*, but does not cite it.

[4] *V.C.*, *V.B.R.L.*, v (*Life*, pp. 29, 73).

[5] Pasqual (ii, p. 70) says "to Montpellier or Perpignan," and neither *V.C.* nor *V.B.R.L.* (*Life*, pp. 30, 73) is of any help (*cf.* p. 276, below). The probabilities are in favour of Montpellier.

on a guerrilla warfare on his nephew's Catalonian frontiers, where we last saw him, came to an end in 1286; for France, under the threat of abandonment, forced upon him a treaty with Alfonso. Two years later, it is true, James was again nibbling at Catalonia, but that was because Alfonso had himself broken the treaty and the King of France had allowed "his very dear uncle" to retaliate. Alfonso appealed to the Pope, Philip to Edward I; and James had the hardihood to challenge his nephew to a duel, to be fought, under Edward's auspices, at Bordeaux. Fortunately Edward was wise enough to do nothing, and, in March 1290, the Pope sent legates to Montpellier—as well he might—to treat for peace.[1]

The next year an agreement was drawn up (February 19, 1291), from which, however, as the Pope had to point out, the restitution of Mallorca was omitted. No sooner was this set right than Alfonso died (June 18, 1291)—he was but twenty-seven years of age—leaving both Aragon and Mallorca to his brother James (now known as James II of Aragon), who at that time was ruling over Sicily. At the moment things looked hopeful for the other James, for the new king of Aragon was neither as unfriendly nor as ambitious as Alfonso had been, and Nicholas IV wrote (August 11, 1291) to the Mallorcan authorities, commanding them to obey not the nephew but the uncle.[2] Then Nicholas died, and James of Aragon, as was natural enough in those days, retained his secure possession of the coveted island. Not until Boniface VIII succeeded to the papacy did matters move again in the direction of justice.

It was in June 1295 that the new Pope proclaimed the *status quo ante bellum* with regard to Mallorca: the elder James was to rule in the island, but to hold it from the younger, exactly as he had held it from Peter. This decision was embodied in the Treaty of Anagni,[3] but

[1] Lecoy de la Marche, i, pp. 293-305. For the challenge, *cf.* Zurita, bk. iv, chap. 111.

[2] Lecoy de la Marche, i, p. 309.

[3] Zurita, bk. v, chap. 10; Aigrefeuille, i, pp. 152-3; Lecoy de la Marche, i, pp. 338-47.

much diplomacy was necessary, and a little fighting, before Mallorca was actually restored to its rightful sovereign, who protested the while, bitterly and vigorously, but quite ineffectually, against the conditions on which he was permitted to hold it.[1]

From even this brief outline of events we can conclude that, when James and Ramon met once more, the sovereign was suffering from disillusionment no less than his subject. True, Boniface had allowed James of Aragon until Christmas Day, 1297, for the restoration, but hope deferred had for a long time been making the heart sick, and Ramon, after his own experiences with Boniface, was not at all the man to reassure his lord and master.

We may infer, nevertheless, from past history, that the conversation of the two friends would not be confined to politics. Each would have much to tell ; and no doubt, apart from exchanging reminiscences and grievances, they soothed their spirits once again with controversial theology. Further, from time to time, their conversation could not but turn upon Miramar and the possibility of its re-establishment ; for, though Lull's horizon was far wider now than when the college was founded, he still had great affection for it and belief in its potentialities in the future.

Again, since in or about October 1297 Lull went straight from James' residence to Paris,[2] it is reasonable to suppose that he gave him some advice, at the least, as to the best way of approaching his ambitious nephew, Philip the Fair, with whom, on his former visit, he had had little success. Not a word of the results of his approach has come down to us, from which fact the conclusions naturally drawn are negative. Ramon certainly seems to have spent most of his time in Paris in writing and lecturing.

At the end of February 1298[3] he completed a book entitled (briefly) the *Declaration of Ramon by means of*

[1] Aigrefeuille, i, p. 154 (Document of August 23, 1295).
[2] *V.C.*, *V.B.R.L.*, v (*Life*, pp. 30, 73).
[3] *Cf.* Pasqual, ii, pp. 71–2, *Vindiciae*, i, 224, and references in n. 2, p. 277.

a dialogue. The full title, which is a long one,[1] shows that it is directed against the opinions of certain Averroistic philosophers ("contra theologiam, quae domina est philosophiae") which had been condemned, in 1277, in the form of two hundred and nineteen articles, by Etienne Tempier, Bishop of Paris.[2] The book is of particular interest as the first of Ramon's attacks on Averroism. In a forest near Paris, sad and desolate as ever, he meets a thirteenth-century Socrates who blames the Bishop for his action and undertakes to justify the beliefs which were censured. Ramon, nothing loth, proposes a philosophical debate on each of the articles, which is duly held and described in detail : when it is over, either party, as is the usual proceeding in such cases, claims the victory. In the end, they decide to submit their arguments to the actual Bishop of Paris, and to the Chancellor, Rector and masters of the University.

We can pass briefly over a *Tractate of Astronomy*, which had been completed at Paris in October 1297,[3] and over the *Contemplation of Ramon*,[4] an opuscule also written in Paris, probably a little later, of which the exact date, however, is not known.[5] During the octave of the Assumption, 1298, Lull completed another of his

[1] *Declaratio Raimundi per modum dialogi, edita contra aliquorum philosophorum et eorum sequacium opiniones erroneas et damnatas a Venerabili Patre Domino Episcopo Parisiensi.*

[2] *Cf.* also Pasqual, ii, p. 72, *H.L.F.*, No. 235, pp. 333–4. As the heresies in question were taught by Boetius, it seems likely that this book is identical with that referred to in the 1311 catalogue and elsewhere as 'Liber contra errores Boetii et Sigerii' (*cf.* p. 346, below). The *Declaratio* was first printed by Otto Keicher (*op. cit.*, pp. 95–221).

[3] *Tractatus novus* (or *Liber*) *de Astronomia* ; cf. *H.L.F.*, No. 169, p. 309 ; Longpré, col. 1107.

[4] Its alternative title is *Liber de decem modis contemplandi Deum.* At the end of the book we read that the author desires to present it to the King of France, and submits it first to the masters of theology in Paris for their revision. (Cf. *H.L.F.*, No. 213, p. 324, Longpré, col. 1104.) For its complement, *Liber quomodo contemplatio transeat in raptum*, *cf.* Rubió y Balaguer : "Los códices, etc," p. 322.

[5] The *De gradibus conscientiae* or *Declaratio conscientiae,* which follows this treatise (see Pasqual, ii, p. 71), *H.L.F.* (No. 162, pp. 305–6) believes not to be by Lull, while admitting that he did write a treatise *De conscientia* which is not known ; *cf.* Longpré, col. 1098.

numerous 'Disputations,' the title of which [1] recalls the *Desconort* in its re-introduction of a hermit with whom Ramon debates. This hermit, as it soon appears, is not the unlettered fatalist of the poem : he is devoted to Scholastic philosophy, has studied theology in Paris, and, when Ramon, still sorrowful at his failures, encounters him by the banks of the Seine, is immersed in the *Sententiae* of Peter Lombard. The content of the *Disputatio Eremitae et Raymundi* consists in Ramon's explanation to him, by means of the *Ars Magna*, of certain of the *Sententiae* which he cannot understand. Examples of the type of question answered have already been given ; many of the questions most commonly debated in the Middle Ages occur in this book. "Can God damn Peter and save Judas ?" [2] and "Can God make matter to exist without form ?" [3] are variants of the better known "Can God create that which He cannot destroy ?" Another familiar one is that which discusses if an angel can pass from one place to another in a moment of time.[4] The mediaeval interest in the angelic world is reflected in a number of other questions : Can a wicked angel repent ? Can one angel speak with another, and, if so, how ? [5] More fantastic questions are those which ask if Adam and Eve could have cohabited in the Garden of Eden before first taking food,[6] and if a child slain in its mother's womb by some persecutor of the Faith is purged from original sin through the baptism of blood.[7] An interesting reply to another [8] declares that the Blessed Virgin had no stain of original sin, the Holy Spirit having prepared the way for the Incarnation by her sanctification as the sun prepares the day by means of the glorious dawn.[9]

It is worth noticing that at the end of this book the hermit does not accept Ramon's explanations unquestioningly, but only says that he will examine them with

[1] *Disputatio Eremitae et Raymundi super aliquibus dubiis quaestionibus Sententiarum magistri Petri Lombardi.* Salz., vol. iv (cf. *H.L.F.*, No. 22, pp. 140–4).

[2] Bk. i, q. 36. [3] Bk. ii, q. 56. [4] Bk. i, q. 29.

[5] Bk. ii, qq. 49, 54. [6] Bk. ii, q. 80. [7] Bk. iii, q. 123.

[8] Bk. iii, q. 96. [9] The passage is quoted on p. 408, below.

care[1]—a conclusion as typically Lullian as are the conditions laid down by Ramon for the holding of the debate in due form and order, and not reserved for the books in which Christians argue with unbelievers.

During the greater part of this sojourn in Paris, Ramon was attempting, perhaps a little half-heartedly and spasmodically, to persuade the King of France and the University of Paris to undertake some part of the tasks which he had set in vain before Boniface, and establish the long-since mooted schools of languages.[2] Eloquent letters are extant which he addressed at this time (1298–9) to the King, to the University,[3] and to a friend of his own. Results there would appear to have been none, and, sick at heart, Ramon turned to the making of books again.[4]

In October 1298 a new work, entitled the *Tree of the Philosophy of Love*,[5] was "finished by Ramon, near the city of Paris," taken to the city, and presented there "to great lords and to masters and their disciples," who were begged "to correct it, according to their philosophy." In the epilogue of the book, from which the foregoing quotations are taken, Ramon is urged to present it, in Latin, "to that most noble lord, the wise and good King

[1] "Quia habes alium modum extraneum," he adds, "quam habeant moderni magistri . . . adhuc non bene assuevi nec habituavi tuas rationes."

[2] Denifle et Chatelain, ii, pp. 83–4: "Epistola Raymundi Lull ad Universitatem Parisienem, quam laudibus extollit, quamque hortatur ad porrigendum preces suas regi, ut fundetur Parisiis studium Arabicum, Tartaricum et Graecum." The essential passage in this letter begs for the foundation in Paris of a "studium Arabicum, Tartaricum et Graecum, ut nos linguas adversariorum Dei et nostrorum docti, predicando et docendo illos, possimus in gladio veritatis eorum vincere falsitates, et reddere populum Deo acceptabilem, et inimicos convertere in amicos."

[3] This letter is quoted in the preceding note. For the others, *cf.* Martène et Durand, *Thesaurus novus anecdotorum*, etc. (Paris, 1717), i, pp. 1315, 1317. For their dates, see Longpré, col. 1080. It is not difficult to suppose that Ramon made such appeals more than once, in which case P. Longpré's supposition falls to the ground. Further (see p. 204 above) the passage which he quotes from *Felix* deals with conversation, not letters.

[4] Two other letters written by Lull about this time, to Venice, are described by Longpré (col. 1082).

[5] Or *Arbre de Filosofia d Amor*, the title of its original Catalan. It is also frequently known as the *Philosophia Amoris*, and Lull himself refers to it, in his Latin works, by several titles: e.g., *Arbor sive Ars Philosophiae Amoris* and *Philosophia boni Amoris*.

of France, and likewise in the vulgar tongue to the most noble, wise and good Queen of France, to the end that it might be made known throughout the whole kingdom."[1]

From the opening lines of the book, it is fairly clear that Ramon had come to Paris for the purpose described in the letters just referred to, and that he had been entirely unsuccessful. He was there, he tells us, " that he might work great good by means of knowledge, the which thing he could not bring to its fulfilment and end, so he considered how he might work great good by means of love, wherefore he purposed to make this *Tree of the Philosophy of Love*." [2] In order to do this, he retires to the usual " fair wood," which is " near Paris " and " thickly planted with trees," for the purpose of meditation. He can hardly be said to have failed in this book to " work great good," for, though as a whole it is very unequal,[3] being in places prolix, involved, and even dull, it is as delightful and as profitable a book to dip into as Ramon ever wrote. It moves in various and varied mediums—in maxim and allegory, subtlety and simplicity, poetry and prose, exposition, meditation and prayer. Never for long is it devoid of grace and charm. Mn. Riber, with his unfailing sensitiveness and insight, contrasts its beauties with the cumbrousness of the *Tree of Science*,[4] remarks on its reminiscences of the Provençal Courts of Love, and hazards the conviction that its author would have won his laurels at the Jocs Florals of Toulouse. More appealing still is its unmistakable fervour, the sincerity of a single-minded lover of beauty, of one entirely devoted to God. It is not a mystical treatise, but it abounds in that unquenchable desire which

[1] *Arbre de Filosofia d Amor*, ed. Rosselló (the edition cited throughout and abbreviated *A.F.A.*), pp. 178–9 ; *T.L.*, pp. 127–8.

[2] *A.F.A.*, p. 3 ; cf. *L.A.A.*, 86 (*Bl.*, p. 424).

[3] For this reason, in translating it into English (*The Tree of Love*, London, 1926), I have abridged it considerably, summarizing in an introductory essay the parts not translated.

[4] *Vida abreujada*, p. 42. The comparison is hardly translatable with any literalness into sober English : " Una rosa al peu d'un cedre, un arbrissó àgil i gràcil de branques fines com a nervis, de tremolenca joventut de fulla, de tèbia soca llisa com un braç humà. Sembla una ombrel·la fresca del verger d'Amic i Amat."

is the raw material, as it were, of all mysticism. Its concluding words illustrate the spirit in which it was written :

> And Ramon entreats his Beloved, as vehemently as he may, that the book may ever be kept by Him, and that many good lovers may serve and honour Him because of it, and that they may be mighty warriors against false love, which is contrary to the love of God.[1]

The artificiality of the *Tree of the Philosophy of Love* is inherent in its plan, and an analysis of the book will make clear the extent of it. In the heart of his " fair wood " Ramon descries a lady, clad in costly apparel, making great lamentation. She is Philosophy-of-Love, and her sorrow is great because men court her sister Philosophy-of-Knowledge, make " many books and many arts " in the sciences, and neglect entirely the art of love. Ramon consoles her by telling her of his *Ars Amativa*, and of this new book on the philosophy of love which it is in his mind now to make. She departs, and he sets to work, planning his volume on the lines of the *Tree of Science* : dividing it, that is to say, into seven parts, dealing each in turn with roots, trunk, boughs, branches, leaves, flowers, and fruits. The roots are the eighteen *començaments* of the *Ars Amativa*,—goodness, greatness, duration, power, wisdom, will, virtue, truth, glory, difference, concordance, contrariety, beginning, mean, end, majority, equality, and minority. These are defined fully, after which come some " cogitations " by the Lover upon the properties and works of love and the relations between Lover and Beloved. The second section discusses the " form " and the " matter " of love with an artificiality which is too seldom relieved by such flashes of poetry as are to be found throughout the book. The third section deals with the " boughs " of the tree, or rather with three of them only, the " conditions," the " questions," and the " prayers " of love. Each of these is considered in relation with the eighteen " roots " of love in turn. The " conditions " are aphorisms, by means of which the " questions " are answered and which

[1] *A.F.A.*, pp. 178–9 ; *T.L.*, p. 127.

are also made the basis of the "prayers," so that they form, as it were, the skeleton of the entire section.[1] The fourth part describes the "branches"—"liberality, beauty and solace of love," and with this part the style of the book completely changes, its artificialities become fewer, and the narrative element makes a welcome re-appearance.[2] Snatches of dialogue between Love, the Lover, and the Beloved, or between more conventional characters, which have characterized the earlier books, now take on more importance, and for pages together comprise the whole argument.

With the fifth section[3] begins the history of the first of two successive lovers with whose adventures most of the remainder of the book is occupied. It describes "the leaves of the tree of love," which are the lover's sighs, proceeding both from yearning and from pain, the tears that love makes him shed, and the fears that come from consciousness of sin. The Lover of the story, through overmuch sighing, weeping, and fear, falls grievously sick, and is visited by the Physician of love, who, in words already quoted,[4] prescribes "a medicine that shall give him frenzy, that love may cause him to speak as a fool, for they that speak of love in manners most like to those of fools are they that are in truth the sanest."[5] The lover drinks the potion, but finding himself "in straiter travail of love than heretofore,"[6] cries out that the physician has poisoned him, and that night, while all are sleeping, makes his escape.[7]

After some time he is recaptured, and bound to his Beloved "with many cords of love . . . that he might not flee from Him, nor from the trials of love."[8] He is likely to be condemned to death, but the Lady of love pleads for him, and he is allowed Life-of-Love as an advocate, who, following the fashion of the mediaeval Courts of Love, pleads against Death-of-Love for him. After

[1] See *T.L.*, pp. 6–7.
[2] *Ibid.*, pp. 8–9.
[3] *Ibid.*, pp. 16–75.
[4] See pp. 240–1, above.
[5] *A.F.A.*, p. 106 ; *T.L.*, p. 35.
[6] *Ibid.*
[7] Possible reminiscences of Ramon's defection are traceable throughout this part of the story.
[8] *A.F.A.*, p. 108 ; *T.L.*, p. 38.

a debate which is interesting intrinsically, as well as for historical reasons, judgment is given against the criminal, who confesses his sins, draws up and signs his testament and makes a humble prayer of great beauty to the Beloved, "for by prayer there comes from Beloved to Lover grace and pardon."[1] But when all is done, and he lies down to die, Death-of-love is found to have no power over him, and it is only by taking him to the Holy Land, and showing him the Holy Places, that the enemies into whose power he has been delivered can cause him to die from the very strength of his devotion.

There follows an account of the burial of the Lover which is of great beauty:

When the Lover was dead, the servitors of love bathed and washed him with the tears that he had shed for love's sake, the which tears had been laid up by Remembrance-of-Love; and they wrapped him in fair white samite, whereby it was signified that he had been cleansed from his sins. Over that white samite they spread another cloth of samite that was crimson, the which was to signify that the Lover was a martyr for love's sake. And over the samite of crimson they spread samite of gold, in significance that the Lover had been proved and had remained ever loyal to his Beloved and to Love. After this they set the body of the Lover upon a bed of patience and humility, and, bearing candles lighted at the flame of love, they brought it into the church of love.

When the body of the Lover was brought into the church of love, the prayers were sung by Life-of-love, who was vested in sanctity and virtues, for the soul of the Lover had departed to the true life, to be for ever with his Beloved. The Roots of love made their responses to Life-of-love, and the servitors of love bore the candles.

Many and long and solemn were the prayers that were recited at the burial of the Lover, and Life-of-love preached, and praised the Lover greatly, and recounted the griefs and trials which he had borne as a good and loyal lover. The ladies and the servitors of love wept sorely when they heard the many praises of the Lover which the preacher of love recounted, and they had very great sorrow and grief at the death of the Lover, whereto they had been accessory and consenting.

In a fair coffin, wrought of love, glory, truth, humility, and

[1] *A.F.A.*, p. 117; *T.L.*, p. 50

piety, the servitors of love placed the body of the Lover, and the palls, the candles and the bed they gave to the poor who begged for alms, for the sake of love, more than for their necessities of eating and sleeping.[1]

"The flowers of love," begins the sixth part of the book,[2] "are three—to wit, the glories, the praises and the honours of the Beloved, in Whom the soul of the Lover has glory."[3] A new lover is chosen by the Lady of love, and his praises of the Beloved are rehearsed, together with his exhortations to his fellow-lovers, to the "servitors of love," and to the "ladies of love," who sadden him by their reminders that "few love the Beloved more than all things besides, wherefore well-nigh the whole world is lost and has forsaken the end for the which it was created."[4] At last they decide to attempt to stir men up to the love of God by making a journey of praise through the world. But their experiences are unhappy. First, they visit "a fair church, in the which many men sang the honours of the Beloved."[5] But among these men are seven that do Him dishonour.

For even as they sang they thought upon sins which they were to commit. One thought unlawfully upon a woman whom he greatly loved; another, who desired to have a fat capon which belonged to his neighbour, considered how he might steal it; a third thought how in another church he might obtain a certain dignity; another was wroth because he had not the honourable place in the quire; another was angered with a companion who sang better than he; another was slothful and desired to sleep; and another considered how he might slay a man who had spoken to him insultingly.[6]

Next, they see "a great school wherein a master taught many disciples,"[7] but some of these disciples desire learning for unworthy motives. A monastery yields no better result: one monk is a slave to pride, and another to hypocrisy, while at the royal court, where the King is to all appearance just and honourable, his

[1] *A.F.A.*, pp. 130–1; *T.L.*, pp. 66–8.
[2] *T.L.*, pp. 76–100.
[3] *A.F.A.*, p. 137; *T.L.*, p. 76.
[4] *A.F.A.*, p. 148; *T.L.*, p. 90.
[5] *A.F.A.*, p. 150; *T.L.*, p. 93.
[6] *A.F.A.*, p. 151; *T.L.*, p. 94.
[7] *Ibid.*

motives are unworthy and he "dishonours the Beloved in his intention."[1] Then the Lover and his companions go through the capital, and find that all the Beloved's commandments are broken openly. And, taking counsel in a "fair meadow" outside the city, they find that their desire is "to leave the world, and to be no more among men, but rather to dwell in the woods with birds, beasts and trees, for these dishonour not the Beloved."[2]

The conclusion of the narrative is striking, not only as it stands, but because beneath it we may read the feelings of Ramon the man, who is speaking to us in his own character. It may be quoted in full:

Then the Lover and the ladies of love entered a forest, and found therein a pilgrim returning from his pilgrimage, who asked them whither they were going. The Lover and the ladies of love recounted to him the intention for the which they were leaving the world and purposed to dwell in the forest. The pilgrim rebuked them sternly, saying that they should return to the world to live among men, and not be idle, to the end that the Beloved should have servants who should rejoice in His honours, and should bring Him honour, and whensoever He is dishonoured should have grief and sadness. "And have ye consolation," said the pilgrim, "by reason of the justice which the Beloved will work in the world to come upon them that in this world do Him dishonour. For none will have defence against the Beloved, neither will any be able to deny or hide from Him the dishonour which they have done Him. Return ye therefore to the world, and look to it that the Beloved may have many good servants and that the world may have truth and be in good estate."[3]

Of the last section of the book,[4] dealing with the fruit of love—God Himself, the work of God, and happiness—it is unnecessary to write, since it consists entirely of the familiar aphorism and dialogue recalling the *Book of the Lover and the Beloved*. It was perhaps in the main this final section which led Costa i Llobera to describe the whole *Tree of the Philosophy of Love* as being of the substance of its more widely known predecessor, yet overlaid with the method of the *Ars Magna*.[5] Of parts

[1] *A.F.A.*, p. 153; *T.L.*, p. 98.
[2] *A.F.A.*, p. 154; *T.L.*, p. 99.
[3] *A.F.A.*, p. 154; *T.L.*, pp. 99–100.
[4] *T.L.*, pp. 101–26.
[5] *A.F.A.*, p. xi.

of the book this is true enough. Its weaknesses, which we may readily admit, appear greater to-day than they really are because Lull assumed his readers to be familiar with his well-defined methods, which modern readers are not. But other parts—both purple passages of some length and paragraphs culled here and there—have a vividness, force and beauty which rank them with Lull's best writing. His power in sustained narrative, as we have seen, never again touched the same heights after the publication of *Blanquerna*, and in fact he attempted this kind of art again but little. The fantastic allegory of the *Tree of the Philosophy of Love* is attractive enough in itself, but as a story it is misty and vague. In narrative, in characterization and in anecdote the book must rank even below *Felix*. Only in its imagery, and possibly in its dialogue, is it higher than that romance, and on a level with *Blanquerna*.

One interesting feature of this book has not before been pointed out by any critic. Ramon seems completely immersed in his subject : his pet themes are for the time forgotten, or purposely laid aside. There is hardly a mention of Jews, Mohammedans or Tartars, whose conversion he so earnestly desired. Missionary colleges, military orders and crusades fall completely into the background. Ramon's past failures and future projects alike disappear : first things are set first, and the supreme place is given to the supreme end of man—to glorify God and to enjoy Him for ever hereafter. Not the foreground alone, but the whole picture in the author's mind is filled by the loving yet commanding figure of the Beloved. Commanding, because if *methods* of conversion do not find a place in the book, the *fact* of conversion is given an important one. Lull does not forget Our Lord's last orders to His followers, and the *Tree of the Philosophy of Love* is in essence, though not in every particular, a book of refreshment and encouragement to all who are obedient to those orders and are following the injunctions of the pilgrim.

The book is meant for actives. Mystical outpourings, in the strict sense of the adjective, it has none, nor does it extol the life of the hermit. Neither the first lover, who fled from the trials of love and from love's physician, nor the second lover, who was fain to retire from the world like Pope Blanquerna, gets his way: the latter is reproved sternly, the former condemned to die. And if both win high praise at last it is for labouring in the vineyard of the Beloved and bearing the burden and heat of the day. For the second lover "returned to the world, and went into far countries to bring honour to the Beloved, and endured many trials and much grief and sorrow."[1] While to the first lover his one defection—so like Ramon's—was freely and fully forgiven, and his tombstone was allowed to bear words which might well be written of Ramon himself:

> Here lies a Lover, who has died for his Beloved, and for love . . ., who has loved his Beloved with a love that is good, great and enduring . . ., who has battled bravely for love's sake . . ., who has striven against false love and false lovers . . ., a Lover ever humble, patient, loyal, ardent, liberal, prudent, holy and full of all good things, inspiring many lovers to honour and serve his Beloved.[2]

[1] *A.F.A.*, p. 154; *T.L.*, p. 100.

[2] *A.F.A.*, p. 131; *T.L.*, pp. 68–9.

CHAPTER XIV

1299–1305

Ramon Lull in Paris (*continued*). Relations with Le Myésier. Verse writings: the *Song of Ramon*, the *Dictat*. Prose: the *Book of Prayer*: its singular qualities. Return to Barcelona and Mallorca: disputations with Jews and Moslems. The *Medicine for Sin*. Minor prose works. Journey to Cyprus and Armenia. Return to Mallorca: the *Thousand Proverbs*. Genoa and Montpellier. The *Liber de Fine*.

IN June 1299 was completed a book upon another series of fifty questions which Lull solved by his *Art* at the request of his friend and disciple, Thomas Le Myésier, Canon of Arras, during this same visit to Paris.[1] Le Myésier [2] is a man of considerable importance in Lullian history. By many scholars he is thought to be the author of the contemporary biography of his master from which we have been quoting in this study: the evidence for the theory is small, it is true, but the fact that the manuscript containing the best Latin text of that biography and a list of Lull's writings dated 1311 was bequeathed by him to the Sorbonne in 1336 connects him definitely with the contemporary life. His personality and physical appearance are probably preserved in the celebrated Karlsruhe miniatures which En Jordi Rubió has studied with great industry and written upon very suggestively[3]: we may be sure that if we knew more of Le Myésier we should know more of Ramon Lull.[4]

[1] *Liber super quaestiones magistri Thomae Attrebatensis* (*H.L.F.*, No. 71, p. 249). On the date, see Pasqual, ii, p. 77; *cf.* also Alòs: *Los catálogos*, etc., p. 70; Longpré, col. 1094.

[2] Pasqual, ii, pp. 78–9; *cf.* Longpré, col. 1085, and the note next following.

[3] "El Breviculum, etc." (See Bibliography below.)

[4] As this book goes through the press I hear that M. Langlois is working upon Le Myésier in the Paris Archives.

Between philosophy, astronomy and mathematics,[1] polemic and allegory, Lull wrote so much about this time that one is in danger of overlooking the simple and pathetic verses known as the *Song of Ramon*,[2] conjecturally assigned to the year 1299 also.[3] The *Song* consists only of fourteen monorimed stanzas, each of six octosyllabic lines, but it is deservedly the best known of its author's poems : for intensity, vividness and human appeal it is nowhere surpassed by him, while his never-failing facility, both in language and in rime, lends it considerable effect.

In words already quoted,[4] Ramon outlines, with swift, telling strokes, the story of his conversion and the foundation of his beloved Miramar, passing thence to describe his message as a preacher and the nature of his *Art*. Up to this point there has been no suggestion of grief in the poem, but now it becomes as elegiacal as the *Desconort*. The writer is "old, poor and despised" ; none will bring him help in his plans, which are more ambitious than he can accomplish. He has sought much from the world and given it much, but he is "little known and little loved." [5]

[1] Here may be noted the following treatises, of which the first is largely metaphysical (Pasqual gives some extracts from it in *Vindiciae*, i, p. 329) and the second geometrical: *Liber de quadratura et triangulatura circuli* (June 1299: *H.L.F.*, No. 160, p. 305 ; Longpré, col. 1094) ; *Liber de nova et compendiosa geometria* (July 1299: *H.L.F.*, No. 170, p. 309. Pasqual, ii, p. 75, has June). Both were written in Paris.

Pasqual (ii, p. 79 ; *cf.* Av. p. 615) adds to Lull's productions of this epoch in Paris an opuscule entitled *De congruo adducto ad necessariam rationem* (1299), which was written in opposition to certain Parisian theologians who attacked his teaching. *H.L.F.* (No. 227, p. 331) entitles the tract *Quaestio utrum illud quod est congruum in divinis ad necessariam probationem possit reduci, salvo mysterio fidei.*

[2] *Cant de Ramon.*

[3] Pasqual, ii, pp. 84–5 ; *Obras rimadas*, p. 363 ; *H.L.F.*, No. 98, p. 267. There seems to be no evidence whatever for this conjecture, which *H.L.F.* goes so far as to state as a fact. The poem might well have been written several years earlier.

[4] See p. 130, above.

[5] Sóm hom vell, paubre, menyspreat,
no hai ajuda d'home nat
e hai trop gran fait emperat.
Gran res hai del món cercat,
mant bon eximpli hai donat :
poc són conegut e amat.
(*Cant de Ramon*, viii.)

In language that recalls one of the loveliest images of the *Book of the Lover and the Beloved*, he protests that his desire is to die in the ocean of love.[1] The thought drives depression from his spirit ; his melancholy departs, and he is once more his former self, outlining his aspirations and dedicating himself anew to their fulfilment. Only once again, and for a moment, is he pathetically despondent :

> To work great good, where'er I go,
> Is my desire, but naught can do,
> Wherefore I suffer ire and woe.[2]

Then instantly he recovers himself :

> Holiness, life and sanity,
> God grant me, joy and liberty,
> From sin and evil keep me free.
> His am I, wholly, trustingly :
> And neither devil or man is he
> That has dominion over me.[3]

During the late summer of the year 1299, a great desire came to Ramon to return for a time to his native island, which he had not seen (as far as the evidence of his writings testifies) for something like twenty years. It had not actually been restored to James of Mallorca by his nephew until August 9, 1298, eight months later than the day which Boniface had stipulated.[4] But presumably, after the elder James and the younger had met

[1] Vull morir en pèlag d'amor (ix ; cf. *L.A.A.*, 235, *Bl.*, p. 447 ; *cf.* p. 372 below).

[2] On que vage cuit gran bé far,
e a la fi res no hi puc far,
per què n'hai ira e pesar.
(xi, 1–3.)

[3] Santedat, vida, sanitat,
gauig, me do Déus e llibertat,
e guard-me de mal e pecat.
A Déu me són tot comanat :
mal esperit ne hom irat
no hagen en mi potestat.
(xiii.)

[4] So Lecoy de la Marche, i, p. 359. Other accounts differ as to the actual day of the official restitution, but all give the year as 1298. (*Cf.* Dameto, ii, p. 6 ; Aigrefeuille, i, p. 155.)

"like father and son,"[1] come to terms on the question of allegiance, and taken up their new possessions—for James of Aragon was awarded Corsica and Sardinia—they would depart to these respective territories. Nothing could be more natural, therefore, than that Ramon should think of going to Mallorca also.

He was engaged, at this time, upon another brief work in Catalan verse,[2] the *Dictat* (or *Writing*) *of Ramon*, consisting of one hundred and eight couplets, mainly didactic and doctrinal, and couched in his tersest and most maxim-like style.[3] The *Dictat* is hardly poetry, but some of its couplets have a peculiar mnemonic power which perhaps justifies their perpetuation, and must certainly have recommended them to missionaries and preachers :

More wondrous is the Incarnation
Than a thousand thousand worlds' creation.

A God made man we can better love
And understand than a God above.[4]

In writing the *Dictat* it seems possible that Ramon had in mind its use in a preaching mission of his own in Barcelona and in Mallorca. He begs the King of Aragon to summon Jews and Saracens to argue about their faiths with Franciscans, Dominicans and others, the results of which arguments will, of course, be their conversion.

Let these, good King of noble race,
In Barcelona first take place.[5]

The body of the *Dictat* is concerned with the funda-

[1] Lecoy de la Marche, i, p. 359.

[2] And possibly also a work in prose—the *Principia philosophiae complexa*—which Pasqual (ii, p. 95) lists as having been begun at Paris, and finished in Mallorca in 1300 ; cf. *H.L.F.*, No. 130, pp. 292–3, Longpré, col. 1091, and pp. 298 n., 343 below.

[3] There is a Latin version of this work at Munich entitled *Compendiosus tractatus Raymundi de articulis fidei.* For bibliography, see Longpré, col. 1105.

[4] Mays val un hòm deificar
Que mil milia mons crear.

Car Deus s es homenificat
Es mays entés e mays amat.

(iv, *Obras rimadas*, p. 378.)

[5] The doggerel, bad as it is, is hardly as pronounced as in the original :
Humil rey d'alta corona,
Començem en Barcelona.

mental Christian verities. The first part, and perhaps the most important, demonstrates the necessity for the existence of a God, from the argument of design and also from the implications of a contrary assumption. The couplets jingle merrily :

If God be not, both wrong and right
At death are lost and ended quite.

* * * * *

If God be not, no worth have we :
No worth have all things that we see.

* * * * *

If God be not, pray tell me where
Is he that made this world so fair.

And at the end Lull concludes, with great satisfaction :

Now have we proved for all to see
And shown that God perforce must be.[1]

The five later parts defend, in much the same manner, the Unity of God, the Trinity, the Incarnation, the Creation of the world—refuting the Mohammedan dogma that the world is eternal—and the Resurrection of the flesh.

From the dedication of the *Dictat*[2] it would appear

[1] Si Deus no es, tot quant es tort
E tot lo be 's pert en la mort.

* * * * *

Si Deus no es, no valem res
E per no res es tot quant es.

* * * * *

Si Deus no es, ¿ e quí ha mes
Tant bell ordre en ço que es ?

* * * * *

Provat es donchs e demostrat
Que Deus es de necessitat.

[2] To St. Louis (who had died nearly thirty years before) and King James II of Aragon :

A honor del Sanct Spirit
Començá e finí son escrit,
Ramon, en vinent de Paris,
El comana a Sanct Loys,
E al noble rey d'Aragó
Jacme en l'encarnació
De Christ mccxc nou.

that Lull wrote it as he was actually journeying from Paris to Mallorca. Probably the greater part, if not the whole, was composed at Barcelona, where he made a short stay, and, about the end of 1299,[1] wrote a *Book of Prayer*,[2] at the command of the King of Aragon, for the use of himself and his consort. " This book," he says at the end of it,

> was made at the request of the most high and noble lord James, King of Aragon, and of the most high and noble lady Blanche, Queen of Aragon, his wife, who commanded Ramon to make this book, which should give instruction and teaching, that those who know not how to pray to God should learn to pray to Him, and that those who love Him not greatly should learn to love Him.[3]

A better title for the book than that given to it would be " Book of Prayer and Meditation," since both these elements have a place and it is difficult to disentangle them. Twelve chapters, nine of which are very brief and three a great deal longer, describe different aspects of prayer. The first is addressed to the one God, the second to the Holy Trinity, the third to God under six of His Divine attributes in turn. A long chapter entitled " Of our Lord God Jesus Christ " next applies certain incidents in the life of Christ to the spiritual life of the Christian, after which brief chapters comprise meditations on the Blessed Virgin, the angels, Christians and infidels. Finally come prayers for the departed, for parents and friends, and for oneself, the last-named considering in turn the seven virtues and the seven deadly sins as subjects for meditation. A brief general thanksgiving closes the book, save that some manuscripts have also an " instruction for loving God " which goes into the proper use of the book in some detail.

The *Book of Prayer* is entirely devotional, devoid of erudition and scanty in references to Ramon's beloved

[1] *Libre de Oració*, ed. Rosselló (*Obras*, vol. ii, p. xiii).

[2] Pasqual, *H.L.F.* (No. 230, p. 332) and others entitle it the " Book of (thirteen) Prayers," but the title of the original Catalan edition is as in the preceding note. See Rogent i Duràn : *Bibliografía*, etc., p. 346 ; Longpré, col. 1104.

[3] *Libre de Oració* : " De la fi d aquest libre " (*ed. cit.*, p. 267).

ideals and projects. It contains not a single allusion to any of his other writings—a rare occurrence in Lull—and it has two further striking characteristics, one of which, were its authorship not certain, might lead us to attribute it to another hand.

First, it is lyrical and emotional to a degree seldom reached by Lull's writings. At best, these qualities make it the more attractive : the fervour of some of its simplest petitions might well give them a life as long as that of the language in which they were written. But we also find, in the tendency, for example, to dwell upon the physical aspects of the Passion, an emotionalism which we should to-day consider exaggerated. Throughout the book, too, occur passages which are best described as purely lyrical, some of them being in rimed prose, after the Arabic model, a device which emphasizes their nature.[1]

Closely connected with this lyricism is another characteristic which it is very rare indeed to find in a genuinely Lullian work—a quite feminine profusion of exuberant figures of speech. Can this have been meant to attract the fancy of Queen Blanche? It can hardly be attributed to Oriental influence, so unusual is it even in Ramon's most poetical works. Still less can it be a sign of decadence, for it is absent from later books. There would seem, then, to be some personal reason underlying it, possibly a re-reading, about that time, of the *Song of Solomon*, which has clearly influenced the book. Be it as it may, the most confirmed Lullist receives a surprise when he comes upon such passages as these :

Thou, Divine Will, art a flower of rose, of violet,[2] of eglantine, and of lily, which blossoms and bears fruit both in the righteous and in sinners ; a flower of love that makes men love Thee and

[1] The reader may consult, for example, chap. iv, § ii (De Nativitat) and the opening of chap. vi (Dels Angels). These are perhaps the two most marked examples in the book. *Cf.* also *Blanquerna*, chap. 49 (*Bl.*, p. 183), *A.C.*, p. 9, note, and p. 177, above.

[2] The word *viola*, in literary Catalan, old and modern alike, is the Spanish *alelí*, or scented stock, but in the current language it also denotes the violet, and may always have done so.

desire Thee, and causes them to weep as they love, honour and serve Thee.[1]

I will understand and remember those springs of love in Thy crown of thorns, whence issued flowers of crimson hue, blood-red roses, flowers sweetly scented, which ran down Thy Head, Thy Face and Thy Body, staining them with crimson.[2]

I beg Thee, O Lord, to . . . illumine my heart with the brightness of love, and to clothe and adorn it with roses, violets and the virtues, that sighs may issue therefrom, opening mine eyes that the white flowers of weeping and tears may issue thence.[3]

Of hope I make lily flowers, roses and violets, whence issue sweet love and perfume when I am in sadness, sighing and tears. . . . To have hope in Thine eternal and infinite power, and in Thy will, wisdom and virtue, which are the fulness of hope, is a crown of roses and violets, rubies, diamonds, carbuncles, emeralds and sapphires.[4]

And the ornateness of the chapter upon the Blessed Virgin is unparalleled in all Lull's writings, so sober, as a rule, is his taste, and so restrained his imagination :

Thou art the dawn that dost illumine sinners upon the troublous sea, and likewise when the sea is calm, smooth and still. . . . Star that dost illumine heaven and earth and sea, illumine thou my sinful heart with thy love. . . . Star that dost illumine all stars else, descend to those that love and call upon thee. . . . Queen of queens, virgin above all virgins, carbuncle, ruby, emerald and sapphire among precious stones, to thee I give in bondage all the strength of my body and my spirit. . . . Thou, O Empress, art a spring whence flowers of crimson flow to the heart of the sinner. . . . A garden art thou where roses are plucked, and lilies and violets of sweet perfume, and apples sweet to the taste.[5]

Even to a reader who finds the hyperboles of the book unpleasing, and its metaphors without power, there is something very attractive in the devoutness of the

[1] Chap. iii (*Obras*, p. 199).

[2] Chap. iv, § iii (*Obras*, p. 203). *Cf.* (p. 205) the similar comparison of the blood and water that issued from Christ's side at the Crucifixion with "flowers red and white," and (p. 211) the author's return to the figure of the crown of thorns.

[3] Chap. iv, § v (*Obras*, p. 209).

[4] Chap. xi, § vi (*Obras*, p. 233).

[5] Chap. v, *passim*. These are mere fragments, extracted for the sake of space : the whole chapter should be read.

Book of Prayer. It lifts the curtain hiding Ramon's inner life, which one is tempted to neglect for the crowded activity of his outward life, and reveals a soul that was very childlike and very near to God. In the body of the book there is no reference to the sovereigns for whom it was written : if we assume in the recipient knowledge of a few common mediaeval terms, it might have been written for a man of no learning and little culture, for a youth at his marriage, almost for a child. It is more prolix than are most of Ramon's works : and the prolixity is strange in one so practised in the writing of proverbs. But it well deserves its place next to the *Tree of the Philosophy of Love* in Rosselló's collected edition, and the editor might well have prefixed to it one of Ramon's best known apostrophes :

> O ye that love, if ye will have fire, come light your lanterns at my heart ; if water, come to my eyes, whence flow the tears in springs ; if thoughts of love, come gather them from my meditations.[1]

Evidently it was Lull's intention to spend some time in his native country, for while he was at Barcelona he obtained audience of the King of Aragon, who had not long returned from a sanguinary but victorious engagement at sea against his brother Frederic in support of the papal policy. About the same time Lull was granted a special permission, dated October 30, 1299,[2] to enter all the synagogues and mosques in the royal dominions and to preach there the true faith.[3] There was nothing

[1] *L.A.A.*, 173 (*Bl.*, p. 437).

[2] This date is previous by two months to that given as the date of the King's return, *e.g.* by Zurita (Bk. v, chap. 40), and by other authorities—a strange inconsistency. It is true that the document (which is quoted in the next note) bears the date of no year, but the preceding and following documents in the register are both of the year 1299. En Jordi Rubió has kindly gone into this chronology with me in some detail, and we conclude that the Chancellor must have signed the permit instead of the King, a proceeding for which there are precedents.

[3] Rubió y Lluch, *Documents*, etc., xiv (i, pp. 13–14) :

. . . Concedimus et damus licenciam magistro R° Lulii quod, electis per eum quinque vel sex probis hominibus et sibi adhibitis, possit predicare in sinagogiis judeorum diebus sabbatinis et dominicis, et in mesquitis sarracenorum diebus veneris et dominicis, per totam terram et dominacionem

unusual, of course, either in this or in the complementary decree for which Lull asked in his *Dictat*. Throughout the thirteenth century, owing mainly to the zeal of the Dominicans, such attempts to convert Jews and Moors were made continually in Aragon,[1] where both races were treated with comparative tolerance and even friendliness, not least by the very friars who strove with them in argument. The *Pugio Fidei*[2] of Ramon Martí (1278) was a powerful weapon of conversion and a spur to determined proselytizing. In 1263 James the Conqueror had ordered his Jewish subjects to sit at the feet of the Friars Preachers, and we read of a debate, held in the same year at Barcelona, in the King's presence, between a converted Jew appropriately baptized Paul (Fr. Pau Cristià) and turned Dominican, and a rabbi of Gerona, Moses ben Nachman. In the same year, Jews and Saracens were ordered to attend a Dominican mission; two years later, another debate, held also in the King's presence, ended in a public scandal, the Jewish speaker being accused by the Dominicans of blasphemy, so that the Pope had to be called in to settle the quarrel.[3] In 1268, again, complaints that the Jews of Barcelona and Lleida (Lérida) were ill-treated led to their being granted a royal dispensation from attending Christian missions outside their own quarter; together with this favour,

nostram, et exponere judeis et sarracenis predictis fidei catholice veritatem admissis religiosis quibuscumque ad predicacionem ipsam accedentibus. Nos enim damus per presentes, firmiter in mandatis, universis et singulis aljamis judeorum et sarracenorum tocius terre nostre, quod ipsi, diebus predictis sub forma predicta, audiant et audire teneantur prefatum magistrum R. Lulii, et si voluerint, oportunitate captata, possint respondere ejus predicacioni et exposicioni, non tamem cogantur nec cogeri possint eisdem super premissis si noluerint respondere.

[1] Alfonso the Wise, in Castile, was doing good service at about the same time to the same cause by ordering the translation into Castilian of the sacred books of Moslems and Jews "to the end that it may clearly appear" (the quotation is from Juan Manuel's *Libro de Cetrería*) "that all that was in their law was a figure of this law which we Christians have, and that both Jews and Moors are in great error, and are in the way wherein their souls will be lost."

[2] For an account of this interesting work, see Menéndez y Pelayo: *Historia de los heterodoxos españoles*, Madrid, 1917, vol. iii, pp. 251–55.

[3] On these debates, and James the Conqueror's treatment of Jews, see Tourtoulon, bk. iv, chap. 3.

they were granted that of not being forced to admit into their synagogues more than ten Christians at a time, accompanying a Christian preacher. Such essays at toleration make us smile to-day, but they also indicate what was regarded as intolerance, and it is greatly to the Conqueror's credit that he not only resisted papal attempts to reverse his policy but protected the Jews as well as suffering them, thereby incidentally enriching his dominions and giving an example of both policy and generosity to those who came after him.

It is as well to realize how ordinary was Ramon's request, coming from an accredited Christian preacher, for otherwise we should be surprised to find that he remained a very short time at Barcelona. Either the permission accorded him was less than that which he asked for or he had made some wholly distinct requests which were not granted him[1] : for whatever reason, he made little use, as far as Barcelona was concerned, of his privileges, but soon after the turn of the year took ship to Mallorca.[2] Here (for he was still nominally in the King of Aragon's dominions) he began a preaching mission immediately, anxious to profit by his experiences with the heathen abroad in the interests of the heathen at home.[3]

Hardly had he arrived in Mallorca, and concluded a book which he had begun while still in Paris,[4] than he set to work on a verse *Application of the "Art General,"*[5]

[1] These can be the only interpretations of *V.C.* (*Life*, p. 30 : E com hagués soplicat lo dit rey sobre algunes utilitats de la sancta Fè catòlica e veés que no aprofitava, tornà s en Mallorque) and of *V.B.R.L.* (*Life*, p. 74 : sed videns, se parum vel nihil super talibus obtinere, regressus est Majoricas).

[2] Not earlier, because James of Aragon did not return to Barcelona till December 1299 ; not later, because Ramon had been in Mallorca long enough to publish a book there (*cf.* text below) in the March of 1300. Zurita (according to Pasqual, ii, p. 93) says that James had already left Barcelona when Ramon gave up his importunity. But for that matter Zurita (bk. v, chap. 42) says that James was still in Barcelona on March 21, 1300, so he is clearly wrong somewhere.

[3] *V.C.*, *V.B.R.L.*, v (*Life*, pp. 30, 74).

[4] The *Principia philosophiae complexa*, 1300. See p. 343 n., below. The original form of this work is Catalan ("Començaments de philosophia") ; *cf.* Longpré, col. 1091.

[5] *H.L.F.*, No. 100 (pp. 268–9) ; *Obras rimadas*, pp. 384–85.

which he completed by March 1301.[1] In its twelve hundred lines he shows how to apply the *Art* in turn to theology, philosophy, logic, law, medicine, rhetoric and moral science. It is scarcely necessary to say that the medium of verse is used simply for its mnemonic value, the treatment being in no way poetical.

The same would hardly be said of the *Medicine for Sin* (" Medicina de Peccat ")[2] which was finished in July of the same year. This is a huge work of some six thousand lines, arranged in stanzas each containing ten octosyllabic couplets, occasionally diversified in length, or by the use of more irregular metres,[3] or by the suppression of stanzaic form altogether.[4] The five sections, dealing respectively with contrition, confession, satisfaction, temptation and prayer, are very unequal, both in length and merit, and occasionally wander considerably.[5] The section on prayer, sometimes catalogued as a separate poem,[6] has a certain unity of its own ; it exalts the Essence of God, describes His attributes, incites the reader, by these and other considerations, to prayer, and finally deals with prayer in general under the five headings of quantity, quality, time, place and manner.

[1] The book ends :

Es en Maylorca la ciutat
 Aquesta nòu escrit acabat,
Al nombre d'encarnació
 Mil et trescents con Deu hom fó,
Al mes de Mars. . . .

H.L.F. interprets this as March 1300.

(*Obras rimadas*, p. 422.)

[2] *H.L.F.*, No. 101 (pp. 269–70).

[3] *e.g.*—a bold and telling example—

Temptació
De mal angel e bò
Vuyl ensercar en est sermó ;
Car vuyl mostrar
Com se puscha hom guardar
Al començament, com vol far
Alquna re.

(iv, i : *Obras rimadas*, p. 491.)

[4] As in the two final sections, *passim*.

[5] Notably the second section, on Confession, which treats at length of the Human Nature and the Passion of Christ, of the Blessed Virgin and of the saints—who plead for the penitent.

[6] See *Poesies*, p. 153.

The poem, incredible as this may seem to those who read it, was compared favourably by Torras i Bages[1] with the "starry autos" of Calderón. Few would give it such extravagant praise as this. It has not on the whole, or for long together, very much of the essence of poetry. It is vivid, lively and emphatic, written often in the staccato style of the verse proverbs, fluent, sometimes eloquent, and characterized especially by a wonderful richness of rimes, both single and double. Too frequently its matter is very arid, and it is with relief that we turn from the subtleties of its theological disquisitions to simple and naïve descriptions such as that, in the last section, of the Infant Jesus,[2] to the rare nature passages hardly surpassed by Lull anywhere :

> When shines the star at peep of day
> And all the flowers in glad array
> Wait for the sun to make them gay
> With floods of radiant light,
> Then that same hope that makes them bright
> Fills me with gladness and delight,
> For I trust in the Lady of love alway.[3]

and to the rather more frequent passages which, though hard to render efficiently in another language, are in their original Catalan of real force and eloquence :

> Who's He that all things can create
> And pardon sins, however great ?
> Who in a moment can destroy
> The world and all that we enjoy ?
> Who gives the harvest, flower and grain ?
> Who makes a man to rise again ?
> Who gives him joy that never ends ?
> Who is most loyal and true of friends ?

* * * * *

[1] See *Poesies*, p. 259.

[2] V, vii : *Obras rimadas*, p. 583.

[3] Quant par l'estela en l'albor,
E s'apareylon tut li flor,
Qu'el sòl montiplich lur color
D'esperança,
Mi vest alegrança
D'una douçor confiança
Qu'ay en la dona d'amor.
(II, xxiv "De Esperança" : *Obras rimadas*, p. 466.)

One, only One, all this can do—
All this, and more than I can show.
He is the God that loves alway :
Him do I praise, to Him I pray.
Before Him, I, a sinner, bend :
He gives me pardon and grace to amend.[1]

In the autumn and winter of 1300 Lull was again hard at work writing prose opuscules of some merit.[2] In September he completed (in Catalan) the *Book of the Being of God*, in which he deduces eight corollaries from the principal truth which man knows about God,—namely, that He is. According to the prologue, he intended to translate this book into Arabic and to use it "in disputations with Saracens, Jews and pagans," for which reason he writes only of the Trinity in Unity, and not of the three Persons considered singly, the Christian doctrine of the Trinity being so great a stumbling-block to the heathen.[3] Allied to this work is the *Book of the Knowledge of God*, finished (also in Catalan) in the following month and intended to be used similarly. With the same reservation as in the earlier work, it summarizes Lull's teaching on the Divine Nature.

[1] ¿ Quí es que puscha res crear
Ni negun peccat perdonar ?
¿ Quál es cell qui pòt destruir
En un punt lo món e delir ?
¿ Quí fá florir e fá granar ?
¿ E quí pot hom ressucitar ?
¿ E quí dona gloria 'l cèl ?
¿ E quí es ver amich faèl ?
. . . . . .
No es mas sòl un qui qu'eu say
Qui ha tot quant dich, encar may ;
Aquel qui es bò Deu d'amor,
Lo qual prech, reclam e aor,
Que'm dó sa joya e'm perdó
Mos peccats on penedent só.
(V, vi : *Obras rimadas*, p. 581.)

[2] Pasqual (ii, p. 95) ascribes to July 1300 Lull's free translation into Latin of the *Dictat*, entitled *Compendiosus tractatus de articulis fidei* ; *cf.* Longpré, col. 1105.

[3] *Libre del Es de Deu*, Pròlech (ed. Rosselló, pp. 440–1). Cf. *H.L.F.*, No. 174, p. 311, Rubió y Lluch, *Sumari*, etc., pp. 293–94, and *ed. cit.*, pp. xxv–xxvii.

As we have made many books, wherein we have said much of God . . ., we now make this book, towards the end of our life (*en la derreria dels nostres dies*), wherein we reduce to the conclusions which follow all that we have said of the Essence of God and His Trinity.[1]

The substance of the book consists in the putting of twenty-five fundamental questions upon the Nature of God, and answering each question in turn by developing five axiomatic truths.

November saw the completion of a third work, the *Book of Man*,[2] the threefold aim of which is described as being to lead men to a knowledge—both corporal and spiritual—of themselves, so that, by reflecting on their own nature, they may learn to know their fellow-men and the God-Man. The first distinction describes the body and the soul of man and their functions, repeating much from the *Book of the Rational Soul* and making excursions into natural philosophy. The second is concerned with death, both physical and spiritual. The third treats of prayer, and is in reality a short instructional treatise, almost complete in itself. It contains twenty-two short prayers to God, forty to Jesus Christ, and nineteen " praises " of Christ, much after the manner of the *Song of the Three Children*.[3] Finally come thirty-five paragraphs entitled " De Precationibus," some of them addressed to Christ and others to Our Lady. In these, and especially in the exuberance of their metaphors,[4] we see clearly the influence of the *Book of Prayer*.

The Catalan *Book of God and of Jesus Christ*,[5] finished

[1] *Libre de Conexença de Deu*, Pròlech (ed. Rosselló, p. 376). Cf. *H.L.F.*, No. 175, p. 311, Pasqual, *Vindiciae*, p. 327, Rubió y Lluch, *Sumari*, p. 294, and *ed. cit.*, pp. xxii–xxiv.

[2] *Liber de Homine, Libre del home*. Salz., vol. vi. Cf. *H.L.F.*, No. 45 (pp. 215–17), Longpré, col. 1094. There is a Catalan MS. of this work in the British Museum (MS. Add. 16431, fols. 1–99).

[3] Salz., vi, pp. 48–57.

[4] *E.g.*: Tu es luna coeli misericordiae. . . . O Domicella amoris, rubinus, smaragdus, topasius et saphyrus . . . Clara et lucens fontana. . . . Arbor vitae . . . . Porta Paradisi, Palatium in quo est omne bonum (Salz., vi, pp. 57–61).

[5] Frequently referred to as the " Book of God " (*Libre de Deu*) : see ed. Rosselló, pp. xvii–xxii and *H.L.F.*, Nos. 47, 176 (pp. 219–20, 312). A number of other books with this or a similar title are attributed to Lull, but they are probably by one or more of his followers. This book is the only one of the title which is undoubtedly genuine. Its Latin version is in Salz., vol. vi.

in December 1300, is described in its prologue as being "explained as best we are able, that men may understand it. Howbeit in a few places we shall speak of God subtly." The subtlety consists principally in suggestions of the doctrine of the Trinity, made in the first part (" Of God ") to prepare the reader—and especially the heathen reader[1]—for the second part (" Of Jesus Christ "). Where Lull finds it essential to preach the Trinity of Persons, he is at particular pains not to divide the Substance.[2] In each part are asked and answered, concerning God the Father and God the Son respectively, the same ten fundamental questions which we find in the *Art General* : Is He ? What is He ? Whence is He ? Wherefore is He ? etc. The answers, which comprise the whole of the book, are concise and cogent, yet overwhelming in their number and cumulative effect. The *Book of God and of Jesus Christ* and the *Book of Prayer* are, both in style and method, as unlike as it is possible for two theological books to be. One is evidential, the other devotional : of neither can the reader easily believe that it was written by a man of nearly seventy. The *Book of Prayer* has all the fervour of youth. The *Book of God and of Jesus Christ* has a command and an array of argument as remarkable as the energy and power which enabled its author to compose such a book in the space of a few weeks and in the midst of other occupations.

While Lull was still in Mallorca, there came news from the East which, for all his years, stirred him into the activity of boyhood. "The Great Tartar," as the Khan of Tartary was called, "had conquered all the kingdom of Syria." [3] The boasted crusades and martial exploits of Christian armies had been insufficient to drive

[1] The introduction clearly states that the book is meant principally for the use of missionaries and for the defence of the Catholic faith (*ed. cit.*, p. 273).

[2] As in pt. i, chap. 5 (" Es demanat quant es Deus " : *ed. cit.*, pp. 302–7) : " God is one, and there are neither two Gods nor more, for if there were two or more . . . neither would be God. . . . Since there is one God only, He can be infinite, etc., etc."

[3] *V.C.*, v (*Life*, p. 30). *V.B.R.L.* paraphrases (p. 74) : " Imperator Tartarorum Cassanus Regnum Syriae fuisset aggressus, illudque totum suo dominio ambiret."

the Moslems from their secure possession of the Holy Places. But deliverance had come from another source, and one long looked to with expectation. So friendly to Christianity were the Tartars that, with Palestine under their rule, there would undoubtedly be the fullest freedom there for Christians. And in a new field of Catholic activity, especially in a field that had formerly belonged to the Prophet, there was work for Ramon Lull to do, and to do quickly !

Losing little time, he set sail, probably early in 1301,[1] for the Holy Land, and had progressed as far as Cyprus when "he found that the news was false."[2] What had actually happened was certainly sufficient to account for the rumour. The Khan had indeed gained a victory, at the end of December 1299, over the combined forces of the Sultan of Egypt and the King of Syria, driving them back into Egypt and declaring himself lord of Syria. So great had been the effect of the news in Europe that Boniface VIII had publicly predicted the forthcoming deliverance of the Holy Places from the Moslems (April 7, 1300). But during this campaign news had been brought to the Khan of the rebellion of a kinsman in Persia, as a result of which he hastened there with all possible speed after his victory, without waiting to consolidate it in person ; whereupon the treachery of his subordinates in Syria caused the country to return to its former allegiance. Hence Ramon, landing at Cyprus, found his hopes frustrated and his plans for the future checked. Even he must have been nonplussed for the moment.

His active mind, however, and his recent experiences at home soon suggested to him what work he might do for the Faith.[3] Catalans were as well known in Cyprus as in Northern Africa on account of their commercial activities. So Lull petitioned King Henry of Cyprus to

[1] Not earlier, for the Catalan verse "Application" of the *Art general*, consisting of 1200 octosyllabic lines (*H.L.F.*, No. 100, pp. 268–69) was probably only finished, in Mallorca, in March 1301 (*cf.* p. 298, above).

[2] *V.C.*, *V.B.R.L.*, v (*Life*, pp. 30, 74).

[3] Both *V.C.* and *V.B.R.L.* make a short homiletic digression here, quoting in the vernacular, not too exactly, from the Bible. (*Life*, pp. 30–1, 74.)

gather together such heretics as were in his kingdom[1] and authorize him to preach to them. Afterwards, he added, he would visit the Sultans of Babylon and Egypt and the King of Syria, so that he might bring the peoples of all these countries into the unity of the Catholic faith.

The King received the proposal without enthusiasm, but did not reject it,[2] so Ramon began to hold disputations, with what result is not known.[3] While in Cyprus that autumn, he had another escape from death, for, during an illness which laid him low, a cleric[4] and a servant who were in attendance upon him gave him poison. Nothing is known of the motives for this crime,[5] but Ramon apparently feared its repetition when he discovered it. He took no action against its authors, but although not yet well, left the place immediately for Famagusta, a south-eastern coast-town, at that time of considerable importance. Here he found a warm welcome from the Master of the Temple, who lived at Limisso (the modern Limasol) not far away, and lodged him in his house there until his health was fully restored.[6] Then Ramon went on his way.[7]

[1] *V.C.* says merely "certain heretics"; *V.B.R.L.* specifies: "infideles atque schismaticos, videlicet, Jacobinos, Nestorinos, Momminas" (*Life*, pp. 31, 74–5). By "Momminas" I understand "Maronitas" to be meant and assume a scribal error, following Sollier ("Momminas non novi, puto legendum Maronitas") who reads "Momminas" where the Parisian MS. of *V.B.R.L.* has "Momminos."

[2] ". . . de la qual cosa lo dit rey de Xipre hac poca cura" (*V.C.*, v, agreeing with *V.B.R.L.*, v: *Life*, pp. 31, 75).

[3] Unless we count the statements: "no cessà de confondre los dits heretges ab preycacions e disputes" (*V.C.*, v) and the "viriliter operari," etc. of *V.B.R.L.*, v (*Life*, pp. 31, 75).

[4] *V.C.*, "capellà," *V.B.R.L.* "clericus." *Cf.* Pasqual, ii, p. 98, n. *V.B.R.L.* adds: "qui non ponentes Deum ante conspectum suum, suae salutis immemores, cogitaverunt viri Dei bona scelerosis manibus extorquere" (*Life*, p. 75).

[5] Longpré (col. 1083) surmises that it was "afin d'enlever son bagage."

[6] This seems to be what is meant by the phrases used by *V.C.*: "Fo alegrement rebut per lo mestre del Temple qui era en la ciutat de Limiso, e tingué l en sa casa fins que hagué recobrada la salut" (*V.C.*, v. So also *V.B.R.L.*: *Life*, pp. 32, 75).

[7] Lull's *Rhetorica nova* was written in the monastery of St. Chrysostom, near Mt. Bufavento, in the north of Cyprus, and is dated September 1301 (cf. *H.L.F.*, No. 74, p. 251); his *Liber de natura* (*H.L.F.*, No. 68, pp. 247–48; Longpré, col. 1107) is dated "Famagusta, December 1301." These two books help to fix the chronology of this period.

Before returning homewards by the usual sea-route, and touching at Rhodes and Malta,[1] Lull appears to have travelled from Cyprus to the mainland, an adventurous journey if not a long one. This we infer from the statement in a minor work of his[2] that it was written "in Alleas, civitate Armeniae, anno 1301."[3] The work in question resembles a number of others in being a manual of elementary instruction in the fourteen articles and the seven sacraments and is of no significance. It may well have been written for ill-instructed Christians whom Lull met in Asia: the prologue, indeed, suggests this.

From Alleas to Mallorca was a long journey,[4] and part of it Ramon beguiled by making a new "book of proverbs," which contains a thousand in all,[5] divided into fifty-two "chapters" according to their subjects. A very cursory glance at the book is sufficient to show that of the simplest proverb form he had by now become a master: his terse monosyllables, read in their original Catalan, are unforgettable.

Ama pus bon cosi, que mal fiyl.[6]
Hom auar a tart riu.[7]

[1] We gather this from references in the *Liber de fine* (see p. 316, below; *cf.* Pasqual, ii, p. 101).

[2] *Que deu hom creure de Deu* (or *Quid debet homo credere de Deo*). Cf. *H.L.F.*, No. 177, pp. 312–13; Longpré, col. 1098. Pasqual (ii, p. 101) dates this book January 1302; a Catalan version extant in MS. at Munich gives the same date.

[3] *V.C.*, *V.B.R.L.* simply record that he went from Limasol to Genoa (*Life*, pp. 32, 75–6), but the evidence of the book seems conclusive. Alleas, according to *H.L.F.*, is el-Ayyas, or Layas, a town of which only ruins now remain, situated opposite to Alexandretta and in the mediaeval principality of Armenia, which is quite distinct from the modern Armenia, where many commentators assume that Lull went. See p. 318, n. 4, below.

[4] Lull may, for all that the available evidence tells us to the contrary, have crossed to the mainland and returned to Cyprus before going home. If he was at Famagusta in December 1301 (n. 7, p. 305) this is very likely, and the contemporary life would then be correct.

[5] That he wrote this book (*Libre de mil proverbis*) while on his journey is clear from his own statement (*Obras*, i, p. 489): "Aquests prouerbis feu e dicta maestre Ramon Lull de Maylorca, venent d oltra mar, en l any de nostre Senyor Deu Jhesu-Christ m.ccc.ij." Cf. *Obras*, i, pp. 383–489; *H.L.F.*, No. 259, pp. 367–69; Obrador, *Viatge*, etc., p. 608.

[6] Love a good nephew better than a bad son (*L.M.P.*, v, 4; *Obras*, i, p. 395).

[7] A miser seldom laughs (*L.M.P.*, xli, 10; *Obras*, i, p. 467).

Tot hom glot viu poch.[1]
Ama mes ta fe que ton fill.[2]
Si est mal volgut, est pobre.[3]

Needless to say, not all the thousand are so essentially proverbial as these. Here and there, most noticeably in the sections on confession and satisfaction, Ramon loses the knack of the proverb-writer and finds himself penning whole series of single-line instructions. Here and there, again, we find him condensing sentences from the *Book of Contemplation*, *Blanquerna* and *Felix*,[4] putting into their briefest form his well-known views on prelacy and secular government.[5] But there are really very few of the *Proverbs* which are not fairly satisfactory in form, nor is there in the book much meaningless repetition. A small proportion of the thousand maxims are trite and dull, and a good many more are but slight variations of other proverbs, well-known religious truths, texts from Holy Scripture, and the like. The great majority, however, are of notable variety and reach a very high standard, amply justifying Ramon's aim in composing them :

> Since man has been created to know and love and remember and honour and serve God, therefore we make these *Thousand Proverbs*, to give doctrine therewith that men may be ever mindful of the end for which they were created. And since the proverb is an instrument which briefly certifies truth concerning many things, and the manners are many and diverse wherein a man is straitly bound to love and honour God and to have charity to his neighbour as to himself, therefore do we make many proverbs concerning all these manners.[6]

Some of them are of interest chiefly for their quaintness, which even touches obscurity :

Make thou thy lineage gentle with humility.[7]
Love rather God's work in thee than thy work in Him.[8]

[1] The glutton's life is a short one (*L.M.P.*, xlii, 20 ; *Obras*, i, p. 469).
[2] Love thy faith more than thy son (*L.M.P.*, xvi, 16 ; *Obras*, i, p. 418).
[3] If thou hast the ill-will of others, thou art poor (*L.M.P.*, l, 1 ; *Obras*, i, p. 483).
[4] *E.g.* ii, iii, *passim* ; viii, 7 ; xxxv, *passim* ; xxxix, 1–6.
[5] *E.g.* ii, iii, *passim*.
[6] *L.M.P.* " Del Pròlech " (*Obras*, i, pp. 383–84
[7] Ab humilitat fas ton linyatge gentil (*L.M.P.*, xxvii, 13 ; *Obras*, i, p. 441).
[8] *L.M.P.*, i, 8 (*Obras*, i, p. 386).

In others the thought is better worth preserving than the expression :

The more thy memory and understanding are fixed on God, the greater will be thy love and fear of Him.[1]

He that fears God more than he loves Him loves himself more than God.[2]

Greater than any gift of thine is the gift that thou hast of the poor man who asks aught of thee for the love of God.[3]

A great number are more worldly-wise than one might have expected from Lull, and these, together with some of his spiritual and ethical proverbs, are characterized chiefly by their shrewdness :

Consort not with a man who desires to buy thy house.[4]

Speak not to thy neighbour either of his wife or of thine.[5]

Tell not thy neighbours what thou eatest in thy house.[6]

Let thy conscience be neither too broad nor too narrow.[7]

If thou reprove an angry man, thou shalt soon become angry likewise.[8]

Temperance and riches are sisters.[9]

Others are of importance for the study of Lull's thought, and it will not be amiss here to quote from the very significant proverbs which exalt faith as opposed to reason :

With faith believe thou the truths that thou understandest not.

By faith thou shalt attain to knowledge.

Disbelieve not all the things that thou canst not understand.

First comes belief, and afterwards understanding.

Faith illumines the paths of truth with the light of love : understanding concerns itself with knowledge.

Faith is near to the will and far from the understanding.[10]

[1] *L.M.P.*, i, 4 (*Obras*, i, p. 385).
[2] *L.M.P.*, i, 5 (*Obras*, i, p. 385).
[3] *L.M.P.*, xxxv, 20 (*Obras*, i, p. 456).
[4] *L.M.P.*, viii, 17 (*Obras*, i, p. 402).
[5] *L.M.P.*, ix, 8 (*Obras*, i, p. 403).
[6] *L.M.P.*, ix, 9 (*Obras*, i, p. 403).
[7] *L.M.P.*, xxi, 6 (*Obras*, i, p. 427).
[8] *L.M.P.*, xlvii, 7 (*Obras*, i, p. 478).
[9] *L.M.P.*, xv, 9 (*Obras*, i, p. 415).
[10] *L.M.P.*, xvi, 1, 2, 4, 5, 20, 21 (*Obras*, i, pp. 417–8).

This seems the most suitable place to discuss the relation to these proverbs, if any such exists, of the three other similar collections known or believed to be by Lull. That of 1296, to which reference has already been made,[1] stands by itself entirely, and the single "Book of Proverbs" which the catalogue of 1311 mentions is probably either this or the collection just described. Another collection of proverbs, not extant, would seem to be distinct from these, for Lull sent them to James II "king of Aragon, Valencia and Sardinia and Count of Barcelona," describing them, in an accompanying letter the date of which is unknown,[2] as "a book which I have newly made,[3] called a 'book of proverbs,' wherein are many subtleties."[4] These proverbs were meant, as the letter shows, for the *infantes*, who were to learn from them divine and worldly wisdom. They may conceivably be identical with the "instructional proverbs" (*proverbis d'ensenyament*) which were first printed in 1882 by Morel-Fatio and considered by him as certainly authentic.[5] These, however, are rimed, consisting of one hundred and seventy-four octosyllabic couplets, and the probability is that we have in them a fourth collection of proverbs—a supposition by no means unlikely when it concerns

[1] See p. 273, above.

[2] It is dated "apud Montempesulanum, octo dies infra cadragesimam." As Lull was at Montpellier in 1307, the day mentioned of that year (which would have been February 7) is generally assumed as being the *terminus ad quem* for these proverbs. A reference in the letter ("Propono stare Avenione cum Domino Papa in curia supra negotium quod jam scitis") would rather indicate 1309, as will later appear. So would the preceding words: "Postquam a vobis recessi, multa pericula mihi evenerunt. Pauper sum. . . ."; (*cf.* pp. 333 ff. below. As Lull was also in Montpellier in February and March 1309, this date seems the more likely; cf. *H.L.F.*, pp. 368–9).

[3] Unless "newly made" means "re-fashioned," the collection can hardly be identical with any of the others here mentioned. But there is a case for supposing that it does mean this.

[4] See Rubió y Lluch: *Documents*, etc., xxxiv (i, p. 41). . . . Tramito vobis, domine, unum librum quem feci de novo, de proverbis nominatum, per Petrum de Oliveriis, in quo libro multe subtilitates continentur, que sunt utiles ad sciendum, in tanto quod homo laycus sciens ipsas erit supereminens in intellectu omni alii layco qui non sciat: et hoc, domine, poteritis cognoscere per libri rubricas et prossessum. Quare, domine, erit bonum quod infantes hunc adiscant ad hoc ut regnare sciant.

[5] "Proverbes rimés de Ramón Lull," in *Romania*, xi, 1882, pp. 188–202; cf. *H.L.F.*, pp. 263–4, 368–9, and Obrador, *Viatge*, etc., pp. 606–7.

a writer as prolific as Ramon. A few examples will be quoted to show the secular character of the maxims, which seldom mention God, still less the dogmas of the Church. It is significant that many of them treat of the choice of companions.

> These saws are made for education,
> That by them we may have salvation.
> Ramon would send them far and wide
> That all men may be edified.[1]
>
> Trust not a man that never will
> Reprove thee when thou doest ill.[2]
>
> To him that takes thy coat away
> Lend not thy knife another day.[3]
>
> He who needs not his life to mend,
> God makes that man to be His friend.[4]

After his return to Mallorca, where he may possibly have been in July 1302 when the city did homage to James of Mallorca's son Sancho,[5] Ramon visited Montpellier and Genoa. Whether he went to these cities in that order, or in the reverse, or whether perhaps he stayed at Montpellier and thence went to Genoa and back, cannot with certainty be stated. The silence of the contemporary biography on the Montpellier visit[6] would of itself suggest that the stay there was a brief one ; against this, however, must be set the long list of opuscules which Ramon published in that city between September 1302 (when he finished, in Mallorca, his *Book of the Trinity and Incarnation*[7]) and

[1] Proverbis fas d'ensayament
per que hom vinga a salvament,
Los quals vol tremetre Remon
a tots los homens d aquest mon. (Nos. 1, 2)

[2] Not vulles en hom fiar
que no t reprèn de ton mal far. (No. 21)

[3] No vulles prestar ton coltell
A çell qui ha tolt lo mantell. (No. 126)

[4] Qui perfetament esta bo
Deus lo fa de si companyó. (No. 157)

[5] On October 19, 1302, Sancho did homage in turn to the King of Aragon.

[6] See *Life*, pp. 32, 76.

[7] *Liber de Trinitate et Incarnatione* (*H.L.F.*, No. 205, pp. 321–2 ; but see also Golubovich, p. 380, Alòs, *Los catálogos*, etc., p. 50, and Longpré, col. 1100, on this book and the connection of it with *De secretis Sacratissimae Trinitatis et Incarnationis*). *H.L.F.* (No. 229, pp. 331–2) gives also a *Liber de sermonibus factis de decem praeceptis*, dated from Mallorca in October 1302.

the April of 1304.[1] In this same period only three books were published at Genoa, and all of them in February 1304[2]—a fact which points to one stay only, and that short. But, as none of the Montpellier treatises bears a date between April and October 1303, it may well be that another visit to Genoa was made in that summer, and was both preceded and followed by a longer sojourn in Montpellier, after which came a second visit to Genoa the following winter.

A few only of these treatises deserve mention. In the *Dispute between Faith and Understanding*[3] Lull returns to

[1] The list is as follows: APRIL 1303: *Liber de Praedestinatione et libero arbitrio* (*H.L.F.*, No. 224, p. 330; Longpré, col. 1099). OCTOBER 1303: *Disputatio Fidei et Intellectus* (*H.L.F.*, No. 26, pp. 158–62). NOVEMBER 1303: *Liber de lumine* (on the physical qualities and symbolism of light), (*H.L.F.*, No. 87, pp. 259–60; Longpré, col. 1107). ?DECEMBER 1303: *Liber de regionibus sanitatis et infirmitatis* (*H.L.F.*, No. 85, pp. 258–9; Longpré, col. 1108). JANUARY 1304: *Liber de intellectu* or *Ars intellectus* (*H.L.F.*, No. 140, p. 297); *Liber de voluntate* (*H.L.F.*, No. 141, pp. 297–8); *Ars Juris* (*H.L.F.*, No. 73, pp. 250–1). FEBRUARY 1304: *Liber de memoria* (*H.L.F.*, No. 142, p. 298); *Liber de significatione* (*H.L.F.*, No. 228, p. 331; Longpré, col. 1094). MARCH 1304: *Liber de consilio* (*H.L.F.*, No. 220, p. 328; Longpré, col. 1108). APRIL 1304: *Liber de investigatione vestigiorum productionis divinarum personarum* (*H.L.F.*, No. 206, p. 322. *Cf.* Alòs, *Los catálogos*, p. 85).

There was also published in or about the year 1304 the *Ars generalis ad omnes scientias*: the exact date of this work is not known. Pasqual places here the *Liber de modo applicandi novam logicam ad scientiam juris et medicinae* (ii, p. 104; cf. *H.L.F.*, No. 167, p. 307; Longpré, col. 1094), presumably because it completes and quotes the *Logica nova* (see next note).

On the possibly genuine *Liber qui continet confessionem* and *Liber de confessione*, see H.L.F., pp. 337–8 and p. 362, n. 1, below. On Pasqual's ascription of a second *Ars Juris* to Montpellier (January 1304), see *H.L.F.*, pp. 308–9. A third *Ars Juris* (if indeed there are three) is dealt with on p. 335, n. 1, below. Alòs believes that Lull wrote four, the fourth being an *Ars de Jure* or *Ars Juris naturalis*, also written at Montpellier in 1304. (Not in *H.L.F.*; see Alòs, *Los catálogos*, etc., pp. 10, 65–6; Longpré, col. 1094.)

[2] *Lectura Artis quae Brevis practica Tabulae Generalis intitulata est* (*H.L.F.*, No. 36, pp. 188–90; *cf.* p. 247, above); *Liber ad probandum aliquos articulos fidei per syllogisticas rationes* (*H.L.F.*, No. 218, pp. 326–7; Alòs, *Los catálogos*, p. 52; Longpré, col. 1098); and *Logica nova* (*H.L.F.*, No. 56, pp. 242–3). The attribution of the last of these books to Genoa in May 1303 (Longpré, col. 1094) seems unlikely to be correct; one MS. says that it was written in Catalan at that date and translated into Latin at Montpellier in July 1304. For the *Logica brevis et nova* (mentioned in the Catalogue of 1311) and the probably spurious *Logica parva*, see *H.L.F.*, Nos. 57, 58, p. 243; Longpré, col. 1096; Rogent i Duràn, *Bibliografía*, etc., pp. 2, 47, 64 and index (*sub* Lull); and Alòs, *Los catálogos*, p. 73.

[3] *Disputatio Fidei et Intellectus*, Salz., iv. On the MSS., see Longpré, col. 1098.

a problem which he had treated on several occasions, as we have already shown. The present treatment is probably a development of the slightly drawn allegory in *Blanquerna*.[1] Understanding and Faith debate whether the articles of religion can be proved by reason, and the former tells the story (repeated by Lull elsewhere[2]) of a Christian who proved to a Saracen king the falsity of Mahomet's teaching but would not prove to him also the truth of Christianity because (he said) the faith cannot be demonstrated by "necessary reasons." "You have done me ill service," replies the King, "for before I was at least a Mohammedan, and now I am neither Mohammedan nor Christian."[3]

Faith objects to the moral of this story that if the truth of Christianity were demonstrable there would be no merit in belief. Understanding, after indulging in a not very apt similitude and some mild invective, replies with an equally unanswerable argument. "If the Trinity be not demonstrable," he says, "God will be the cause of damnation. For all unbelievers will be damned; and if the truth be not demonstrable and God grants them not faith to believe without understanding, they cannot be saved. But we know that Divine Goodness wills the salvation of all men; wherefore the truths of religion must be demonstrable."[4]

To this Faith replies that God does grant faith to infidels who have the will to believe or understand, and returns story for story by relating the anecdote told of Alain de Lille,[5] who found a child with a glass in its hand trying to measure the volume of water in a great river. As much chance of success had the child—so runs the argument—as have men who try to prove the doctrine of the Holy Trinity.[6]

Understanding answers that they can be successful if aided by Divine grace. "I have no wish to destroy you," he continues, patronizingly. "You will be useful

[1] Chaps. 43–4 (*Bl.*, pp. 161–6). [2] See pp. 317, n. 4, 338–9, below.
[3] Salz., iv, p. 2; *cf.* also p. 4 (§ 5). The story is here told very briefly.
[4] Salz., iv, p. 4.
[5] Here he is described simply as "quidam magnus clericus Christianus."
[6] Salz., iv, pp. 4–5.

to men without great intelligence. But those who *can* understand, *should* understand. There seems little will to believe left in the world to-day. We must prove our religion to be true if we would have it accepted."

"I am hard, it is true," returns Faith, who is no great debater. "I am hard, but I have more merit."

"But what is the use of that," is the retort, "if there are none who win it?"[1]

The argument grows warm, and at last Understanding induces Faith to discuss with him, "per syllogismos Raymundi," four representative articles, dealing respectively with the Trinity, the Incarnation, the Creation of the world, and the Resurrection of the dead. The debate is a long one, and at last Faith grows weary. "That proves that I am right," cries Understanding, much in the manner of the argumentative bully at school.[2] Faith walks away in disgust, whereupon Understanding follows her with soft words, until they reach the inevitable hermit, who of course represents Ramon's point of view, and seals Understanding's arguments with his mild and general approval, saying that a book shall be prepared containing a report of the discussion and presented to the Pope, the Cardinals, and various of the Universities.[3]

Throughout their debate, the disputants are so anxious to score points off each other that their arguments lose much in attractiveness. The truest thing said by either of the two is probably Understanding's observation that unbelievers can come to faith through understanding and to understanding through faith. But the book as a whole might easily have been made much better.

The chief interest of another work of this period, the *Book of the Ascent and Descent of the Intellect*,[4] is rather in the curiousness of its plan, and the way in which this is worked out, making the book a sort of encyclopaedia upon all branches of knowledge. An old edition has the

[1] Salz., iv, pp. 4–5. [2] *Ibid.* p. 25.

[3] Notably Paris, Montpellier, Toulouse and Naples. Salz., iv, p. 26.

[4] *Liber de ascensu et descensu intellectus* (*H.L.F.*, No. 62, p. 245; *cf.* Rogent i Duràn, *Bibliografía*, etc., pp. 46–8; Longpré, col. 1094), finished at Montpellier in March 1305.

quaintest of illustrations, representing the ladder, so often mentioned by the Fathers, whereby the spirit of man may ascend, through a knowledge of created things, to a knowledge of God. The eight steps in the engraving, labelled in turn " stone, flame, plant, beast, man, heaven, angel, God,"[1] lead to the closed door of a house among the clouds bearing the words " Sapientia edificavit sibi domum." To the right are the other degrees, inscribed in two concentric circles—round the outer of these, the twelve degrees " whereby the understanding passes to understand things and the secrets of each thing,"[2] and, round the inner, the five ways in which the understanding may work.[3] The engraving and the preface together describe the method of this " book or art." By the seven steps in turn, the understanding mounts or " ascends " to the eighth, but, while on each step, it " descends " to consider the properties of each, according to the twelve degrees of the outer circle and the five manners of the inner. Some of the questions considered show Lull's ever-inquiring interest in natural science : they are still represented in enquirers' books—the so-called " children's " encyclopaedias—of to-day :

> When a stone is warmed, where does its coldness go ?
> When a candle is put out, where does the flame go ?
> Why can a male engender a female ?
> Why does the magnet attract iron ?
> What advantage has a tree from its leaves ?
> Why does rue strengthen the eyes, and the onion weaken them ?

Not dissimilar are the questions on mankind, the angelic beings, and the heavens. Of these sufficient examples have been given in earlier chapters.

In December 1304 Ramon published in Montpellier a treatise of more weight than importance—a new *Ars Magna*, applied to the art of preaching and called the *Ars Magna Praedicationis*.[4] The first part of this book

[1] Lapis, Flamma, Planta, Brutum, Homo, Coelum, Angelus, Deus.

[2] Actus, Passio, Actio, Natura, Substantia, Accidens, Simplex, Compositum, Individuum, Species, Genus, Ens.

[3] Sensibile, imaginabile, dubitabile, credibile, intelligibile.

[4] *H.L.F.*, No. 246, p. 338.

only is concerned with the application of the *Art*, the second part consisting of one hundred sermons for Sundays and festivals of the Saints, designed to serve as illustrations of its author's principles.[1] One service done by this work to Lullian scholarship is the long way which it goes towards disproving the authenticity of a "Book of the Conception of the Blessed Virgin Mary, free from original sin."[2] Attributed to Ramon by a number of writers, it has been claimed for him chiefly by uncritical partisans. The construction of the book, in which two Roman priests argue with a Jacobite on Our Lady's Conception, is not unlike that of a Lullian work, and each of the disputants is as "fidelis, verax, caritativus et pacificus" as any character in Lull's writings. The book is dated, however, from Avignon in December 1304, and though that city is near enough to Montpellier to make possible its publication there in the same month as the work known to be genuine,[3] the unlikeliness that Lull would be in Avignon on December 7 and following days (as the book states that he was) and both before and after that date be in Montpellier is by no means a negligible argument.[4]

It may possibly have been the interest aroused by the new "Ars Magna" in Montpellier that led Lull to re-popularize his original *Art* in the city by publishing an *Introductorium magnae Artis Generalis*, which he

[1] Pasqual (ii, pp. 105–6) gives some brief extracts from the sermons, none of which, however, is particularly notable, except Sermon 92, which praises the Franciscans. *Cf.* Rubió y Balaguer ("Los códices lulianos, etc.," p. 329) who corrects the erroneous statement of *H.L.F.* that there are only 58 sermons.

[2] *Liber de conceptu virginali.* Pasqual (ii, pp. 106–10, and *Vindiciae*, i, pp. 431–4) upholds Lull's authorship of this book vehemently. He is followed by Bové, Mn. Avinyó and others. *H.L.F.* (No. 80, p. 257) briefly rejects it. P. Longpré (cols. 1110–11) gives a concise and useful bibliography on the question of its authenticity. Rogent i Duràn (*Bibliografía*, etc., pp. 14–15) discuss other possible authors.

[3] This is the assumption of Pasqual (ii, pp. 106–7) who urges it (ii, pp. 107–110) with great vehemence.

[4] A stronger and perhaps conclusive one is the reference in the prologue to a decree by the King of Aragon, given at Valencia "on the 14th of March of this same year," maintaining the dogma of the Immaculate Conception. This seems to refer to the similar decree of John I of Aragon, given at Valencia on March 14, 1394 (5), and if this is so the book is one of the late imitations of Lull which abounded for long after his death.

completed on March 8, 1305.[1] A much more important work, however, brought out there in the month of April, was the *Liber de Fine*,[2] a book of no great length, but strongly personal, and thus of considerable interest, although it repeats a good deal that is found in Lull's earlier writings.

The prologue, after lamenting the state of the world, and the preponderance in it of unbelievers over Christians, describes the author's renunciation of his possessions, and the efforts which he has made to excite princes, cardinals and popes to missionary zeal. He has made many books to expose the errors of unbelievers: this book shall be the last of all, hence its title. "I can do no more than I have already done," is his cry. "I find none who will lend me in any way effective help. So I set down my arguments in final form and order, once and for all,[3] that on the Day of Judgment I may stand guiltless and unafraid in this respect before the company of Heaven—nay, before God Himself."[4]

There are signs in the arrangement of the book of the care with which it has been planned. The first section, which deals with Ramon's ideas on disputations with unbelievers, is divided into five parts, relating respectively to Saracens, Jews, schismatics, Tartars and pagans. On the institution of four monasteries for missionary training, "in locis competentibus et amenis,"[5] he becomes

[1] Or 1306? (N.S.): see p. 323, n. 1, below, and *H.L.F.*, No. 131 (p. 293). At about the same time he completed the *Liber de ascensu et descensu intellectus*, referred to above (pp. 313–4) more naturally, and the *Liber de demonstratione per aequiparantiam* (*H.L.F.*, No. 30, pp. 170–2; Longpré, col. 1099).

[2] *Libellus de Fine, in quo traditur modus et doctrina, quo possunt omnes infideles ad Fidei Catholicae veritatem breviter reduci, et Terra Sancta e manibus infidelium recuperari.* The quotations and references which follow are taken from the edition published at Palma in 1665. See on this book: *H.L.F.*, No. 242, p. 337; Pasqual, ii, p. 112, and *Vindiciae*, i, p. 248; A. Gottron, *Ramon Lulls Kreuzzugsideen*, Berlin, 1912; Riber, *Vida i actes*, etc., pp. 194–207.

[3] *De Fine*, pp. 3–4: Et quia feci multos libros contra homines infideles, et ad exaltationem humani intellectus, ut ad omnes scientias sit artificialiter generalis, libellus iste finis omnium erit dictus, cum quo excuso me Deo . . . quoniam in isto opere facere plus non possum, ex eo quia quasi solus sum in tractando, et neminem quodammodo invenio, qui me juvet; sed propono finaliter Domino Papae, et aliis quibusdam Principibus, seu Rectoribus fidei Christianae mittere librum istum.

[4] *Ibid.*, p. 5.

[5] *Ibid.*, p. 8.

eloquent. Brushing aside as unimportant the question of their comparatively trivial cost, he addresses himself to the Holy Father and the Cardinals of the Church, showing how blessed and how greatly rewarded they will be if they take up the matter seriously. Let them set about it now : more than a thousand years have produced no better plan, and soon the night when no man can work will be upon them.[1]

There follow references to his own books[2] and travels,[3] some of which are cited elsewhere, and descriptions of the beliefs of various religious bodies with which we are already familiar.[4] Then a burst of eloquence closes the first section of the book :

> Ah, Holy Catholic Church ! Thou seest how many are thy enemies, and how many more thou wilt have, if thou remain in idleness and set not about these things whereof we have treated.[5]

The reference here is primarily to the perils of a Tartar (or Tartar-Moslem) invasion,[6] which leads the author naturally to his second section, on armed crusades. The " two swords " of the Betrayal in Gethsemane are interpreted as figuring " that ye must do battle both with preaching and with arms against men that are unbelievers." [7] To this interpretation Lull has in effect been long committed. In the second section, divided into seven parts, he treats of military projects, rather more fully than in his earlier writings. The greatest stress is laid upon a theme which since the fall of Acre had come more and more into prominence—the unification of the military orders [8] under a leader of whom little is said here

[1] *De Fine*, p. 12 : Ha Papa Domine, qualiter eritis benedictus ! et o Domini Cardinales, qualiter eritis remunerati ! Et ille maxime Dominus Cardinalis, qui istud officium pertractabit ! Incipite, pro Deo, incipite : nam mors venit, et mille anni sunt jam praeteriti, in quibus melius negotium inceptum non fuit. . . .

[2] In which occurs the phrase : " In pluribus libris meis, in lingua Arabica et Latina " (p. 17). See p. 193, n. 3, above.

[3] See pp. 147–8, above.

[4] Including the story, told once again (see pp. 312, 338–9), of the Saracen king (" qui Murmiamoli vocabatur ") and the religious who left him suspended between Islam and Christianity (pp. 52–4).

[5] *De Fine*, p. 57. [6] See pp. 248–50, above. [7] *De Fine*, p. 13.

[8] *Ibid.*, pp. 61–2 : " Faciat de ordine Templi et militiae Hospitalis et Alamanorum et de Heucles, et etiam Calatrava . . . unum ordinem."

save that he is to be a king's son,[1] and is referred to as Bellator Rex. Various plans are outlined for the campaigns against the heathen which he might pursue. One possible campaign is to Syria, by way of Turkey and "Armenia"[2]: this is long and difficult. Nor are other Eastern schemes more practicable: one is costly,[3] another unhealthy,[4] a third—the Tunisian expedition—was tried without success by St. Louis.[5] A more clearly practicable campaign would be in Southern Spain, whence Bellator should proceed to Ceuta, thence to the more thickly populated region of Tunis and ultimately to the Holy Land.[6]

Amid all this matter-of-fact planning, the note of rhetoric is not lost. There is a touching description of the sad state of Jerusalem, made more vivid by contrast with the splendour of papal Rome. Oftentimes has Ramon himself seen the Holy Father—"ornatum, illuminatum," surrounded by his Cardinals,—saying Mass in St. Peter's and praising Christ our Lord. But there is "another altar" which he has also seen: one of its two lamps is broken, and its city is made desolate, though it is excellent above all cities else. Alas, that we are Christians and that this should yet be so![7]

Then, turning from the depressing past and the

[1] See p. 264, above. [2] See p. 306, above.

[3] *De Fine*, p. 80. This is the journey, which some suppose Ramon to have made, "ad quandam insulam, quae Raised appellatur, quae est prope Alexandria situata."

[4] *Ibid.*, p. 80. This is an expedition by sea, "versus Cyprum in Armeniam. . . . Istae terrae omnibus non sunt sanae, pro ut scio, quia fui, et etiam via longa." This very clear reference makes the deductions drawn up on p. 306 above fairly safe.

[5] *Ibid.*, p. 81; *cf.* p. 54.

[6] *Ibid.*, p. 82. "Hispania, videlicet Andaluzia, ubi est Almaria, Malica et Granata; hic est locus amaenissimus et laudabilis plus quam alter." On one side is the sea; on the other, Christian Spain.

[7] *Ibid.*, pp. 69–70. Sed aliud altare est, quod est exemplar et Dominus omnium aliorum, et quando vidi, in ipso duae Lampades solae erant, una tamen fracta est, Civitas depopulata est, eo, quia quasi 50 homines non morantur, sed hic multi serpentes in cavernis commorantur; et illa Civitas est excellentissima super omnes alias Civitates: et hoc intelligo quo ad Deum; sed quoad nos quid est? Et dedecus quale est, in quo est, a quo venit, et quantum est videatis. Et non ne sumus christiani, aut quid sumus?

uncertain present to the glorious future, Ramon breaks forth into eulogy and prayer :

> Ah, devout and faithful King, whosoever thou art, what honour will be thine in Heaven and upon the earth, when thou shalt present thy son for the accomplishment of this task, so good, so great and so worthy. How great will be thy joy when thou seest this thy son raised to this lofty dignity and highly exalted with honour ! . . . Ah, Jesus Christ our Lord God, descend Thou among us, complete and perfect this work and bring it to the holy end which Thou desirest.[1]

The third section of the book, which is the least important, describes the *Ars Magna*, its divisions and its developments.[2] Unfortunately, from the modern reader's standpoint,—though probably not from its author's—it conveys the impression of bathos, but its last lines, written in the spirit of the *Desconort*, cannot fail to recapture one's sympathies :

> Langueo, et vivo in tristitia, et dolore, et vado per mundum universum ; et qui me impedit audiat, si mentales aures habeat, quantum contra bonum publicum hic consistit.[3]

Is there only disconsolateness in those lines ? Surely there is desire and defiance. Seventy-three years of age, weary and oft-defeated Ramon might be, but while life was left in him he would fight for all that he held dearest, and the book which he described as marking the end marks in reality a fresh beginning. Ten years had passed since Boniface had sent him away from Rome empty ; he must try his fortune once again with one of Boniface's more sympathetic successors.

[1] *De Fine*, pp. 70–1.
[2] "De Arte Generali et de 20 Artibus specialibus."
[3] *De Fine*, p. 123.

CHAPTER XV

1305–1309

Clement V succeeds to the Papacy: Lull has an interview with him at Lyons. Lull again in Paris: his meeting with Duns Scotus. Second African mission: success and failure at Bugia. His debates in captivity: Ramon and Hamar. Departure from Bugia. Shipwreck off Pisa. Lull in Pisa, Genoa and Montpellier. Visit to the Pope at Avignon.

THE writing of the *Liber de Fine* meant that Ramon Lull had once more seen an opportunity of pressing his desires upon the Pope with some confidence that they would receive fulfilment. So long as Boniface wore the tiara he might eschew the Papal Court with a clear conscience. But Benedict XI, who succeeded in 1303 to the See of Peter, took an early occasion of easing the strained relations which had existed between the Papacy and the French King, and when, after a brief reign, he was followed by Clement V[1] (a Frenchman, Archbishop of Bordeaux, and a friend of King Philip from his youth) Lull may well have thought that his star was in the ascendant.

Clement was elected on June 5, 1305, and at the end of August travelled from Bordeaux to Montpellier by easy stages. Lull probably saw the new Pope at Montpellier, where Clement stayed four days, being met there by the Kings of Aragon and Mallorca[2] and holding some kind of conference with them.[3] That the former King as well as the latter was favourably inclined to Ramon's

[1] Pasqual (ii, pp. 112–3) wrongly makes Clement succeed Boniface.

[2] Devic et Vaissette, ix, p. 285.

[3] From October 7 to 11, 1305. *Cf.* Zurita, Bk. v, Chap. 68; Devic et Vaissette, ix, p. 285: *Disputatio Raymundi Christiani et Hamar Saraceni* (Salz., iv, p. 47) implies that Ramon was present at the conference, the exact date given for which varies.

wishes at the time we infer from the fact that, on Midsummer Day 1305, he had granted him as a recompense for his services a pension for life [1]; at a rather later date, too, it is said, he endeavoured, though unsuccessfully, to obtain for him a canonry.[2] What more probable than that he had secured an audience for him with the Holy Father, or at the very least had promised to intercede personally on his behalf? This is the more likely because Ramon himself records that, at that interview of the Kings with the Pope, the conversation turned on the possibilities of a new crusade, for which King James of Aragon offered " his person, his throne and his treasure," afterwards presenting Clement with a copy of the *Liber de Fine*. " And of this I am certain," adds Lull, " for I was there."[3]

This does not, of course, necessarily mean that he was at the actual conference, but may merely indicate his presence at the time in Montpellier. Apart from a brief visit to Barcelona in the preceding August,[4] he seems to have remained there between his return from Genoa and this time; and when Clement, refusing to go to Rome as his Cardinals desired for his coronation, left by way of Nimes for Lyons, where he elected to be crowned instead, Ramon followed him, and in all

[1] See Rubió y Lluch, *Documents*, etc., xxxi (i, p. 39). The terms of the concession are generous enough to indicate real cordiality: " Damus et concedimus vobis de gratia speciali, duos solidos barchinonenses habendos et percipiendos diebus singulis toto tempore vitae vestrae quibus fueritis in partibus dominationis nostrae, supra proventibus et exitibus nostris vicariae civitatis Barchinonae, donec nos ipsos duos solidos barchinonenses die qualibet recipiendos in abtiori et magis idoneo loco, vobis duxerimus assignandos. Concedimus etiam vobis quod quandiu vos sequutus fueritis curiam nostram, habeatis et percipiatis, qualibet die qua in curia nostra fueritis super eisdem proventibus et exitibus dictae vicariae, portionem ipsam duplicatam, scilicet quattuor solidos barchinonenses computatis in eis dictis duobus solidis ad vitam vobis ut predicitur assignatis."

[2] Finke: *Acta Arag.*, i, p. 880. The document cited bears the date of May 22, 1309. Lull's not being in holy orders was, of course, no disqualification for a canonry, but I am not at all convinced on other grounds that our Ramon Lull is here referred to.

[3] *Disputatio Raymundi Christiani et Hamar Saraceni.* Salz., vol. iv; cf. *H.L.F.*, p. 155.

[4] Of this there is no other testimony than that the *Liber de erroribus judaeorum* (*H.L.F.*, No. 256, p. 334) was published by Lull in Barcelona in August 1305.

probability witnessed the coronation. This took place in the church of St. Just on November 14: it was a brilliant spectacle, attended, as was natural, by Philip the Fair and a great company of the French nobility, and also by the two James II's, of Aragon and of Mallorca.

Soon after his arrival at Lyons, Lull had audience of the Pope and put before him his case for the establishment of monastery-colleges, as well as his more recently conceived military projects, with all the eloquence of one who feels success, long deferred, to be within his reach at last.[1] But once again he failed to arouse the Pope's enthusiasm,[2] and once again there was reason for his failure. The King of France was pressing Clement for the suppression of the Templars, and even more strongly for a formal condemnation of the acts of his late enemy Boniface VIII, which it was naturally the Pope's desire to avoid granting. While the King was demanding that the name of Clement's great predecessor should be erased from the Papal records, his body disinterred, his bones burned and their ashes flung to the winds, it would be hard enough for the Pope to give his attention to projects for the teaching of Oriental languages, to say nothing of taking practical steps to carry them into effect.

In all probability Ramon Lull underestimated or was ignorant of the difficulties which beset the way of the newly crowned Pope when he presented himself before him. If so, the shock of unexpected failure would have been the greater. Intense depression was followed by a not unnatural exaltation of spirit, under the influence of which Ramon shook off the dust of Lyons from his feet and, in about January 1306, probably returned for a brief space to Mallorca.[3]

[1] *V.B.R.L.*, v (*Life*, p. 76) specifies the place. *V.C.* vi (*Life*, p. 33) reads only: "En temps de papa Climent quint partí s lo reverent mestre de la ciutat de París e venc s en al sant Pare," etc. Neither *V.B.R.L.* nor *V.C.* specifies any of the projects which Lull put forward except that of the colleges: from the *Liber de Fine*, however, we may be sure that he urged the others also.

[2] "De la qual cosa axí lo sant Pare com los cardinals hagueren poca cura ne ansia" (*V.C.*, vi; *V.B.R.L.* agrees: *Life*, pp. 33, 76).

[3] Pasqual ignores this Mallorcan visit (ii, p. 116) and supposes that Lull went from Lyons to Montpellier, but he is led astray by believing the *Ars Brevis* (p. 335 below) to have been written there and not at Pisa. Mn. Galmés (p. 72)

Before June of the same year he was in Paris,[1] where each time that he visited the great University he was more and more sought after and revered.[2] But, since he had last been there, a new and resplendent star had appeared in the academic firmament : Duns Scotus, a young Franciscan, whom rumour credited, as it had credited Ramon, with supernatural illumination, and who, at the command of the General of his Order, had left throngs of pupils at Oxford to go and teach his new philosophy at the Sorbonne.

Of his first meeting with Ramon, the story is told that the white-bearded apostle was sitting at the feet of the young teacher, giving clear signs, perhaps absent-mindedly, of his agreement or disagreement with different points of the lecture. Duns Scotus, thinking to rebuke what he took to be the ignorant presumption of an old man whom he had not seen in his audience before, turned upon him with a question ridiculously elementary :

" Dominus, quae pars ? "[3]

To which Ramon, in no way surprised into silence, calmly answered :

" Dominus non est pars, sed totum."[4]

sends Lull to Paris from Lyons, thence to Pisa, and, in 1307, to Mallorca. This assumes omission as well as error at this point in *V.C.*, which is undoubtedly wrong in putting the Paris visit before that to Lyons, and, after the account of Lull's failure with Clement, says merely : " Per la qual cosa lo dit reverent mestre elevat tot en esperit venc en Mallorque." (*Life*, p. 33 ; *V.B.R.L.*, pp. 76–7, agrees.) I know of no clear evidence which proves Lull to have been in Mallorca in 1306 as well as in 1307, and Mn. Galmés may well be right. At the same time, *V.C.*, though undoubtedly faulty once, as shown above, connects the return to Mallorca so definitely with the failure that I am inclined to assume two sojourns in Mallorca instead of one.

[1] So that he may have written the *Introductorium magnae Artis generalis* (see p. 316, n. 1, above), as Salzinger asserts that he did, in Montpellier, and completed it there on March 8, 1306 (*cf.* Pasqual ii, p. 116), though the year 1305 is likelier. *H.L.F.* (p. 293) curiously remarks that no MS. of this work is extant, and believes it to be a fragment of another ; actually it was printed in 1515, 1635 and 1637, as well as being translated into Castilian and French. (Rogent i Duràn, *Bibliografía*, etc., pp. 53, 177–9.)

[2] *V.C.*, v (*Life*, p. 32) and *V.B.R.L.*, v (*Life*, p. 76) are both reticent about his doings at Paris, limiting them to the " reading " of the *Art* (*V.B.R.L.* adds " efficaciter ") and the compilation of " divers books."

[3] " What part (*i.e.* of speech) is *Dominus* (Lord) ? "

[4] " The Lord is no part, but the whole."

And his eulogists have it that, as he spoke, he stood up in the hall and silenced both lecturer and audience with a magnificent improvisation upon the perfection of the Divine Nature. It is even said that, under the same inspiration, Ramon wrote a book entitled *Dominus quae pars? sive Disputatio Raymundi cum Scoto*. He was certainly as capable of writing the book as of delivering the panegyric, but nothing other than the alleged title is known of it.[1]

Several short works he did write at Paris, by one of which his stay is approximately dated.[2] Another,[3] almost certainly written at this time,[4] is a "petition" addressed to the "professors and bachelors of the University of Paris," asking them—"quanto humilius et ardentius potest"—either to draw up a summary of the arguments most fitted to convert the heathen, or to approve and ratify those which he himself proceeds to enumerate,—namely, twenty syllogistic arguments on the Trinity, and twenty on the Incarnation.

In the beginning of this opuscule, Ramon describes himself as a man who has mastered Arabic, and is returning to preach to the infidels among whom he has already laboured. This suggests that it was composed very shortly before he left the Sorbonne,[5] for at the beginning of 1307 he went from Paris, by way of Montpellier,[6] to Mallorca, and thence upon a new African

[1] *Cf.* Riber: *Vida i actes*, p. 210.

[2] The *Liber facilis scientiae* (*H.L.F.*, No. 31, pp. 172–3) is dated, in many, but not in all copies, June 1306 (see p. 345, n. 1, below), and the *Quaestiones supra Librum facilis scientiae* (*H.L.F.*, No. 32, pp. 173–4) were written in the same year.

[3] *Supplicatio Raymundi professoribus ac baccalaureis Studii Parisiensis*. Salz., vol. iv; cf. *H.L.F.*, No. 28, pp. 166–8; Golubovich, p. 386.

[4] In several copies it is dated 1310, but is quoted in the *De Convenientia Fidei et Intellectus in Objecto* (1308: see p. 338 below) which makes 1306 the most likely date.

[5] The suggestion is confirmed by an almost precisely similar reference to himself in the *Disputatio Raymundi Christiani et Hamar Saraceni*, which, as will be seen, was written immediately after the experiences now to be related.

[6] Pasqual (ii, pp. 120–1) quite needlessly sends him to Pisa and then back to Mallorca, but this (see p. 334 below) is almost certainly inaccurate. If the letter of Ramon to James II of Aragon is correctly dated February 7, 1307 (see p. 309 above) this would no doubt be the approximate date of his passing through Montpellier on his way to Mallorca.

campaign, landing at Bugia, a town some hundred miles east of Algiers.

It would hardly appear to have been a suitable time for the descent of a proselytiser upon the town. The devastating eight-years' siege of Tlemcen—the longest and perhaps the most remarkable that ever took place in North Africa—was just dragging to a weary close. Algiers chose the same year to declare its independence, and fruitless attempts were made to subdue it. Some eighteen months before Ramon's arrival, there had been war between the kingdoms of Bugia and Tunis, and Bugian troops had taken and sacked Constantine. Nor was the disturbed condition of these states the worst omen for Ramon's missionary enterprise. For more than a year a religious reformer called Saâda had been attacking Mohammedan orthodoxy in the city of Bugia and the surrounding country, and contemporary accounts point to the extreme inflammability, at the time, of the popular temper.[1]

How much of all this Ramon knew it is impossible to say : he was certainly in the habit of selecting unpropitious moments for his entrances on the stage of publicity. Nor did he begin his mission as tactfully as at Tunis. "When he was in the midst of the market-place,"[2] says the contemporary biography,[3] "forgetful of the peril of death, he began to cry in a loud voice : 'The law of the Christians is holy and true, and the sect of the Moors is false and wrong, and this am I prepared to prove.'" Again and again he repeated this daring challenge, until a furious mob, already exasperated by one religious agitator, had gathered around him tumultuously, intent upon his death.[4]

They seem, however, to have been prudent enough to ask the authorization of the Kadi, or chief judge of the city—the contemporary chronicler calls him

[1] Mercier, ii, p. 248. [2] *Lit. plaça*, or principal square.

[3] *V.C.*, vi. So also *V.B.R.L.*, vi (*Life*, pp. 33–4, 77).

[4] *V.C.* has "una gran multitut de moros qui ab gran avalot lo volgueren matar"; *V.B.R.L.* is more definite: "irruerunt multi nefandis manibus super eum, volentes ipsum penitus lapidare." (*Life*, pp. 34, 77.)

" bishop "[1] who, desirous of seeing the venerable orator for himself, sent his officers[2] to bring Lull before him. What happened may be related in the words of the contemporary Catalan biography :

When [Ramon] was led into his presence, the Bishop began to speak with him, saying : " How is this that thou hast committed folly so great, attempting to impugn the law of Mahomet, when it is certain that every one that impugns it shall die a cruel death ? " Then answered the said reverend master : " The true servant of God must fear no peril of death in showing forth the truth to infidels who are in error and bringing them into the way of salvation."

To which the Bishop made answer : " Thou speakest truth. But which is that law that is erroneous and false ? Is it of the Christians or of the Moors ? I would fain hear thy arguments, if thou hast any, whereby thou dost prove thy law. Tell them to me, for I will hear[3] them willingly."

Then the said reverend master made reply : " It pleases me. Give me a place that is convenient, wherein are thine own learned men, and I will prove to thee, by necessary reasons, that the law of the Christians is holy and true."[4]

A place and a time were duly appointed, and the debate was held. Only part of it has been recorded, but this is of as great interest as the report of the Tunisian sermon, and may also be quoted *verbatim*.

" I ask thee,"[5] enquired the said reverend master of the Bishop : " Is our Lord God Sovereign Goodness ? "[6] The Bishop made answer that it was so. Then the said reverend master, desiring to prove the Holy Trinity, argued thus : " All sovereign

[1] *Lo bisbe*. *V.B.R.L.* : " Antistes sive Episcopus civitatis " ; *cf.* below, " erat enim Episcopus famosus in philosophia " (*Life*, pp. 77–8). This suggests that the Mufti is meant, which word is accordingly used by Pasqual and others. But the narrative as a whole indicates rather that a civil officer is in question, hence other biographers render the word as Kadi.

[2] *V.C.*, " saigs " ; *V.B.R.L.*, " nuncios."

[3] Or " solve " (*i.e.* answer effectively) according as we read *l'ascoltaré* or *la soltaré* (*Life*, p. 35, n.).

[4] *V.C.*, vi (*Life*, pp. 34–5). *V.B.R.L.* (pp. 77–8) follows closely, except that it makes the debate take place there and then. *V.C.* is probably correct here.

[5] *V.B.R.L.* prefixes the words : " Conveniamus ambo in aliquo communi, deinde rationem necessariam tibi dabo " (*Life*, p. 78).

[6] *V.B.R.L.* : " Estne Deus perfecte bonus ? " (*Life*, p. 78).

goodness is perfect in itself, so that it has within itself all good, and has no necessity to work any good thing apart from itself whatsoever. Therefore, since our Lord God is Sovereign Goodness eternally and without beginning, it follows that our Lord God has no necessity to work any good apart from Himself; for, were it otherwise, there would be in Him neither sovereign goodness nor perfection.

"And, since thou deniest in God eternal generation—namely, in the Person of the Son—it follows from this that before the creation of the world our Lord God had less of goodness than after He created it; for perfection is to produce good of itself, and it would be a great error that our Lord should grow more in perfection at one time than at another. I believe, on the other hand, that the goodness of our Lord is eternally diffusive of good, and this pertains to Sovereign Good, that God the Father, eternally, of His own goodness, should engender God the Son, and that of both these should be produced the Holy Spirit." [1]

At this reasoning, we learn from the chronicler, the Kadi "marvelled," and "answered never a word, but commanded that he should be thrown forthwith into prison." At this summary judgment the fury of the waiting mob broke out, and they demanded leave to stone him. This, however, the Kadi forbade, saying that in due time a trial in proper form would take place, "for," explains the chronicler, "he desired that he should be condemned to death by trial and judgment." [2]

So the mob could only show its wrath with Ramon by insulting him as he was led away to prison. Some belaboured him with sticks, others hurled stones at him, others struck him with their fists, and those who could

[1] *V.C.*, vi (*Life*, pp. 35–6). *V.B.R.L.* gives the latter part of the argument ("And since . . . Holy Spirit") more clearly and (I think) more satisfactorily, thus.

Et quia tu negas Beatissimam Trinitatem, posito, quod non sit, Deus non fuit perfecte bonus ab aeterno, usque quo produxit bonum mundum in tempore: tu autem credis creationem mundi, et ideo Deus fuit magis perfectus in bonitate, quando creavit mundum in tempore, quam ante; cum bonitas sit magis bona diffundendo se, quam existendo otiosa; hoc autem habeo pro te: pro me vero habeo, quod bonitas ab aeterno in aeternum sit diffusiva; et hoc est de ratione boni, quod sui ipsius sit diffusivum: quoniam Deus Pater bonus de sua bonitate generat bonum Filium, et ab utroque bonus Sanctus Spiritus est spiratus (*Life*, pp. 78–9).

[2] *V.C.*, *V.B.R.L.*, vi (*Life*, pp. 36, 79).

get near enough pulled at his long, white beard.[1] The Kadi's officers did their best to protect him but without much success, and it can only have been a relief to the venerable preacher when he found himself safely in the foul closet [2] of the prison which was to serve as a dungeon for him, and loaded with heavy chains.[3] It was but a literal counterpart of the mystical experience which he had described allegorically more than once :

> Imprisoned was the Lover in the prison of Love. Thoughts, desires and memories held and enchained him lest he should flee to his Beloved. Griefs tormented him ; patience and hope consoled him. And the Lover would have died, but the Beloved revealed to him His Presence, and the Lover revived.[4]

Meanwhile, the Kadi took counsel with the other authorities [5] as to Ramon's fate, and they resolved by a majority to put him on his trial, to kill him if he was found to be a man of learning and therefore dangerous, but, if he seemed to be a harmless fanatic, to let him go.[6] One of the Moors who was present at this council, however, had known something of Lull at Tunis.[7] " Beware ! " he said to them. " Make him not to come here before you all, for he will bring against our law such arguments as it will be impossible to answer." [8] The warning was heeded, and a new opinion now found favour, that the most politic action would be to transport him to another dungeon, more loathsome still, where he would

[1] *V.C.*, *V.B.R.L.*, vi (*Life*, pp. 36–7, 79). The latter version has the phrase " per barbam, quae sibi prolixa fuerat, acriter tractus."

[2] *V.C.* has " a la privada de la presó " (*cf.* Cast. " excusado," " retrete ") ; *V.B.R.L.*, " reclusus est apud latrinam carceris latronum," but also " postea vero positus est in quadam domicula ejusdem carceris " (*Life*, pp. 37, 79).

[3] *V.C.* alone (*Life*, p. 37) gives the following details of the imprisonment : " Per los saigs fonc deffensat, axí com los era estat manat per lo bisbe. . . . (A la privada de la presó lo meteren) ab una grossa cadena al coll."

[4] *L.A.A.* 168 (*Bl.*, p. 436).

[5] *V.C.* : " los satrapaços de la ley " ; *V.B.R.L.* : " clerici legis " (*Life*, pp. 37, 79).

[6] *V.C.*, *V.B.R.L.*, vi (*Life*, pp. 37, 79–80).

[7] *V.B.R.L.*, vi (*Life*, p. 80) alone suggests this ; *V.C.* (p. 37) being less definite : " Quidam eorum, qui transfretaverat Genua Tunicium cum Raymundo, quique audiverat sermones atque rationes suas frequenter."

[8] *V.C.*, vi (*Life*, p. 37). *V.B.R.L.* (p. 80) reads similarly.

probably die from his privations.[1] The thing was done ; but, before any ill effect could ensue, the Catalans and Genoese, who traded as freely in Bugia as in Tunis, petitioned that their fellow-Christian might have better treatment. They, no doubt, or some of them, were among the most influential of the Christian merchants, and their prayers prevailed.

In another and " more tolerable " prison[2] Ramon remained for about six months—approximately from May to November 1307. He seems to have been treated there with real kindness, and allowed, not only to receive visitors, but to debate with well-disposed Moors upon the very subjects for discussing which in public he was deprived of his liberty. " Each day," says the contemporary biography :

> Each day came the Moors, praying him to be converted to the law of Mahomet, and offering him infinite treasures, honours and women. But he, like one that was established on immovable rock—that is, in the fervent love of his Master Jesus—answered them saying : " And if ye yourselves will renounce this your false sect, and will believe in the Holy Name of Jesus, I promise you eternal life and treasures that will never fail you." [3]

The curious result of these debates which Lull carried on with his adversaries, while in captivity, the chief of them being a " learned Moor named Hamar," [4] was an agreement, proposed by Lull himself,[5] by which

[1] *V.C.*, but not *V.B.R.L.*, suggests the motive (*Life*, pp. 37–8, 80).

[2] *V.C.* : " un altre loc pus soportable " ; *V.B.R.L.* : " in locum decentiorem " (*Life*, pp. 38, 80).

[3] *V.C.*, vii (*Life*, p. 39). *V.B.R.L.* (p. 80) agrees.

[4] This quotation, and the substance of the paragraph (apart from the passages cited from *V.C.*), are taken from the *Disputatio Raymundi Christiani et Hamar Saraceni*. That this is genuinely autobiographical may be inferred from the opening words of the prologue : " Quidam homo Christianus Arabicus cujus nomen erat Raymundus . . . ivit ad quandam civitatem Saracenorum, cujus nomen erat Bugia, in qua ipse predicando et laudando sanctam Catholicam Fidem, in platea a Saracenis fuit captus, percussus et in carcere positus " (Salz., iv, p. 1).

[5] From a reference in *Disputatio* (Salz,. iv, p. 46), it would appear that such books (written, of course, by Moslems) were common in Bugia, " quorum unum vidit Christianus, dum erat in carcere."

either side was to compose a book proving his law to be true,[1] copies of each book to be sent to the chief authorities in Christendom and Islam. Hamar's only stipulation was that he should be allowed to begin, for—he naïvely added—his arguments would be found unanswerable. Lull readily consented and set about his part of the task with alacrity, thinking that here at last was a chance for him to get a full and adequate hearing.[2] He began his book in Arabic, sending the Kadi a summary of it when it was nearing completion, as a basis for his adversaries' portion.[3] But Satan—as the old Catalan biography phrases it—saw that this would never do, for " along that road all these souls would go to Paradise." The enemy of truth arranged, therefore, that the King of Bugia, who was at that time in Constantine, not far away, should come to hear of the matter and order that Ramon should be expelled immediately, and if he returned be put to death.[4]

So the volume planned was not at that time completed.[5] It appeared, nevertheless, in the following year in Latin—written, of course, by Ramon alone, to encourage Christians and Saracens to dispute " by reasons, and not by authorities," [6] and entitled the *Disputation of Ramon the Christian and Hamar the Saracen.* Though probably somewhat conventionalized by the circumstances of its composition, it is a work of quite unusual biographical interest, giving a further insight into

[1] *V.C.*, vii ; *V.B.R.L.*, vi (*Life*, pp. 39–40, 80–1).

[2] Or, as *V.C.* puts it (*Life*, p. 40), " havía confiança en nostre Senyor que en aquella forma ell los convertiría." (*V.B.R.L.* omits this.)

[3] The *Disputatio* (Salz., iv, p. 46) suggests that the Mufti is meant rather than the Kadi : " Raymundus Christianus posuit in Arabico praedictas rationes et facto libro misit ipsum ad Episcopum Bugiae." *Cf.* p. 326, n. 1, above.

[4] *V.B.R.L.* agrees with *V.C.*, but leaves Satan out of the narrative (*Life*, pp. 40, 81).

[5] *V.C.* makes this quite clear, though *V.B.R.L.* is silent on the subject : " En aquesta forma lo dit reverent mestre no pogué acabar la dita obra la qual ab gran alegría havía ja be enantada" (*Life*, p. 40).

[6] *Disputatio*, p. 46, " De ordinatione vel De fine libri." His account of the composition of the book is : " Et ille (Raymundus) existens Pisis recordatus fuit praedictarum rationum, quas habuit cum supradicto Saraceno, et ex illis composuit hunc librum in latino, et misit ipsum Domino Papae et Reverendis Cardinalibus."

Ramon's methods as well as into some of his ideas upon missions.

The Saracen, who is allowed to begin the argument, as in the actual debate, takes his first stand upon the common ground between himself and his adversary—namely, the existence of seven " essential conditions " of the Godhead.[1] From this position he proceeds to argue that neither the existence of a Trinity nor the possibility of a Divine Incarnation is compatible with the idea of God.[2] The " accidents " of generation, human existence and death cannot be postulated of God. Were an incarnation of the Godhead necessary to the eternal purpose, the Almighty would have taken, not man's imperfect nature, but the nature of the angels. Much argument on these lines follows, and Hamar endeavours to reinforce his conclusions by promising Ramon many beautiful and noble maidens, if he will but change his faith, to say nothing of a great house, and riches, honour and peace.[3]

Ramon, in answer, throws scorn upon these material ideals. Eternal glories have nothing to do with earthly things. Riches and honour upon earth last only for a few years : the rewards of the Christian faith relate to the everlasting world to come. " But I promise thee," he adds, " that if thou dost leave thy false and diabolical religion, and acceptest mine, thou shalt have the reward of life eternal ; for my religion has its root and increase, not in force and warfare, like thine, but in preaching and in the shedding of the blood of the blessed martyrs." [4]

These words introduce Ramon's arguments, which are divided into two parts. In the first part he proves the Trinity and the Incarnation, by adopting the same seven " conditions " which Hamar has laid down, but also terming eleven Divine " qualities," enumerated by Hamar, co-essential dignities of the Godhead.[5] Having completed his most important proofs, he next adduces forty *signa* in defence of the Catholic position : the ten commandments, seven sacraments, seven virtues, seven deadly sins and nine ordinances of Holy Church.[6] With

[1] Salz., iv, p. 2. [2] *Ibid.* [3] *Ibid.*, p. 12.
[4] *Ibid.* [5] *Ibid.*, pp. 12–34. [6] *Ibid.*, pp. 34–46.

these the controversial part of the book ceases ; when the Saracen has heard Ramon's arguments he remains pensive for a time, then sighs, and finally goes away without desiring to continue the discussion.

Upon either side there are some telling arguments. Ramon's strongest points are a most potent comparison between the Allah of Islam and the Holy Trinity of the Catholic faith, and contrasts between the practices of the rival faiths and the lives of their founders. It is interesting to observe that he definitely sets the Jewish faith above that of Islam, describing the former as "good" and the latter as "false and erroneous"[1] : elsewhere he has sometimes been less severe with the Moslem than with the Jew.

For the benefit of Pope and Cardinals, to whom copies of this book are to be sent, Ramon gives some further views upon the religious problems of the East.[2] After making the complaint, not for the first time, that Christians do not offer converted Moors, as they should do, amenities such as those which Hamar offered him, he goes on to counsel more worldly wisdom in dealing both with Saracens and with Tartars. From them "the whole of Christendom is in the greatest danger." It is only seventy years, he says, since the Tartars "came out of the mountains," yet their three emperors have lands "of more than twice the extent of those of Christian and Saracen rulers together." There is the Great Khan,[3] who has "the land of Prester John" in the east ; Cotay, surrounded by proselytizing Saracens ; and Carbenda, lord of Persia as far as India, who became converted to Islam, with all his soldiery, in the time of his brother Casan. These empires offer unrivalled opportunities to Christian missionaries, of which so far only Nestorians and Jacobites, "who hate the Latins," have taken advantage. He therefore proposes to the Pope three things : first, the establishment and endowment in

[1] Salz., iv, p. 34. Contrast p. 67, above. [2] *Ibid.*, pp. 46–7.

[3] *Ibid.*, p. 47 : "Major imperator . . . magnus Canis (seu Cham) et possidet terram Presbyteri Joannis ; et ultra istum imperium versus partes orientales nescitur alter dominus, nisi ipse."

perpetuity of " four or five monasteries " where missionaries in training—religious and secular alike—may learn heathen languages ; next, the unification of the military orders [1] into one new order, bearing a fresh name, to be stationed permanently on the borders of Saracen territory ; thirdly, the levying of a tithe on the whole of the Church for the conquering of the Holy Land. The second and most interesting of these proposals develops to some extent the corresponding suggestions in the *Liber de Fine*. The kingdom of Granada should be the first objective of the unified order, for " its foundations are upon a rock " —*i.e.* there are Christian states around it. Then Barbary should be surrounded with Christian outposts, for it, too, is comparatively near at hand. And lastly should come Palestine, most distant and most difficult of the three, care being taken not to begin these operations in Syria, " whose foundations are on sand," Persia and the territory of the fanatic Carbenda being so near it.[2]

On leaving Bugia, Ramon was met by further adventures no less startling than those which he had undergone already. He had been placed on board a ship bound for Genoa, strict orders having been given to the captain that he was to land him on Christian territory only.[3] As they reached Pisa, a storm sprang up, the ship was wrecked some ten miles from land, and a handful of the passengers alone escaped in a boat. Among them was Ramon. He had been able to save nothing, either of his books or of his clothing. Helpless and naked he landed, and in some fashion made his way from the shore to Pisa.[4]

[1] Salz., iv, p. 47 : " scilicet de Ordine Templi, Hospitalis et Hospitalis Allemannorum, Vellensium et Calatravae et Sepulchri." *Cf.* pp. 233, 317–18, above.

[2] *Ibid.* : " Sed non vadant primo in Syriam, in qua fundamentum est arenosum et labile et circa ruinam a longe per Infideles circuitum." *Cf. ibid.*, pp. 46–7 : " Et sic non convenit, quod Rex Franciae, nec etiam aliquis alius eat in Syriam, cui Persia est vicina, alias Carbenda et Soldanus statim venirent contra Christianos."

[3] *V.C.*, vii : " Manaren al patró de la nau ab grans penes que no l lexás en neguna terra de moros." *V.B.R.L.*, vii : " Praeceptum est Domino dictae navis, ut in terra illa non sineret hunc virum amplius remeare."

[4] *V.C.*, *V.B.R.L.*, vii (*Life*, pp. 40, 82).

There, it is needless to say, he was honourably received by the citizens, and taken by one of them into his house.[1]

Ramon must now have been about seventy-five years of age. In the course of a few months he had gone through two voyages, a shipwreck, a trial for his life, a long imprisonment under the foulest conditions, and maltreatment, at least once, at the hands of a mob. But neither his body nor his mind, still less his indomitable will, was disposed to rest.[2] He betook himself for a period of tranquil study to the monastery of St. Dominic,[3] near Pisa, and at once set to work to write again. Here he wrote, in Latin, the *Disputation* which has just been described, and also the *Ars generalis ultima*.[4] This last book he had begun some two and a half years earlier in Lyons, but probably had to re-commence from memory, unless, by chance, he had left the manuscript in Europe before setting sail for Bugia.[5] About the same time

[1] The accounts of the shipwreck in *V.C.*, *V.B.R.L.* vii, are confirmed in almost every detail by Ramon's own account (*Disputatio*, etc., p. 46): "Et incontinenti Saraceni ipsum miserunt in quandam navem tendentem Genuam, quae navis cum magna fortuna venit ante portum Pisanum, et prope ipsum per decem milliaria fuit fracta, et Christianus vix quasi nudus evasit: et amisit omnes suos libros et sua bona."

[2] Both *V.C.* and *V.B.R.L.* draw attention to his energy at this point (vii, *Life*, pp. 40–1, 82): "Jatsía fos molt antic de dies, emperò no cessava de servir a son creador, etc." "Vir Dei, licet jam esset antiquus et debilis, semper tamen labori pro Christo insistens, etc."

[3] This is the general belief of biographers, but see *H.L.F.*, Nos. 143, 158, 180, 237, 255; Rogent i Duràn (*Bibliografía*, etc., p. 404); Golubovich, i, pp. 383, 385 on the names Donnino (Domnino) and Domenico.

[4] *H.L.F.*, No. 51, pp. 236–7; Keicher, p. 44. The significance of the adjective will not escape the reader. Both *V.C.* and *V.B.R.L.*, vii (*Life*, pp. 41, 82) append a eulogy of this work to the account they give of its composition; that of *V.B.R.L.* is the fuller. A Catalan text, now lost, is believed to have been the original form of the work. The earliest printed copy known of any of Lull's writings is of the *Ars generalis ultima* (Venice, 1480: Rogent i Duràn: *Bibliografía*, etc., p. 1).

[5] The fact that this *Ars* was begun "at Lyons, on the Rhone, in the month of November 1305" is stated without comment at the end of the book. Pasqual (ii, p. 121) is so certain that it was not re-commenced from memory that he sends Ramon, without evidence whatsoever, from Paris to Pisa, and from Pisa to Mallorca, instead of from Paris to Mallorca direct, so that he shall have been able to leave his manuscript there before going to Africa. If this really happened, it was particularly obliging of the shipwreck to take place off Pisa.

(January 1308)[1] he completed also a *résumé* of this book which is known as the *Ars brevis*[2] and during four centuries enjoyed an outstanding popularity.[3]

The Latin works written at Pisa[4] are of small importance, being for the most part re-statements of earlier works. The *Hundred Signs of God* seeks, as its name implies, to enumerate all the signs which reveal God to man, expounding each very briefly. The *Book of Clerks* professes to teach in six lessons the beginnings of Christian doctrine, to which (says the author) even clerics are often strangers.[5] At the end Lull " dedicates and sends it " to the " venerable University of Paris, and principally to its Chancellor, Rector, Dean and other chief members." [6] In doing so, he alludes to his attempt to win the Pope's ear at Lyons, begging them ever to bear in mind his three requests[7] and to help him to obtain their fulfilment.

But this marvellous old man did much more in Pisa than write books. Here he seems to have found the spirit that more than once he had looked for in vain at Rome. " Desiring to incite the commune of the city of Pisa to the service of Christ," [8] he proposed to the council of the commune that some among them should take the cross and " become knights of Jesus Christ to conquer the Holy Land " [9] : he proposed, that is to say, at an age

[1] Salzinger's attribution of the *Ars brevis quae est de inventione mediorum juris* or *Ars brevis juris civilis* (a work for the instruction of ignorant jurists) to Montpellier, January 1308, is combated by Pasqual (ii, p. 116), who dates it 1306. (See also *H.L.F.*, No. 168, pp. 308–9 ; Alòs : *Los catálogos*, p. 72 ; Longpré, cols. 1094–95 ; and p. 311, n. 1, above.)

[2] *Ars brevis, seu Compendium et Isagoge Artis Magnae* (the *Artificium sive Ars brevis* of *H.L.F.*, No. 50, p. 236). It has also other sub-titles.

[3] *Cf.* index (*sub* " Art Breu ") to Rogent i Duràn : *Bibliografía*, etc.

[4] Those not yet mentioned are : *Liber ad memoriam confirmandum* (*H.L.F.*, No. 143, pp. 298–9), *Liber clericorum* (*H.L.F.*, No. 78, pp. 255–6), *Liber de centum signis Dei* (*H.L.F.*, No. 180, p. 314). The last two are dated May 1308 ; the *Disputatio*, etc., is dated April 1308. *Cf.* Pasqual, ii, p. 142 ; Longpré, col. 1099.

[5] The Latin text of 1499 is reproduced, together with a French translation *en regard*, in *Obres*, i, pp. 295–386. The editor collated this text with another fifteenth century edition which is in the Biblioteca Provincial, Palma.

[6] *Obres*, i, p. 385. [7] See pp. 332–3, above, and *Obres*, i, pp. 385–6.

[8] *V.B.R.L.*, vii (*Life*, p. 83).

[9] *V.C.*, vii (*Life*, p. 41). Cf. *V.B.R.L.* (p. 83).

when most men have long since betaken themselves to a life of leisure, to assist in the foundation of a new military order and start recruiting for a new Crusade.

How much of the work in this connection he intended to do himself is uncertain. Most probably he knew that the Grand Master of the Hospitallers, Foulques de Villaret, had journeyed from Cyprus to Poitiers, and was even now in conference with Clement V upon the subject of the projected Crusade.[1] But in any case it was no new one to him: long before, in poem, narrative and proverb, he had preached it:

> Do thou inflame
> With love our threefold powers, O blessed Maid,
> That we may go to Syria, unafraid,
> The souls of unbelievers fierce to tame
> And give to Christians peace in Jesus' name.[2]

Certainly Ramon could not have been disappointed in the people of Pisa. They received his proposal warmly, and sent him to the Papal Court with letters of recommendation and assurances of their support to bear to the Pope and the Cardinals. On his way there, about May 1308,[3] he made a brief halt at Genoa, where he had also received much kindness, and here he was welcomed even more warmly: many devout persons[4] offered freely to help him, and a sum of over thirty thousand florins[5] was collected.[6]

[1] He left Cyprus at about the beginning of 1307, and was at Poitiers from August 8, 1307, to August 12, 1308, the Grand Master of the Temple being there also. (*Cf.* Delaville le Roux, p. 279.)

[2] *Blanquerna*, Chap. 76 (*Bl.*, p. 300).

[3] The date, and the brevity of Lull's stay there, are fixed by the facts that he brought out, in the same month of May 1308, the *Liber Clericorum* at Pisa, and the *Ars Divina* (or *De Arte Dei*: *H.L.F.*, No. 181, pp. 314–5) at Montpellier. He could not, therefore, well have written an *Ars brevis . . . juris* at Montpellier in January 1308, as he was then at Pisa (*cf.* p. 335, n. 1, above); nor the *Liber de venatione substantiae, accidentis et compositi* there (*H.L.F.*, No. 139, pp. 296–7; Longpré, col. 1095) in February 1308.

[4] So *V.C. V.B.R.L.* has "devotae matronae atque viduae plurimae . . . aliique civitatis ejusdem nobiles." (*Life*, pp. 41, 83.)

[5] So *V.C. V.B.R.L.* reads "triginta quinque millia florenorum." On the mention of the florin, see p. 129, n. 1, above.

[6] *Cf.* Finke, *Acta Arag.*, vol. ii, No. 556; Longpré, col. 1084.

Armed with letters, promises and money,[1] Ramon went boldly forward. Soon after his coronation at Lyons, Clement V had definitely refused to go to Rome, and, having spent some time at Bordeaux, Poitiers and Toulouse, decided to fix his court at Avignon. That city had been ceded by Philip the Fair to Charles II of Naples in 1290, but Clement would have found himself in quite a French environment when, early in 1309,[2] he took up his residence there, far from the quarrelsome Italians of his day, whom he neither trusted nor understood. Towards Avignon, then, Lull journeyed, but first he went to Montpellier, which drew him, in old age as in youth, irresistibly. In the very month of his arrival he published one lengthy but little-read work, the *Ars Divina*,[3] which, he says, has been offered to Clement and to Philip[4]; in the October of 1308 he completed a *Liber de novis fallaciis*[5]; in the November, a *Tractatus de experientia realitatis Artis Generalis*[6]; in the December, the *Excusatio Raymundi*[7]; and in the

[1] Pasqual (ii, pp. 143–5), with righteous indignation but somewhat clumsy sarcasm, cites a trenchant criticism of Lull's action by the Dominican chronicler Brovio.

[2] The exact chronology of the Pope's movements varies with different authors, but it seems most likely that he left Poitiers on or about August 12, 1308, and did not arrive in Avignon till April 1309 (Devic et Vaissette, ix, pp. 310–12). His route would in that case be: Poitiers, Bordeaux, Agen, Toulouse (Christmas 1308), St. Bertrand de Comminges, Montpellier (February 26, 1309), Narbonne, Montpellier, Nimes, Avignon. Others make him arrive at Avignon much earlier.

[3] See p. 336, n. 3, above, and Longpré, col. 1099.

[4] This, no doubt, was done at a conference held by the King and the Pope in, or soon after, May 1308, for Lull would naturally take the first opportunity, not only of presenting his book to the Pope, but also of reporting to him the generosity of the Genoese and the Pisans. This conference should not be confused with an earlier one held in May 1307. Clement remained in Poitiers after this, but Philip went away, and returned for the later meeting, at which the decision was made to call the Council of Vienne. (*Cartulaire général des Hospitaliers de Saint-Jean de Jérusalem*, iv, 4748 ff.; Devic et Vaissette, ix, pp. 298–302; Pasqual, ii, p. 146.)

[5] *H.L.F.*, No. 151, pp. 301–2; Longpré, col. 1095.

[6] *H.L.F.*, No. 135, p. 295; Pasqual, ii, p. 147; Longpré, col. 1095. Lull makes bold claims for his *Art* in this work and challenges his readers to propound a question which he cannot solve by it.

[7] Not known by Salzinger, nor mentioned in *H.L.F.* Pasqual, however, had seen it, and from internal evidence dates it credibly (ii, pp. 148–9) as above. It cites the *De experientia realitatis Artis Generalis* and is dated "December," neither place nor year being mentioned.

February of 1309, still being at Montpellier, a *Liber de substantia et accidente*.[1]

Ramon was still finding inspiration in Montpellier. In the following month (March 1309) he completed three[2] further works there. The first, which has the clumsy title *Liber de convenientia quam habent fides et intellectus in objecto*,[3] is, though very short, by no means without interest, but repeats a good many ideas from the earlier *Dispute between Faith and Understanding*. The book presents, as it were, a synthetic solution of the problem so many times stated, on the lines of the proverb : " First comes belief and afterwards understanding." But though the author, after demonstrating by twelve syllogisms certain articles of religion, advocates the unity of faith and understanding, he does not fail first of all to drive home the great importance of the latter. Did not the Lord Jesus, he argues, tell St. Thomas to test with his own senses the reality of His appearance ? Did not St. Peter exhort us to be always ready to give reasons for the faith that is in us ? Did not St. Augustine seek to prove the doctrine of the Trinity ? And what of the *Summa* of that " vir sapiens et Catholicus," St. Thomas Aquinas ?[4]

The " narratives " which advocate the union of understanding and faith might be considered by some readers as forming merely a defence of understanding. The story of the Saracen prince who could not be converted,[5] retold with considerable detail, is one of them. It now appears that the incident is a real one, for " I saw the friar with his companions," says Lull, " and talked with them." The prince is a " certain learned king of

[1] *H.L.F.*, No. 66, p. 247. On the " Book of Proverbs " which he may have written at this time, *cf.* p. 309, n. 2, above. On the *De aequalitate actuum potentiarum animae in beatitudine*, see Longpré, col. 1099.

[2] Four, if we include *De propriis et communibus actibus divinarum rationum* (*H.L.F.*, No. 207, p. 322 ; Longpré, col. 1099), as written at Montpellier in April 1309. Some writers, however, believe Lull to have been in Paris in that month.

[3] Salz., vol. iv ; cf. *H.L.F.*, No. 29, pp. 168–70, Rubió y Balaguer, " Los códices, etc.," p. 323, Longpré, col. 1099. One MS. only of this work dates it 1304 ; the remainder as above.

[4] Salz., iv, pp. 2–3.

[5] See pp. 312, 317, n. 4, above.

Tunis, called Miramamolinus,"[1] and is convinced of his errors (" for he was a reasonable man ") by a Catholic friar who is by no means learned, but argues effectively from the immorality of Mahomet's teaching. When it comes to positive instruction, however, all that the religious can do is to recite the Apostles' Creed in Arabic and say : " Believe this and be saved." The king replies by banishing so futile a teacher from his dominions.[2]

The second narrative is no less familiar. A Saracen philosopher meets a Latin, a Greek, a Jacobite and a Nestorian in argument. None of the four can convince him of the truth of Christianity, and as a result he complains bitterly that he has to be damned through no fault of his own, for he cannot believe that which he does not understand.[3] The pamphlet—for it is no more—ends with the author's solemn disclaimer of responsibility for those whom he has warned and instructed as to how they may bring the whole world into good estate, and who will take no steps to do it.[4]

Lull's second work to be completed before he left for Avignon was a little-known *Liber de majori agencia Dei*,[5] and the third a *Book on the Acquisition of the Holy Land*,[6] addressed to the Pope, and aiming no doubt at following up his successes in Pisa and Genoa. In this book he outlined the expected course of such a crusade as he had been preaching, and such as Clement also was meditating in conjunction with Templars and Hospitallers, even while Philip was planning the destruction of the Order of the Temple. Lull's new idea is that, since the Christian hosts have more galleys than the Saracens, the holy war

[1] Miramamolinus is a corruption of Amir-al-mumenim (" Prince of True Believers ") and is not a name but a title. There was, however, a tendency at this time to use Oriental titles as proper names.

[2] " Et tunc Rex fecit ipsum vituperari, et ejici illum Fratrem e suo Regno," Salz., iv, p. 4.

[3] *Ibid.*

[4] The three emperors of the Tartars are again named and the argument (p. 5) is similar to that described on p. 332, above.

[5] Alòs, *Los Catálogos*, etc., p. 73. The book is in the catalogue of 1311, but is not mentioned by Salzinger, Pasqual or *H.L.F.*.

[6] *Liber de Acquisitione Terrae Sanctae* (*H.L.F.*, No. 254, p. 342, Longpré, col. 1109) written about March 1309. See Bibliography, No. 78a.

should begin on sea. Once the Christians are masters of the ocean, they can attack by land. From Constantinople (which had now been in Christian hands for more than a century) an army will devastate Syria. This accomplished, to subdue Egypt will be comparatively easy, especially if the parallel crusade, which Lull has always yearned for, can be carried on in Spain and Northern Africa with Granada and Ceuta as its objectives. This is the argument of the first part of the book. Alas, for Ramon's hopeful plans and easy rhetoric! These things were never to materialize. No doubt they might have done so had petty jealousies and rivalries been swallowed up in the ocean of love. But that was not the way of fourteenth-century Europe.

The two latter parts of Lull's book, which discuss missionary work, contain very little that is new to us. He builds his three language schools light-heartedly at Rome, Paris and Toledo, and with a wave of his *Ars Magna* disperses all the arguments of faithless and zeal-less Christians who see a lion in the missionary's way everywhere.

To those conversant with the history of Clement's papacy, it is hardly necessary to describe the result of Ramon's interview with the Holy Father at Avignon, shortly after the end of March 1309.[1] "When he saw that he could accomplish naught," says the chronicler wearily, "he went away."[2] Quite possibly his own recent successes, and Clement's negotiations with the military orders, may have given him confidence, but how he could ever have hoped to accomplish anything of importance at this juncture is a marvel. At the moment of his arrival, the process of Boniface VIII, demanded by Philip and agreed to by Clement reluctantly and after long delay, was actually in progress, and had not yet passed beyond its initial stages, while the other question on which King and Pope were opposed—the suppression of the Templars—was being worked out at the same time by means of an investigation of charges against the Order. Practical

[1] Longpré, col. 1085. [2] *V.C.*, *V.B.R.L.*, vii (*Life*, pp. 42, 82).

enough in many ways, Ramon was rash and inconsiderate—even in old age—in others, and no one can blame Clement for his pre-occupation at the moment with matters of such vital import and on which feelings on either side ran so high.

The powerful Foulques de Villaret, it may be added here, was no more able than Ramon to carry out the projected Crusade—if he ever really desired to do so. On leaving Poitiers, he travelled through France to Florence and Pisa, returning to Clement at Avignon some three months after the Pope arrived there. He had collected fifty-seven galleys and made arrangements upon a large scale for provisions. His plan that his Order should leave Cyprus for Rhodes, and use that island as a crusading base, found favour : it is said that Clement himself gave ninety thousand florins to further it. The Kings of England, France and Navarre looked with favour upon the idea of a fresh attempt to conquer the Holy Places. Charles of Naples sent many vessels for the adventure. In Germany, as well as in Italy and France, there was an unusual outbreak of enthusiasm. Men and boys enrolled in large numbers ; women flung down their jewels for the cause of the Cross. Preparations were completed for the inauguration of the Crusade and for a meeting of the Crusaders at Brindisi. Surely enough, in the spring of 1310, the Grand Master, with a numerous fleet, sailed thence for Rhodes, and on August 15 of that year, having picked up reinforcements at Cyprus, took it. There, whether by misfortune or by design, the projected Crusade came to an untimely end. The Knights Hospitallers became the Knights of Rhodes. And that was all.[1]

[1] Delaville le Roux, pp. 279–80 ; Vertot, ii, pp. 63 ff., *passim*.

CHAPTER XVI

1309–1311

Lull's last visit to Paris: his campaign against Averroism: minor works written there. He attends the Council of Vienne. His *Petition to the General Council* and poem entitled *The Council.* His experiences on the journey described in the *Phantasticus.* Results of the Council.

It might have been supposed, when Ramon left Avignon, after a short stay, in the spring of 1309, that he would have returned to Barcelona, where stirring events were in progress. The King of Aragon had remained unmoved by the efforts of the Grand Master of the Hospitallers, for he was himself planning an expedition, called for popularity's sake a " Crusade," against the Moors in the south of Spain. This objective was, as we have seen, one greatly favoured by Lull, and it is surprising that he apparently took no great interest in it. In the result, he was justified. Castile and Aragon joining forces, James made a good beginning by besieging Almería both by sea and by land. But Granada came to its rescue ; there was a notable defection among the Castilian leaders ; and in the end the siege had perforce to be ingloriously raised.[1]

Meanwhile Ramon had travelled northwards to Paris, where once more he visited the University, and lectured both upon the *Art* and upon many other books which he had written.[2] Never, it would seem, had he

[1] Zurita, bk. v, chaps. 78 to 85.

[2] It is supposed that he wrote in Paris, soon after his arrival there, an opuscule entitled *De conditionibus figurarum et numerorum* (Pasqual, ii, p. 155 ; not in *H.L.F.*). To the year 1309 are also commonly attributed an *Ars mixtiva theologiae et philosophiae* (November 1309 : *H.L.F.*, No. 172, p. 310 ; Longpré, col. 1106) and *De pervertione entis removenda* (December 1309 : *H.L.F.*, No. 158, pp. 304–5). In the following January was published a *Metaphysica*

been heard so gladly and by such vast numbers as now. "There came to hear him, not students alone, but also a great multitude of masters, who affirmed that (his) holy science and doctrine was corroborated not only by philosophical arguments, but also by the principles and rules of sacred theology."[1] If there were some who "averred that the holy Catholic faith could not be proved," Ramon did not despair of converting them, but "made divers books and treatises" in which he combated their opinions.[2] These we shall shortly notice.

Ramon stayed in Paris—for the last time, as it proved,—for over two years, from the spring of 1309 to the autumn of 1311.[3] During this period he received not only the practical homage of crowded lecture-rooms, but also public testimony of a kind more durable. In 1310, on "the Tuesday after the octave of the Feast of the Purification" (February 10), a body of forty masters in the University drew up, at Ramon's request, and "of their own free will," a statement approving the *Ars brevis* and styling it "good, useful and necessary, containing nothing contrary to the Catholic faith, but many things in support of the said faith." And this testimony was not only to be published, but to be repeated, literally and *viva voce*, to Master Raymundus Lull himself, for which purpose a deputation was to wait upon him in his house, "in vico buqueriae Parisiensis, ultra parvum pontem

nova (*H.L.F.*, No. 61, pp. 244–5), and in February a *Liber novus physicorum* (*H.L.F.*, No. 60, p. 244; Longpré, col. 1108), and a *Liber de ente infinito* (*H.L.F.*, No. 199, pp. 319–20; Longpré, col. 1100). The *Ars mixtiva* is possibly the same book as the *Principia philosophiae complexa*, which *H.L.F.* and Pasqual list separately (see pp. 291, 298 n., above).

[1] *V.C.*, vii (*Life*, p. 42); cf. *V.B.R.L.*, vii, pp. 83–4.

[2] *V.C.*, vii (*Life*, p. 42). *V.B.R.L.* (p. 84) expands these few words into the following passage, which is not found in *V.C.*:

Sed quia propter dicta commentatoris Aristotelis, scilicet Averrois, videbat quam plurimos a veritatis rectitudine praecipue fidei Catholicae nonnullos deviare, dicentes: Fidem Christianam quantum ad modum intelligendi esse impossibilem sed opinabantur, eam veram esse quantum ad modum credendi, cum sint Christianorum collegio complantati, ideo Raymundus via demonstrativa et scientifica hujusmodi conceptum eorum nitens improbare eos ad redargutionem multipliciter reducebat; quoniam si Fides Catholica secundum modum intelligendi est improbabilis, impossibile est quod sit vera; super quo siquidem libros fecit.

[3] The letter quoted by Finke (p. 321, n. 2, above) is dated May 22, 1309.

versus Sequanum."[1] We may fairly see behind this document an abortive attempt made in Paris to undermine Lull's teaching, and an enthusiastic counter-rally to his side of the most important elements in the University.[2]

In the following August, Ramon had audience of King Philip at Vernon, as a result of which the King gave him a letter of general commendation, describing his character and work in the highest possible terms.[3] Soon afterwards, at the King's special request, the Chancellor of the University caused a further examination of Lull's works to be made, and, as a consequence of this, there was drawn up a new and no less laudatory document than the preceding one.[4] As this, however, is dated September 1311, we are unduly anticipatory in alluding to it now.

[1] The document is quoted *in extenso* by Denifle (*Chartularium*, etc., Letter 679) and also by Pasqual (*Vindiciae*, i, pp. 276–7, n.). The masters named, it says, and others to the number of forty, "asseruerunt . . . per eorum juramenta, non ut dolo, metu, vel fraude ad hoc inducti, sed sua spontanea voluntate, ad requisitionem Magistri Raymundi Lulli Catalani de Majoricis, quod ipsi a dicto Magistro Raymundo Lull audiverunt per aliqua tempora Artem seu scientiam, quam dicitur fecisse seu adinvenisse Magister Raymundus, quae quidem Ars seu scientia sic incipit: *Deus cum tua gratia, sapientia et amore incipit Ars brevis, quae est imago Artis generalis* . . . Asseruerunt etiam dicti Magistri et omnes alii, ut praedicitur, per eorum juramenta coram praefatis juratis nostris, quod dicta Ars seu scientia erat *bona, utilis, necessaria*, prout ipsi perpendere poterant, seu etiam judicare et quod *in ea nihil erat contra Fidem Catholicam*, seu etiam dictae fidei repugnantia; *multa autem ad sustentationem dictae fidei, et pro ipsa facientia, in dicta scientia seu Arte, ut dicebant, poterant inveniri*. . . ." This is the principal part of the testimony, which after Lull's death was often quoted and made use of in defence of his teaching.

[2] Denifle, in annotating the document (see last note) asks why this and later testimonies were made to Lull's orthodoxy when no one doubted it. The only possible reply is that there must have been those that doubted it, and there may well have been many at such a time of turmoil in the University.

[3] "Notum facimus," it says, "quod nos audito Magistro Raymundo Lullio, exhibito praesenti, ipsum esse virum bonum, justum et Catholicum reputamus, et ad confirmationem et exaltationem fidei Catholicae firmiter insistentem. Quapropter nobis placet, quod ipse ab omnibus orthodoxae fidei cultoribus, et praecipue subditis nostris, tractetur benigniter, ipsique favor benevolus impendatur, quem gratum habebimus et acceptum: in cujus rei testimonium praesentibus litteris nostrum fecimus apponi sigillum. Datum apud Vernonem, secunda die Augusti, Anno Domini 1310" (*Chartularium*, etc., Letter 684; Pasqual, *Vindiciae*, i, p. 282, n.).

[4] It is dated "Anno Domini 1311 die Jovis post Nativitatem Beatae Mariae Virginis." The essential part reads: "De illustris Regis Franciae speciali mandato et quantum occupationum frequentia patitur, diligenter inspectis quibusdam operibus, quae Magister Raymundus Lullius edidisse se dicit; testamur nihil nos invenisse in illis, quod bonis moribus obiret et sacrae Doctrinae

The books written by Lull during his last stay in Paris are for the most part directed against Averroism.[1] It was in 1198, and therefore more than a hundred years earlier, that the Spanish Moor, Ibn-Rushd, commonly known as Averroes, had died in disgrace for opinions which the orthodox Moslem found heretical. He had

Theologicae sit adversum ; quin potius in dictorum serie et tenore, pro humani fragilitate judicii scribentis zelum fervidum et intentionis rectitudinem pro fidei Christianae promotione . . ." (*Chartularium*, etc., Letter 691 ; Pasqual, *Vindiciae*, i, p. 291, n.). On these three documents, *cf.* Bové (" R. Lull y la lengua latina ") pp. 72–82 ; Keicher, pp. 29–30 ; Longpré, cols. 1085–6.

[1] Besides those mentioned in the text above and below, they include : *Liber de Praedestinatione et Praescientia* (*H.L.F.*, No. 225, pp. 330–1 ; Longpré, col. 1100) ; a brief treatise against fatalism, supplementary to that of 1303 (not certainly, but probably, written at Paris in April 1310) ; *De naturali modo intelligendi* (*H.L.F.*, No. 145, pp. 299–300 ; Longpré, col. 1106 ; completed in May 1310 at the Chartreuse of Vauvert, near Paris) ; *De venatione medii inter subjectum et praedicatum* (Pasqual, *Vindiciae*, i, p. 281, *c.* July 1310) ; *De conversione subjecti et praedicati per medium* (*c.* July 1310) ; *Liber de possibili et impossibili* (*H.L.F.*, No. 157, pp. 303–4 ; Keicher, p. 56 ; Longpré, col. 1106 ; October 1310) ; *De fallaciis quas non credunt facere aliqui qui credunt esse philosophantes, contra purissimum actum Dei verissimum et perfectissimum* (*H.L.F.*, No. 150, p. 301 ; Longpré, col. 1106 : *c.* October 1310) ; *Liber de correlativis innatis* (*H.L.F.*, No. 63, p. 246; February 1311) ; *Liber de syllogismis contradictoriis* (*H.L.F.*, No. 149, pp. 300–1 ; Longpré, cols. 1106–7 : February 1311 : addressed to Philip the Fair) ; *De divina unitate et pluralitate* (*H.L.F.*, No. 183, p. 315 ; Longpré, col. 1100 : March 1311) ; *Liber de Deo ignoto et mundo ignoto* (*H.L.F.*, No. 184, pp. 315–6 : June 1311) ; *Liber facilis scientiae* (Salz., vol. iv ; cf. *H.L.F.*, No. 31, pp. 172–3 ; Longpré, col. 1100 : June 1311, but see p. 324, n. 2 ; this book contains contradictory suppositions, true and false, an understanding of which will lead to the " easy knowledge " of God) ; *Quaestiones supra Librum facilis scientiae* (Salz., vol. iv ; cf. *H.L.F.*, No. 32, pp. 173–4) ; *De forma Dei* (*H.L.F.*, No. 182, p. 315 : July 1311) ; *De existentia et agentia Dei* (*H.L.F.*, No. 185, p. 316 : August 1311) ; *Liber in quo declaratur quod fides sancta catholica est magis probabilis quam improbabilis* (*H.L.F.*, No. 79, p. 259 : August 1311) ; *De perseitate et finalitate Dei*, also called *De ente, quod simpliciter per se et propter se est existens et agens*, and attributed both to September 1309 (probably in error : see p. 350, below) and to September 1311 (*H.L.F.*, No. 200, p. 320 ; *cf.* No. 179, p. 313, which apparently does not refer to the same work) ; *Duodecim principia philosophiae* (also called *Liber lamentationis philosophiae*), attributed to (? February) 1311 (*H.L.F.*, No. 55, pp. 241–2 ; Keicher, p. 60 ; Longpré, col. 1106). The *Liber de trinitate in unitate permansive in essentia Dei* (*H.L.F.*, No. 208, p. 323) may have been completed in April 1310, as it asserts, but hardly in that case, as it also asserts, in Montpellier. Longpré (col. 1099), who has studied one of the MSS. at Rome, thinks the date to be April 1305, when of course (pp. 315–20 above) Lull was in Montpellier. The *Liber de ostensione per quam fides catholica est probabilis atque demonstrabilis* (*H.L.F.*, No. 216, p. 325 ; Longpré, col. 1100) was probably written during this stay in Paris.

rendered a great service to the Europe of his day by his interpretation of Aristotle, who became known in the West very largely through his influence. The commentaries on Aristotle written by him were being translated during the thirteenth and fourteenth centuries, both by Jews and by Christians, and not only these, but also his own philosophical ideas, had become widely popular in the Christian universities of Europe by the centenary of his death. Schoolmen and Averroists constituted two rival forces among Aristotelians, fighting battles on questions as fundamental as monopsychism, personal immortality, fatalism, and free-will.[1] "Ille maledictus Averroes," as the young Duns Scotus would call him, had more followers after his death than during his lifetime, while it is to be doubted if even the outraged orthodoxy of his own countrymen was more fundamentally offended than that of the schoolmen when his teachings were found to cut across their most cherished principle, —the unification of philosophy and religious belief.

Nowhere in Europe did the conflict rage more fiercely than in Paris. At the very beginning of the thirteenth century Averroes' commentaries were forbidden there, and the prohibition seems to have caused Averroism to flourish. About the time when Pope Alexander IV exhorted Albertus Magnus to write his treatise *De unitate intellectus contra Averroem* (1256), a teacher of the forbidden philosophy was raised up for it in Siger of Brabant, who continued for nearly twenty years to expound and foment Averroism in spite of prohibitions and persecutions unnumbered, roundly denouncing not only Albertus Magnus but many other anti-Averroistic teachers, including even St. Thomas Aquinas himself.

It was after 1270, when the Bishop of Paris solemnly condemned Averroism, that the hottest stage of the battle was arrived at. Almost yearly there were issued decrees against Siger of Brabant, Boetius of Dacia, Bernier of Nivelles and other leading Averroists. In 1277, four years before Siger's assassination, matters were brought to a head by the formal condemnation of no less than

[1] This subject is treated at greater length in Longpré, cols. 1119–22.

two hundred and nineteen propositions extracted from the heterodox leaders' teaching.[1] Among them we find some of Averroes' chief doctrines, and others held not by himself but by his followers. There was the theory that one creature only—a first Intelligence—is produced directly by God, and that all other creatures are produced by such intermediaries. There was that form of fatalism in which celestial bodies are made to determine terrestrial happenings, and a moral determinism familiar to later ages. Another of these doctrines, strongly opposed by the schoolmen, was the unity of human intellect, and an even more abhorrent theory was that of the two truths—the ideà that what is true in theology may be false in philosophy, and *vice versa.*

Over thirty years later [2] we now find Ramon attacking this same teaching vehemently, alarmed at its still growing vogue and encouraged by the increasing attention paid in the University to his venerable presence.[3] An historian as impartial in this matter as Renan has described him as the hero of the Averroist crusade.[4] In May 1310 he published a *Liber de efficiente et effectu*, maintaining God to be the efficient cause and the world His effect.[5] In July 1310 he completed a book "reproving certain errors of Averroes," [6] and rebuking those who listened to that philosopher, claiming that he wrote only for the understanding while the Fathers wrote for belief. Averroes was a Saracen, and knew no better, says Lull, but that so-called Christians should follow him is unthinkable.[7] In the following January he published one

[1] *Cf.* p. 277, above.

[2] *Cf.* Keicher, *art. cit.* iii, "Averroismus und Lullismus," pp. 49–85.

[3] The interested reader should not miss the sixth and seventh of the Karlsruhe miniatures referred to above (p. 288) in which Lull and Averroes figure.

[4] *Averroès et l'Avérroïsme*, Paris, 1866, p. 255.

[5] *H.L.F.*, No. 67, p. 247 ; Longpré, col. 1107.

[6] *Liber reprobationis aliquorum errorum Averrois.* Pasqual, ii, pp. 163–4 ; *H.L.F.*, No. 165, pp. 306–7 ; Longpré, col. 1106.

[7] *Liber reprobationis*, etc., *cit.* Keicher, p. 53, n.: "Si (Averroes) erravit, non est mirum, cum fuit Saracenus et ignoraverit, quicquid in prima distinctione fuit dictum ; sed mirandum nimium est et dolendum de Christianis quibusdam qui dicunt se esse philosophos et adhaerent istis opinionibus Averrois secundum modum intelligendi, ut dicunt cum audiverunt illa, quae in prima distinctione dicuntur."

hundred syllogisms on the Holy Trinity, to be used in Averroistic argument.[1] In April 1311 he gave to the world ten discourses,[2] which he had himself pronounced, on the ten chief errors of Averroes. In these he thunders against the corruption of Paris by Averroism, and begs the King to intervene in this process of contamination by forbidding the fashionable heresies to be taught. Of a different nature is the *Dispute of Ramon and an Averroist*,[3] which in a calmer manner considers five of the problems[4] at issue between Averroists and Catholics, and works out solutions which to their author at least are satisfactory.

A rather different, though related, book was completed in August 1311 and entitled *Concerning a Question very lofty and profound*.[5] In it a Christian and an infidel meet near Paris, whither the infidel is going in order to demonstrate to the philosophers the frivolity of the Christian religion. The Christian, on the other hand, is leaving for some Moslem country to confound the philosophers of Islam by invincible arguments. The discussion between them, as to whether each can demonstrate the mistakenness of the other's objections to his faith, is based on practical grounds ("ut evitemus prolixitatem disputationis") and fills the remainder of the treatise.

Yet again Ramon varied the nature of his output in a work in which he returns some part of the way towards his former allegorical manner. Its very title, in the midst of so many abstract titles, is attractive: *Of the Birth of*

[1] *Liber contradictionis inter Raymundum et Averroistam, de centum syllogismis circa mysterium Trinitatis* (*H.L.F.*, No. 70, pp. 248–9; Keicher, p. 57; Longpré, col. 1106).

[2] *Sermones contra errores Averrois* (April 1311: *H.L.F.*, No. 164, p. 306; Keicher, p. 54).

[3] *Disputatio Raymundi et Averroistae.* This is undated, but seems to be assignable to the end of 1310 or the beginning of 1311. *H.L.F.*, No. 166, p. 307; Keicher, p. 54.

[4] *Viz*: (i) Utrum intellectus extra sensum et imaginationem faciat scientiam. (ii) Utrum hoc quod intelligit Averroista per Commentatorem Aristotelis contra sanctam fidem Catholicam sit vera intellectio. (iii) Utrum Deus sit ens simpliciter existens et agens. (iv) Utrum Deus sit per se magis amabilis quoad nos quam intelligibilis. (v) Utrum divina potestas sit tantum infinita per suam possificationem, quantum est infinita per aeternificationem.

[5] *Liber de quaestione valde alta et profunda.* *H.L.F.*, No. 217, pp. 325–6; Longpré, col. 1107.

the Little Child Jesus.[1] Planned, so its author tells us, on Christmas night 1310, it was written in Paris in January 1311 and sent to Philip the Fair.[2] Its form is semi-dramatic. On the eve of Christmas, six ladies, named Prayer, Praise, Charity, Contrition, Confession and Satisfaction, who have retired from the world, are speaking together of Jesus Christ, adoring Him at His manger and praising Him in carol and in psalm. They have come to the manger at the counsel of Prayer : sick at heart for the wrongs of the world, they had at first resolved to wander in desert places where no evil could touch them. But on reflection they become convinced that the true remedy for their depression lies not in the solitary life but in greater devotion. So they have come to worship the Christ-Child, and to find in Him the means of converting the hearts of men.[3]

Arrived at the manger, they give in turn their reasons for making the pilgrimage,[4] are admitted by Justice and Mercy, who guard the entrance, and are addressed by twelve allegorical characters (" Reginae duodecim seu imperatrices ") who represent the twelve eternal attributes of God.[5] In such admiration and wonder are our six ladies left by these addresses that they somewhat unimaginatively declare them to be a panacea for the ills which they deplore.[6] Singing each a canticle to the Blessed Virgin Mary, they beg her to pray her Son to move the hearts of men—especially the heart of King Philip, that he may expel from Paris Averroes' books and teachings. After which, " greatly consoled," they depart.

[1] *De natali parvuli pueri Jesu* ; cf. *Life*, pp. 44, 85 ; *H.L.F.*, No. 53, pp. 237–40. As the versions of this work differ, the description of it which follows is an eclectic one. The quotations are made from the Paris edition of 1499.

[2] *Cf.* Pasqual, ii, pp. 165–6.

[3] Adeamus ipsum cum audacia. Reclamemus cum fiducia, qui tantum humiliatus est, ut ipse nos exaudiat ; quatinus a cordibus hominum extirpemus vicia et inseramus virtutes (chap. vi).

[4] Chaps. viii–xiii.

[5] Or " Dei rationes eternae " (chaps. xv–xxvi).

[6] . . . que si gentes audirent et intelligerent talia verba ardua et amena, in toto mundo non esset nisi unus populus Christianus a Christo puero nato Deo et homine ita nominatus (chap. xxvii).

In one manuscript Ramon then addresses Philip in person, since a copy of the book is to be sent to him.[1] In another, there follows an exposition of a number of his well-known projects, after which the Blessed Virgin exhorts the ladies to go and bear these projects to the court of the King of France.[2] On the way they meet Ramon, an old man with a long beard and a countenance expressive of great sorrow. He has done his best, he says, that Jesus, the Child that to us is born, may be honoured of prelates and princes, but in vain. He recounts his failures and his successes, but chiefly his failures. So the ladies invite him to follow them, and they go to the royal court together.

While Ramon was still in Avignon he must have heard of and discussed the forthcoming general council which Clement V, while still at Poitiers, had decided to convoke, and, by a bull dated August 12, 1308, summoned to meet in October 1310 at Vienne. Although the purpose of the council was largely to deal with the Templars, there were many other far-reaching matters to be discussed, and it is more than possible that Lull determined, long before it was held, to be present at it and to put forward his requests once more in what might well be a sympathetic atmosphere. In actual fact, the meeting of the Council of Vienne was postponed by one year, as neither the investigation concerning the Templars nor the process of Boniface VIII was concluded. When at length it was opened, on October 1, 1311, Ramon was present, quite resolute in his determination to be heard.

Before leaving Paris, in mid-September, he had written one final pamphlet[3] against the Averroists, which he

[1] Chap. xxviii in edition of Paris, 1499. The original MS. dedicated to King Philip is in the Bibliothèque Nationale of Paris (lat. 3323).

[2] Cf. *H.L.F.*, *loc. cit.*

[3] *Liber de ente, quod simpliciter per se et propter se est existens et agens* (*H.L.F.*, No. 200, p. 320; *cf.* p. 345, n. 1, above). This is not found in the old catalogues of Lull's writings, but has all the appearances of being genuine and is commonly taken as such.

proposed—so he tells us in the prologue—to take to the Council and use there to turn public opinion in the direction he desired. His other objects in attending the Council are summed up in the contemporary biography, as follows :

> He resolved . . . to propose three things for the honour and reverence and increase of the holy Catholic faith : first, that there should be builded certain places where certain persons devout and of lofty intelligence should study divers languages to the end that they might preach the holy Gospel to all nations ; second, that of all Christian knights there should be made a certain order, which should strive continually for the conquest of the Holy Land ; third, that in opposition to the opinion of Averroes, who in many things has endeavoured to oppose the Catholic faith, men of learning should compose works refuting these errors aforementioned and all those that hold the same opinion.[1]

These brief proposals can be considerably amplified on the authority of none other than Ramon himself. In the ten clauses of his *Petition to the General Council*,[2] he again suggests for his colleges Rome, Paris and Toledo ; enjoins upon the future unified military order,[3] as a first task, the occupation of Ceuta and Constantinople, to serve as bases for further attacks[4] ; and with respect to

[1] *V.C.*, viii (*Life*, p. 43). *V.B.R.L.* (pp. 84–5) expands the third clause, and, for "certain places," in the first clause, reads "locus sufficiens." With this passage and a mention of the *Liber de Natali Pueri* the contemporary biography comes to an end, stating that up to this date Lull "has made more than an hundred and twenty and three volumes of books in honour of the Holy Trinity," and adding a eulogy of his fervour, virtue and learning and a reference to the dissemination of his books throughout the world, and especially in Paris, Genoa and Mallorca. See p. 365, below. On the catalogue of Lull's works which is appended to the Latin biography, see *H.L.F.*, p. 72, and Alòs: *Los Catálogos*, etc., pp. 14–15.

[2] *Petitio Raymundi in concilio generali*, etc. *Cf.* Pasqual, ii, pp. 191 ff; *H.L.F.* No. 252, pp. 340–41 ; Longpré, col. 1109.

[3] Did Ramon, we may wonder, know anything of an anonymous petition addressed to Philip the Fair, proposing the use of the Templars' wealth for the foundation of a unified "royal order," incorporating all other Christian military orders ? The first Grand Master was to be the King of Cyprus, and after his death Philip's second son (? Bellator Rex) was to succeed him (Vertot, ii, pp. 92–3).

[4] See p. 340, above.

Averroism generalizes his proposal into an embargo upon the teaching of all philosophy that is contrary to Christianity. Part of his *Petition* is concerned with uprooting superfluous luxury from the Church, and the abolition of plurality of offices, on which, however, less insistence is laid than might have been expected of the author of *Blanquerna*. Another part recommends the substitution of syllogistic for declamatory discourses by Christian orators in the mosques and synagogues of Christian countries, where sermons should be preached on Fridays and Saturdays respectively. Another desires that Christian usurers be forbidden to make wills and that their oaths be not accepted. Another, again, suggests that the number of salaried judges should be increased, and that the science of law, being "very prolix and diffuse," should be reduced to syllogistic form, reference here being made to Lull's own *Ars Juris*. Another aims at reforming the science of medicine by exalting experience and experiment at the expense of authority. Another seeks to alter the dress and tonsure of the clergy, the tonsure to be uniform and the dress to be sober, economical and distinct from the attire of the layman. And, most important of all, the *Petition* calls for the subsidizing of the new Crusade by secular princes, under penalty of excommunication, as well as by the utilizing of certain sources of ecclesiastical revenue, comprising a tithe of the Church's wealth.

At the same time as this *Petition* in prose, Ramon wrote a poem, full of vigour and enthusiasm,—"un dels més graciosos i gentils del sant juglar"[1]—called *The Council* (*Del Concili*). It consists of some eight hundred lines, in duorimed stanzas of seven lines each, comprising a series of open letters, in verse, to Pope, Cardinals, princes, prelates and religious, and a number of allegorical stanzas addressed to Contrition, Satisfaction, Devotion and Prayer, who are begged to accompany Ramon on his southward journey.

It would appear that he was somewhat restive at the

[1] Torras i Bages, p. 261.

postponement of the Council, and certainly, though hopeful, as always, he was none too confident of its results. In a brief introduction to his poem, he urges those attending it to make due spiritual preparation, not to believe all they hear, and to guard against wilful deception. Then he openly addresses the 'Senyor En Papa quint Clement,' urges him to delay the Council no longer, and prays for God's blessing on Pope and Council both. The recipients of his remaining open letters are exhorted more straitly and with much more definiteness. The Cardinals must see to the apportionment of a tithe for the projected Crusade. The prelates, so well provided for by God, must give as has been given them and revise their standards of values :

> Boast not, my lords, your gorgeous rings,
> Fine horses, clothes and such like things.
> Your retinue no profit brings
> If prudence from its actions wings
>   A speedy flight ;
> And boldness in an evil plight
>   Is more than might.[1]

"Princes, dukes and marquises" must contribute personal service. In exhorting the secular powers, Ramon is perhaps at his best :

> A knight that truly loves God's Son
> No rest will know till His work be done,
> And all the Holy Land be won.
> God aids His chosen cause, and none
>   Can say Him nay.
> So, king and emperor, to the fray !
>   Let us away !

[1] Senyors prelats, no val anell
ne gran cavall, ne bell mantell
ne gran flota de mant donzell,
si en sos faits no ha capdell
   discreció,
e que sia ardit e pro
   quan és raisó. (ll. 338–44.)

Kings, emperors, barons, to the field !
Soon will your valour [1] stand reveal'd.
Let reason be your sovereign shield ;
Clad in God's love, ye cannot yield
To any foe.
So call to prelates, high and low :
" Lords, let us go ! " [2]

Nor is the duty of the religious any less binding. They must preach a crusade with one voice. They must go to Ultramar and build monasteries there. They must counsel the Pope well and fearlessly. They must do all that they can to aid the cause of God without thought of harm or disgrace :

The contémplative, the monk profest
In the fear of God sets up his nest.
No threat or attack disturbs his rest ;
No sloth must e'er his life infest.
Nay, let him raise
A crusading zeal in these our days
To God's high praise.[3]

Of the allegorical stanzas, which are all in the same vigorous style—the style of a youth rather than of a man

[1] *I.e.* true worth ; *cf.* p. 32, above.

[2] Cavaller qui bé sap amar
en conquerir tot Ultramar
en nulla res no deu dubtar ;
pensar pot que Déus vol aidar
a sa honor ;
vagen, doncs, rei, emperador,
ab gran vigor.

Rei, emperaire e baró,
cras veirem si seran bo,
ne de raisó fan ganfanó
e de l'amor de Déu gonilló ;
e que als prelats
diguen : nòs som aparellats
senyors, anats ! (ll. 212–25.)

[3] Religiós contemplatiu,
temor de Déu està son niu,
no tem menaces ne null briu
ne no vol ésser sejorniu.
Vai preïcar
que anem tuit en Ultramar
per Déus honrar ! (ll. 359–65.)

of nearly eighty—the best are those to Devotion. What avails a stout helm for the head, without thee, Devotion, cousin of Will and Goodness? Thou and I will go to Vienne together, to weep and to pray: we will cry aloud continually till our prayers be granted us:

> He that loves truly knows not fear.
> No task's too mean, or too severe,
> For a servant who his Lord holds dear.
> Then leave we affright behind us here,
> And take our fill
> Of boldness, season'd with good-will,
> Sauce for all ill.[1]

"Come thou too with us, Prayer," ends the poem, "and let us be good companions. Come not unless thou desirest, for no good will result thus. But if thou art inspired by love, God will aid thee. As for Ramon, he will do what he may, by raising his standard and preaching to those whom God has given authority."[2]

At the conclusion of the poem is a hymn—in which Ramon speaks of himself by his full name—describing various virtues and vices which may be expected to be present at the Council, and praying, in a frequently recurring refrain, for showers of blessing to water a parched land. As a whole, it is a remarkable piece of work, not least because of its strikingly popular form, which contrasts with the weighty matters dealt with and the importance of the persons addressed. As Torras i Bages truly says, "our own age could not understand, and would consider intolerably audacious, the exhortations and even the rebukes which the Beat Ramon directed to Pope, Cardinals, prelates, princes, religious,—and that not in letters written in Latin, or by means of diplomatic communications, or even with the fervour of

[1] Qui bé ama, no ha paor,
ne res no es té a deshonor.
Pus que de Déus és servidor
al nostro hostal lleixem paor;
e ardiment
sia nostre pa e piment,
e bon talent. (ll. 618–24.)

[2] ll. 625–701.

a preacher of the Gospel, but in the language and the style of a troubadour. Yet Ramon's reverence for authority, and his faith in its Divine right, were unquestioning. His voice is that of a privileged servant giving a warning to his master, not through any affectation of pride, but simply from his genuine affection towards the family. To-day, alas, that happy familiarity between governor and governed is lost, and such admirably sincere language as Ramon's is no longer possible."[1]

In the inaugural discourse of the Pope to the Council, which turned on the question of the Templars, the reconquering of the Holy Land and the reform of the clergy, one at least of Ramon's projects was referred to, and it is by no means improbable that his representations about the projected Crusade, as well as on the foundation of missionary colleges, carried some weight, though he was clearly less qualified to speak of the first matter than of the second. He appears to have remained at Vienne until the termination of the Council in May 1312, occupying his spare time with the writing of a number of books,[2] of which by far the most interesting is the "Dispute of a Cleric and Ramon the fantastic," generally known by an abbreviation of its Latin title,[3]—*Phantasticus.*

This book, like the *Disputation with Hamar*, is probably a reproduction, or an expansion, of Lull's personal experiences. Two travellers are going to the

[1] Torras i Bages, p. 261.

[2] The *Benedicta tu in mulieribus,* bearing internal evidence of early date, is nevertheless dated from Vienne in October 1311, and is often considered as spurious (see p. 408, below). It is included in *Obres,* vol. i, but Obrador, its editor, who originally believed it to be genuine, abandoned that belief (contrast him in *Revista luliana,* i, pp. 93–102 and in *Obres,* i, p. xxxvi; only five years separate these judgments). *Cf.* Pasqual, ii, p. 190; *H.L.F.*, No. 82, pp. 257–8; Av., pp. 510, 630; *Obres,* x, pp. xv, xvi; Alòs, *Los Catálogos,* etc., pp. 66, 78; Rogent i Duràn, *Bibliografía,* etc., pp. 295–6.

The *Liber de ente reali et rationis* was completed at Vienne in December 1311 (*H.L.F.*, No. 69, p. 248) and the *Liber de ente simpliciter absoluto* in March or April 1312 (*H.L.F.*, No. 201, p. 320; Longpré, col. 1100). The latter book is closely related with the *De ente quod simpliciter,* etc., of 1309 or 1311 (pp. 345, 350 above); Custurer, who alone of commentators knew both MSS., says that it is only a revised form of this book; Pasqual (*Vindiciae,* i, pp. 372–3) lists all three.

[3] There is an edition (cf. *H.L.F.*, No. 54, pp. 240–1) published in 1499 at Paris, and a Catalan version at Palma (*cf.* Rogent i Duràn, *Bibliografía,* etc., pp. 20–23).

Council : one is a cleric, named Peter, and the other, Ramon, a layman. " I have often heard of you," says the cleric, " as a most fantastic person. Pray, what are you going to do at the Council ? "

Ramon describes his ideals, whereat Peter the clerk laughs heartily. " I had heard of you as a fantastic man," he cries, " but now I know you as the most fantastic of the fantastic. Only a hopeless dreamer could conceive such schemes as these." " Let us consider that," says Ramon. " Perhaps I am less fantastic than you. We will relate each of us his life's history."

The clerk first tells his story, which is almost a picaresque novel in little. He was a peasant's son, and began his career by begging. Then he was enabled to study for orders, graduated at the University in arts and law, became a priest and an archdeacon, collected many important benefices and has used the wealth which has accrued to him through these in helping his numerous relatives to live more comfortably and to better their social positions. He is followed on horseback by his three nephews, to each of whom he has given a rich benefice, and he is now bound for the Court, where the offer of an important bishopric awaits him. His servants and horses are numerous ; his expenditure is on the munificent scale which befits his wealth. He, certainly, is not fantastic, but discreet and prudent.

Ramon replies to this autobiography with the story which we already know. " I have been married," he says, " and had children ; I have been well-to-do, lascivious and worldly.[1] Everything that I had in the world I have left that I might honour God, procure the greater good of my neighbour, and exalt our holy faith. I have learned Arabic, and laboured to convert the Moors. I have been bound, imprisoned and assaulted. For five and forty years I have laboured to move Christian princes and prelates that they may promote the common weal of the Church. Now I am old and poor, yet still I have the same purpose, and I trust that, with the grace of God, I may persevere therein even unto death. Does such

[1] See p. 17, above.

a life as this seem to you fantastic ? Let your conscience judge, as God Himself will judge you."

This simple yet noble *apologia* is followed by a dispute between the two men as to which of their stories is the less fantastic. Peter the Clerk says that it is his, because he is the happier and the more honoured by men. Ramon replies that it matters not how troubled one's life is if the public good be served by it, illustrating his arguments freely from his own experiences. They part—in Lull's usual style—without being reconciled ; and, indeed, reconciliation between the two ideals of two such contrary types of man would hardly be credible.

CHAPTER XVII

1311–1315

Ramon Lull returns to Mallorca. His comments on the results of the Council. Foundation of the Lullian School. Lull's testament. His visit to Sicily, brief return to Mallorca, and departure on his third African mission. His landing at Bugia, experiences in Tunis, and probable return to Bugia. His martyrdom. Problems of fact and chronology. Burial at Palma. Lull's tomb to-day.

As soon as the Council of Vienne was over, Lull returned to his native island, staying, for a short time only, at his favourite Montpellier, on the way.[1] For once the stay must have had sorrowful memories for him : the unfortunate James II of Mallorca, who so often had made the city his home, had died in Mallorca a year previously (May 28, 1311).[2] His last years, one is glad to think, were comparatively happy. His nephew James, who was of a conciliatory disposition, found that his uncle bore him no grudge for a situation, now past, which had been made by neither, but supported him constantly, as in the siege of Almería, and even lent him much money.[3] It is not hard to imagine Ramon's feelings at the loss of one who had been to him, in turn, pupil, master and

[1] Here he wrote the *Liber de locutione angelorum* in May 1312. *H.L.F.* (p. 336) thinks that the title should rather be *De locatione angelorum*, and that the book is concerned with the question, discussed at great length by St. Thomas Aquinas, of the occupation of material place by the spiritual substance of an angel. It was known in the eighteenth century, but seems to be no longer extant.

[2] *Thalamus parvus*, p. 344 ; Muntaner, chap. 255 ; Lecoy de la Marche, i, p. 363. Zurita (bk. v, chap. 97) gives the date, possibly by a printer's error (for it only occurs once), as MCCCXII. This is quite wrong : King Sancho confirmed his predecessor's privileges on July 4, 1311.

[3] " 160,000 tournois d'argent au coin de Saint Louis et du meilleur alloi, que son neveu promit de lui rendre au bout de trois mois, et qu'il ne lui rendit pas." (Lecoy de la Marche, i, p. 363.)

sovereign, besides proving at all times a sympathetic friend and a constant, if too often an impotent, well-wisher. He had arrived at an age when new friends are made no longer, and it may well have been with a premonition of his own passing from this world that he visited the spots in Montpellier which he and his royal lord had known for more than half a century. After crossing to Palma, he would doubtless make a pilgrimage to James' grave in the new Cathedral, and to what had once been the munificent foundation of Miramar, now almost forgotten.

Once in Palma—the date would not be later than the beginning of July 1312—Ramon set himself once more to write in earnest. His first task was to record some of his opinions upon the work and achievements of the Council of Vienne,[1] which seem not to have fallen far below his expectations. Two of its decisions, in particular, delighted him. The first was the resolution passed upon the teaching of the languages of the heathen, in regard to which his suggestions had been very moderate. Where he asked that three central colleges should be established,[2] the Council decided to found five—a parent institution at Rome,[3] and branch schools at Bologna, Paris, Oxford and Salamanca. The Oriental languages—Hebrew, Arabic and Chaldaean—were to be taught in these, and permanent provision, as Ramon had recommended, was to be made by the Church for the expenses of the Rome and Salamanca colleges.[4] King Philip took it upon him to finance the college at Paris, and the colleges of Oxford and Bologna were to be supported by secular princes.

A second decision, probably only less welcome because it fell short of Ramon's hopes, was that which enjoined upon the Knights of St. John the prosecution of the armed propaganda which the Templars had for so long neglected, the Templars' possessions being allotted

[1] In *De participatione Christianorum et Saracenorum* (July 1312: *H.L.F.*, No. 255, pp. 343–4).

[2] See pp. 340, 351, above.

[3] Or, more exactly, "ubicumque Romanam curiam residere contigerit."

[4] Denifle, *Chartularium*, etc., Letter 695.

to them for this purpose.[1] Clement had been most anxious not to sacrifice this Order, and only consented to its suppression under great stress. Probably, after the events of the past few years, he had little more confidence in the outcome of the injunctions to the Hospitallers than had Ramon,[2] who in his book shows his feelings unmistakably, and recommends the concentration of Pope and princes on the work of the seminaries. For some reason he seems to have placed his confidence in Frederic of Sicily,[3] who was now firmly seated upon his throne. To him he dedicates this commentary which he has written upon the Council, together with other works of the same period ; he invites him, further, to approach the King of Tunis, in order to arrange a conference, with his sanction, between leading doctors of Christendom and Islam. So far carried away is Ramon by this suggestion that he not only sketches what he considers may be the happy results of its adoption, but he outlines the course which it may take, details the probable Mohammedan arguments, and provides the Christian doctors with replies !

There had been other hopeful events at the Council of Vienne, though by no means all of them fulfilled their promise. A month after the promulgation of Clement's unwilling acquiescence in the suppression of the Templars, Philip of France, contented at last with his success in one particular, even though his attack on Boniface's memory had been defeated, offered to take the Cross if a new Crusade were set on foot within six years. Not only would he do so himself, but he would bind his eldest son to take his place if he should himself die within the appointed period, and he would also answer for the support of the flower of his nobility. None more joyful, we may be sure, than Ramon, when it was resolved in the Council to prepare for such a crusade, and to raise an ecclesiastical tithe in all Christendom for six years. That

[1] Except the Spanish possessions, which went to the warfare against Granada. (Vertot, ii, p. 112.)

[2] *Cf.* the criticisms recorded by Vertot, *loc. cit.*

[3] *Cf.* p. 296, above. P. Longpré (col. 1087) aptly points out that he had been in relations with Frederic as long before as 1296, and cites references.

the Crusade never materialized was not the fault of the Council, nor was Ramon to know it, for, before the six years were over, he was dead.

Again, Clement required the bishops who attended the Council of Vienne to deliver written proposals for the reforms in the Church which many besides Lull felt to be essential to its progress. Unfortunately, the loss of the Acts of the Council prevents our knowing the exact course which these matters took, but it is probable that a very large number of suggestions were received, that as a result of them decrees were made, and that these would have been duly promulgated but for the death of Clement. Some of them were published by John XXII, in 1317.

Between July 1312 and May 1314 Ramon wrote some forty books and pamphlets, at only a few of which we shall attempt to glance here.[1] Of those which were written in Mallorca, two or three only are of interest. The *Book of the Seven Sacraments* consists of dialogues between a Catholic and an unbeliever, in which the former completely silences the latter.[2] *A Book of Virtues*

[1] Those not mentioned either in the text or in the following notes (here or on p. 367) are: *Liber differentiae correlativorum divinarum dignitatum* (July 1312: *H.L.F.*, No. 209, p. 323; Longpré, col. 1100); *Liber de quinque principiis quae sunt in omni eo quod est* (August 1312: *H.L.F.*, No. 161, p. 305; *cf.* Alòs: *Los Catálogos*, etc., p. 80); *De novo modo demonstrandi, sive ars praedicativa magnitudinis* (probably September 1312: one of the books in which Lull writes against alchemy: it follows the method of contraries used in the *Liber facilis scientiae*, and not the syllogistic method: it is addressed to Frederic of Sicily, who is asked to enforce its circulation: *cf.* Salz., vol. iv; *H.L.F.*, No. 33, pp. 174–6; Alòs, *Los Catálogos*, etc., p. 80); *Liber de Pater Noster* and *Liber de Ave Maria* (October 1312: these are not mentioned in *H.L.F.*; *cf.* Pasqual, ii, pp. 210–11); *Liber de operibus misericordiae* (February 1313: *H.L.F.*, No. 226, p. 331); *Liber de virtute veniali atque vitali* (April 1313, dedicated to King Sancho: *H.L.F.*, No. 250, p. 340; *cf.* Longpré, p. 1101). There is also an *Ars infusa* of this date, but of doubtful authenticity, which summarizes the *Ars brevis* (p. 335 above), and a *Liber de septem donis Spiritus Sancti* (*H.L.F.*, No. 232, pp. 332–3). See also for this period, *H.L.F.*, No. 244, p. 337, which discusses the authenticity of a *Liber de confessione* or *Ars confessionis*, assigned by Pasqual (*Vindiciae*, i, p. 315) to 1312; also Alòs, *Los Catálogos*, p. 79; *Obres*, i, xxxiii, ff; Longpré, col. 1100, No. 50.

[2] This book, *Liber de septem sacramentis ecclesiae*, though given by Pasqual (ii, p. 210) as having been written in October 1312, is apparently referred to in the catalogue of 1311, so that unless it is another work with the same or a similar title that that catalogue indicates, it belongs to an earlier period (cf. *H.L.F.*, No. 231, p. 332).

and Sins (January 1313),[1] written in Catalan and translated into Latin, discusses discrepancies between the preaching of morals and the practice of what is preached, prints no less than one hundred and thirty-six sermons, and outlines a method of instruction, beginning with philosophical principles, passing to the principles of theology, and deducing rules of life from both. A third work with a lengthy title,[2] sometimes shortened to *Quae lex sit magis bona*, follows familiar lines in maintaining the superiority of Christianity over the religions of the Saracens and the Jews, but it is of interest for the respectful tone in which Islamic teaching is alluded to, and for its conclusion. In this, James II of Mallorca's successor, King Sancho, and the Bishop of Mallorca, Guillem de Vilanova, are asked to put the book into circulation and compel the Jews of the island to learn from it, while Christian merchants, going to Saracen cities, are urged to make use of its arguments in their constant endeavours to convert their clients. Frederic of Sicily is addressed in this book also.

During this visit to Mallorca Lull accomplished another of the practical tasks which were never far from his mind—making a legacy, as it were, to the island which he was soon to leave for ever. There is no evidence that he made, or contemplated, any effort for the restoration and re-establishment of Miramar. One likes to think that he kept its memory green, as a man will keep the memory of his firstborn. But in six-and-thirty years, as Quadrado well points out,[3] his horizon had widened

[1] *Liber de virtutibus et peccatis* (*H.L.F.*, No. 247, pp. 338–9). Also known, together with several other works, as *Ars major praedicationis*, but not to be confused with the *Ars magna praedicationis* of 1304 (see Alòs, *Los Catálogos*, etc., pp. 52, 79, 80.) To it Lull added in February 1313 an *Ars brevis praedicationis*, summarizing the larger work and explaining certain obscurities in it (*H.L.F.*, No. 248, p. 339; Rubió y Balaguer: "Los códices," etc., pp. 335, 338).

[2] *Liber per quem poterit cognosci quae lex sit magis bona, magis magna et magis vera* (February 1313), *H.L.F.*, No. 219, pp. 327–8; Longpré, col. 1101. This may have been composed first in Catalan.

[3] Su idea, no encerrada ya en este peñón, traspasaba los mares, dilatábase por los continentes, era acogida por las universidades, apoyada por los reyes, adoptada en pleno concilio ecuménico de Viena, que en la corte romana y en París y en Oxford y en Bolonia y en Salamanca mandó instituir cátedras de lengua hebraica, arábiga y caldea para predicar la fe a los infieles; mas ¡ ah !

vastly, and he had but recently seen the apparent fulfilment of those hopes of which Miramar was but the germ. His legacy to the island was a " Lullian School " (*Escola lul·lista*), which at a later date developed into the Estudi General, or Lullian University, of Mallorca.[1] In this he had the encouragement, and probably the practical help, of both King and Bishop.

When once again, after spending less than a year at home, Ramon planned another journey overseas, he appears to have had the idea that he would never return. So, like the Lover in one of his own books, he sends for a " faithful scrivener " and draws up a testament (April 26, 1313) " concerning the things which he had held in trust for his Beloved." [2] One such, a spiritual testament, he had indeed made already :

> He bequeathed his body to the worms that they might devour it, and to the dust of the earth that the wind might scatter it, and none might remember it any more ; for many a time had he adorned it and clothed it with fair garments that men might speak of it and he himself have in it vainglory.
>
> He bequeathed his heart to desires and sighs, and his eyes, with their weeping and tears, to those lovers of the Beloved that do penance for love's sake ; and he bequeathed to them likewise his imagination, to imagine therewith the wonders of the glory of his Beloved, and the pains of hell and the torments of the devils. And he bequeathed to his Beloved his memory, understanding and will. And he bequeathed to men that are sinners the fear which he had of his Beloved by reason of his sins.[3]

Now he turns his mind for a time to worldly things. His wife, apparently, has died, but his son and daughter, Dominic and Magdalene, and his son-in-law, Peter de Sentmenat, are still living, for he makes his two children his part-heirs, and his daughter's husband one of his four

¡ cuán penoso había de serle ver morir en la tierra nativa el primer germen sembrado por sus manos, antes que brotaran los transplantados a otro suelo ! (*Recuerdos de Miramar*, p. 16.)

[1] See p. 382, below.

[2] *T.L.*, p. 49. For details regarding the testament, see Bofarull, *op. cit.*, and Keicher, pp. 43–4. Its text is reproduced in various places, and is most conveniently consulted in Av., pp. 523–5.

[3] *T.L.*, p. 49.

executors. There can have been little to leave them which was of value. Had he not made that clear, eighteen years earlier, in the *Desconort ?*

> . . . Never did I see
> Or think on wealth or honour graspingly ;
> And with the heritage that fell to me
> Ever have I been liberal and free :
> My very children are in poverty.[1]

Among the bequests which deserve mention are legacies to both the Dominican and the Franciscan orders, to various convents of women and to orphan children. Ten of his own works—they are mainly, though not wholly, those written during the past twelve months—he desires to have copied on vellum in Romance and Latin,[2] together with a collection of his sermons : one copy, in Latin, is to be sent, " for the love of God," to a Carthusian monastery near Paris where he has often worked, and another copy to Genoa. Nor does he forget his earlier havens of refuge, for a coffer full of books which is in his son-in-law's house is bequeathed to the monastery of La Real,[3] his association with which goes back some fifty years.

[1] (N'eremità, cert siats que) anc mais cobeitat
de deners ni d'honors a mon coratge plac,
e en aquest negoci de mon patrimonat
hai tota hora despès e n'hai tan llarguejat
que li meu infant n'estant en paupertat.
(*Desconort*, xviii.)

[2] " Mando quod fiant inde et scribantur libri in pergameno in romancio et latino ex illis libris quos divina favente gracia noviter compilavi videlicet : *De viciis et virtutibus et de novo modo demonstracionis. Et de quinque principiis. Et de differencia correlativorum. Et de secretis sacratissime Trinitatis et incarnacionis. Et de participatione christianorum et sarracenorum. Et de loqutione angelorum. Et de virtute veniali et vitali. Et de peccatis venialibus et mortalibus.* (These two are probably one work.) *Et de arte abreviata sermocinandi. Sermones autem illi scripti quos perfeci et compilavi sunt in summa centum octuaginta duo.* Item est ibi *liber de sex sillogismis.*" On *De secretis* etc., for which three dates have been proposed, see Longpré, col. 1100 ; on the " sermons," and *De sex sillogismis*, see Alòs : *Los Catálogos*, etc., p. 52.

[3] The reference, at the close of the contemporary biography (*Life*, pp. 45, 86), to the dissemination of Lull's books " in the city of Paris in a Carthusian monastery, and in the city of Genoa and in the city of Mallorca " suggests that this biography should be dated at about the same time as the testament. (See p. 351, n. 1, above.)

The remainder of his money, and such of his books and copies of books made by order of his executors as remain undisposed of, he bequeathes to his executors to distribute upon his behalf—"for the love of God, and for the good of my soul and of theirs"—wherever they think best. He makes characteristically loving provision for the future of those of his books that are to be given away. The church that accepts them is to place them in a chest, to secure them by means of a chain, and to allow any persons belonging to that church to see and read them when they desire. These provisions regarding his own works are the most interesting parts of the testament. Certainly Justice, Prudence and Charity were among Lull's executors [1]; and many, both rich and poor, must have been the better for his dying as for his living. "He may have willed," says Mn. Riber, aptly, "that the dust of his body should be scattered to the four winds, but he willed more effectively a scattering of the fruits of his ardent and irradiant spirit." [2]

The testament is dated April 26, 1313, and Ramon must have set off upon his travels within a week or two of its completion, since he began a new book [3] while at sea in May 1313, and finished it, according to the final words of the book itself, in the same month at Messina.

For Lull's new destination was Sicily. So far as we know he had never been there before, though he may easily have called at the island on his travels, and long ago Gaufredi had given him recommendations to the Sicilian Franciscans. Probably much had passed between him and King Frederic before he now left Mallorca: from the frequent references to the King, and the exhortations addressed to him in Lull's books of this period, we conclude that the octogenarian missionary looked upon him as his chief hope among secular princes. Never did he write more feverishly than now—inspired, no doubt, by Frederic, and by the approval of the

[1] *T.L.*, p. 50. [2] *Vida i actes*, p. 239.

[3] *De compendiosa contemplatione*. Neither Salz., nor *H.L.F.*, knows anything of this, but Pasqual (ii, pp. 219–20) had apparently seen it, as he cites the first and last words in the original Latin and describes its content. It has been re-discovered in recent times by Senyor d'Alòs ("El manuscrito, etc.," p. 103).

Archbishop of Monreale, to whom also he refers in these opuscules. Between the May of 1313 and that of 1314 he produced over thirty works.[1] Practically none of these is of any interest to-day, except the *Hermit's Consolation*,[2] a kind of antithesis to the *Desconort*. In it Ramon, walking through the usual forest of his narratives, meets a disconsolate hermit whose good but wavering

[1] The list, given below, of those not mentioned in the text, will show that Ramon began writing in the late summer after his arrival in Sicily and wrote incessantly until early in May :

OCTOBER 1313 : *Liber de ente absoluto* (*H.L.F.*, No. 202, pp. 320–21) ; *Liber de accidente et substantia* (*H.L.F.*, No. 66, p. 247 ; *cf.* Alòs : " El manuscrito," p. 103, Longpré, col. 1101) ; *Liber de medio naturali* (*H.L.F.*, No. 155, p. 303) ; *Liber de actu majori* (*H.L.F.*, No. 238, p. 335) ; *Liber de venatione Trinitatis per substantiam et accidentem* (*H.L.F.*, No. 139, pp. 296–7). NOVEMBER 1313 : *Liber de loco minori ad majorem* (*H.L.F.*, No. 156, p. 303) ; *Liber de perfecta scientia* (*H.L.F.*, No. 159, p. 305) ; *Liber de inventione divina* (*H.L.F.*, No. 186, p. 316) ; *Liber de divina sanctitate* (*H.L.F.*, No. 187, p. 316) ; *Liber de esse infinito* (*H.L.F.*, No. 204, p. 321) ; *Liber de Trinitate trinissima* (*H.L.F.* No. 210, p. 323) ; *Liber de potestate infinita et ordinata* (*H.L.F.*, No. 188, pp. 316–17). DECEMBER 1313 : *Liber de creatione* (*H.L.F.*, No. 222, p. 329) ; *Liber de Essentia et Esse Dei* (*H.L.F.*, No. 189, p. 317) ; *Liber de concordantia et contrarietate* (*H.L.F.*, No. 221, pp. 328–9) ; *Liber de natura divina* (*H.L.F.*, No. 190, p. 317) ; *Liber de quinque praedicabilibus et decem praedicamentis* (*H.L.F.*, No. 59, pp. 243–4). JANUARY 1314 : *Liber de Deo majore et minore* (*H.L.F.*, No. 192, p. 317) ; *Liber de potestate pura* (*H.L.F.*, No. 198, p. 319) ; *Liber de intelligere Dei* (*H.L.F.*, No. 191, p. 317) ; *Liber de voluntate Dei infinita et ordinata* (*H.L.F.*, No. 193, pp. 317–8). FEBRUARY 1314 : *Liber de affirmatione et negatione* (*H.L.F.*, No. 153, p. 302) ; *Liber de vita Dei* or " de vita divina " (*H.L.F.*, No. 178, p. 313) ; *Liber de majori fine* (also called *De fine et majoritate* (*H.L.F.*, No. 243, p. 337) ; *Liber de divina justitia* or " de justitia Dei " (*H.L.F.*, No. 194, p. 318). MARCH 1314 : *Liber de esse perfecto* (*H.L.F.*, No. 203, p. 321) ; *Liber de objecto finito et infinito* (*H.L.F.*, No. 154, pp. 302–3) ; *Liber de memoria Dei* (*H.L.F.*, No. 195, p. 318). APRIL 1314 : *Liber de civitate mundi* (date not certain : *H.L.F.*, No. 153, p. 306 ; some interesting notes in Longpré, col. 1102) ; *Liber de multiplicatione quae fit in essentia Dei per divinam trinitatem* (*H.L.F.*, No. 211, pp. 323–4). MAY 1314 : *Liber de consilio divinarum dignitatum* (not the same book as in *H.L.F.*, No. 220). For *Liber de perseitate Dei*, see Alòs " El manuscrito, etc.," p. 109.

Pasqual (but not *H.L.F.*) also gives (ii, p. 222) *Liber de definitionibus Dei* (SEPTEMBER 1313 : MS. at Innichen and in *Ottob. lat.*), and *Liber de divinis dignitatibus infinitis et benedictis* (OCTOBER 1313 : MS. in *Ottob. lat.*). Rubió y Balaguer (" Los códices, etc.," pp. 321, 325–6) gives *Liber propter bene intelligere, diligere et possificare* (OCTOBER 1313 : MSS. at Innichen and in *Ottob. lat.* ; not previously known). Alòs (" El manuscrito, etc.," p. 106, *Los catálogos*, etc., p. 84) gives *De divina unitate* (NOVEMBER 1313 : MSS. in *Ottob. lat.*).

[2] *Consolació d'ermità*, written in Catalan in August 1313 (*H.L.F.*, No. 260, pp. 369-71). For the Latin version, made in May 1314, see Alòs : " El manuscrito, etc.," pp. 115-27 ; for bibliography, Longpré, col. 1101.

resolutions he strengthens by means of argument, much as he himself had been strengthened, though in another fashion, by the hermit of the poem.

Besides writing in Sicily, it is to be presumed that Ramon held discussions with the King, the Archbishop and others, concerning the best methods of converting the Jews and the Saracens who were to be found in that newly tranquillized island. But, old as he was, the idea came gradually to him that he would return once more to Africa and make a last effort by his preaching to evangelize some part of the country. With the desire came also the opportunity. The moment, as it chanced, was extremely favourable, for the King of Bugia had just concluded a ten years' treaty (November 23, 1312) with the peace-loving Sancho of Mallorca, and with Bugia Ramon was already familiar. So, about May 1314, he left Sicily for a brief stay in Mallorca, proceeding thence, on August 14 of the same year, to Bugia. On Rome, on Paris, even on Montpellier, he now turned his back. Changes were taking place in the world he had known: Clement V, for example, had died that April, but Ramon was not interested in even the name of his successor. These things were now to him as of the world, worldly. He was going on his last mission "into a far country to do honour to his Beloved"[1]: as it proved, and as he may perhaps have suspected, he was going at last to meet Him.

That Ramon set out from Mallorca for Bugia, and that he arrived at his destination, we know from a letter in the Mallorcan archives, in which he reports his landing to some fellow-citizens, including two Franciscans, who had come on board at Palma to take leave of him.[2] Precisely what he did next is not clear. For some reason he left Bugia for Tunis,[3] where at the end of the year he received letters from James II of Aragon, dated from

[1] *L.A.A.*, 167 (*Bl.*, p. 436).

[2] Custurer, pp. 58, 542; Sollier, *Acta Sanctorum*, pp. 649, 673.

[3] Not, presumably, for political motives, for the treaty between the two kings guaranteed mutual freedom and protection to each other's subjects; *cf.* Custurer, p. 539 (who dates the treaty 1313) and E. Aguiló, in *B.S.A.L.*, vol. xv, p. 217.

Lleida on November 5, 1314.[1] One of these was addressed to himself and briefly acknowledged a communication of recent date. It is to be supposed that Ramon, who was clearly proceeding with more than usual caution on this visit,[2] had asked for introductions to assure him against a possibly hostile reception, for of the other two letters one was addressed to the King of Tunis [3] and the other to Joan Gil, an Aragonese painter and interpreter (*torcimany*) to that King. The former, which is quite affectionate in its references to Ramon, may be quoted :

From us, James, by the grace of God King of Aragon, etc., to the most noble and most honoured Miralmomonin Bujahie Zacharie, King of Tunis, son of Almir Abhalabber, son of the Almirs. We give thee greeting as a King whom we greatly love and to whom we desire that God may give much honour and increase of good. King, we make thee to know that we have understood that our subject Ramon Lull is in thy city of Tunis, wherein it pleases him to dwell and to be. Wherefore, King, since we are acquainted with the said Ramon, and know that he is a man that is good and learned and of upright life, and love him, we pray thee that it may be thy will and pleasure, for our honour, to have and to hold the said Ramon in thy grace, and for this we shall be greatly beholden to thee. Given in the city of Lleida, four days having passed of the month of November, in the year of Our Lord one thousand three hundred and fourteen.[4]

Ramon's life at Tunis must for a time have been comparatively peaceful : his preaching tours to the villages were devoid of incident and his disputations with learned men in the cities quite amicable. No doubt the recommendations to a temporarily friendly monarch were of great value to him. So few enemies had he that his thoughts turned again to his writings, and we find

[1] Arxiu de la Corona d'Aragó, *cit.* Rubió y Lluch, *Documents*, etc., liv, lv, lvi (i, pp. 62–4).

[2] Pasqual (ii, p. 230) and others affirm that Lull disguised himself by wearing an *alquasis* or Moorish cloak on this visit to Africa. If so, the quotation of *L.A.A.*, 167 (p. 368 n. 1 above) is particularly appropriate, for the Lover of that versicle disguised himself. But the evidence which Pasqual cites seems to me quite inconclusive.

[3] Rubió y Lluch : *Documents*, etc., liv (i, p. 62).

[4] Rubió y Lluch : *Documents*, etc., lv (i, p. 63). Both these letters are dated from Lleida, November 4, 1314.

him in July 1315 addressing King James and begging him to arrange for a certain Fra Simó de Puigcerdà, a former pupil of his, to be sent to him, in order to help him translate into Latin some of his recent works, embodying his disputations with the Saracens. Are we to see in this request for a collaborator evidence that at the age of eighty-three Ramon at last found his powers failing him—his eyesight, perhaps, or his memory? It is impossible to say. All we know is that the King complied with his request, for there exist two letters from him to the Guardian of the Franciscan Convent at Lleida and the Provincial of the Order in Aragon, dated from Barcelona on August 5 and October 29, 1315, respectively.[1] The first of these specifies one of the books—an *Ars Consilii* [2]—and adds that there are a number more, written all in Romance: the second gives the total as fifteen.[3] In the interval between the two, Fra Simó had been consulted, and the result was that he was sent to Tunis as Lull had asked.

Very little information has come down to us about these books which he was to translate, or indeed about any of Lull's works written in Tunis. Two of them were published in December 1315: the *Liber de Deo et mundo* [4] and the *Liber de majori fine intellectus amoris et honoris*.[5]

[1] Arxiu de la Corona d'Aragó, *cit.* Rubió y Lluch, *Documents*, etc., lviii, lix (i, pp. 65–7); Finke, *Acta Arag.*, ii, pp. 900–1.

[2] This is to be distinguished from the *Liber de consilio*, nemtioned in *H.L.F.* (No. 220, p. 328) and written in 1303 (see p. 311, n. 1, above), and the *Liber de consilio divinarum dignitatum* of May 1314 (p. 367, n. 1, above). *Cf.* Alòs: "El manuscrito ottoboniano, etc.," p. 111. The explicit of the Latin MS. states that its first form was Arabic, that Lull translated this into Romance, and afterwards had it turned into Latin.

[3] "Scire vos volumus nos litteram recipisse a discreto Raimundo Lulli in partibus Tunicii nunc agentis, per quam significavit nobis se, ex quo fuit Tunicii, quindecim libros condidisse super quibusdam disputacionibus quas habet cum Sarracenis, etc."

[4] *H.L.F.*, No. 196, pp. 318–9. The only copy known of this work is at Munich, in the same MS. as that which follows.

[5] *H.L.F.*, No. 146, p. 300; *cf.* Alòs: "El manuscrito, etc." Here may be mentioned three opuscules described by Golubovich, p. 398, and clearly relating to this or an earlier mission in Africa. With P. Longpré, however (cols. 1102–3), I incline to the belief that they are extracts from longer works. The *Liber de Deo et suis qualitatibus infinitis*, discovered by Senyor d'Alòs in Rome, is, though undated, also connected with a mission and with Tunis.

The latter is actually dedicated to the Mufti of Tunis; this, considering the nature of its contents, is eloquent evidence to the cordiality of Lull's relations with those whom he was striving to convert. An ancient tradition, which this dedication confirms, describes the white-bearded octogenarian—"corpore iam senex, animo vero semper virens"[1]—as being more successful in this mission than in any before. Five converts in particular figure in the version of it given by Joan Ot Menorca, and these are said to have been among the most influential and learned Moors of the city.

Was it for this reason that the tolerance accorded to the aged missionary ceased? Or was it because he felt that his work in Tunis was ended that he undertook (as nearly all tradition asserts) the long journey westwards again to Bugia? No one can say. But what happened when he reached that city can be quickly told, so scant is our knowledge of the details. Flinging caution to the winds—perhaps because of the impunity with which he had taught at Tunis, perhaps (who knows?) because he was as truly inspired now as ever he had been half a century before at Randa—he went out boldly into the streets, proclaiming in a loud voice the truth of the religion for which he had spent his life.[2] A hostile crowd, no less furious than any from which in the past he had escaped, collected around him. Someone took up a stone. The rest of the story followed quickly.[3]

Unresistingly,—nay, triumphantly—the aged Lover of Christ suffered the cruel stones to work their will upon him. The moment of his going hence had come—the moment for which he had yearned, as a youthful convert, in his *Book of Contemplation*, and had never shrunk from save when forgetful of his Beloved. "Thy servant and subject, O Lord," he had written in his youth, "has very great fear of dying a natural death . . . for he would fain have his death the noblest that is, namely,

[1] Bouvelles (see p. 15, n. 1, above).

[2] *Cf.* Pasqual, ii, pp. 234–6.

[3] Pax, followed by later writers, has tales of imprisonment and torture for which there is no early testimony.

death for Thy love."[1] He had his wish. It may be, as the legend has it, that his assailants left him all but dead, and that two Genoese merchants, Esteva Colom and Luis de Pastorga by name,[2] begged his body from the civil governor, and, finding that there was life in it, took it on board a Genoese boat that was about to sail. If that story be true, Ramon gave back his spirit to God as he came in sight of his native island ; this perhaps he would have desired above all, who had longed to die in the very ocean of love.[3] Or it may have been to a dead body that those pious merchants, whose names have come down to us for remembrance, rendered the last offices. There is appropriateness in picturing the martyr, who had fought for so many years that he had strength to fight no more, sinking beneath the tempest of his adversaries' blows, which "were to him as flowers and as a bed of love."[4] Then it was that "the Beloved revealed himself to His Lover, clad in new and scarlet robes," that He "stretched out His Arms to embrace him" and "inclined His Head to kiss him."[5] Then, like the earliest Christian martyr, the faithful soldier and servant had the last vision of his earthly life, and with it the first glimpse of Paradise.

Considering the large number of Lullian manuscripts extant—especially those containing his authentic and apocryphal writings—it is astonishing how scanty is the

[1] *L.C.*, chap. 160 (*Obres*, iv, pp. 363-4).

[2] Legend has made great play with Colom's name, representing him as the ancestor of the celebrated Columbus (*Cat.* : Colom ; *Cast.* : Colón). It has even been suggested that Lull knew of the existence of an American continent, and passed on the secret to Esteva Colom with his last breath, prophesying that a descendant of his (Colom's) would discover it! See Av., pp. 229–37 (Chap. 18 : "En Llull descubreix l'América") ; and Salvador Bové : "Lo Beat Ramon Lull y 'l descubriment de les Americques" in *Revista luliana*, vol. i, 1901, pp. 105–14.

[3] "Vull morir en pèlag d'amor" (*Cant de Ramon*, l. 49). See p. 290, above.

[4] *L.A.A.*, 36 (*Bl.*, p. 416) ; *cf.* a stanza of the well-known Mallorcan *goigs* :

Us aparella Bugia
aquell vermell vestiment
que l'amor vos abellía :
de les pedres del torrent
dolça us es la pluja dura
qui us ha tot empurpurat.

[5] *L.A.A.*, 91 (*Bl.*, p. 425).

testimony, not only to the details of Lull's martyrdom—for we have no certain evidence as to either the date or the place or the manner of it—but even to the very fact that he was martyred at all.[1] Traditions, inscriptions, pictures and references [2] have no doubt a considerable cumulative effect ; but we may feel some surprise that, as En Jordi Rubió remarks, in a thoughtful little essay already quoted, all the known editions of Lull's works prior to 1506 speak of him merely as " master " or " hermit " and only a single edition published in 1491 at Seville contains a statement that he was stoned to death, adding that he died from the effects of the stoning, at Tunis.[3] It was not, as far as is known, until 1506, in a Valencian edition of Janer's *Ars metaphysicalis*,[4] that he was given the title of " martyr," nor was his office published until that date.[5]

It is clear from the letters of James II of Aragon above mentioned that Ramon Lull was alive, and in Tunis, near the end of 1315, so that the dates traditionally given for his stoning and death—June 29 and 30, 1315, respectively—can no longer be accepted. We have already commented in this narrative upon the passion of his biographers for the attribution of the principal events in his life to prominent saints' days,[6] and there are other indications of pious overlayings in all the stories of his martyrdom commonly told. That he died in 1315 is stated at the end of the fifteenth-century

[1] Gaston Paris (*Revue historique*, 1897, vol. 63, pp. 375–7) was so struck by this, and by the evidence given on p. 374, n. 1, below, that he considered " de plus en plus douteux le martyre qu'il aurait souffert en Afrique."

[2] Pictorial evidence goes back as far as the decade after Lull's death. See Av. : *Història del lulisme*, pp. 54–5.

[3] " Ramon Llull," in *Revista dels Llibres*, Any ii, 1926, p. 89. Pasqual (*Vindiciae*, i, p. 356) is a little less definite. A medical examination of Lull's remains, made on December 5, 1611, in connection with the process of canonization, supports the tradition (*cf.* Buades, *art. cit.*).

[4] Rogent i Duràn : *Bibliografía*, etc., p. 34.

[5] *Ibid.*, p. 35 : " Officium gloriosissimi et beatissimi martyris magistri Raymundi Lulli, qui passus est pro Christi nomine in Tunici civitate."

[6] See p. 8, above. The critical reader who is curious to read a modern defence of the dates June 29–30 will find one in Av., pp. 530–38, on the tone and manner of which it would be uncharitable to comment. Pasqual's argument (ii, pp. 231, 247 ff.) is only less interesting because it is the product of a writer who lived in an age less critical and exact than our own.

British Museum manuscript of the *Hermit's Consolation* [1]; if we accept this statement—as we reasonably may in the absence of documentary evidence to the contrary—and allow him to have gone to Bugia after the Latin opuscules appeared, we are forced to place his death between the end of December 1315 and the following March—counting the days of the year 1316 from Lady Day, as was then the custom. This seems quite a satisfactory supposition.

The manuscript reference, if accepted, makes it impossible to imagine Ramon as succumbing before his assailants in Bugia itself, nor is there any tradition of weight to support this little held belief. But it also contradicts the well-founded legends which embroider the theory, very generally accepted, that he died at sea. That he was borne to the Genoese ship, dead or alive, seems likely, and it will be readily understood that the civil authorities of a city recently bound to a friendly state by treaty would have no desire to break a newly sealed compact by refusing a reasonable request made by Christian and Aragonese merchants of some standing. As to the rest, there are so many stories that one may safely take one's choice, almost the only constant factor being the names of the two merchants, which vary hardly at all. Bouvelles, Cornejo, and others make these merchants see an immense pyramid of light proceeding from a heap of stones ; examining it, they find Lull's body beneath. Seguí and his imitators then put them on a boat bound for Genoa, which, after two days, " found itself miraculously off Mallorca," whereupon " the holy man yielded up his soul to his Lord and Creator." This particular version of the legend continues that, on landing, the merchants said nothing of Lull's dead body, meaning to take it with them to Genoa. But their ship refused to sail again, thus confounding their nefarious projects ! So they landed once more and published the truth abroad,

[1] En l any de nostro senyor Mil cccxv fina sos dies mestra Ramon llull en la Ciutat de Mallorque segons es stat atrobat en hun libre molt antich en lo peu del demunt dit libre o tractat apellat de consolacio dermita. Deo gracias amen.

taking the body to St. Eulalia, where Ramon's parents were buried, after which the Franciscans interred it in their convent.

The last statement, at least, is true enough. In a chapel of the beautiful church of San Francisco at Palma, the relics of Ramon Lull still lie, and have lain, with one brief interruption, since the chapel was built in 1448, when, after being exposed for an entire day to the veneration of the faithful, they were solemnly placed at rest there.[1] Not long since, at the sexcentenary (June 12, 1915), they were re-interred in a coffin of cedar wood, on which was engraved a part of the wonderful epitaph of the Lover already quoted from the *Tree of Love*.[2] The coffin rests within an urn of alabaster, and the urn within a tomb of seven panels representing the seven liberal arts, garnished appropriately with fantastic beasts and flying angels. Never for long without those who come to venerate it is the body of one who to the people of Mallorca, if not in the eyes of the Church, is a blessed saint.[3] We have followed that body, with due reverence, to its last resting place : let us now see what fate has befallen the work of its indomitable spirit.

[1] For a fuller history of Lull's bodily remains, see Av., pp. 543, ff.

[2] See p. 287, above.

[3] I have been criticized in the English press for the statement that " in his own country Lull receives the . . . homage of a saint " (*B.L.B.*, p. 11). In everything but official devotion this is indubitably true, and has probably always been so. For brevity, I content myself with three selected testimonies. The first, dated 1478, is reproduced fully in Av. : *Història del lulisme* (pp. 275–6) ; the second is from Pasqual's *Examen de la crisis, etc.* (1749), vol. i, p. 5 : " Todo un reino tan Católico como el de Mallorca venera al B. Lulio por santo " (Feyjóo, *Cartas*, etc., i, Letter 22 also admits this, p. 391 below) ; the third is from a discourse by Mn. Miquel Gayá Bauzá in 1900 (*Revista luliana*, iii, pp. 93–101) and begins : " En Ramón Llull es un sant," the thesis of the discourse being that, so far as orthodoxy will permit, he should be so regarded.

CHAPTER XVIII

The history of Lullism. Veneration of Lull's memory in Mallorca. Its persecution by Nicholas Eymeric and the results. The spread of Lullian teaching. Attempts to secure Lull's canonization and their outcome. Dominican persecutions in the eighteenth century. Feyjóo and Pasqual. Lullism in the nineteenth and twentieth centuries: great names. Miramar and Randa.

RAMON LULL was hardly in his tomb when there began to form about his head a double halo of sanctity and science. The cult both of the man and of his work began early in Mallorca, and, less markedly, on the mainland also. This was partly due, no doubt, to the support and encouragement of Guillem de Vilanova, who, as we have seen, looked approvingly on the Lullian School, and, till his death in 1320, would have done all in his power to assure its progress and keep green the memory of its founder.

As the generation which had known Lull in the flesh passed away, and the events connected with his martyrdom and burial came to be surrounded with their first incrustation of pious legend, a chance happening struck the popular imagination so forcibly as to raise Ramon at once to the heights inhabited only by candidates for the honour of canonization. About the year 1350 a fire broke out in the sacristy of the church of San Francisco, destroying all that was there with the single exception of Lull's sepulchre. This preservation, which the spirit of the time did not hesitate to dub miraculous, was the occasion for an examination to be made of Lull's remains and for their solemn transference to a place of greater honour, where they remained till the building of the chapel a century later. At the same time a record was made of the occurrence, a later copy of which is, if its genuineness can be admitted, a valuable testimony to the circumstances and date of Lull's martyrdom.[1]

Ample evidence exists, supplied alike by the friends of Lullism and its enemies, as to the veneration with which its author was regarded,[2] and to the celebrity which was being gained for his writings, both in Mallorca and elsewhere. But about this time began the virulent persecution of Lull's teaching which was to last for centuries, and which, though it eventually died down without apparent result, is probably responsible for the somewhat grudging recognition which Rome has made of our hero's sanctity. His arch-persecutor was the Dominican inquisitor Nicholas Eymeric (1320–99), a man whose remarkable energy and talents were accompanied by a degree of obstinacy and violence no less unusual.[3] In his fierce and fanatical attempts to prove that Lull's works contained heresies we see something more than a perverted enthusiasm for the unity of the Church and an exaggerated individual enmity: we see a particular expression of the antagonism between two powerful religious orders. The well-known story of Dominic's girding himself with Francis' cord to symbolize his desire for the unification of their two societies recurs almost tragically to the memory when one reads of the acrimony with which these societies fought over the man who in his lifetime knew both so well, considered long and seriously entering the one, and eventually allied himself with the other.

[1] Custurer, Dist. 1, Cap. 3.

[2] Mn. Avinyó, for example (*Història del lulisme*, p. 61), quotes Clasqueri, Archbishop of Tarragona (1373), as saying: "Idem quoque [Raymundus] jam defunctus cultum et scolam, ut Christi Martir ac Doctor Illuminatus, quotidianis plane incrementis, precipue apud conterraneos, obtinuit . . . absque eo quod unquam circa sui cultum vel scolam scandalum aliquod insurrexerit; sed omnia quiete ac pacifice quoad utrumque sunt introducta, promota et custodita."

And Eymeric (*Directorium Inquisitorum*, Pt. ii, Q. 9, No. 5) makes no difficulty about testifying to the vogue of Lullism: "Raymundus praedictus est in coelis Beatus, et pro tali habendus a suis sectatoribus et nominandus . . . multos sequaces habuit atque habet hodie . . . quae doctrina erat plurimum divulgata."

[3] See Grahit, *op. cit.*; Quétif-Echard: *Scriptores Ordinis Praedicatorum*, Paris, 1721, vol. i, pp. 714–7.

It was in 1366 that Nicholas Eymeric began his lengthy campaign against Ramon Lull, denying his sanctity and inspiration, reviling his reputation and character, describing him as a heretic, an ignoramus, and a necromancer,[1] appealing against him to Gregory XI, whose chaplain he was, producing (in 1376) a condemnatory bull by that Pope now generally considered to have been a forgery,[2] and extracting from Ramon's genuine and apocryphal works one hundred propositions [3] which it was not difficult to brand as heretical. Menéndez y Pelayo, examining Eymeric's propositions, describes some of them as mere cavilling, others as drawn from pseudo-Lullian works generally but erroneously ascribed to the master, and others again as admitting quite clearly of two senses—the one heretical and the other orthodox.[4] In this brief sketch it is impossible to examine them ; in the next chapter we shall touch on Lull's orthodoxy, and subscribe to Menéndez y Pelayo's judgment upon his teaching: " audacious indeed, fraught with danger if you will, but assuredly not heretical." [5]

The documents of that time suffice to reflect the seriousness with which Eymeric's accusations were taken. In 1372, by the bull *Nuper dilecto*, Gregory XI ordered the Archbishop of Tarragona to collect Lull's numerous writings, to consider them in relation to the charges which had been brought against them, and if he discovered in them doctrinal errors, to burn them.[6] As a result of the

[1] " Condemnavit [Gregorius XI]," says a typical passage of his *Directorium Inquisitorum*, " doctrinam ejusdem Raymundi Lulli, Catalani, Mercatoris, de Civitate Majoricarum oriundi, laici, phantastici, imperiti, qui quamplures libros ediderat in vulgari Catalanico, quia totaliter grammaticam ignorabat ; quae doctrina erat plurimum divulgata, quam creditur habuisse a Diabolo, cum eam non habuerit ab homine, nec humano studio, nec a Deo, cum Deus non sit doctor haeresum nec errorum : licet ipse Raymundus asserat in libris suis, quod eam habuit in quodam monte a Christo, qui sibi (ut dixit) apparuit crucifixus ; qui putatur fuisse Diabolus, non Christus."

[2] Custurer, *Disertaciones históricas*, etc., Disertación ii ; Gazulla, *op. cit.* ; Ivars : " Los Jurados, etc.", pp. 107–9 ; Longpré, cols. 1136–7. For the text of the bull (Conservationi puritatis, dated January 25, 1376) see Duplessis d'Argentré : Collectio judiciorum, vol. i, p. 248.

[3] Villaronga, *art. cit.*

[4] *Historia de los heterodoxos españoles*, Madrid, 1917, iii, p. 272.

[5] *Ibid.*

[6] Rubió y Lluch, *Documents*, etc., ccli (June 5, 1372), i, p. 241.

examination of over twenty of Lull's works, no error was found in them at all.[1] Two years later we find Gregory sending for one of Lull's books ("quendam librum Raymundi Lulli") himself.[2] In 1377 Peter IV, ever a defender of Lull,[3] petitions the Pope to have one of Ramon's works examined at Barcelona[4]; in 1386, shortly before his death, he recommends to him some of his subjects who are going to plead with him in Lull's favour.[5] Eymeric, meanwhile, has been exiled from Aragon[6] and taken refuge at the Papal Court of Avignon. Peter's successor, John I, had none of that resoluteness of character which had distinguished both himself and his ancestor, Peter III; he seems to have known little about the controversy when he succeeded, and to have followed throughout the line of least resistance, with dire results for the Lullists. Eymeric returns from Avignon, is received into the new King's favour, and, quick no doubt to appreciate the significance of his artistic and pleasure-loving temperament, prevails upon him, only a few months after his accession, to prohibit Lullian teaching and cause the books of the master, so far as is possible, to be called in.[7] But soon opposing forces get to work upon the King, pointing out that Lull's writings have received the approbation of high authority: in 1388 we find John I declaring that propositions extracted from the *Tree of Love* and condemned are "veri et Catholici,"[8] declaiming to the authorities of Valencia against Eymeric's unjust persecution,[9] writing in a similar sense to the Pope,[10] and shortly afterwards to the University of Paris to ask if

[1] The Archbishop's report is quoted by Mn. Avinyó in his *Història del lulisme*, pp. 91–2.

[2] Rubió y Lluch, *Documents*, etc., cclxxvii (September 30, 1374), i, p. 259.

[3] In 1369, for example, he decreed that the *Art General* might be taught in his dominions (Rubió y Lluch, *Documents*, etc., ccxxx, ccxxxi, October 10, 1369), i, pp. 222–4.

[4] Rubió y Lluch, *Documents*, etc., cclxxxvii (January 7, 1377), i, pp. 268–9.

[5] *Ibid.*, ccclxxv (March 15, 1386), i, pp. 336–7.

[6] *Ibid.*, cclxxx (March 11, 1375), i, p. 261.

[7] *Ibid.*, ccclxxxviii (October 30, 1387), i, pp. 347–8.

[8] *Ibid.*, cccxv (April 25, 1388), ii, p. 306. On the history of the re-examination of these propositions, see Av.: *Història del lulisme*, pp. 110, ff.

[9] Arxiu de la Corona d'Aragó, *cit.* Av.: *Història del lulisme*, p. 130.

[10] *Ibid.*, p. 131.

Lull's writings have indeed been approved and are kept there.[1] Evidently the replies to this and similar queries made elsewhere were satisfactory, for in the following year King John is writing to the Pope again. Will he charge the Bishops and theologians of Valencia and Mallorca to re-examine *in their contexts* the propositions of Ramon Lull that have been condemned, and will he see that Eymeric is *not* among the investigators on this occasion ?[2]

It was at about this time that John broke definitely with Eymeric, of whom in 1387 he wrote as " religiosum et dilectum nostrum fratrem,"[3] but who in 1394 is a " diabolicus et depravatus homo."[4] He now turns definitely in favour of Ramon Lull, addresses the Pope, both indirectly and personally,[5] in defence of his memory,[6] exclaims against his " unjust persecution " by Eymeric,[7] describes him as " vir magisterio decoratus " and " a Deo excelso ingenio illustratus,"[8] and permits his works to be taught publicly once more, giving rooms in his own palace for the purpose, though making the rather important proviso that the writings on theology shall not be expounded.[9] Long before this Eymeric's enemy Ermengaudi, who superseded him as Inquisitor for Aragon, had defended Lull, discovering and announcing that certain of Eymeric's propositions were not to be found in the book from which they were said to have been taken.[10] Once the calumnies of the former Inquisitor were made clear, both Barcelona and Valencia attacked him mercilessly, and it is unnecessary to follow him with any fulness into his discredited and declining old age. Lull's descendants and followers caused the Papal archives to

[1] Rubió y Lluch, *Documents*, cccxciv (July 23, 1388), i, p. 352.
[2] *Ibid.*, ccccii (June 1, 1389), i, pp. 358–60.
[3] *Ibid.*, ccclxxxviii (October 30, 1387), i, p. 347.
[4] Arxiu de la Corona d'Aragó (March 23, 1394), *cit.* Av.: *Història del lulisme*, p. 163 ; *cf.* also pp. 155–6.
[5] *Ibid.*, ccccxv (June 12, 1391), i, pp. 368–9.
[6] *Ibid.*, ccccxvi (August 1, 1391), i, p. 370.
[7] *Ibid.*
[8] Arxiu de la Corona d'Aragó, *cit.* Av. : *Història del lulisme*, p. 134.
[9] *Cf.* Ramon d'Alòs : *Sis documents*, etc., p. 5.
[10] Custurer, pp. 239–40.

be ransacked for the bull which Gregory was supposed to have issued—without result. Later, in the time of Martin V, the Lullists again raised the question of its spuriousness, and judgment was again given in their favour.[1]

The fifteenth century saw Lull's teaching reinstated in authority, principally through the reputation of a few able Lullists such as Joan Llobet (d. 1460). Long before Eymeric's *Directorium* was first printed (1503), his diatribes against Lull were recognized as being ridiculous. On March 24, 1419, the so-called bull of Gregory XI was officially declared to be spurious.[2] In what was later the University of Cervera there was a Chair in Lullian science ("the which is a science right holy and good") as early as 1403.[3] In Barcelona we hear of a lady named Margarita Safont de Pere making over her property to the Lullian School there in 1431.[4] Royal licences and approbations were issued in 1399, 1415, 1425, 1446, and 1449; the last of these, signed by Alfonso V of Aragon, cites a number of previous licences.[5] In 1457 John II of Aragon (then regent only) gave a permission similar to these in its general nature, lauding Ramon to the skies and specifying which of the many subjects treated in his writings were to be taught.[6] On September 5, 1478, he authorized the restoration of the monastery and school on Mount Randa which had fallen into decay, and ordered the royal arms to be carved upon the buildings as a sign of his favour.[7] The restoration was made possible by the munificence of a lady, Beatrice de Pinós,[8] and, in 1481, another pious lady, Agnes Pax

[1] Menéndez y Pelayo: *Historia de los heterodoxos españoles*, Madrid, 1917, p. 278.

[2] Sollier: *Acta Sanctorum*, pp. 485–90; A. Ivars, "Los Jurados, etc." pp. 99–100.

[3] Ramon d'Alòs: *Sis documents*, etc., pp. 13–14. See also his interesting comments on this matter (p. 7).

[4] Bofarull (*op. cit.*) gives a detailed history and description of this School, which flourished greatly throughout the fifteenth century.

[5] Av.: *Història del lulisme*, pp. 249–51.

[6] Ramon d'Alòs: *Sis documents*, etc., pp. 14–15.

[7] Rotger y Capllonch: *Historia del Santuario y Colegio de Nuestra Señora de Cura*. Lluchmayor, 1915, p. 17.

[8] Custurer, Dist. I, cap. 4.

de Quint, founded a Chair of Lullian Science in this reorganized school, expressing a wish that its first holder should be the theologian Pedro Daguí (Pere de Gui).[1] Accordingly, we find Daguí coming from Barcelona to give the first lecture of his professorship in the Cathedral of Palma before a great audience including the Lieutenant-General, the Bishop and the magistrates of the city.[2] He seems to have resided and lectured there, with brief intervals, for at least seven years.[3] His teaching was certainly attacked during this time for unorthodoxy, but he was not the man to suffer such accusations placidly: setting off forthwith for Rome with some of his disciples, he justified himself energetically before Sixtus IV, securing a complete vindication.[4] His pupils were many and distinguished, and his fame, which emerged victoriously from every attack upon it, led the Randa School to flourish as it had not done since the early years of the preceding century[5]—and as it was not to do again, for soon Lullian science came to be taught less conveniently and centrally in Randa than in the newly founded (1483) Mallorcan " University " (Estudi General) of Palma,[6] and the College became reduced to the status of a grammar school.[7]

Though the glorious dawn of the Renaissance had quenched many feebler lights in Paris, and among them

[1] R. d'Alòs: *Sis documents*, pp. 10, 19–21; *cf.* Rogent i Duràn: *Bibliografía*, etc., pp. 6–13 and index (Gui).

[2] Rotger y Capllonch, pp. 19–21; Av.: *Història del lulisme*, pp. 281–2.

[3] It was in the next year (1482) that Daguí brought out in Barcelona his *Janua Artis excellentissimi Magistri Raymundi Lulli*, which was reprinted in Rome in 1485 to mark his victory over his detractors (*cf.* Rogent i Duràn: *Bibliografía*, etc., pp. 6–8).

[4] Menéndez y Pelayo: *Historia de los heterodoxos españoles, ed. cit.*, pp. 286–7; Av.: *Història del lulisme*, pp. 285–8. A second and less determined attempt to brand Daguí as a heretic was made before Innocent VIII in 1484. This failed even more ignominiously than the last.

[5] Av.: *Història del lulisme*, pp. 309–33, gives a lengthy account of Jocs Florals held at Palma in Lull's honour in 1502 which speaks volumes for the enthusiasm of the people.

[6] *Ibid.*, pp. 513, ff. It was raised to University rank on April 17, 1673 (this is the " Lullian University ") and in 1692 was reconstituted as the " Universitat Luliana Reyal y Pontificia de Mallorca."

[7] Rotger y Capllonch, *op. cit.*, pp. 22–36: the history of the School is there related in some detail.

that of Lullian teaching, this began gradually to reconquer favour in the sixteenth century,[1] spreading once more from Mallorca to Barcelona,[2] Valencia and elsewhere in Aragon, and thence into Castile and beyond,[3] while Lullian schools were being founded in other places than Palma. We know, for example, that there was such an endowed school at Barcelona in 1478,[4] and that at Valencia Jaume Janer was teaching in another in 1500.[5] No less a personage than Cardinal Cisneros was responsible for the introduction of Lull's doctrines into the renowned University of Alcalá, which he founded in 1508, appointing one of Lull's biographers, Nicolás de Pax,[6] professor of Lullian science there (1518). Cisneros also formed a Lullian library [7] and subsidized an edition of Lull's works. In every way, indeed, he was enthusiastic for him. "I have a great affection," he wrote on October 8, 1513, "for all the works of the Doctor Ramon Lull, Doctor most illuminate, for they are of great importance and utility; wherefore be assured that I shall continue to favour him in every way that I can, and shall labour that his works may be published and read in all the schools." [8]

Among Lull's other apologists in the fifteenth and sixteenth centuries were many interesting personalities, only a few of whom there is space in this brief survey so

[1] Av.: *Història del lulisme*, pp. 256, 376–9.

[2] On the important part played by Barcelona in the publication of Lull's works before 1500, see Rogent i Duràn, *Bibliografía*, etc., p. 3.

[3] It was spasmodically in evidence in Paris. Bernardo de Lavinheta, for example, was teaching Lullian science there in 1515. The first known printed edition of one of Lull's works comes from Venice in 1480 (see p. 334, n. 4, above); the next oldest editions known are dated from Barcelona in 1481–2, 1488–9, Rome 1485 and Seville 1491.

[4] Menéndez y Pelayo, *op. cit.*, p. 284.

[5] Torras i Bages, p. 265; Rogent i Duràn: *Bibliografía*, etc., pp. 15–16 and index (Janer).

[6] He also translated the *Desconort* into Castilian ("Desconsuelo muy piadoso del iluminado Doctor Raimundo Lulio Mallorquin: autor del Arte General. Traducido en lengua castellana por Nicolás de Pachs. Mallorca, 1540"). See Av.: *Història del lulisme*, pp. 370–4; R. d'Alòs: *Los catálogos*, etc., pp. 55–67; Rogent i Duràn: *Bibliografía*, etc., pp. 78–9.

[7] An inventory of this has been published by Ramon d'Alòs (*Los catálogos* etc, pp. 55–67).

[8] *Cit.* Menéndez y Pelayo (*op. cit.*, p. 287).

much as to mention.[1] An attractive figure is Ramon de Sibiude (or Sabunde), known to the general reader through Montaigne : it is generally held, though some writers dissent from the view, that his debt to Lull was great.[2] Alfonso de Proaza was a Valencian supporter to whom we owe an edition (1515) of the *Ars inventiva veritatis*, subsidized by Cisneros, and an important catalogue of Lull's writings.[3] At the Council of Trent, Joan Vileta,[4] a Canon of Barcelona, was the successful champion of Ramon's teaching, which, on September 1, 1563,[5] was declared to be perfectly orthodox, the prohibition placed on it a few years earlier by Paul IV being thereupon removed. On returning to Barcelona, Vileta signalized his victory by re-establishing there the Lullian School, which had lapsed, by republishing some of Lull's writings and by lecturing on them himself, drawing audiences which, for their size and enthusiasm, must have rivalled Lull's own audiences, long years before, in Paris.[6] Much more might also be written of the Lullists Joan Llobet and Jaume Janer, already referred to, and of foreigners who spread Ramon's doctrines, such as Bessarion, the fifteenth-century Greek Bishop of Nicea, the German Cardinal Nicholas of Kuss (Cues), and the Italian Pico de la Mirandula.[7]

In the sixteenth and seventeenth centuries appeared a number of biographies of Ramon Lull, which, if written too exclusively in the hagiographical style, and with little critical method, at least bear witness to a sustained interest in their subject. Charles Bouvelles

[1] Others are mentioned in Bover (*Biblioteca de escritores baleares*), Av. : *Història del lulisme, passim.*

[2] See, *e.g.*, Menéndez y Pelayo, *op. cit.*, pp. 279, ff. ; Probst, *Le lullisme de Raymond de Sebonde* ; Salvador Bové : *Assaig sobres el filosoph Ramon Sibiude*, Barcelona, 1896.

[3] *Cf.* Ramon d'Alòs : *Los Catálogos*, etc., *passim* ; Rogent i Duràn : *Bibliografía*, etc., pp. 51–2.

[4] Rogent i Duràn : *Bibliografía*, etc., pp. 90–1 and index.

[5] " post exactam excussionem scrupulosumque examen per biennium fere non interruptum " ; *cf.* Ramon d'Alòs : *Sis documents*, pp. 10–11, 21–4. For the later history of the prohibition see also J. Pou y Martí, pp. 6–8.

[6] Torras i Bages, p. 266. For an inventory and catalogue of Vileta's Lullian library, see *Los Catálogos*, etc., pp. 67–83.

[7] Av. : *Història del lulisme*, pp. 250, ff.

(Bovilius) wrote the first of these, in 1511, publishing it in Paris [1]; the biography of Pax came out at Alcalá in 1519; that of Seguí, a Canon of Mallorca, in 1606 [2]; a less known one by Antonio Daça in 1611 [3]; a biography and "defence" of Lull by Sánchez de Lizarazu in 1613 [4]; and a brief, compendious sketch by the Irish friar, Luke Wadding, in the third volume of his Franciscan Annals (*Scriptores Ordinis Minorum*) in 1650. This is only a short selection from a list which would be many times its length if it included minor biographies and reprints: Seguí's biography, more fantastic, if possible, than the rest, has been on the whole more generally followed, and has exercised an influence out of all proportion to its merits. Of editions of this period, one of the most famous, though by no means the best, is Joan Bonlabi's Valencian edition of *Blanquerna* (1521) which also contains a biographical outline.[5] Mention should be made, too, of a large number of French biographies, French editions and translations into French of Lull's works (1617–88) which demonstrate his popularity in France in the seventeenth century.[6]

Daguí, besides rendering many other services to his cause, succeeded in interesting the Catholic Monarchs in Ramon Lull, and was afterwards appointed by them an honorary chaplain. This was but the prelude to the events of an era in which Lullian doctrines were in favour with kings and popes. A very definite pronouncement approving them was made by Innocent VIII in 1502, and it is said on good authority, though no documentary

[1] Its title is *Epistola in vitam Raemundi Lullii Eremitae*. The date, 1514, often given to it, is that of a second edition, published in Paris also; *cf.* Av.: *Història del lulisme*, pp. 361–3; and Rogent i Duràn, *Bibliografía*, etc., p. 43, which explains the mistaken description of this work as having been first published at Amiens.

[2] *Vida y hechos del admirable Doctor y Mártir Ramon Lull*; *cf.* Rogent i Duràn: *Bibliografía*, etc., pp. 133–4; Av.: *Història del lulisme*, pp. 438–41.

[3] *Vida y milagros del Doctor Iluminado y santo mártir Raymundo Lulio de la tercera orden*, Valladolid, 1611 (*cf.* Rogent i Duràn: *Bibliografía*, etc., pp. 143–4).

[4] *Vita incliti et admirabilis Doctoris Raymundi Lulli*, etc. (*cf.* Rogent i Duràn: *Bibliografía*, etc., pp. 147–9).

[5] Rogent i Duràn: *Bibliografía*, etc., pp. 68–70; *cf.* p. 119 n, above.

[6] *Ibid.*, pp. 157–233.

evidence survives, that Leo X, who was Pope from 1513 to 1521, declared him to be Beatus.[1] But the first determined and influential attempt to secure the canonization of Ramon was not begun till late in the sixteenth century under the advocacy of Philip II of Spain, at whose suggestion Seguí's biography had been written, who had ordered a new catalogue of Lull's works to be made (March 9, 1578) and who had later sent to Mallorca (March 19, 1583) for a number of Lull's works for the Escorial library.[2] About this time an attempt made in his name by the anti-Lullists to get Lull's works on the Index once more had been signally defeated. Now, by a royal order dated 1594, the most important documents and data relative to the works afore-mentioned were sent to him, together with the report drawn up after an examination of Lull's remains at Palma. Probably Philip died before any result could come of this, but his son, Philip III, took up the matter and kept it before the Roman Court for many years. We read of a number of processes held at Palma in support of the canonization, with the approval of the Bishop. One of these took place in 1605, in order to prove certain miracles; another, in 1607, to prove miracles since reported; more miracles in 1612; more still in 1617, and each time a new process.[3] A letter dated August 16, 1611, is extant from Philip III to Paul V, in which the King begs the Pontiff to expedite the proceedings in Rome. A year later, when the 1612 process ends, an earnest petition for Lull's canonization goes to Rome from Mallorca, Catalonia and Alcalá University.[4] A document in existence signed by the Spanish Ambassador in Rome reports that certain letters on the subject have been received, adds that the Cardinals

[1] Av., pp. 550–1. Similar cases of lost bulls of beatification and canonization are cited, and it is pointed out that the seventeenth-century processes assumed beatification and were concerned with canonization only.

[2] Bover: *Biblioteca*, etc., i, p. 87; Av.: "Catàlech," etc., p. 409. Seguí, who is perhaps hardly an unbiassed witness, testifies that Philip would sit up at night over *Blanquerna*; *cf.* Av.: *Història del lulisme*, pp. 439–40, 446.

[3] Blanch, *op. cit.*; *Acta Sanctorum*, pp. 679–91.

[4] Custurer, *cit.* Av., pp. 553–4.

seem well disposed towards the proposition, and begs that the twenty books by Lull which have been asked for previously should be sent to the Sacred Congregation as soon as possible.

There our information, for the time being, ends. But it is not to be supposed that, because the representations described petered out at Rome without effect, Ramon was denied the cultus of beatification, or official veneration, either in Mallorca or on the mainland. Urban VIII, in 1625, published a bull which forbade such honour being paid to those who had not been canonized or beatified, or who alternatively had not enjoyed such cultus for at least a hundred years without interruption or protest by authority. It is noteworthy that this prohibition in no way altered Lull's status in Mallorca. It was affirmed at a later date by Cepeda [1] and by Pasqual [2] that some such cultus ("aliqua species cultus sacri") had been paid to him before the Beatification by Leo X, and for at least a century before the unsuccessful process.[3] Pasqual also testifies that books "printed in Italy, France, Germany and Spain," at the very beginning of the sixteenth century, term him "Saint or Beatus or Martyr." [4] Certainly his Office and Mass were used in Mallorca in that century, the probability being that Leo X restricted their use to that island.[5] "In times past," says Vicens Mut, writing in 1650, "his particular Office was used, and some say that Pope Leo X permitted and granted a Proper Mass to be celebrated on the day of his martyrdom. But now we use only the Common of Saints, which is done with great solemnity and devotion." [6]

If the seventeenth century distinguished itself by the devotion of the Franciscans to Lull's memory,[7] the

[1] See Av., pp. 555–6. [2] *Vindiciae*, i, p. 356.

[3] Some of the relevant documents of the process are cited in Av., pp. 548 ff.; *cf.* Custurer, Disertación i ("Del Culto Inmemorial del B. Raymundo Lullio").

[4] *Vindiciae*, i, p. 356. [5] Av., p. 552, n. 1.

[6] *Vida del Venerable Mártir Raymundo Lulio*; *cf.* Av., pp. 551–2.

[7] On March 7, 1642, for example, Lullian teaching was ordered to be carried on in the Franciscan province of Mallorca, an order extended to the whole of Spain by the Chapter-General of 1688 (Sollier, *Acta Sanctorum*, p. 731).

eighteenth was to see a violent renewal of persecution, much though not all of which is attributable to the Dominicans. So petty was this in many of its manifestations that it is unnecessary to follow it in great detail. A few typical incidents will show its nature.

One June morning in 1699 an image of Ramon Lull disappeared from the University in Palma, and six days afterwards fragments of it were found in the precincts with a paper attached bearing the words "Inter haereticos locum," and others in the Franciscan convent, near the cell of the friar who occupied the University Chair of Lullian theology. The incident caused great excitement. The Bishop challenged the culprit to prove Lull's heresy, but no culprit appeared, a suspect was tried and acquitted, a great festival of reparation was held in the following August,[1] and in time the matter dropped.[2]

Whether as further reparation, or for other reasons, the *causa pia* was taken up again early in the eighteenth century. Josef Antoni de Cepeda, a fervent Lullist, who was then ruling the diocese, placed himself at the head of this movement, ordered a new inspection of Lull's remains, which was carried out in 1748, declared the cult of Lull, in 1749,[3] to be valid, and authorized prayers for his intercession during droughts which came in the two years following.[4] But for the indifference of Charles III, who then ruled Spain, some progress might have been made with the *causa pia*, for the attitude of Clement XIII was distinctly a friendly one. The Dominicans in Mallorca, needless to say, opposed these proceedings vehemently, and, as a consequence, were deprived of their Chairs in the University (1752) until a royal order (1761) rescinded this obvious injustice. In 1755, the year in

[1] The text of the sermon preached in the Cathedral by a Jesuit priest on that occasion is still extant. See Joan Bta. Torroella in *Revista luliana*, vol. ii., pp. 270–6, 304–11.

[2] Av.: *Història del lulisme*, pp. 543, ff.

[3] The text of the declaration is given in Av., pp. 555–6, together with that of a number of eighteenth-century documents (pp. 557–9) which show Rome's concurrence in the cultus paid to the Beatus.

[4] Av.: *Història del lulisme*, pp. 583, ff.

which Damián Cornejo's biography of Lull (1686)[1] was reprinted in Mallorca, numerous acts of vandalism are reported, such as the quenching and breaking of lamps before images of Lull, and it is clear that on both sides, about this time, there was much bad feeling.[2]

Cepeda's two successors in the Mallorcan diocese were both convinced Lullists, but in 1772 a Dominican Bishop, Juan Diaz de la Guerra, was elected, and from his entry into Palma on October 25 of that year he seems to have determined to put an end to the cult which his Order so deeply resented. The next five years are a record of feuds which reached the point of pitched battles.[3] It is said that Guerra plotted persecution in Dominican convents by night ; he may well have done so, for the lengths to which he went could hardly have been the result of one man's enmity. He rifled the library of the College of Sapiencia, founded in 1634 by a namesake and admirer of Lull. He cancelled the feasts of Ramon Lull (January 25 and June 30) in the diocesan almanac. He prohibited the giving of alms for the cult and even confiscated the collection plates. He seized portraits, images and harmless manuscripts. He forbade the use of the name of Ramon Lull as a name in baptism. He impounded even the moulds, blocks and standing type of printers when these bore any relation to the hated hero. Against his fanaticism, Lull's adherents, who of course grew steadily in numbers, could do little. What they could do, however, they did, keeping guard over Lull's tomb lest the Bishop should desecrate that also and complaining bitterly and strongly to the King. They had some success : a royal order arrived which prevented the conversion of the Sapiencia into a hospice (1776) ; further commands (1777) were that images and pictures of Lull that had been removed should be replaced, and the

[1] *Vida admirable del inclito mártir Raymundo Lulio*, Madrid, 1686 (Rogent i Duràn: *Bibliografía*, etc., pp. 229–30, 287–8, 347).

[2] The effects of the repercussion of this feeling in Rome are described in Armengual, p. 72, and Av. : *Història del lulisme*, pp. 586, ff. The latter relates the events of these years in Mallorca in much greater detail than is possible or desirable here.

[3] Av. : *Història del lulisme*, pp. 605–41.

excommunicate on Lull's account should be reinstated; and about the same time a boat arrived at Palma bearing the welcome tidings that the Bishop had been promoted to the see of Sigüenza.

While to the edification of none and to their own eternal discredit the Bishop and his followers were brawling, a great outburst of Lullian activity was taking place both in Spain and abroad. At the very beginning of the century, or, more correctly, at the end of the preceding one (1700), a Jesuit priest named Jaume Custurer (1657–1715) published his *Historical Dissertations* on Ramon Lull in Mallorca,[1] while in 1708 another Jesuit, the Belgian, P. Sollier (1665–1740), published in Antwerp a no less famous study of Lull's life and works in the *Acta Sanctorum*, incorporating the contemporary biography in its Latin version.[2] More important still was the work of Ivo Salzinger (1669–1727), to whom we owe the monumental edition of a large number of Lull's Latin works published at Mayence from 1721 to 1742,[3] and whom the Lullian University of Mallorca honoured and rewarded with the degree of Doctor. Salzinger includes in his first volume a more nearly complete text than Sollier's of the Latin contemporary life, the importance of which became clear when it was contrasted with biographies like those of Bouvelles and Pax. It is curious that the Catalan text, which differs notably from the Latin, and has long been known, has only quite recently been published[4]; and even more so that both Seguí and Wadding speak of having actually seen an autobiography of Lull, written, according to the first, at the request of Philip the Fair, and, according to the second, for James II of Mallorca.

The eighteenth century witnessed a great activity in Mallorcan publications of Lull's writings, but it was also

[1] See Bibliography, No. 135, and Rogent i Duràn: *Bibliografía*, etc., pp. 241-6.

[2] See Bibliography, No. 60, and Rogent i Duràn: *Bibliografía*, etc., pp. 253–5. Sollier was for many years president of the Congregation of Bollandists.

[3] On this edition, see Rogent i Duràn: *Bibliografía*, etc., pp. 264–84.

[4] See pp. viii, 351, above, and Bibliography, No. 61, below.

characterized by attacks on his memory, made by means of books and pamphlets, hardly less vehement, though certainly less crude, than the attacks already described in Mallorca. One of the best known of the polemists was Benito Jerónimo Feyjóo (1676–1764),[1] who, professing unwillingness to enter the fray, did so nevertheless with considerable zest and a surprising lack of humour.[2] The *Art* he ridiculed from beginning to end—and precursors, it must be allowed, had already made his task easy. Nor had he any difficulty in rebutting the extravagant claims made for Lull in Mallorca, where (says Feyjóo) he is venerated as a saint and referred to as the "trumpet of the Holy Spirit."[3] When, however, he contends that the uselessness of the *Art* is proved by the fact that it has never found favour nor has been taught publicly save in Mallorca, we suspect him of bolstering up his not impregnable case with generalities.[4] And he has, of course, no more conception than most of his contemporaries that there is any good in Ramon's works outside the *Art*. He was taken up by the Lullists without delay, notably by P. Fornés, a disciple of Salzinger's, who published a *Liber apologeticus Artis Magnae* at Salamanca in 1746,[5] and by one with a greater and more enduring name than Fornés' three years later.

This was the Cistercian monk Antoni Ramon Pasqual (1708–91),[6] Abbot of Ramon's beloved La Real and professor of philosophy in the Lullian University of Mallorca, who, in 1749–50, published in two volumes a reply to Feyjóo, and a defence of "the purity of Lullian doctrine and the utility of the Lullian Art and Science."[7]

[1] *Cartas eruditas y curiosas*, vol. ii, Letter 13, pp. 158–98. (The second edition—Madrid, 1750—is that used here and below.) Less important is vol. i, Letter 22, on the same subject; *cf.* Menéndez y Pelayo: *Historia de los heterodoxos españoles*, ed. 1880–1, iii, pp. 71–84; Rogent i Duràn: *Bibliografía*, etc., *passim*.

[2] *Ibid.*, p. 175.

[3] *Ibid.*, pp. 168, 197; *cf.* p. 375, n. 3, above.

[4] *Ibid.*, p. 190.

[5] *Cf.* Rogent i Duràn: *Bibliografía*, etc., pp. 315–17.

[6] Rogent i Duràn: *Bibliografía*, etc., p. 309, and index.

[7] *Examen de la Crisis del R.P. Maestro D. Benito Gerónimo Feijóo sobre el arte luliana*, per . . . el R.P. A. R. Pasqual. Madrid, 1749–50, 2 vols; *cf.* Rogent i Duràn: *Bibliografía*, etc., pp. 325–6.

With exaggerated modesty (as it now seems to us) he compares his opponent to Goliath and himself to a puny David : examining and disposing of Feyjóo's criticism, he goes on to defend his hero's character, work and teaching, the second volume broadening into a general exposition of the whole content of the Lullian writings. Without making claims for Ramon which would seem in his day to be in the least excessive, he holds him up to universal admiration as one " whose virtue and perfection appear to me indisputable, . . . a Mallorcan patriot of whom the whole world might be proud." [1]

But something much better than this " defence and illustration " of Lull's teaching came out of these controversies. Twenty-nine years later, in 1778, was published Pasqual's *Vindiciae lullianae*,[2] from the first part of which—a biography of Lull—we have more than once quoted. The polemical part of this work is now quite out of date, and the biographical part has of course in many of its findings been superseded. But it stands out head and shoulders above the biography and criticism of its time, and, indeed, it has served as the basis of much of the later criticism that has appeared, even down to the twentieth century. Nor must we omit to mention Pasqual's bibliographical work, for though his tables of the writings of Lull have now in many respects to yield to fuller knowledge, they have still to be reckoned with by the student, being based to a great extent upon actual acquaintance with the works listed and not merely on the work of predecessors. As well as the *Vindiciae*, Pasqual wrote a biography in Castilian, similar to the Latin biography but not identical with it, and published only in the year 1890. From this, which is handled and consulted more conveniently than the *Vindiciae*, most of our quotations of Pasqual are taken.

Since the events briefly recorded above, there has been little hostility on the part of the Dominicans to the veneration of Ramon Lull, and, on the other side, little progress with the *causa pia*. Any misgivings which might have

[1] *Examen*, etc. Prólogo.
[2] Rogent i Duràn : *Bibliografía*, etc., pp. 359–61.

existed as to the beatification of Ramon Lull by Leo X were removed by the confirmatory act of Pius IX, who, on September 11, 1847, allowed the use of the Office and Mass in Mallorca, assigning it to July 3,[1] and, on February 4, 1858, extended this use to the whole Franciscan Order.[2] On April 11, 1905, at the request (February 13, 1904) of the Bishop and clergy of Mallorca, the cultus was confirmed by Pius X,[3] and although, not unnaturally, Mallorcans and many other devotees of the Beatus throughout the world would like to see an extension of the Office and Mass, so that he may be *in via ad canonizationem*, the attempts which have been made to effect this have not, up to the present, been successful.[4]

It may be added here that the possibilities of Ramon's canonization are remote—not merely, as Mallorcans frequently assert, because they have too little influence at Rome, but also, and principally, because the orthodoxy of Ramon's writings is not unimpeachable. This may be thought unfair, for he submitted all his writings to the Church's correction, and she has pronounced in their favour more than once. But only in a general sense, it may be replied : it is not difficult to find passages of dubious orthodoxy. Further the fact that he was martyred for the Catholic faith has unhappily never been unanswerably demonstrated. The little that is known of his death makes it impossible for a Postulator to show that he was killed *in odium fidei* ; and, since there is presumptive evidence that his vigorous methods of attack and the boldness of his character may themselves have antagonized the Mohammedans and caused the final attack on him, the burden of proof lies with the Postulator. Up to the present the Promotor Fidei has not been able to accept his arguments as conclusive. It seems unlikely, therefore, that Ramon's beatification will for the present be extended.

For some time before it was duly confirmed, and

[1] The text of this is given in Av., pp. 560–1. [2] Av., pp. 562–3.

[3] The complete reply of Rome, in its Latin text, will be found in Av., pp. 564–87.

[4] *Cf.* S. Bové : "Història del culte sagrat y publich que 's dona al B. Ramon Lull." In *Revista luliana*, i, pp. 32–8.

continuously since the confirmation, Ramon's spirit has been allowed to rest untroubled by the clamour of controversy. It has almost seemed as if he who in life had disputed unceasingly was to be the subject of disputes for ever. He had fought the good fight until he fell, and for centuries men had wrangled over his body. But now at last we come to the period in which he enters into the kingdom of immortality. While his work was in fashion, while the modes of thought to which he was accustomed still prevailed, none could say what would be his fate in the future. But to-day the *Ars Magna* and its progeny are one and all discredited ; the exaggerations of scholasticism are laughed at ; one half of Ramon's schemes are seen to have been fantastic visions and the other half have for so long been accomplished in their essentials that we cannot easily imagine the time when they were considered daring reforms. Such upheavals of thought would have buried the work of a lesser man under their ruins. But Ramon Lull is great, and his work not only lives still, but enjoys a secure and growing reputation.

As we shall see in the next chapter, the establishment of this reputation implies a complete reversal of values, which has been brought about by the devoted labours of a few Mallorcan and Catalonian Lullists, during the latter half of the nineteenth century and the early years of the twentieth. Their contributions to Lullian studies have been both manifold and varied : searching for manuscripts, preparing editions, considering biographical problems, compiling bibliographies, examining with especial care the sources of Lull's writings, and applying themselves to the problems which are raised by the history of his ideas. Although first-rate critics like Menéndez y Pelayo have also borne a share in this task, and valuable work by a large number of Mallorcans and others has been published in such reviews as the extinct *Revista luliana*, the *Museo Balear*, and the bulletins of the Lullian Archaeological Society and the Academy of Barcelona, it will not be invidious to single out a small number of devoted men who have done most to make Lullian studies what they are.

Josep Maria Quadrado (1819–96) and Marian Aguiló (1825–97) are two of the earliest of these. Aguiló—poet, philologist and antiquarian—is remembered by Lullists chiefly for his editions of Lull's works.[1] Quadrado, an indefatigable historian and journalist, had an unrivalled knowledge of Mallorca, the story of the conquest of which he related, as well as its history in the fifteenth century. It is unfortunate that, like his successor Obrador, he never wrote the extensive work on Lull of which he often spoke, but made most of his direct contributions to the subject through the medium of pamphlets and articles.[2] But the indirect debt of Lullists to him is recognized by all.

Geroni Rosselló (1827–1902), to whom we owe, not only some volumes of Lull's prose, but the sole edition of the poems which approaches completeness,[3] was a lifelong enthusiast and student of the Beatus. A prominent Mallorcan poet, recently deceased, has called him "the incarnation of Lullism in our island."[4] He was writing on Lull up to the time of his last illness. Mateu Obrador (1853–1909) continued his work, going farther afield than he, to Munich, Milan and Venice, in search of manuscripts and early editions, and handling the results with the sureness and the zeal of the scholar born. Lullian studies have also been furthered, in one direction or another, by Antoni Rubió i Lluch (b. 1856), Josep Torras i Bages (1846–1916), Miquel dels Sants Oliver (1864–1920), Joan Maura (1841–1910) and Miquel Costa i Llobera (1854–1922). Nor must we forget the contributions of foreigners like Adam Gottron and J. H. Probst or the influence of the long article on Lull in the *Histoire littéraire de la France*. The author of this, it is true, is unsympathetic in his attitude to Ramon as a man, but the information which he has collected and set out is invaluable to the student, though

[1] See Bibliography, No. 66, below. He also frequently published short poems and selections. See Manuel de Montoliu : *Manual d'història crítica de la literatura catalana moderna*. Barcelona, 1922, pp. 275–6.

[2] In the *Unidad Católica*, *Museo Balear*, and elsewhere.

[3] See Bibliography, Nos. 65, 68, below.

[4] Juan Alcover : *El Lulismo en Mallorca*, etc., p. 12.

some of it is already out of date and it sorely lacks the elementary apparatus of an index.

The sexcentenary of Ramon's martyrdom was kept in 1915, and, though overshadowed by the death, four months before the festival, of Mgr. Campins, the beloved Mallorcan Bishop who had planned such great things for it, was nevertheless the occasion of many solemnities. Ten years earlier, a " Comissió Editora Lulliana " had inaugurated a modern edition of Lull's Catalan works, in many volumes, of which a substantial proportion was to be completed by the festival. In spite of unforeseen difficulties, ten such volumes had in fact appeared in 1915, and others have since been published. With the early volumes of this edition will be associated the names of Mateu Obrador and Antoni Maria Alcover ; with the later volumes, the name of Salvador Galmés. To estimate the full importance of this magnificent work is impossible. It has made accessible those of Lull's writings which to modern ideas are by far the most attractive. It has revealed to many Catalonians who read no Latin and know of him only by name and tradition the real nature of his genius. And it has given the world at large three things at least which, had they been possessed by past ages, might have entirely changed the history of Lullian appreciation : the vast and complete *Book of Contemplation*, a reliable text of *Blanquerna*, and, more recently, the complete *Tree of Science*. To the same desire to make Lull known throughout the world as engendered this edition must be ascribed a number of recent biographies—all, unhappily, partial, but complementary. Such are the admirably compact little *Vida compendiosa* of Mn. Galmés (1915), the exquisitely written *Vida i actes* of the poet Mn. Riber, his slighter and more popular *Vida abreujada* (1921), and the longer but by no means satisfactory biography of Mn. Avinyó (1912). Much valuable scientific work which cannot be detailed briefly but is reflected in our Bibliography is being performed by a group of younger Catalan scholars in Barcelona. The leaders of this group are En Ramon d'Alòs and En Jordi Rubió i Balaguer, whose joint

Memoria, published by the Institut d'Estudis Catalans in 1914, is a very useful and significant contribution to the history of Lullian studies, and of much greater importance than its length and nature would suggest. Finally, mention must be made of the admirable and detailed article on Lull by P. Ephrem Longpré in the *Dictionnaire de Théologie Catholique* (1927), which is in reality a critical study in outline quoted frequently in this book for its bibliographical information, and of the still more recently published bibliography (1927) of the known editions of Lull's works between 1480 and 1859 which has been many years in the making, is chiefly due to the labours of N'Estanislau Duràn and the late Elíes Rogent, and has been completed and seen through the press by En Ramon d'Alòs.

A feature of Lullian studies in the twentieth century has been the serious attention given by Arabic scholars to Lull's Oriental sources. The conclusions to which their researches have led them are such as to arouse both interest and expectation, though they have perhaps not seemed to unbiassed students as important as their authors have thought them. Julián Ribera, for example, in 1899,[1] found resemblances between the *Hundred Names of God*, *Blanquerna* and the *Book of the Lover and the Beloved*, and works of the Moslem philosopher and mystic Mohidín Abenarabi,[2] especially his *Alfotuhat*. The verbal similarities, Ribera freely acknowledges,[3] are but slight, and his findings are based largely upon general resemblances, and upon the assumption that Lull knew more Arabic than Latin, having " learned no Latin in the schools," yet being a " distinguished master " in Arabic.[4] This assumption, probably, few will be inclined to grant.

More recently, Don Miguel Asín Palacios, a brilliant pupil and follower of Ribera,[5] best known in this country

[1] " Orígenes, etc." (Bibliography, No. 211).

[2] *Ibid.*, pp. 212–13. Ribera goes so far as to say of Mohidín (p. 200): " [Su] vida, opiniones y sistema son como un retrato anticipado de la vida, opiniones y sistema del filósofo mallorquín." He does not, however, marshal much evidence to support so strong an assertion.

[3] *Ibid.*, p. 215.

[4] *Ibid.*, pp. 192–3.

[5] See Miguel Asín : " Mohidin " (Bibliography, No. 104).

by his arresting work on *Dante and Islam*, has taken a somewhat aggressive line with those who still maintain Lull's essential originality. As justification of this he has adduced some similarities of thought between Lull and Mohidín Abenarabi,[1] alleged further reminiscences in Lull of the latter's works, and discussed characteristic details of Lull's writings and geometrical method, such as the use of letters as symbols for ideas, of the word *dignitates* for the Divine attributes, of figures which suggest Arabic love-poetry rather than Hebrew or Christian, of conceptions of the Beloved which are Oriental or clothed in Oriental dress.

It is too early to give a considered judgment on these matters, which have not yet been studied as fully and as systematically as is possible. The ideas of Ribera and Sr. Asín Palacios have been vigorously combated, not always without *parti pris*, and the most ardent of the combatants, such as Mn. Salvador Bové (1869–1915), have tended rather to rush to the opposite extreme, to deny that Lull used Arabic sources at all, and to endeavour to derive his work (in so far as they will allow it to be derivative) from the Bible and the Fathers only.[2] The truth is probably that Lull frequently followed Moslem literature in matters of detail, but that it had little or no influence upon his intellectual formation and only a subsidiary influence upon his work anywhere.

Two signs of progress of another kind in nineteenth-century Lullian history may be commented upon to conclude this chapter. It was a happy day for the domain of Miramar when it first attracted, and was bought by, a wealthy young man of thirty—a descendant of Rudolf of Habsburg, the late Archduke Louis Salvator of Austria.[3] From 1867 to 1915 (when he died) the Archduke spent a great part of his life on the extensive

[1] *Abenmasarra y su escuela*, Madrid, 1914.

[2] See Bové : *El sistema científico luliano* ; Probst : *Caractère et origine*, etc. (Bibliography, Nos. 126, 200) ; P. Longpré (cols. 1132–3) gives an opinion on the controversy, and also develops (1133–4) the view, already put forward by others, that Lull probably derives more than has been supposed from Roger Bacon.

[3] Cf. *Obras*, i, pp. 9–19.

estate, which he set himself to beautify and enrich, as a memorial to one whose earliest and purest Christian ideals were centred upon its future. Many a traveller during those years, availing himself of the kindly hospitality which built and maintained a guest-house for pilgrims to Miramar, has spent days among the woods and cliffs which overhang the still, blue Mediterranean, and speak, not of the strife and ambition which brought the missionary college to ruin, but of the loving idealism which founded it and the tranquillity which reigned in it while it lived. Nor did the Archduke forget Ramon's continual preaching of the doctrine of the Holy Trinity and the "great devotion" which "the people of those parts conceived . . . to the virtues of the altar of the Holy Trinity which was in the church."[1] For the tourist to visit in the estate there are the cave and the spring which tradition has named after Ramon, and the carefully chosen miradors whence the views on a clear summer's day are unrivalled. For the pilgrim there is the tiny chapel of the Holy Trinity, where, on Trinity Sunday, the people flock from all over the island for the festival.

The Archduke has gone, and, through his country's adversity, his fortune has dwindled to nothing, but it may be hoped that his example, once given, will be followed in successive generations by others. More recent is the resuscitation of Randa, Ramon's other shrine, set in a country less luxuriant than that of the north-western Sierra, but speaking even more eloquently of his character, and richer in memories of both his life and teaching. During the nineteenth century it fell into a lamentable state of desolation, and it was not until the appointment to the diocese of Mgr. Campins, a patriotic Mallorcan by birth, education and residence, that there began for it a new era of prosperity. After some years of preparatory restoration, a small community of Franciscan tertiaries was installed there in 1913, the walls were rebuilt, the chapel was restored, and for the first time in its history the Sacrament was reserved there. With the revival of the festival of the Mare de Deu

[1] *Blanquerna*, chap. 98 (*Bl.*, p. 408).

de Cura, who is venerated there, the inauguration of pilgrimages from all over the island, and the sex-centenary celebrations crowning all, the renaissance of devotion in Randa may be considered complete.

Here, above all other places in Mallorca, and indeed elsewhere, the pilgrim may lose himself in Ramon's past and live his very life in imagination. So austere is the situation of Mount Randa, so extensive is the view from its summit, so convincing are the terrace and the cave which tradition makes Ramon's dwelling-place, that it only needed a Franciscan community to imbue it with his spirit. Even the fact that the Lullian science is no longer taught there is symbolical, for the Lull whom Randa presents to us now is not the figure of mediaeval times—an outworn shell—but the figure concealed beneath the shell, who lives and breathes and is immortal.

To present in its essential outline that figure, once hidden but now fully revealed, is the task remaining to us which will be attempted in the final chapter.

CHAPTER XIX

Ramon Lull to-day. Claims made for him in the past as prophet, philosopher, alchemist, theologian, etc. Beginnings of the modern orientation of Lullian studies at the time of the Catalan renaissance. Lull as patriarch of Catalan literature,—as an immortal personality,—as active and contemplative in one,—as a typical Franciscan.

By the very magnitude of his literary achievements, Ramon Lull deserves a niche in literary history. The dynamic quality of his temperament, denied one form of expression principally by causes beyond his control, found an outlet in another form which none could forbid him, and the result is astonishing to consider. The Sicilian Mariano Accardo Sículo, who was well known as a Lullist in the sixteenth century, makes him the author of three thousand works. Custurer, on Mut's authority, quotes a more modest statement of Joan Llobet that he had himself read over five hundred of Lull's books, and adds that "others say his works amount to a thousand, and others that they exceed three thousand and even four."[1] We need not credit these assertions in order to rank Lull as one of the most fertile writers of the Middle Ages. Before the Council of Vienne, the contemporary biography declares that his works number "more than an hundred and twenty and three"[2]; the two catalogues of 1311 and 1314 together, though omitting many Lullian writings known to be genuine, raise this total by thirty[3]; and Pasqual, whose attempt to draw up a complete list is more successful than most such

[1] Custurer, pp. 539–40; *cf.* pp. 337–8, Av., p. 589, and Alòs: *Los Catálogos*, etc, p. 9.

[2] *Life*, p. 44; *cf.* p. 351, n. 1, above.

[3] Alòs: *Los Catálogos*, etc., pp. 14–17.

efforts have been, arrives at the respectable sum of two hundred and fifty.[1]

But we must not confuse magnitude with greatness, and the Latin genius has always tended less towards concentration than towards self-dispersal over a wide field of activity. We are concerned rather with quality than with quantity. Wherein lies Ramon Lull's greatness? What is there of permanent value in his writings? These are questions which have been answered in many different ways during the last six centuries. From the standpoint of to-day we can answer them best by looking back, first of all, over the period that has intervened since his death and taking stock of the claims that have been made for him.

Much of his vogue during the Middle Ages, and not a few of the extravagances uttered in his defence, are traceable to a belief that the *Ars Magna* would do what its author claimed for it; that, as he himself held, it was perfect and indestructible, being in no sense his own work, but directly and literally inspired by God. Some such belief as this underlies the foundation of the Lullian schools, lectureships and like institutions, and the opposition to Lull's writings by those who thought them heretical was all the fiercer because of the importance attached to them by their defenders. Strange as it may seem to us, there really were those who could take seriously the refrain:

> Tres sabios hubo en el mundo,
> Adán, Salomón y Raymundo.[2]

and there were even those who could quote the notorious remark, attributed to one Pere Rossell, that the Old Testament was the work of God the Father, the New Testament of God the Son, and the writings of Ramon

[1] *Vindiciae*, i, pp. 369–74. This list includes a few translations as separate works and counts two parts of the same book, in some places, as two books. This, however, does not greatly modify the total, to which that arrived at in the present biography is about equal; *cf.* Alòs: *Los Catálogos*, etc., pp. 43–4.

[2] "There have been three wise men in the world: Adam, Solomon and Ramon." The lines were frequently quoted on both sides in the controversies of the eighteenth century.

of God the Holy Spirit.[1] The reaction against these absurdities was bound to come. In due time the man who has been described as being "before Dante himself, the great popular philosopher of the thirteenth century"[2] was ridiculed for his philosophy, not only by polemists in Spain like Feyjóo, but abroad, in mere allusiveness, by novelists like Rabelais[3] and scientists like Francis Bacon.[4] To-day Ramon's importance as a philosopher is only historical.[5] He may be "in some respects one of the most remarkable figures in the history of mediaeval philosophy,"[6] but he is principally remembered as one of the most curious and picturesque.

Nor is he taken more seriously as (if the usual sense of the term be adhered to) a theologian. His campaign against the Averroists, and his stalwart defence of the unity of philosophy and theology, excite our admiration still, but they excite nothing else, so far removed from us is their epoch. Ink, if not blood, was freely and unprofitably spilt over the question of whether or no Ramon exalted the understanding unduly and claimed that the truths of revealed religion could be proved by intellectual processes without the aid of faith. To-day it seems clear enough that, whatever of heresy can be extracted from his writings by the method of isolating passages from their context,[7] Ramon had not the slightest intention of despising or underrating the importance of faith. Again and again he declared its supremacy. Faith is necessarily higher than intellect, even as oil is higher than the water above which it floats.[8] Far from desiring to make any

[1] Pujols, *op. cit.*, p. 53.

[2] Probst, *art. cit.* (*Criterion*, vol. iii, p. 210).

[3] "Laisse-moi l'astrologie divinatrice et l'art de Lullius, comme abus et vanités" (*Pantagruel*, chap. 8).

[4] He describes the *Ars Magna* as "methodus imposturae, quae tamen quibusdam ardelionibus acceptissima procul dubio fuerit." (*De Augment Scient.*, lib. vi, cap. 2 : ed. Wirceburgi, 1779–80, ii, p. 94).

[5] A summary of Lull's philosophy, brilliant in its concentration, will be found in Longpré, cols. 1113–19.

[6] Wm. Turner : *History of Philosophy*, Boston, 1903, p. 394.

[7] *Cf.* Menéndez y Pelayo : *Historia de los Heterodoxos Españoles*, Madrid, 1917, bk. iii, chap. 5, *passim* ; Longpré, cols. 1122–6, and pp. 378–80, above.

[8] *Ars Magna*, chap. 63 : Et sic fides ascendit super intellectum, sicut oleum ascendit super aquam.

opposition between the Articles and faith, he affirms that they cannot be proved without its aid.[1] It is faith which illumines the understanding[2]; or, to change the metaphor, the understanding mounts by means of it[3]; or again, faith and understanding are a man's two feet, each being equally necessary to anyone who possesses both.[4] Before understanding can function in these lofty spheres, the possibility of there being mysteries of religion must be known (which is the work of faith),[5] and there must further be the "habit of faith," which comes from the grace of God,[6] a predisposition towards belief, "a presupposition by faith that the fourteen articles can be proved."[7] And, even if this be present, the kind of proof that can be urged is a proof *per aequiparantiam*[8]: not absolute but relative—a process of argument which frequently is concerned only with what is congruent or "fitting"[9]—a "Demonstratio, sive Persuasio," in no way appearing, as rationalistic proof

[1] *Liber de convenientia fidei et intellectus in objecto*, pt. i (Salz., iv, p. 4): "Et ideo ego, qui sum verus Catholicus, non intendo probare Articulos contra fidem, sed mediante fide; cum sine ipsa non possem probare; nam Articuli sunt per superius, et meus intellectus est per inferius, et Fides est habitus, cum quo Intellectus ascendit super suas vires."

[2] *Liber de quatuordecim articulis*, etc. Prologue (Salz., ii, p. 1): "Fides est illuminatio intellectus," etc.

[3] *Ars Magna*, chap. 63: Fides est medium cum quo intellectus acquirit meritum, et ascendit ad primum objectum, quod quidem influit intellectui fidem, ut ipsa sit intellectui unus pes ad ascendendum; *cf.* n. 1 above.

[4] *Ibid*: Et intellectus habet alium pedem de sua natura, videlicet intelligere: sicut homo ascendens scalam cum duobus pedibus. Et in primo scalone ponitur pes fidei. Et in illomet pes intellectus ascendendo gradatim.

[5] *Liber mirandarum demonstrationum*, bk. iii, chap. 49 (Salz., ii, pp. 160–62); *Ars inveniendi particularia in universalibus*, dist. ii, pt. 1 (Salz., iii, pp. 3–4).

[6] *Brevis practica Tabulae Generalis*, pt. iii, chap. 3 (Salz., v, p. 32). Cf. *Disputatio Eremitae et Raymundi*, etc. (Quaest. 113, § 1, Salz., iv, p. 97); *Disputatio Raymundi Christiani et Hamar Saraceni*, pt. ii, chap. 3, sig. 22 (Salz., iv, p. 41: a brief and clear statement); *Liber de Homine*, dist. ii, pt. iib (Salz., vi, p. 34).

[7] *Liber de quatuordecim articulis*, etc. Prologue (Salz., ii, p. 1).

[8] *Liber de demonstratione per aequiparantiam*. Prologue (Salz., iv, pp. 1–2). Cf. *Disputatio Raymundi Christiani et Hamar Saraceni*, pt. ii, chap. 20 (Salz., iv, pp. 33–4).

[9] Though as Costa y Llobera says (Prologue to *Obras*, vol. ii, p. xix), for the frequently repeated word *coué* ("it befits") is not infrequently substituted the phrase *coué de necesitat*.

would do, to limit God,[1] but negatively of supreme importance, since no infidel can destroy it.[2]

If the failure by missionaries and other teachers in Lull's day to make use of apologetics exasperated him into over-insistence upon their efficacy, the fact is not surprising. His general position on this important subject is that of St. Thomas Aquinas, who upheld apologetics and made use of "necessary reasons" to prove all but a few of the higher truths of Christianity. The differences between him and Ramon are partly of emphasis and partly of method. Ramon sought, on the one hand, to press the unbelievers as closely as he could towards acceptance of the doctrines of the Holy Trinity and of the Incarnation: perhaps, in his passionate antagonism to the much bruited belief that what was true according to faith could be false according to reason, and *vice versa*, he pressed them sometimes too far. On the other hand, he used his arguments too little for defence and too much for attack, for they were frequently negative rather than positive. Again this is an excess of the enthusiast, readily pardonable by those who live in an age when so much love has grown cold. Whether or no Ramon stepped for a moment, now and then, beyond the boundary line of orthodoxy is no longer a matter of prime importance: it is swallowed up by other considerations as the less is by the greater.

Another question which excited past ages but which may now be considered as finally put to rest is the long-debated one of whether or no Ramon was an alchemist. So great was his fame that for centuries after his death

[1] As Lull himself says (*Desconort*, xxvi) in reply to an imaginary criticism:

> . . . És ja damunt provat
> que la fe es pot provar, si bé n'havets membrat;
> e si bé es pot provar, no es segueix que creat
> contenga e comprena tot lo éns increat,
> mas que n' entén aitant com a ell se n'és dat. . . .

[2] *Liber de convenientia fidei et intellectus in objecto*, pt. i (Salz., vol. iv, p. 4): Non autem dico, quod probem Articulos Fidei per causas, quia Deus non habet causas supra se, sed per talem modum, quod Intellectus non potest rationabiliter negare illas rationes, et possunt solvi omnes objectiones contra ipsas factae, et infideles non possunt destruere tales rationes vel positiones; talis est ista Probatio, sive dicatur Demonstratio, sive Persuasio, vel quocunque alio modo possit dici, hoc non curo, quia propter nostrum affirmare vel negare nihil mutatur in re.

the works of others were foisted upon his reputation, both of set purpose, by men who were anxious that their writings should receive attention, and unconsciously, by critics who genuinely believed them to be his.[1] It is understandable enough, in view of Ramon's interest, which his genuine works attest, in natural science,[2] that some of these apocryphal writings should be treatises on alchemy. The surprising fact is that, in spite of strong internal evidence to the contrary,[3] they should ever have been attributed to him by men so well informed as Salzinger and Rosselló, the latter of whom could say that Lull's "chief title to glory and immortality is as a chemist."[4] Fortunately the vast majority of Lullian scholars have taken a saner view, recognizing that Ramon himself, in works known to be genuine, repeatedly attacked the alchemists' pretensions[5]—a fact which,

[1] Some of these were written by a converted Jew named Raimundo de Tárraga, who lived in the fourteenth century, and wrote alchemical works, as well as others which were condemned by Gregory XI.

[2] Torras i Bages (pp. 222–3) considers that the *Liber Chaos* alone is sufficient to decide in the affirmative the question of whether Lull was an alchemist. It is right to add that he qualifies this noun with the words: "prenent aquest nom en la significació de naturalista experimental."

[3] The pseudo-Lullian *Libro de la quinta esencia*, for example, is described as having been finished in Paris in 1319. The *Epistola accurtationis lapidis philosophorum Raymundi Lullii ad Regem Robertum* is said to have been presented to a "Roberto Anglorum Regi," who never existed. Luanco cites these (pp. 33 ff.) and other examples.

[4] *Obras rimadas*, p. 112.

[5] The most important passages from these works only can be cited:

I. *Quaestio.* Utrum Alchymia sit scientia?

Dico, quod non, et hoc probo sic. Suppono, quod sit magnum bonum, magnum verum esse, quod Alchymia non sit scientia, et quod hoc intelligere et amare sit magnum bonum, magnum verum esse; et si contraria suppositio est vera, de necessitate sequitur, quod Alchymista habeat ita magnum vigorem bonum et verum artificialiter, sicut agens naturale naturaliter, et quod hoc intelligere et amare sit magnum bonum, magnum verum esse, quod est falsum et impossibile: ergo concluditur quod Alchymia non sit scientia, sed sit figmentum. (*De novo modo demonstrandi*; Salz., iv, p. 16.)

II. Unum metallum in speciem alterius metalli converti non potest. . . . Forma, quam Alchimista extraneae materiae dat, brevi tempore in corruptionem perducitur. (*Liber principiorum medicinae*, dist. vi, chap. 20; Salz., i, p. 31.)

III. *Quaestio.* Utrum Alchymia sit in re vel in ratione tantum?

Quod nullus artifex potest aliud animal transferre in aliud, vel aliam plantam in aliam, similiter nec Alchymista potest transmutare aliam speciem metalli in aliam, etc. (*Quaestiones per Artem Demonstrativam seu Inventivam solubiles*, 166), Salz., iv, p. 165.

apart from other considerations, is surely final. It may be added that not a single alchemical work is attributed to Lull in either the contemporary biography or the contemporary catalogues, and that the earliest known manuscript of such a work dates only from the fifteenth century. The *coup de grâce* to the alchemical legend was given in 1870 by a Spanish scientist of repute, Luanco,[1] and since that time few writers have upheld it.[2]

One of the results of the belief in Lull the alchemist was the neglect of many of his genuine works in favour of sensational and ephemeral books attributed to him which he never wrote. Nearly all the early catalogues include a large number of spurious works: hardly any writer before Pasqual can be said to shake himself free from them. A further source of exaggeration in this regard was the cataloguing as distinct works of several editions of the same book bearing each a slightly different title, a practice which has not failed to confuse modern bibliographers also.

Another question, of entirely secondary importance, over which long controversy has raged, is whether or no Ramon is to be numbered among the earliest defenders in Spain of the dogma of the Immaculate Conception of Our Lady. During the centuries of strife now past no title was claimed for Lull more vigorously by his partisans than "first defender of the Immaculate Conception." [3]

IV. *Quaestio.* Utrum Alchymia sit possibilis?

Elementativa habet veras conditiones, et una species non se transmutat in aliam speciem. Et in isto passu Alchimistae dolent et habent ocasionem flendi. (*Ars generalis ultima*, pt. xi, sect. v, chap. 15.)

Other and less definite indications will be found in *Liber Demonstrationum*, *Liber Chaos*, *Felix*, *Liber super quaestiones Atrebatenses*, *Arbre de Sciencia*; *cf.* Borrás y Rullán, *Espíritu*, etc., pp. 79–81.

[1] *Ramon Lull considerado como alquimista*, Barcelona, 1870.

[2] Exceptions are Torras i Bages (pp. 222–6), Mn. Avinyó (Av., pp. 306–10), and Fr. Querubín de Carcagente (in *Revista luliana*, 1902, i, pp. 114–122). P. Longpré (cols. 1111–12) gives a useful bibliography of this question.

[3] To quote the *gozos* (Cat. *goigs*) supporting the project for Lull's canonization:

> Hagamos bien a la Causa Pía
> del santo Mallorquín mayor,
> de la Fe gran defensor
> y defensor de María.

A large part of Mn. Avinyó's *Història del lulisme* is devoted to this question.

The title has also been keenly contested. It has been too generally assumed that its applicability to Lull depends on the genuineness of the *Benedicta Tu* [1] which is at best uncertain.[2] Actually an answer can be given from Ramon's authentic works, for, though he is as a rule very reticent in them on the subject, there is a passage, already alluded to,[3] in the *Dispute between Ramon and the Hermit*, which, since this book is certainly genuine and there is no evidence of interpolation, puts the matter beyond doubt.

In this passage Ramon states clearly that he considers the Blessed Virgin to have been born without stain of sin whatsoever.[4] The hermit with whom he is disputing replies rather weakly that all humanity was corrupted by original sin, and Our Lady, being conceived before the Redemption, contracted this like everyone else. "Before a house is actually built," answers Ramon, "its end—*i.e.* habitation—is conceived. Just so the Redemption was a part of God's plan before it was effected: everything was made ready for it, and part of the preparation was the sinlessness of Our Lady." [5]

Clearly then, Lull was an upholder of the Immaculate Conception; but, welcome as the fact may be to many, it is merely a side issue, to emphasize which unduly is to obscure, as past ages have done, Lull's real greatness.

[1] See p. 356, n. 2, above. [2] See p. 356, n. 2, above.

[3] See p. 278, above.

[4] The most important part of the quotation runs:

. . . Nisi Beata Virgo fuisset disposita, quod Filius Dei de ipsa assumeret carnem, scilicet quod non esset corrupta, nec in aliquo peccato sive actuali sive originali, Filius Dei non potuisset ab ipsa assumere carnem; cum Deus et peccatum non possint concordari in aliquo subjecto . . .

Sicut Deus non assumpsit hominem sed humanam naturam, sic semen, de quo fuit Beata Virgo, non assumpsit peccatum a suis parentibus, sed sanctificationem a Sancto Spiritu, qui "sic preparavit Viam Incarnationis per Sanctificationem, sicut sol diem per auroram." (*Disputatio Eremitae et Raymundi super aliquibus dubiis quaestionibus sententiarum magistri Petri Lombardi*: bk. iii, quaestio 96: "Utrum Beata Virgo contraxerit Peccatum Originale": Salz., iv, pp. 83–4.)

[5] Finis Recreationis fuit ante conceptus, quam fuit Recreatio, et Filius Dei, qui concepit et voluit finem, sic et multo melius praeparavit et ordinavit omnia pertinentia ad Recreationem a principio usque ad finem, sicut bonus artifex praeparat et ordinat materiam camerae a principio usque ad finem. . . .(*Ibid.*, p. 84).

Nor is service rendered either to Our Lady or to Ramon's reputation by attempts to find further proofs where they do not exist [1] and basing unjustifiable assumptions on those we have.[2] The claim, so frequently urged and so entirely unsubstantiated, that Ramon is the originator of the famous "Potuit, decuit, ergo fecit," is typical of too much Lullian apologetic.

In the foregoing pages we have passed in brief review some of the principal reasons for which Ramon Lull has been judged an immortal. They range from that which he himself alleged—that he was the divinely inspired exponent of a method for converting the whole world—to the preposterous and even ludicrous claims at which he would have been the first to be astonished.[3] He is the discoverer of nitric acid, of a Great Elixir, even of America ! [4] "He has been represented as a troubadour, a disillusioned Don Juan, a naturalist, a jurisconsult, a musician, a mathematician, a chemist, a navigator, a theologian . . . as everything except what he was,"[5]—as what he *was*, and is now recognized to be, in contradistinction from what he *did*, or possibly may have done.

To reveal Ramon Lull as he was, is and probably

[1] The chief of these is the claim of Lullian authorship for the *Liber de conceptu virginali* (see p. 315, above).

[2] See, on this subject, Pasqual, ii, pp. 107 ff., Av., pp. 395–403, 510–11, and the Catalan edition of *Liber de conceptu virginali*; Ramon Arques y Arrufat: *Lo dogma de la immaculada en la literatura catalana antiga*, Barcelona, 1905, chap. ii ; M. Gayá Bauzá : "El amor de María según el Doctor Iluminado," in *Revista luliana*, iii, pp. 203–8, 248–50 ; J. Pijoan : "De com lo Beat Ramon Lull va escriure lo llibre de Santa María," *ibid*, iii, pp. 285–6 ; Pedro Arolas y Vergés : "Ramon Llull y la immaculada," *ibid.*, iv, pp. 43–8 ; Borrás y Rullán : *María S.*, etc. (which contains some very unconvincing quotations). The Biblioteca Provincial of Palma has a vast collection of memorials and other kinds of ephemeral literature bearing on this subject.

[3] See J. F. de Masdeu : *Historia crítica de España*, etc., i, p. 39.

[4] See *Raymund Lully's Great Elixir, a dramatic poem* (London 1869), which incorporates and amplifies these traditions, making Lull an alchemist before he became a monk ; also Av., chap. 18 : "En Llull descubreix l'América."

[5] Miquel Ferrà, p. 7. In quoting this one need not hold that the author's conclusion expresses the whole of the truth : "Y s'és fet d'ell un trovador, un Don Juan desenganyat, un naturalista, un jurisperit, un músic, un matemàtic, un químic, un nàutic, un teòlec . . . tot menys allò que fou essencialment per damunt qualsevol altra cosa : un generós utopista i un místic excels d'ànima roenta."

will be for generations, is the only task which now remains to us. We shall present him under three aspects.

The beginnings of the modern orientation of Lullian studies may with a little ingenuity be traced back to Pasqual's *Vindiciae* in the eighteenth century, the first volume of which is quoted still with perhaps a little too much deference, though in it, as in the entire work, can be found the germ of much that has since come to flower. But the first evident traces of the present-day conception of Lull are found early in the nineteenth century, when the Catalan renaissance brought him into prominence as one of the heroes of Catalonia and its language. It was an imposing gallery of portraits that diligent search in the neglected and well-nigh ruined ancestral castle brought to light: James the Conqueror, Arnau de Vilanova, Ramon Muntaner and Bernat Metge are figures that will stand proudly anywhere. And Ramon of the Barba Florida stood worthily among them. To him was largely due the fact that of modern European languages Catalan was the first to take a place beside Latin as the instrument of philosophy. He, and none other, was the herald of the glories of Catalan poetry,[1] so pre-eminent, after so long an eclipse, to-day. He, again, was the greatest precursor, if not actually the first, of that noble company of religious writers, ascetics and mystics both, who flourished during the Golden Age in Spain.[2]

Having regarded Lull thus, and having set him upon a pinnacle which he fully deserved to occupy centuries before, it was essential for these Catalan writers, not only

[1] I write this deliberately, for it represents one part of Lull's due. An Englishman may perhaps be a suitable person to hold the balance between the "exagerado apasionamiento" of Ruiz, Bové, and others which Sr. Asín attacks, and the latter's own exaggerated reactions against this when he refuses to consider Lull, a "místico anormal del siglo xiii," as "padre del pensamiento catalán del siglo xx" (*El lulismo exagerado*, pp. 535–6).

[2] All these points have been made by one writer or another in Catalonia, but I know only Obrador to have summed them up as concisely and emphatically as in his edition of *L.A.A.*, p. 24:

Pot ben dirse y assegurar que fins a'n els nostres dies no s'havía atribuít expressament al autor del *Amich e Amat* el concepte que mereix, de pare y patriarca de la nostre poesía; ni fins ara se'l havía colocat en el pre-eminent lloch que li correspon, com a precursor de tots els místichs y ascètichs, no tan sols de Catalunya, sino dels de tota Espanya.

to produce in accessible form the works which justified their action, but to make their reasons for it explicit. Then it was that the extent of Lull's claims to immortality, from the standpoint of pure literature, came to light. Of these we have already given some idea. His prose, at its best, when not impeded by the exigences of convention, is simple, naive, unaffected, as beautiful as the language in which it is written and as direct in its appeal to the intellect as the thoughts which it expresses are to the heart. His verse, unequal indeed, but ranging over a great variety of metres and seldom unworthy of preservation, has much the same charm, with the added distinction of being in the purest Catalan, and less influenced by Provençal than that of most of his contemporaries at a time when Provençal influence everywhere was high.[1] As a poet he is seldom at his best in verse media, but through both his verse and his prose the spirit of poetry shines clearly : the vividness of his allegories, the beauty of his symbolism, the lofty flights of his imagination—all this and more marks him out from his fellows, and, for a long time, from his Catalan followers.[2] Further, as we have already suggested,[3] a comparative study of the beginnings of prose fiction in Europe will make it clear how surprisingly mature is Lull's *chef-d'œuvre* of romances, *Blanquerna*, and how high a place in the early history of the novel must, on his account, be given to Catalonia.

We have no thought of comparing Lull, as others have done and none too happily, with Dante,[4] or making claims for him on the literary side which his Catalan works do not bear out fully. These may safely be left to speak for themselves, for in the last hundred years they have won a secure place in European literature.

[1] En Ramon d'Alòs (*Poesies*, p. 9) even says : " La seva llengua poètica ès essencialment catalana, i ell és, en aquest sentit, més catalá que cap dels seus contemporanis i que la major part dels poetes nostrats dels segles xiv i xv."

[2] " poeta qui fa del nostre llenguatge un altre verger celestial, florit com els de la Umbria, pels aucells de la poesia franciscana" (Miquel Ferrà, p. 17).

[3] *Cf.* pp. 166–7 above.

[4] *E.g.* Torras i Bages, p. 251 : " Lull és poeta com l'Alighieri, de formes nues, de soliditat de matèria, és sa poesia ambrosia que satisfà i delecta als déus, etc."

The point at issue here is that this aspect of Lull's genius was for centuries not apparent. Men wrangled over his theological terminology, and vainly endeavoured to defend or overthrow philosophical works which the progress of thought had already condemned to oblivion. And all the time they could not see that Ramon was "a poet before he was a master of the schools, a man of intuition more truly than a student, and in this sense, if you will, a true 'illuminate.'" [1]

If Lull's position as patriarch of Catalan literature has made him a hero in Catalonia, how much more have his character and life-story made him beloved of the whole Christian world! His personality is in all his writings, and to find it the reader tolerates their length and repetitions, and is rewarded.[2] The suggestion has been made that, in the controversies which raged round those writings, it was Lull's life and character which gave eternal vigour to his defenders rather than any inspiration which they found in the works themselves, or any faith in their future.[3] It is certainly not his writings which have made him a missionary hero among English-speaking peoples, for the authors of the sympathetic if frequently inaccurate biographies of Lull which have appeared in English have not known his Catalan works at first hand and not always a great deal about his Latin works. It may not be out of place to add that the publication in English of the *Book of the Lover and the Beloved* has brought its translator letters from all over the world, from men and women of different religions, races and even colours, and that these correspondents have as a rule remarked less upon the book's content than upon the personality which lies behind it and even upon the over-brief biographical sketch of Ramon Lull which forms its preface. Indeed, the publication of the present

[1] Miquel Ferrà, p. 16.

[2] "Ramon Lull és tot dins cadascún dels seus llibres, i dins cada passatge, com el sol, qui s'emmiralla en cada gota d'aigua. . . . Se repeteixen a l'infinit en tota la seva obra, variades i combinades en mil diferentes formes, les mateixes idèes i les mateixes paraules, els mateixos exemplis, les mateixes equacions lògiques, els mateixos temes obsessionants. . . ." (Miquel Ferrà, p. 21).

[3] *Revista dels Llibres*, Any ii, núm. 14–15, 1926, p. 83.

work has been made possible principally by the interest in Ramon the man of these correspondents and others.

It is not his achievements during a long and troubled lifetime that have made him so compelling a figure. He achieved comparatively little in the practical sphere, and this for many reasons. Not, let it be said most emphatically, from any impotence of temperament which, as the *Histoire littéraire de la France* suggests, blinded him to the "ridiculousness" of his "feverish activity which never led to a single serious accomplishment."[1] This is merely a caricature of a man whose great gift to posterity has been one of dynamic force,[2] and who is a "Loyola manqué" partly because he spent himself as instinct, rather than reason, prompted him, but chiefly because he flourished at a time when ambitions clashed continually in political and religious spheres, when idealism was waning fast and when constructive idealists, in particular, had almost disappeared from Europe. As Ramon's activities began, in his late maturity, to quicken, the dead hand of the fourteenth century was already about to fall upon the Continent—that century in which "heresies and schisms grew apace, false prophets . . . . abounded, fierce wars . . . bathed half Europe in blood, . . . religious orders decayed or followed but weakly in the footsteps of their founders, great theologians were dumb, and art degenerated almost wholly into satire."[3] Was it Lull's fault, we may ask, that Aragon, France, Mallorca and Sicily were continually embroiled in warfare? That the papacy was near its ebb, and successive popes reigned but a few short years without the necessary tranquillity, and sometimes without the disposition, to carry out reforms which Lull was not alone in pressing? That the vitality which inspired the Crusades had come to an end, that the military orders had declined, that the king in whom Ramon centred his

[1] *H.L.F.*, pp. 1–2. I have already dealt briefly with this estimate in my *Studies of the Spanish Mystics*, London, 1927, i, pp. 4–5.

[2] Torras i Bages (p. 206) makes this point well in showing why "sers tan extraordinaris no passen en va pel món."

[3] Menéndez y Pelayo: *Historia de los heterodoxos españoles*, Madrid, 1917, iii, pp. 227–8.

affection, trust and expectations was by force of circumstances unable to carry out his plans as the Conqueror might have done? To these and other such causes Ramon owed the checks which met him at every turn: in other days—either earlier or later—he might have turned failure into brilliant success.

Did any think of Ramon, for example, in 1622, when the process for his canonization had not long been a thing of the past, and when, by the bull *Inscrutabili Divinae* of Gregory XV, was instituted the Sacred Congregation of Propaganda for the extension of the Catholic faith beyond the seas? In one feature after another this foundation was foreshadowed by the *Book of Contemplation* and *Blanquerna*. The Congregation was of thirteen cardinals, who were to have supreme control over the Church's foreign missions, the world being divided (to use Ramon's naive expression) into thirteen parts and to each part being assigned a direct representative of the Holy See. To-day the organization of the Congregation of Propaganda has developed beyond anything that the Beat Ramon, or indeed those of his day, could have imagined. But we may well feel that the essentials of its machine-like efficiency and complexity are to be found in, or are deducible from, his writings.

To be sure, Lull gets no glory for all this: if a few enthusiasts have made ample, even exaggerated claims for him,[1] the vast multitude knows hardly as much of him as his name—he is merely a forgotten precursor. And if we consider the other respects in which his ideals, in advance of those of his contemporaries, were, in one form or another, brought to fulfilment, we shall find no evidence to connect that fulfilment with his influence. Nor need we greatly regret it. Let us suppose that the decisions

[1] A perusal of the Lullian books and pamphlets in the Biblioteca Provincial of Palma will furnish sufficient evidence of this. Pedro Bennazar, for example, in a memorial to Charles II, described him as: "*Fundador de todas las misiones y seminarios del mundo*, nuevo Apóstol de Africa y acérrimo defensor de la purísima concepción de la Reina de los Angeles María SSa." Quite recently, again, Dr. Zwemer, in a biographical sketch of Lull, described him as "first missionary to the Moslems" (see Bibliography, No. 64), a claim challenged with some reason by Bihl (*art. cit.*, p. 336).

of the Council of Vienne had taken root like seed sown in good ground, had borne fruit in Lull's own lifetime and had continued to give harvests to-day. Let us imagine missionary colleges in every Christian province, each bearing upon its portal Lull's name and likeness, with a motto from *Blanquerna* like that which greets the visitor to the little Cura community on the height of Randa. All this, and more, might have come to pass, and yet the primary inspiration of Ramon's life and character would be precisely that which it is at the present day.

He has given us in himself an attractive figure, which, by virtue of the romantic, the picturesque and the poetical in it, makes an appeal to many whom the figure of the recluse, the philosopher, the contemplative, would never touch.[1] To these—actives temperamentally and for the most part laymen—he has shown what is meant by conversion, renunciation and love. He has shown them how a resolute spirit can triumph over weakness and temptation, find its nourishment in hardship, and win its satisfaction by sacrifice and martyrdom. He has shown them what to a soul fired with love, that " wearies not nor is wearied," is meant by a life devoted wholly to the service of God, that spends and is spent, toiling ceaselessly and joyfully with all its powers, with its mind, soul and strength. Is it too much to say that, while the greatest contemplatives endeavour to picture for us the joys of the fruition of God in Heaven, this contemplative-active, so like ourselves yet so different, has given us some foretaste of the joys of those who spend themselves in worship, yet are never spent, who " rest not day and night, saying Holy, holy, holy, Lord God Almighty, which was, and is, and is to come " ?

If it is as an active that Ramon appeals to the present age most widely, he appeals most deeply, and less obviously, as a contemplative.[2] It is a narrow criticism that,

[1] Torras i Bages, for various reasons (pp. 208–10), calls him "Doctor Romàntic," and adds pertinently: "¿ Qué és un romàntic sinó un il·luminat, un home qui no's guia per regles, sinó per sa propia llum ? " (p. 209).

[2] On this aspect of Lull's writings, *cf.* Probst, " L'amour mystique, etc.," and *Caractère et origine*, etc., pp. 91–112.

name, or rather in those which he himself preferred,—the "jongleur" and the "fool" of love. St. Francis' writings were as scant as Lull's were voluminous, but there are striking similarities, both in substance and in style, between them. St Francis' paraphrase of the Lord's Prayer is not at all unlike parts of Ramon's paraphrase in the *Art of Contemplation*, and there are many passages in which we hear in the words of St. Francis the voice of his follower :

> Hail, queen wisdom ! May the Lord save thee with thy sister holy pure simplicity !
> O Lady, holy poverty ! May the Lord save thee with thy sister holy humility !
> O Lady, holy charity ! May the Lord save thee with thy sister holy obedience ! [1]

> I beseech Thee, O Lord, that the fiery and sweet strength of Thy love may absorb my soul from all things that are under heaven, that I may die for love of Thy love as Thou didst deign to die for love of my love.[2]

All the apt phrases with which Fr. Paschal Robinson characterizes St. Francis can be applied to the Beat Ramon as exactly as though they had been written of him : his combination, for example, of "great elevation of thought" with "picturesqueness of expression" and his "deep sense of the spiritual" clothed "with the spirit of romance."[3] Or two other phrases which, true enough of St. Francis, go far towards summing up the character of Ramon :

> He was at once formidably mystic and exquisitely human.
> He had the soul of an ascetic and the heart of a poet.[4]

There, then, we have the Ramon Lull of to-day—and, we may safely predict, of a space of time extending far into the future. A patriarch of literature, an apostle

[1] *Writings of St. Francis of Assisi*, ed. Fr. Paschal Robinson, London, 1906, pp. 20–1.

[2] *Ibid.*, p. 145. "Prayer to obtain Divine Love," attributed to St. Francis by St. Bernardine of Siena and Ubertino da Casale.

[3] *Ibid.*, p. x.

[4] *Ibid.*, p. x.

of religion, and a herald among the mystics. The part of his work which was never destined to be immortal is dead already, and has the interest but of the mummy of a Pharaoh. The part which will live is now, after six centuries, achieving a new degree of popularity. Rubén Darío caught the music of the "nightingales singing among the oaks of his philosophy"[1] : others are attuned to more celestial music still and are asking themselves what it is :

> Les teves ales
> d'àliga són ;
> més ta veu fina
> de rossinyol.
> Ets un apostol
> o un filosof ?
> Ets un asceta
> predicador
> qui del martiri
> cerca 'l palmó ?[2]

Even after another six centuries, though many of the works described in this biography may have found oblivion, it is difficult to see how the name of Ramon Lull can be lost. Even if the virile tongue of Catalonia should be silenced, the apostle and the herald will outlive the patriarch. Reduce Lull's mass of writings, by the fiercest flames of criticism, to ashes, and there still remain *Blanquerna*, and a collection of fragments, unharmed. For these defy criticism and argument ; and while a spark of love for God remains in a human soul, it is unthinkable that Ramon's sublime hymns of love can ever perish.

[1] Sus robles filosóficos están llenos de nidos de ruiseñor.

[2] J. Verdaguer : *Al Beat Ramon Llull* : "Thy wings are eagles' wings, but thy sweet song is the nightingale's. Art thou apostle or philosopher ? Art thou an ascetic and a preacher seeking the palm of martyrdom ?"

SELECT BIBLIOGRAPHY

THIS Bibliography, being intended primarily for the use of English-reading students, includes a larger number of works in English than would otherwise be suitable. It cites most of the works quoted in this book, and a number of others found by the author to be suggestive or otherwise useful. It makes no claim to include more than a small proportion of the numerous works on Lull, and purposely excludes all but the outstanding Lullian editions given in the excellent bibliography of Rogent i Duràn (see below, No. 213), of the philosophical and literary works quoted by Longpré (No. 48, cols. 1140–41), and of the general works on mysticism included by the present author in the bibliography to his *Studies of the Spanish Mystics* (London, 1927), vol. i.

Where a writer uses two different forms of his name (*e.g.* Catalan and Castilian, or Catalan and Latin) for two of his works, one form is used here, throughout, for convenience. Abbreviated titles are employed whenever possible and " Palma " is substituted for " Palma de Mallorca."

I. WORKS OF A GENERAL NATURE

[Encyclopaedias, standard histories of literature and works of reference are not included.]

1. Aigrefeuille, Charles d' : *Histoire de la ville de Montpellier.* Montpellier, 1875–83. 4 vols.

2. Ballester y Castell, Rafael : *Las Fuentes narrativas de la historia de España durante la Edad Media.* Palma, 1908.

3. Binimelis, Juan : *Historia general del reino de Mallorca.* Palma, 1927. [New edition.]

4. Bofarull y Brocá, Antonio de : *Historia crítica de Cataluña.* Barcelona, 1876–8. 9 vols.

5. Bofarull y Mascaro, Próspero : *Colección de documentos inéditos del Archivo General de la Corona de Aragón.* Barcelona, 1847–76, 1910. 41 vols.

6. Bover, Joaquín María : *Historia de la Casa Real de Mallorca.* Palma, 1855.

7. Bover, Joaquín María : *Noticias histórico-topográficas de la isla de Mallorca,* Palma, 1836.

[The second edition (Palma, 1864) is here used.]

8. Bover, Joaquín María : *Del Origen, vicisitudes y estado actual de la literatura en la isla de Mallorca.* Palma, 1840.

9. Bover, Joaquín María: *Biblioteca de Escritores Baleares.* Palma, 1868.

10. Campaner y Fuertes, Álvaro: *Cronicón mayoricense. Noticias y relaciones históricas de Mallorca desde* 1229 *a* 1800. Palma, 1881.
[Detailed, but frequently unreliable.]

11. *Chronica o comentaris del gloriosissim e invictissim rey En Jacme Primer . . . dictada per aquell en sa llengua natural, e de nou feta estampar.* Par Mariano Aguiló y Fuster. Barcelona, 1873.

12. *Chronicle of James I, King of Aragon, surnamed the Conqueror.* Translated by John Forster. London, 1883. 2 vols.

13. Denifle, H. et Chatelain, E.: *Chartularium Universitatis Parisiensis.* Paris, 1889–97. 4 vols.
[The first two volumes are relevant to this study.]

14. Devic, C. de et Vaissette, J.J.: *Histoire générale de Languedoc.* Toulouse, 1872–93. 18 vols.
[A new and revised edition of a standard eighteenth-century work.]

15. Diago, Francisco: *Historia de la provincia de Aragón de la orden de Predicadores.* Barcelona, 1598.

16. Finke, Heinrich: *Acta Aragonensia.* Berlin, 1908. 2 vols.

17. Galindo y de Vera, León: *Historia de las vicisitudes y política tradicional de España en las costas de África.* Madrid, 1884.

18. Giménez Soler, Andrés: "Episodios de la historia de las relaciones entre la Corona de Aragón y Túnez." In *Anuari del Institut d'Estudis Catalans*, 1907, pp. 195–224.

19. *Historia general del Reino de Mallorca.* Escrito por los cronistas D. Juan Dameto, D. Vicente Mut y D. Gerónimo Alemany, 2ª edición corregida e ilustrada con abundantes notas y documentos, y continuada hasta nuestros días por D. D. Miguel Moragues, Pro, . . . y D. Joaquín María Bover. Palma, 1840–1. 3 vols.

20. Lecoy de la Marche, A.: *Les relations politiques de la France avec le royaume de Majorque.* Paris, 1892. 2 vols.

21. Macdonald, D. B.: *Development of Muslim Theology and Jurisprudence.* London, 1903.

22. Mercier, Ernest: *Histoire de l'Afrique septentrionale* (*Berbérie*) *depuis les temps les plus reculés jusqu'à la conquête française* (1830). Paris, 1888–91. 3 vols.

23. Merriman, R. B.: *The Rise of the Spanish Empire in the Old World and the New.* New York, 1918. Vol. i: The Middle Ages.
[An invaluable work of reference for the period, with useful bibliographical information.]

24. Miralles de Imperial, Claudio: *Relaciones diplomáticas de Mallorca y Aragón con el África Septentrional durante la Edad Media.* Barcelona, 1904.

25. Miret i Sans, Joaquim: Itinerari de Jaume I. "El Conqueridor." Barcelona, 1918.

26. Mortier, D. A.: *Histoire des maîtres généraux de l'ordre des frères Prêcheurs.* Paris, 1903. 8 vols.

27. Muntaner, Ramón: *Crónica Catalana del Rey D. Jaume I, etc.* [Catalan and Castilian translation]. Ed. Antonio de Bofarull. Barcelona, 1860.

28. Oliver, M. S.: *La literatura en Mallorca*, 1840–93. Palma, 1903.

29. Quadrado, J. M.: *Historia de la Conquista de Mallorca.* Crónicas inéditas. Palma, 1850.

30. Quadrado, J. M.: *Recuerdos de Miramar: Memoria histórica en el sexto centenario de su fundación.* Palma, 1877.

31. Quadrado, J. M.: *Forenses y Ciudadanos: Historia de las disensiones civiles de Mallorca en el siglo XV.* Palma, 1895 (2nd edition).
[Of secondary and general value.]

32. Rubió y Lluch, Antoni: *Documents per l'historia de la cultura catalana mig-eval, publicats per. . . .* Barcelona, 1908. 2 vols.
[An admirably produced work, of which mainly vol. i is of importance to our subject.]

33. Rusiñol, Santiago: *La Illa de la calma.* Barcelona, n.d.
[Majorcan travel-sketches. Several pages are devoted to Ramon Lull.]

34. Shelley, Henry C.: *Majorca.* London, 1926.
[A general work, combining history and description.]

35. Swift, F. D.: *James the First of Aragon.* Oxford, 1894.

36. Torras i Bages, Josep: *La Tradició catalana: estudi del valor ètic i racional del regionalisme català.* Barcelona, 1892.
[The revised 4th edition, 1924, is here used.]

37. Tourtoulon, Ch. de: *Jacme 1er le Conquérant, Roi d'Aragon.* Montpellier, 1863. 2 vols.

38. Wadding, Luke: *Annales Minorum, seu trium ordinum a S. Francisco institutorum, etc.* Rome, 1731, ff.
[Vols. iii to vi are chiefly relevant to this study.]

39. Zurita, Jerónimo: *Anales de la Corona de Aragón.* Zaragoza, 1610. 6 vols.

II. Works mainly Biographical.

40. Anon: *A Life of Ramón Lull.* Written by an unknown hand about 1311, and now first translated from the Catalan, with notes and an appendix, by E. Allison Peers. London, 1927.
[The 'Life' is the *Vida Coetània*, and the appendix the Latin *Vita Beati Raymundi Lulli*, reproduced from the text of Salzinger. See Nos. 60, 61, below. On the authenticity and correctness of these biographies, see Pasqual: *Vindiciae*, i. p. 4; also Nos. 111, 167, 218, below, and the present study, *passim*.]

41. Avinyó, Joan: *El Terciari Francescá Beat Ramón Llull.* Igualada, 1912.

42. Barber, W. T. A.: *Raymond Lull, the Illuminated Doctor.* London, 1904.
[A brief, popular life, insufficiently informed and in many places incorrect.]

43. Blanch, Mn. Antoni: *Vida del Beat Ramón Llull, Mártir i doctor.* Barcelona, 1907.

44. Brambach, Wilhelm: *Des Raimundus Lullus Leben und Werke in Bildern des xiv Jahrhunderts.* Karlsruhe, 1893.
[Described in "El Breviculum i les miniatures de la vida d'en Ramón Lull de la Biblioteca de Karlsruhe," by Jordi Rubió, in *Butlletí de la Biblioteca de Catalunya*, vol. iii, pp. 73–88. The twelve illustrations of the original are reproduced.]

45. Galmés, Mn. Salvador: *Vida Compendiosa del Bt. Ramón Lull.* Palma, 1915.
[The most reliable of the brief biographies. Draws principally on the *Vida Coetània* for its material, and contains many references to the biographical passages in Lull's works.]

46. Golubovich, P., O.F.M.: "B. Raimondo Lullo." In *Biblioteca Bio-bibliografica della Terra Santa e dell' Oriente francescano.* Quaracchi, 1906, vol. i, pp. 361–92.

47. Histoire littéraire de la France. Paris, 1885, vol. xxix, pp. 1–386.
[Essential for any serious student. The biographical part, however, by B. Hauréau, is violently prejudiced against Lull.]

48. Longpré, P. Ephrem, O.F.M.: "Lulle, Raymond." In *Dictionnaire de Théologie Catholique.* Paris, 1927, vol. ix, cols. 1071 to 1141.

49. Miret y Sans, J.: "Noves biogràfiques d'en Ramon Llull." In *Boletín de la Real Academia de Buenas Letras.* Barcelona, 1915, vol. viii, pp. 101–6.

50. Miret y Sans, J.: "Lo primitiu nom de familia d'en Ramon Llull." *Ibid*, vol. viii, pp. 305–7.

51. Miret y Sans, J.: "La vila nova de Barcelona y la familia d'en Ramon Lull en la xiii[a] centuria." *Ibid*, vol. v, 1910, pp. 525–35.

52. Pasqual, Antonio Raymundo: *Vindiciae Lullianae, sive demonstratio critica immunitatis doctrinae. . . R. L.* Avignon, 1778. 4 vols.
[Vol. i, pp. 1–439, treats of Lull's life.]

53. Pasqual, Antonio Raymundo: *Vida del Beato Raymundo Lulio mártir y Doctor iluminado.* Escrita en castellano por el sabio lulista . . . y publicado ahora por primera vez por la Socd. Arqueológica luliana. Palma, 1890. 2 vol.

54. Quadrado, J. M.: "Primeros años y conversión de Ramón Lull." In *Museo Balear*, i. 1875, pp. 387–410.

55. Riber, Mn. Llorenç: *Vida i actes del reverent mestre i benaventurat mártir Ramon Lull.* Palma, 1916.
[A biography for the general reader rather than the student, drawn mainly from the *Vida Coetània*, and tinctured strongly with poetic feeling.]

56. Riber, Mn. Llorenç: "Ramon Lull en Montpeller y en la Sorbona." In *Revista Quincenal.* Barcelona, 1917, vol. i, pp. 310–39.

57. Riber, Mn. Llorenç: *Vida abreujada del Benaventurat Ramon Lull.* Barcelona, 1921.
[A brief popular life of fifty pages.]

58. Rubió y Balaguer, Jordi: "El Breviculum i les miniatures de la vida d' en Ramón Lull de la Biblioteca de Karlsruhe." In *Butlletí de la Biblioteca de Catalunya*, 1916, vol. iii, pp. 73–88.
[With twelve full-page plates and a note by Ramon d'Alòs.]

59. Sollier, J. B. [Sollerius]: *Acta B. Raymundi Lulli Majoricensis Doctoris Illuminati Bugiæ in Africa Martyris, etc.* Antuerpiæ, 1708.
[See No. 213, pp. 253–77.]

60. *Vida Coetània.* For the Catalan version see British Museum, Add. MS. 16432, fol. 25; *Boletín de la Real Academia de Buenas Letras*, Barcelona, 1915, vol. xv, pp. 89–101; *B.S.A.L.*, 1915, vol. xv, pp. 349–57. For the English translation, see No. 40 above.

61. *Vita Beati Raymundi Lulli Doctoris Illuminati et Martyris.* For this Latin biography see J. B. Sollier, *Acta*, etc. (No. 59, above), vol. v, pp. 660–8; Salz., i, pp. 1–12; Longpré (No. 48), cols. 1072–3; and No. 40 above.

62. Waite, Arthur Edward: *Raymund Lully, illuminated doctor, alchemist and Christian mystic.* London, 1922.
[A brief essay.]

63. Zöckler, O.: "R. Lullus." In *Protestantische Realencyklopädie*, vol. xi, 1902, pp. 706–16.

64. Zwemer, S. M.: *Raymund Lull, first missionary to the Moslems.* New York, 1902.
[A short, readable book, but unreliable as to detail. Written throughout from the standpoint of a missionary.]
For the biographies of Bennazar, Bouvelles, Colletet, Cornejo, Pax, Seguí, Vernon, etc., consult Rogent i Duràn (No. 213, below).

III. Modern or easily accessible Editions of the Works of Ramon Lull, including Selections and Anthologies. (Arranged in Alphabetical Order.)

(*a*) Catalan.

65. *Obras rimadas de Ramón Lull.* Escritas en idioma catalan-provenzal, publicadas por primera vez con un artículo biográfico, ilustraciones y variantes, y seguidas de un glosario de voces anticuadas por Gerónimo Rosselló. Palma, 1859.
[This is the latest edition included in the bibliography of Rogent and Duràn; we therefore begin here.]

66. *Libre del Orde de Cauayleria compost a Miramar de Mallorca per el mestre Ramon Lull.* Ed. M. Aguiló y Fuster. Barcelona, 1879.

67. *Libro de la Orden de Caballería.* Ed. J. R. de Luanco [Catalan and Castilian]. Barcelona, 1901.

68. *Obras de Ramón Lull.* Textos originales, publicados e ilustrados con notas, y variantes, por Gerónimo Rosselló. Palma de Mallorca, 1901–3. 3 vols.
[Vol. i: *Libre del Gentil e los tres savis, Libre de la primera e segona intenció, Libre de mil proverbis.* Vol. ii: *Arbre de Filosofía d'Amor, Libre de Oració, Libre de Deu, Libre de Conexença de Deu, Libre del Es de Deu.* Vol. iii: *Felix de les Maravelles del Mon* (two volumes in one, numbered iii*a* and iii*b* in text above). Prologues to vols. i and iii by M. Obrador Bennassar; to vol. ii by Miguel Costa y Llobera.]

69. *Libre de Amich e Amat.* Text original directament trelladat d'un códiç trecentista. Ab proemi, notes y glosari d'en M. Obrador y Bennassar. Palma de Mallorca, 1904.

70. *Libre apellat Felix de les Maravelles del Mon.* Ed. Gerónimo Rosselló. Barcelona, 1904. 2 vols.
[The publication of this edition was begun in Palma in 1873, but finished early in 1904, in Barcelona.]

71. *Llibre de les besties.* Text original amb prolec, notes bibliografiques i glosari d'en M. Obrador Bennassar. Barcelona, 1905.

72. *Libre de Santa Maria, ordenat per M. Ramon Lull.* Ed. Josep Pijoan. Villanueva y Geltrú, 1905.

73. *Libre de Doctrina Pueril.* Text original, directament trelladat d'un ms. quatrecentista, ab proemi, illustracions y notes d en M. Obrador y Bennassar. Barcelona, 1907.

74. *Obres de Ramón Lull.* Palma de Mallorca, 1906 ff. 13 vols. [In progress.]
[This edition, inaugurated in 1906 by a "Comissió Editora Lulliana," comprises the following volumes: i. *Doctrina pueril,*

Libre del Orde de Cavalleria, Libre de Clerecia, Art de Confessió. ii–viii. *Libre de Contemplació.* ix. *Blanquerna.* x. *Libre de Sancta Maria, Hores de Sancta Maria, Libre de Benedicta Tu in mulieribus.* xi–xiii. *Arbre de Sciencia.* xiv. *Proverbis de Ramon, etc.*]

74a. Consolació d'ermità. Ed. Pere Barnils. In *B.R.A.B.L.*, Barcelona, 1911, vol. vi, pp. 184-195.

75. *Poesies.* Text, notes i glossari de Ramon d'Alòs-Moner. Barcelona, 1925. [A modest but excellently prepared volume of selections.]

76. *Llibre d Amic e Amat, Llibre d Ave Maria.* Ed. M. Olivar. Barcelona, 1927.

(*b*) Latin.

77. *Beati Raymundi Lulli Doctoris Illuminati et Martyris Opera.* Moguntiae, 1721–42. 8 vols.

[See on this, the well-known Mayence edition of Salzinger, Gottron, and Rogent i Duràn, Nos. 151, 213, below.]

78. *Liber de Immaculata Beatissimae Virginis Conceptione.* Noviter impressus una cum versione in linguam cathalaunicam cura et studio Joannis Avinyó, Presbyteri. Barchinone, 1901.

78a. *Liber de acquisitione terrae sanctae,* ed. Longpré. In *Criterion,* Barcelona, 1927, vol. iii, pp. 266–78.

(*c*) English.

79. *The Book of the Lover and the Beloved.* Translated . . with an introductory essay by E. Allison Peers. London, 1923.

80. *The Art of Contemplation.* Translated . . . with an introductory essay by E. Allison Peers. London, 1925.

81. *Thoughts from Blessed Ramón Lull for every day.* Compiled by E. Allison Peers. London, 1925.

82. *Blanquerna—a thirteenth-century romance.* Translated . . . with an introductory essay, by E. Allison Peers. London, 1926.

83. *The Tree of Love.* Translated . . . with an introductory essay, by E. Allison Peers. London, 1926.

84. *The Book of the Order of Chivalry.* Translated and printed by William Caxton from a French version of Ramón Lull's "Le Libre del Orde de Cauayleria," together with Adam Loutfut's Scottish transcript. Edited by Alfred T. P. Byles (London : E.E.T.S., 1926).

85. *The Book of the Beasts.* Translated . . . by E. Allison Peers. London, 1927.

(*d*) Castilian.

86. *Libro del Amigo y del Amado* . . . traducido en lengua española por un devoto del Santo . . . con una introducción de D. Miguel Mir. Madrid, 1903.

87. *Libro de la Concepción Virginal atribuido al Beato Raimundo Lull.* Versión castellana por D. Alonso de Cepeda. Barcelona, 1906.

(*e*) French.

88. *Ars Brevis.* Traduit pour la première fois du Latin en français. Paris, 1901.

89. *Blanquerne l'anachorète, ou 365 questions et réponses de l'ami et de son bien-aimé, por le B. Raymond Lulle.* Genève, 1890.

[Has the Latin and French versions of the *Libre d'amic e amat.*]

90. *Le Livre de l'Ami et de l'Aimé, de Raymond Lulle.* Traduit par M. André. Bruxelles, 1897.
[Another edition: Paris, 1921.]

91. *Livre de l'ami et de l'aimé : petits cantiques d'amour dialogués.* Traduits par A. de Barrau et Max Jacob. Paris, 1919.

(*f*) GERMAN.

92. *Ein Katalanisches Thierepos von Ramón Lull.* von Konrad Hofmann. München, 1872.
[A German edition of the Catalan text of the *Libre de les Besties* from two MSS. in the Münchener Hof- und Staatsbibliothek.]

IV. CRITICAL WORKS ON RAMON LULL AND THE HISTORY OF LULLIAN SCIENCE.

93. Aguiló, Tomás: "Algunos datos bibliográficos relativos a las obras químicas de Lulio." In *Museo Balear*, vol. i, 1875, pp. 423–7.

94. Alcover, Antoni: "Cronica del vi centenari de la mort del B. R. Lull." In *B.S.A.L.*, 1915, pp. 378–88.

95. Alcover y Maspons, Juan: *El Lulismo en Mallorca desde mediados de siglo xix.* Palma, 1915.

96. Alòs, Ramon d': *Los Catálogos lulianos. Contribución al estudio de la obra de Ramón Lull.* Barcelona, 1918.
[A doctoral thesis.]

97. Alòs, Ramon d': *Sis documents per a la història de les doctrines lulianes.* Barcelona, 1919.
[A useful pamphlet published in a limited edition.]

98. Alòs, Ramon d': "El manuscrito ottoboniano lat. 405. Contribución a la bibliografía luliana." In *Escuela española de arqueología e historia en Roma*, Madrid, 1914, vol. ii, pp. 97–127.

99. André, Marius: *Le Bienheureux Raymond Lulle.* Paris, 1900.

100. Anon: "Memoria de los libros que han venido a noticia del Dr. Dimas del illuminado Doctor Raimundo Lullio sin otros muchos que sabe ay en Catalunia, etc." In *Ciudad de Dios*, vol. lxxxi, 1910, pp. 314–323.

101. Antonio, Nicolás: *Bibliotheca Hispana Vetus* and *Bibliotheca Hispana Nova, passim.* Madrid, 1783–88. 4 vols.

102. Asín Palacios, Miguel: "El lulismo exagerado." In *Cultura española*, 1906, vol. ii, pp. 533–41.

103. Asín Palacios, Miguel: *Abenmasarra y su escuela. Orígenes de la filosofía hispano-musulmana.* Madrid, 1914.

104. Asín Palacios, Miguel: "Mohidin." In *Homenaje a Menéndez Pelayo.* Madrid, 1899, ii, pp. 217–56.

105. Asín Palacios, Miguel: "La Psicología según Mohidin Abenarabi." In *Actes du XIVe Congrès International des Orientalistes.* Alger, 1905 (part iii, 1907).

106. Avinyó, Mn. Joan: "Catàlech de documents lulians." In *Boletín de la Real Academia de Buenas Letras de Barcelona*, 1912, vol. vi, pp. 395–420.

107. Avinyó, Mn. Joan: "La Escolástica y el Beat Lull." In *Revista Luliana*, vol. ii, pp. 227–34; vol. iii, pp. 55–61.

108. Avinyó, Mn. Joan : *Història del Lulisme.* Barcelona, 1925.

[Goes down to the eighteenth century only, and contains much irrelevant as well as valuable material. See the criticisms of R. d'Alòs (*Criterion*, 1925, vol. i, pp. 250–58), and P. A. Ivars, O.F.M., in *Archivo Ibero-Americano*, 1926, vol. xxv, pp. 129–35.]

109. Avinyó, Mn. Joan : " Breu exposició del sistema cientific lul·lià." In *Criterion*, 1926, vol. ii, pp. 169–83.

110. Batista y Roca, José María : *Catàlech de les Obres Lulianes d'Oxford.* Barcelona, 1916.

111. Bihl, P. Michel, O.F.M. : " Le B. Raymond Lulle (Etudes Bibliographiques)." In *Etudes Franciscaines*, tom. xv, 1906, pp. 328–45.

112. Blanco, P. Pedro, O.S.A. : " La Apología del Dr. Dimas de Miguel, y el Catálogo de las obras de Raimundo Lulio del Dr. Arias de Loyola. Manuscritos inéditos de la Real Biblioteca de El Escorial." In *Ciudad de Dios*, vol. lxxvii, 1908, pp. 326–333, 412–20, 590–96 ; vol. lxxviii, 1909, pp. 319–24.

113. Blanco, P. Pedro, O.S.A. : " El Catálogo de las obras de Raimundo Lulio del doctor Arias de Loyola." In *Ciudad de Dios*, vol. lxxxi, 1910, pp. 60-4, 132-41, 223-232 ; cf. *B.S.A.L.*. xiii, p. 120.

114. Blanco y Sánchez, Rufino : *Bibliografía pedagógica de obras escritas en castellano o traducidas a este idioma.* Madrid, 1910–12, vol. iv, pp. lii, 688–98.

115. Blanco Soto, P. : *Estudios de Bibliografía Luliana.* Madrid, 1916.

116. Bofarull, Francisco : " El Testamento de Ramón Lull y la Escuela Luliana en Barcelona." In *Memorias de la Real Academia de Buenas Letras*, v, pp. 435–78.

[*Cf.* Gaston Paris' review of this book in *Revue Historique*, 1897, vol. 63, pp. 375–7.]

117. *Boletín de la Sociedad Arqueológica Luliana.* Palma, 1885–1906. (Abbreviated *B.S.A.L* in Bibliography and notes.)

[The most important articles for our purpose in this review are listed separately. The shorter articles are far too numerous to include, but some of them are of very much greater value than others.]

118. Borrás y Rullán, Jaime : *Marta S. y el R. Pontífice en las obras del Beato Ramón Lull.* Sóller, 1908.

119. Borrás y Rullán, Jaime : *Espíritu del Beato Ramón Lull.* Palma, 1909.

120. Borrás y Rullán, Jaime : *Vida popular del Beato Ramón Lull.* Palma, 1915.

[A pamphlet of 32 pages, extremely popular.]

121. Borrás y Rullán, Jaime : *Sistema científico luliano.* Exposición y crítica. Palma, 1916.

122. Borrás y Rullán, Jaime : *Lulismo.* Sóller, 1918.

[Four articles of unequal merit, the best and longest being those entitled " Ramón Lull y el Racionalismo," and " Orígenes del Lulismo."]

123. Bové, Salvador : *La filosofía nacional de Catalunya.* Barcelona, 1902.

124. Bové, Salvador : " Lo Beat Ramón Lull y 'l descubriment de les Amériques." In *Revista Luliana*, vol. i, pp. 105–14.

125. Bové, Salvador : " Breu y sencilla exposició de la Ars Magna Luliana." In *Revista Luliana*, vol. ii, pp. 97–108.

126. Bové, Salvador : " El sistema científico luliano. *Ars Magna.* Exposición y crítica." Barcelona, 1908.

127. Bové, Salvador: "Ramon Llull y la lengua latina." In *Boletín de la Real Academia de Buenas Letras de Barcelona*, vol. viii, pp. 65–88.

128. Bové, Salvador: "Ortodoxia del Sistema y de les doctrines del Beat Ramón Llull." In *Revista Luliana*, vol. i, pp. 285–8, 360–4, 384–7.

129. Buades, A.: "Reconeixement de les despulles des B. Ramon Lull, 1611." In *B.S.A.L.* Palma, 1919, pp. 295–97.

130. Canalejas, F. de Paula: *Las doctrinas del doctor iluminado Raimundo Lulio.* Madrid, 1870.

131. Carreras Artau, Tomás: *Etica hispana. Apuntes sobre la concepción éticojurídica de Ramón Lull.* Madrid, 1914.

132. Carreras Artau, Tomás: *Ramón Lull: programa del curso sobre concepciones éticas en España.* Barcelona, 1915.

133. Casadesús Vila, José: *El Arte Magna de Raimundo Lulio.* Barcelona, 1917.

134. Civezza, Marcellino da, O.F.M.: *Storia universale delle missione francescane.* Rome, 1858, vol. ii, pp. 575–99.

135. Custurer, Jaime: *Disertaciones históricas del culto inmemorial del B. Raymundo Lullio, doctor iluminado y mártir.* Mallorca, 1700.

136. Delisle, L. V.: "Testaments d'Arnaud de Villeneuve et de Raimond Lulle." In *Journal des Savants.* Paris, June 1896.

137. Dmitrewski, Michel de: "Fr. Bernard Délicieux, O.F.M., sa lutte contre l'inquisition de Carcassonne et d'Albi: son procès, 1297–1319." Sec. 14. In *Archivum Franciscanum historicum*, vol. xviii, 1925, pp. 3–32.

138. Ellis, Havelock: "Ramon Lull at Palma." In *The Soul of Spain.* London, 1908, pp. 191–222.

139. Etchegoyen, Gaston: "Versets choisis du Livre de l'ami et de l'aimé." In *Mélanges d'archéologie et d'histoire de l'Ecole française de Rome.* Paris, 1920, vol. xxxviii, pp. 197–211.

140. Etchegoyen, Gaston: "Le Mystique de Raymond Lulle d'après 'Le Livre de l'Ami et de l'Aimé.'" In *Bulletin Hispanique*, 1922, vol. xxiv, pp. 1–17.

141. Ferrá, Bartolomé: "El Sepulcro de Ramón Lull." In *Museo Balear*, vol. i, 1875, pp. 428–34.

142. Ferrà, Miquel: *Ramon Lull, valor universal.* Palma, 1915.

143. Feyjóo, Benito Gerónimo: *Cartas eruditas y curiosas, etc.* Madrid, 2 vols. 1742, 1745.

[See text, p. 391, above, and Rogent i Duràn, *Bibliografía, etc.*]

144. Forteza, Tomás: "Certamen poètich celebrat a Mallorca en honor del B. Ramón Lull. Any 1502." In *Museo Balear*, vol. i, 1875, pp. 443–52.

145. Frost, F. L.: *The "Art de Contemplació" of Ramón Lull.* Baltimore, 1903.

146. Garau, Joan: "Estudi de la doctrina filosófica-teológic qui 's conté en el 'Libre del Gentil y los tres sabis' del Beat Ramón." In *B.S.A.L.*, vol. ix, pp. 33–41.

147. Gayá Bauza, Miguel: "El Amor de María según el Doctor Iluminado." In *Revista Luliana*, vol. iii, pp. 203–8, 248–50.

[This bears on Beat Ramón's attitude to the question of the Immaculate Conception of Our Lady. See on this subject, *ibid*, vol. iii, pp. 220–1; vol. iv, pp. 43–8.]

148. Gazulla, R.P. Faustino D.: *Historia de la falsa bula a nombre del papa Gregorio xi, inventada por el dominico fray Nicolás Aymerich contra las Doctrinas lulianas.* Palma, 1910.

149. Giménez Soler, Andrés: "Documents de Túnez del Archivo de la Corona de Aragón." In *Anuari del Institut d'Estudis Catalans,* 1909–10, pp. 210–259.

150. Gottron, Adam: *Ramón Lulls Kreuzzugsideen.* Berlin, 1912.

151. Gottron, Adam: *L'Edició maguntina de Ramón Lull, amb un apèndix bibliogràfic dels manuscrits i impresos lulians de Maguncia.* Barcelona, 1915.

152. Gottron, Adam: "Die mainzer 'Lullistenschule' im 18. Jahrhundert." In *Anuari de la Societat Catalana de Filosofia,* 1923, vol. i, pp. 229–42.

[A continuation of the foregoing study.]

153. Gottron, Adam: "El Catàleg de la Biblioteca lul·liana del Convent dels Franciscans de Mallorca." In *Butlletí de la Biblioteca de Catalunya,* vol. vi, pp. 146–224. Barcelona, 1924.

154. Gottron, A.: "Neue Literatur zu Ramon Lull." In *Franziskanische Studien.* Münster, 1924, vol. xi, pp. 218–21 (*cf.* also 1914, vol. i, pp. 250, 506, ff).

155. Goyau, G.: *Figurines franciscaines.* Paris, 1921.

156. Grahit Papell, Emilio: *El inquisidor fray Nicolás Eymerich.* Gerona, 1878.

157. Guardia, J. M.: "Littérature Catalane: le Docteur illuminé." In *Revue Germanique et Française,* vol. xix, pp. 200–25. Paris, 1862.

158. Guarnerio, P. E.: "Contributo agli studi lulliani." In *Anuari de l'Institut d'Estudis Catalans,* 1908, pp. 497–519.

159. Haebler, Konrad: *Bibliografía ibérica del siglo xv,* vols. i, ii. Leipzig, 1903–17.

160. Haebler, Konrad: *Ramón Lull und seine Schule.* Leipzig, 1921.

161. Helfferich, A.: *Raymund Lull und die Anfänge der Catalonischen Literatur.* Berlin, 1858.

162. Heredia, Fr. Vicente Beltrán de: "Los Dominicos y los Lulistas de Mallorca en el siglo xviii." In *Criterion,* 1926, vol. ii, pp. 276–96, 418–40.

163. *Homenaje al Beato Raimundo Lull en el sexto centenario de la fundación del Colegio de Miramar.* Palma, 1877.

164. *Homenatge al Doctor Arcangelic lo gloriós martir de Crist Beat Ramon Llull.* Barcelona, 1901.

[An interesting miscellany of poems, articles, etc., by the best-known Catalan Lullists of the beginning of the twentieth century, and others.]

165. Ivars, P. Andrés: "Los Jurados de Valencia y el inquisidor Fray Nicolás Eymerich. Controversia luliana." In *Archivo Ibero-Americano,* Año iii, núms. 16–17, 1916, págs. 68–159; Año viii, núm. 44, 1921, págs. 212–19.

166. Jourdain, C.: "Un collège oriental à Paris au xiiie siècle." In *Excursions historiques et philosophiques à travers le Moyen Age.* Paris, 1888.

167. Keicher, Otto: *Raymundus Lullus und seine Stellung zur arabischen Philosophie.* Münster, 1909.

168. Luanco, J. R. de: *Ramón Lull considerado como alquimista.* Barcelona, 1870.

[See also this author's *La Alquimia en España.* Barcelona, 1889–97.]

169. Manresa, P. Ruperto M. de: *Libro de la Concepción virginal atribuido al Beato Raimundo Lull.* Barcelona, 1906.

170. March, P. Josep M., S.J.: "El P. Jaime Custurer i els seus catàlegs lul·lians." In *Butlletí de la Biblioteca de Catalunya*, 1920, vol. v, pp. 32–44.

171. Martínez Vélez, P., O.S.A.: "La Ciencia Universal: Doctrina de Santo Tomás y Llull." In *B.S.A.L.*, 1908, vol. xii, pp. 161–64, 177–86.

172. Massó Torrents, J.: "Bibliografia dels antics poetes catalans." In *Anuari de l'Institut d'Estudis Catalans*, 1913–14, vol. v, pp. 3–276.

173. Maura Gelabert, Juan [afterwards Bishop of Orihuela]: "Estudios sobre la filosofía de Raimundo Lulio: Naturaleza del alma humana." In *Museo Balear*, 2ª época, vol. i, 1884, pp. 281–96.

174. Maura Gelabert, Juan: "Ensayo sobre la filosofía del Beato Ramón Lull." In *Revista Luliana*, vol. i, pp. 25 ff.

175. Maura Gelabert, Juan: "Lo Beat Ramon Lull, fundador del primer colegi de llenguas orientales." In *Revista Luliana.* Barcelona, 1902, vol. ii, pp. 260–66.

176. Maura Gelabert, Juan: "Psicología Luliana." In *Revista Luliana*, vol. iii, pp. 129–38, 161–71, 225–37, vol. iv, 1–8, 33–7, 49–77.

177. Maura Gelabert, Juan: *El optimismo del Beato Raymundo Lulio.* Barcelona, 1904.

178. *Memoria presentada per l'Institut d'Estudis Catalans als excel·lentíssims senyors president de la Diputació i Alcalde de Barcelona, sobre la celebració del VIe centenari de la mort de Ramón Lull.* Barcelona, 1914.

179. Menéndez Pelayo, Marcelino: "Ramón Lull: discurso leído el día 1º de Mayo del año actual en el Instituto de las Baleares." In *Museo Balear*, 2ª época, vol. i, 1884, pp. 335–42, 361–9, 401–11.

180. Menéndez y Pelayo, Marcelino: *Historia de los Heterodoxos Españoles.* Madrid, 1880; tom. i, pp. 513–39.

[The 2nd and revised edition, Madrid, 1917, iii, pp. 257–89, is used in this study.]

181. Menéndez y Pelayo, Marcelino: *Orígenes de la Novela*, vol. i, Madrid, 1905, pp. lxxi–lxxxviii.

182. Morel-Fatio, A.: "Proverbes rimés de Raimond Lull." In *Romania*, 1882, vol. xi, pp. 188–202.

183. Obrador Bennassar, Mateu: *Doctrines sociològiques lulianes.* Palma, 1905.

184. Obrador Bennassar, Mateu: "Noticia y mostra del llibre lulià 'De Benedicta tu in mulieribus.'" In *Revista Luliana*, vol. i, pp. 93–102.

185. Obrador Bennassar, Mateu: "Ramón Lull en Venecia. Reseña de los Códices e impresos lulianos existentes en la Biblioteca Veneciana de San Marcos." In *B.S.A.L.*, vol. viii, pp. 301–24.

186. [Obrador Bennassar, Mateu]: "Viatge d'investigació a les Bibliotheques de Munich y Milà." In *Anuari de l'Institut d'Estudis Catalans*, 1908, pp. 598–613.

[An account of the Lullian MSS. in these libraries, compiled after Obrador's death, from the notes of his investigations.]

187. O'Neille, Juan: "Ramón Lull: Iconografía," In *Museo Balear*, vol. i, 1875, pp. 435–42.

188. Otto, R.: "Bemerkungen über Ramon Lull." In *Zeitschrift für romanische Philologie*, vol. xii, pp. 511–23.

189. Otzet, Lluis de G.: "La mística luliana." In *Revista Luliana*, vol. ii, pp. 124–9.

190. P., A. de: "El Lulismo en Cataluña." In *Estudios Franciscanos.* Barcelona, 1919, vol. xxiii, pp. 20–5.

The following important articles have appeared while this book is passing through the press :

231. Alòs-Moner, Ramon d' : " Un nou manuscrit, fragmentari, de la *Doctrina pueril.*" In *Franciscalia*, Barcelona, 1928, pp. 1–13.

232. Galmés, Mn. Salvador : " Viatges de Ramon Llull." In *La Paraula Cristiana*. Barcelona, 1928, any iv, pp. 196–225.

233. Rubió Balaguer, Jordi : " Notes sobre la transmissió manuscrita de l'opus lul·lià." In *Franciscalia*, Barcelona, 1928, pp. 335-48.

INDEX

TO THE WORKS OF RAMON LULL (GENUINE AND APOCRYPHAL) DEALT WITH IN THE TEXT

[Short titles are used as far as possible. Heavy type indicates the pages where the work referred to is dealt with at greatest length. No references are given to the Bibliography. The letter "*n*" following the number of a page indicates that the reference will be found among the notes of that page.]

GENERAL INDEX

[No references are made to the Bibliography, and, in entering works which figure in the Bibliography, the authors' names only have been given. Heavy type indicates a somewhat full treatment of the subject referred to. The preceding index should be used to supplement the references here given to Lull's principal themes and to the characters of his fictions. The letter "*n*" following the number of a page indicates that the reference will be found among the notes of that page.]

Printed in England at The Ballantyne Press
Spottiswoode, Ballantyne & Co. Ltd.
Colchester, London & Eton